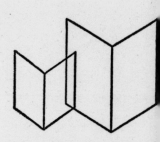

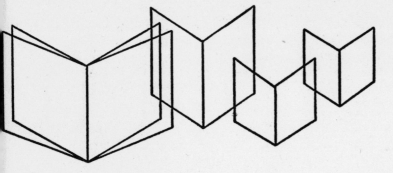

How to become a better reader

PAUL WITTY

Professor of Education

and

Director of the Psycho-Educational Clinic, Northwestern University

SCIENCE RESEARCH ASSOCIATES, Inc., 57 West Grand Avenue, Chicago 10, Ill.

A note to the reader

HOW TO BECOME A BETTER READER is the key that will open many doors to the world about you. It is the tool that will help you to succeed in your studies or in your work. It is the road that will lead you to better reading—for information, for enjoyment, and for a richer life.

What greater reading power will mean to you is indicated by the quotations given here.* What you can do to develop and use this important power is the subject of this book. It tells you exactly how to become a better reader—how much better you become, of course, depends on you.

PAUL WITTY

A BOOK

He ate and drank the precious words,
His spirit grew robust;
He knew no more that he was poor,
Nor that his frame was dust.

He danced along the dingy days,
And this bequest of wings
Was but a book. What liberty
A loosened spirit brings.
—From *Poems: First Series*,
by EMILY DICKINSON

Reading is an adventure, when you go with the poets into the realms of fancy and imagination; you see life with the novelist; you go down to the sea in ships and unto the ends of the earth with the great explorers; the scientist takes you into his laboratory; in biography you are let into the mystery of men's lives; the historian reconstructs the past and gives you glimpses of the future, and the philosopher gives you a glimpse of his wisdom.
—From *The Joy of Reading*,
by HOLBROOK JACKSON

*All quotations are from Alfred Stefferud (Ed.), *The Wonderful World of Books*, (A Mentor Book published by The New American Library of World Literature, Inc., New York; also published by Houghton Mifflin Company). Copyright 1952, by Alfred Stefferud. Reprinted with permission.

Reading is a pleasure of the mind, which means that it is a little like a sport: your eagerness and knowledge and quickness count for something. The fun of reading is not that something is told you, but that you stretch your mind. Your own imagination works along with the author's, or even goes beyond his. Your experience, compared with his, yields the same or different conclusions, and your ideas develop as you understand his.

—From *It's Fun to Read,*

by BENNETT CERF

Each of us must find our own 15-minute period each day [for reading]. It is better if it is regular. . . . The only requirement is the will to read. With it you can find the 15 minutes no matter how busy the day. . . . That means you will read half a book a week, two books a month, 20 a year, and 1,000 or more in a reading lifetime. It's an easy way to become well read.

—From *How to Find Time to Read,*

by LOUIS SHORES

Books extend our narrow present back into a limitless past. They show us the mistakes of the men before us and share with us recipes for human success. There's nothing to be done which books will not help us to do better. They tell us how to live alone and like it, or how to be happy though married. They teach us to grow thin if fat, fat if thin. They tell us how to keep accounts, repair machines, build houses, make love, bury our dead, till our soil, and lose our wrinkles.

—From *Our Reading Heritage,*

by T. V. SMITH

If we read with questions in mind, seeking to get into sympathetic communication with a writer, bearing with him and sticking with him to an end that we reach as quickly as our minds will allow, we will want to read, we will read, and we will be better readers.

—From *A Teacher Looks at Reading,*

by A. B. HERR

Acknowledgments

I wish to express appreciation to Harry Bricker, Ann Coomer, and the SRA book department, who assisted in the preparation of this book; *and to the authors and publishers, who gave permission to reprint selections from their works.*   P. W.

Contents

LESSON 1

Can you learn to read better?

THIS BOOK IS designed to help you *become a better reader.* If you are an average reader, you may be reading this book *now* at a reading rate of about 180 words per minute. And you may be understanding very little—not more than 50 or 60 percent of the ideas presented. Very important, too, you may find little pleasure in reading.

You can change all this. You can improve your rate of reading—perhaps 50 percent or more for many types of reading. At the same time, you can learn to get more out of the things you read. As your reading improves and as your experience with books increases, you will enjoy much more the act of reading. As you go through this book you will gain in rate, in comprehension, and in the joy of reading. *You will become a better reader.*

What will you have to do to read better?

This book will take you step by step along the road to more efficient reading. As the first step, you should plan your own better reading program. In doing so, you should have these things in mind:

1. *Use this book as your guide to better reading.* It is a how-to-do-it book. In studying it, you will not only read about how to read better, but you will also practice better reading. You will learn by doing; and that, of course, is the best way to learn anything.

2. *Make better reading your main goal.* You are probably a busy person. You have many different things to do every day. But if you really want to read better, you will have to make reading improvement your main goal in the weeks just ahead.

3. *Find out how well you now read.* Later in this lesson you will test two of your reading abilities—your reading rate and your reading comprehension. In another lesson you will analyze your present reading skills and habits and will make plans for improving them.

4. *Practice, practice, and practice to read better.* Practice helps to make perfect. Study this book and read other materials for at least one hour every day. The more reading you do the more you will improve your reading.

5. *Watch your reading progress.* From time to time, find out how much you have

improved. To help you measure your reading gains, you will do a general reading exercise at the end of every lesson in this book.

6. *Keep trying to read better.* You will not become a much better reader overnight, or in a day or a week. To make real improvement in your reading, you will have to work at the job over a period of time. As you develop better reading skills and habits, they will help you to continue to improve.

What can you expect along the way toward better reading?

As you use this book to become a better reader, you will have many new experiences. You will enjoy some of these experiences; others may seem unpleasant, at least for a time.

When you start your better reading program, you may feel somewhat uncomfortable. You may have the urge "to go back to the good old days," when most of your reading seemed easy-going and pleasant.

While you continue your efforts to read better, you may, at times, feel discouraged. For example, you may work for a week with only small increases in your reading speed or comprehension.

Yet you should not let these feelings of discomfort or discouragement bother you. Rather, you should recognize that such feelings are quite natural—that they are commonly experienced by people who are learning something new.

You should realize, too, that if you keep up your efforts to improve, you will almost surely make gains in your reading abilities. As these gains occur, your feelings of discomfort and discouragement will decrease and then disappear. You will read with greater understanding and enjoyment. And you will experi-

ence the satisfaction that always accompanies achievement and progress in reading.

To master the lessons in this book, you will have to work hard and steadily. You will probably have to devote about two months to this training before you have sizable gains in your reading rate, comprehension, and vocabulary. At the end of this period, however, you will discover that you have greatly increased your reading power. You will read more, and get more from what you read—results that are well worth the effort and time you put in.

How will this book help you to read better?

How to Become a Better Reader aids you to improve your reading systematically. It encourages you to take a close look at what you are reading. It gives you the "inside story" of how you are reading and of how you should read. It helps you develop the skills and habits that you need for efficient reading.

To find out what is in this book, read the table of contents on pages v-vii. There you will notice that the book is made up of 20 lessons. Each lesson helps you to learn certain ways to read faster and better.

Next, skim this book to get a better idea of its contents. Glance at the pages as you go through the entire book. Read the title of each lesson and the headings; these headings give the main points in that lesson. At this time, do *not* stop to read carefully any of the paragraphs in the book.

As you skim this book, notice that each lesson is made up of two main parts. The first part contains information and suggestions on how you can improve your reading skills and habits. The second part consists of a general reading exercise through which you can test your reading rate, comprehension, and vocabulary. All the general reading exercises are near the back of this book. How to do these exercises is explained on pages 183-185.

How to Become a Better Reader is a self-help book. You can use it without assistance from anyone else. However, if you get some help from a reading instructor, you may get more out of the book and may make more rapid progress.

Whether you study this book alone or with assistance, you alone have the job of becoming a better reader. To do this job well is your responsibility.

This means that when you do a general reading exercise in this book, you always try to make higher scores than you did before. In this way, you compete with yourself, not with anybody else. If your scores keep going higher and higher, you will know that you are becoming a better reader.

In using this book, you should keep a record of your own progress. You do this in the *Progress Folder*[1] that appears at the end of this book. There you record your reading rate, comprehension score, and vocabulary score for each general reading exercise.

Can you learn to read better?

From what you have already read in this lesson, you may be convinced that you *can* learn to read better. Yet you may rightly ask: "Will I have to work two months before my reading shows any improvement?"

You can answer this question by doing the two reading exercises that ap-

pear next. Both exercises are newspaper stories that are at about the same level of reading difficulty. In reading each story, you will determine your rate and comprehension.

To find your reading rate, you will have to time yourself or have someone else time you. For this, you should use a watch or clock that has a second hand.

To check on your comprehension you will take a test that appears just after the story. By means of this test, you will find out whether you understood the main point of the story.

Initial reading exercise 1

Read this story at your ordinary reading rate. Don't push yourself. Just read at your usual comfortable speed.

In the time box, write down your starting time.[2] Then start reading the story.

Time Box

Finishing time	
Starting time	
Reading time	
Reading rate	

SAVES BOY FROM THIRD RAIL[3]

A 22-YEAR-OLD Korean war veteran saved a 13-year-old boy from death by electrocution Monday.

The boy, Nick Calderone Jr., 3502 Wabansia, was playing football with a friend near the abandoned Humboldt

---

[1] If you should not write in this book, you can keep this record in a separate copy of the *SRA Reading Progress Folder*. You can get this copy from your reading instructor.

[2] If you should not write in this book, keep your time record and write your test answers on a separate sheet of paper.

[3] From the Chicago *Sun-Times*, Sept. 22, 1952. Reprinted with permission of the publisher.

Park structure close to the St. Louis Av. station. During the game the ball landed on the tracks.

The boy climbed the structure, reached for the football and fell against the third rail.

Fred Hess, a recently discharged and twice wounded Marine, was repairing his car outside his home at 1625 N. Central Park. He heard someone calling, "Help! Help!"

He climbed to the tracks to find Nick with his head and arm on the third rail as sparks flew.

Hess ran home and got an insulated wire. Not knowing whether the insulation was sufficient, he looped the wire under the boy's arm and lifted it from the rail.

This broke the circuit, and Hess pulled the boy from the rail. The ex-Marine carried him down the catwalk to the boarded-up L station. Hess had to kick his way out of the building.

Nick was taken to North Av. Hospital where his condition was described as fair. Hospital officials say he may lose the use of his right hand.

CTA officials say one reason the abandoned Humboldt Park Line is "energized" with 600 volts of electricity is to prevent thieves from stealing the rails and selling them for scrap.

Now write your finishing time in the time box. Then read this test item and mark a check (✔) at the left of the correct choice.

In rescuing Nick, the young war veteran showed unusual intelligence as well as bravery when he did this:

(A) He quickly kicked the football off the dangerous third rail.

(B) He telephoned the office to turn off the electricity in the third rail.

(C) He carried Nick on the catwalk alongside the third rail.

(D) He used insulated wire to lift Nick's arm from the third rail.

(E) He climbed up to the track when he heard someone calling for help.

Next, figure out your reading time for the story. In the time box, subtract your starting time from your finishing time. The difference is your reading time. Change your reading time into your reading rate; use the table given here. Then write your reading rate in the time box.

Time-to-Rate Table for Initial Reading Exercise 1
(234 words)

Reading time	Reading rate
0:15-0:29	638
0:30-0:44	379
0:45-0:59	270
1:00-1:14	210
1:15-1:29	171
1:30-1:44	146
1:45-1:59	125
2:00-2:14	111
2:15-2:29	99
2:30-2:44	89

(The correct answer to the test is: D.)

Initial reading exercise 2

Read this story at a very fast rate. But keep in mind that you are reading to get the main idea.

In the time box, write down your starting time. Then start reading the story.

Time Box

Finishing time	
Starting time	
Reading time	
Reading rate	

WEALTH COMES TO CRIPPLED VET[4]

By Jerry Thorp

WILLIAM (BILL) SCOBY is rich at 22 in the kind of wealth that eludes many to their graves.

He has earned the earnest affection, admiration and gratitude of not a handful, but hundreds of people. They've decided to let Bill know how they feel about him.

Bill, the son of Mr. and Mrs. John Scoby, 8554 S. 77th Ct., Roberts Park, was an outstanding student at Argo Community High, both scholastically and athletically.

In May, 1951, he was drafted by the Army. Just before going to Korea in October of that year he married his auburn-haired, childhood sweetheart, 18-year-old Arlene Blazevich.

Bill, a medical corpsman, was struck down by enemy mortar fire April 5. His spine was injured so severely that he probably never will walk without braces and crutches.

Bill was brought back to this country and taken to the Army hospital at Fort Campbell, Ky. Arlene quit her office job in Chicago to be near her husband.

She found work at Fort Campbell as a cleaning woman in a guest house.

It wasn't long ago that Bill's friends learned that he will be transferred to the Veterans Administration Hospital at Hines in about a month to complete his recuperation.

They decided he had earned far more than their sympathy.

That's why a neat, one-story frame house is slowly taking shape in Roberts Park at 8542 S. 77th Ct. Mrs. Florence

---

[4]From the Chicago *Sun-Times*, Sept. 22, 1952. Reprinted with permission of the publisher.

Cowgiel, 6159 Archer, is chairman of the committee directing the project.

A lot was donated, anonymously. A trucking firm hauled in necessary top soil for landscaping without charge. A businessman gave an electric pump. A veterans organization supplied funds to buy a heating plant.

A small lumber company donated materials. Labor is being provided without charge. There is only one problem now—plumbing. But Bill's friends aren't too worried. They're sure those materials will come from somewhere.

The house probably will be completed by the time Bill is transferred here. The people who are doing this for Bill and Arlene don't want congratulations.

They figure that he more than made payment-in-full on that grim April day in Korea.

Write your finishing time in the time box. Then read this test item and mark a check (✔) at the left of the correct choice.

Bill's friends are building him a house mainly because they feel that he had

(A) sacrificed so much for them while he was fighting in Korea

(B) given them so much before he went into the Army

(C) married a brave and helpful girl before he sailed for Korea

(D) paid off all his debts before he volunteered for military service

(E) killed and captured many enemy soldiers while fighting in Korea

Now figure out your reading time for the story. Change your reading time into your reading rate; use the table given here. Write your reading rate in the time box.

Time-to-Rate Table for Initial Reading Exercise 2
(350 words)

Reading time	Reading rate
0:30-0:44	568
0:45-0:59	404
1:00-1:14	313
1:15-1:29	256
1:30-1:44	216
1:45-1:59	188
2:00-2:14	165
2:15-2:29	148
2:30-2:44	134
2:45-2:59	122
3:00-3:14	112
3:15-3:29	104
3:30-3:44	97
3:45-3:59	91
4:00-4:14	85

(The correct answer to the test is: A.)

If you are a fairly good reader, you probably answered correctly the comprehension tests in both reading exercises. You probably found, too, that you read the second story at a faster rate than you read the first story. You read more rapidly because you pushed yourself to read faster and because you concentrated more closely on what you were reading.

The two exercises you have just done demonstrate that you can learn to read better and faster. As you are studying the other lessons in this book, you will discover that you can improve your reading more and more. These lessons will help you to read with increasing speed and comprehension. They will aid you in developing better reading skills and habits. And they will bring you many other benefits, as Lesson 2 will show.

What have you learned about better reading?

Read the first statement. If you believe the statement is *true*, mark a + at the left of it. If you believe the statement is *false*, mark a O at the left of it. Answer each of the other statements in the same way.

1. Most persons read about as fast and as well as they can.

2. You can learn to read better by making reading improvement one of your main jobs in the next two months.

3. To improve your reading, you should do some reading every day.

4. During your better reading program, you may sometimes have feelings of discomfort and discouragement.

5. You can expect to improve your reading greatly within a week.

6. In each lesson in this book, you will learn about better reading by practicing better reading.

7. You can improve your reading only if you have the help of a reading instructor.

8. *How to Become a Better Reader* is a book that you can manage without help.

9. You do a general reading exercise in this book to measure your reading enjoyment.

10. You keep a record of your reading improvement in the *Progress Folder*.

Here are the correct answers to this test: (1-0; 2-+; 3-+; 4-+; 5-0; 6-+; 7-0; 8-+; 9-0; 10-+)

Here are the ratings on your scores: Excellent, 9-10; Good, 7-8; Fair, 5-6; Poor, 0-4.

Do general reading exercise 1 (page 186)

Before doing General Reading Exercise 1, read carefully the directions starting on page 183. Then do the exercise to determine your present reading rate, comprehension, and vocabulary.

After completing this exercise, ask yourself these questions: "What is my reading rate? Is it fast enough? What is my comprehension score? Do I understand well enough what I read? What is my vocabulary score? Do I know the important hard words?"

Because you were learning to do a general reading exercise, you probably made lower scores than you will make next time. But your effort has not been wasted. You have taken the first step in becoming a better reader. How this and later steps will benefit you is described in the next lesson.

LESSON 2

How will better

reading benefit you?

IF YOU LEARN TO READ faster and with more understanding, you can do many jobs that require reading with efficiency. And you can save a great deal of time for other activities. These are only a few of the benefits from better reading, as this lesson will show.

You accomplish more in less time

Suppose that you are reading this book at the rate of about 200 words a minute. Suppose that, through your better reading program, you increase your rate to 300 words a minute—up 50 percent. And suppose that you raise your comprehension from 70 percent to 80 percent —up about 15 percent.

You read more. Within an hour of reading time, you can read 50 percent more than formerly. In the same time as before, you can read three chapters instead of two, three books instead of two, and three magazine articles instead of two. During your reading time, you get much more done—and that is an important benefit.

You save time. At your increased rate, you can read 3,000 words in a book,

magazine, or newspaper in 10 minutes instead of 15 minutes. You save five minutes in your reading time, a 33 percent saving. In two hours' time, you can read something that you used to take three hours to read. You save one hour—and that is a real benefit.

And while you read faster than before, you also read more efficiently. You get more from what you read because faster reading and greater understanding tend to go together.

To see exactly how much more you can get done through better reading, study the arithmetic problem that appears next.

The arithmetic of better reading

Question: If you increase your rate by 50 percent and your comprehension by 15 percent, how much more can you accomplish?

Situation: Suppose you are reading a book. The book has one important idea on each page. Each page has 400 words. You read for one hour.

Solution: At your old rate of 200 words a minute, you read one page in two minutes or 30 pages an hour. At your old level of comprehension, you understood 70 percent of the 30 ideas that you came across. You got 21 correct ideas from one hour of reading.

At your new rate of 300 words a minute, you read one page in 1 1/3 minutes or 45 pages an hour. At your new level of comprehension, you understand 80 percent of the 45 ideas that you come across. You get 36 correct ideas from one hour of reading.

Conclusion: Dividing 21 into 36, you find that *within an hour of reading time you are getting about 71 percent more correct ideas than you did before.* Your total gain is much more than your increased rate of 50 percent and your increased comprehension of 15 percent because rate and comprehension together contribute to the correct ideas you get from your reading.

If you are in school, you can make higher marks

Reading is required in about 90 percent of the work done in school or college subjects. In courses in English, social studies, science, or mathematics, for example, you have to spend much time in reading textbooks, additional references, and other materials. To pass these courses, you have to be a reasonably good reader.

From your own experience you probably know that skillful reading and academic success tend to go hand in hand. Good students are usually good readers; and good readers are usually good students. And, of course, many poor students are handicapped by poor reading ability.

Several years ago Dr. Robert C. Aukerman, Jr., made a study of the reading abilities of good students and poor students in a Detroit high school. He se-lected 73 pairs of eleventh-grade pupils. In each pair both pupils had made the same intelligence test scores, but one pupil was a much better student than the other as determined by school marks.

Dr. Aukerman then gave all the pupils a number of reading tests; these tests measured reading comprehension and vocabulary development, in general and in specialized fields such as literature, history, science, and mathematics. From his study, Dr. Aukerman drew these conclusions:

Good students are much higher in general reading ability than are poor students. With few exceptions, they are also higher in the reading abilities and vocabularies that are required in specialized fields.

If you are a student, you can probably make higher school marks by improving your reading. And this is true whether you are a poor, average, or good student.

Nancy, for example, was a superior tenth-grade student in a Chicago high school. She took a seven-week reading improvement course through which she increased her reading rate by 80 percent and kept her comprehension at 90 percent.

After completing the course, Nancy reported its benefits in this statement:

Improving my reading has helped me in several ways.

On my college aptitude tests there is a whole section which tests reading speed and comprehension. I'm sure my reading improvement helped me there.

In my school work I find that I am able to finish much more quickly that reading which does not require note-taking, and in outside reading there's an amazing difference.

I'm doing a term paper on Ghandi and have had to read several books.

Due to my faster reading, I've had more time to work on the paper.

Recently my art teacher asked me to read extra material about Modagliani; I found I was able to read it much faster than ever before. I also comprehended it very well.

I am sure that because of my special reading work I'll be able to do better college work.

By the end of the semester, Nancy had raised her marks in English and Biology from B-plus to A. She became a straight-A student.

If you have a job, you can do it better

In general, the better you read the better you succeed in school or college. And the better you succeed in school or college the better able you are to get the job you want after graduation. In short, the greater your reading power the more likely you are to get ahead in the world of work.

Suppose that you have a job in a business, in a trade, or in a profession. On the job you must get much important information from a variety of printed materials—not only from books, magazines, and newspapers but also from letters, typewritten instructions, and special manuals. If you can read these materials quickly, accurately, and meaningfully, you have a better chance to succeed in your chosen career.

If you are an adult, you may feel that you already read well enough—that you do not need to improve your reading abilities. Or, you may feel that you should read better. However you feel, you will be interested in the editorial appearing next.

A reading exercise

In reading this editorial, measure your reading rate and comprehension.

In the time box, write your starting time. Then read the editorial. Read it as fast as you can, but make sure you understand what you are reading.

Time Box

Finishing time	
Starting time	
Reading time	
Reading rate	

SOME MORE ON BUSINESS READING[1]

By C. B. Larrabee, Editor and Publisher of Printers' Ink

FROM TIME to time in this column, I have talked about the reading habits of business executives. Perhaps the least understandable and most exasperating phase of this subject is not so much a reading habit as a lack of reading habit.

It is the familiar fallacy, the I-haven't-time-to-read fallacy. It usually is uttered most loudly and emphatically by the executive who has time for golf, for interminable business conferences, for long conversations at cocktail bars and for getting tenth row center seats at the big demand shows.

I would be a lot more sympathetic with this executive if I didn't know others who not only seem able to put in a 11-

[1]Reprinted from *Printers' Ink*, June 22, 1951. Copyright 1951 by Printers' Ink Pub. Co., Inc., 205 East 42nd Street, New York 17, New York.

or 12-hour day at the office, when necessary, but also to have plenty of time for business reading plus some recreational reading.

Perhaps I am too hard on the man who hasn't time to read. In many cases the specialists in reading habits are finding that it is not a question of time but of ability.

It may seem presumptuous to imply that a successful businessman, with the usual elementary and secondary school education frequently plus a college degree, doesn't know how to read. But science has found that many men and women who know what the words mean are so slow and inept in their actual reading that it takes them minutes to read material that a skillful reader can cover in seconds.

A few years ago the unskillful reader would have felt he was doing something disgraceful if he took a course in better reading habits. Today this is no longer true. Now in a number of larger communities and in smaller ones, it is possible for adults to take simple, concentrated courses which will teach them not only to read with greater speed, but also with greater understanding.

I think it is most significant that many of the executives who are taking these courses are not the readers with the least ability. Frequently they are men who already read well by ordinary standards. They realize that the more intelligently they read, the more time they literally make for the kind of reading that they feel is so necessary to a proper understanding not only of their jobs but of the world that surrounds their jobs.

Within the last few weeks two of my most valued correspondents have urged me to put more emphasis on this phase of business reading.

From Frank E. Fehlman, for instance, I have a letter saying, "The top psychological brass at Columbia have convinced me that anyone can speed up his reading rate from 10 percent to as much as 50 percent." "But," he adds, "a great many businessmen still read as they did in grade school."

Not everybody can be an expert reader. But in these days where it is necessary for the businessman to read voluminous reports, letters, inter-office memoranda and many other types of reading that are part of the daily business operation, bad reading habits take a toll on business efficiency that is none the less appalling because it is hidden.

Write your finishing time in the time box. Then read this test item and mark a check (✔) at the left of the correct choice.

According to the writer of this editorial, many business executives need more

- (A) time to do their business and recreational reading
- (B) training in the meanings of different words
- (C) skill in reading many things faster and better
- (D) business letters, reports, and magazines to read
- (E) college and university degrees in business methods

Now figure out your reading time for the editorial. Change your reading time into your reading rate; use the table given here. Write your reading rate in the time box.

Time-to-Rate Table for the Editorial
(520 words)

Reading time	Reading rate
0:45-0:59	600
1:00-1:14	466
1:15-1:29	380
1:30-1:44	322
1:45-1:59	279
2:00-2:14	246
2:15-2:29	220
2:30-2:44	199
2:45-2:59	181
3:00-3:14	167
3:15-3:29	154
3:30-3:44	144
3:45-3:59	134
4:00-4:14	126
4:15-4:29	119
4:30-4:44	113
4:45-4:59	107
5:00-5:14	102
5:15-5:29	97
5:30-5:44	93

(The correct answer to the test is: C.)

Next, reread the editorial carefully. Pay special attention to the paragraph that begins, "I think it is most significant." This paragraph points out how reading improvement can benefit a business executive in his everyday work.

You can get more joy out of living

From the reading you do for recreation, you can get satisfactions that come in no other way. If you fill your leisure time with reading, you can gain enjoyment that adds much to the zest of living.

Through reading you can live, in imagination, the lives of others. You can take part in the great events of the past —the discovery of America, the invention of the airplane, the development of wonder drugs, and the first splitting of the atom. In your mind's eye you can project yourself into the fantastic future—riding a jet-propelled space ship on a trip to the moon. You can build castles in the air, Utopias this world will never see.

You can rub elbows with presidents and prime ministers, kings and queens, conquerors and slaves, scientists and explorers, stars of stage or screen. You can be a surgeon performing a delicate operation; an airplane pilot taking off into the wide blue yonder; an engineer bridging tropical rivers—all through reading. For there is a book or magazine for your every interest, your every mood, your every taste.

Such enjoyment is out of your reach if reading is drudgery—that is, if you read slowly and laboriously. But this enjoyment is within your grasp if you can read rapidly, easily, and with understanding.

You can be a better person

Reading can help you become the kind of person you want to be—well-adjusted, socially-liked, well-informed, and more interesting all around.

Through books, magazines, and newspapers you can know yourself better. You can extend your interests and improve your abilities. You can master the skills and acquire the habits that you need for happy and successful living.

Through reading, you can learn to understand other people and to get along with them much better than before. Because you are a social being, you want the recognition and approval of other people, especially of those whom you see every day. You are more likely to win and hold their friendship and respect if you are a well-read person.

People who read much and think about what they read are usually interesting and popular. They almost always have something worth-while to contribute to conversation wherever it occurs—in school, at home, on the job, during social gatherings.

In a real sense, the well-read man is "a man of distinction" wherever he is. And this has been true for many years. As Dr. A. Whitney Griswold, who is President of Yale University, once stated, there was a period in our history when our leaders "found time to read, and demonstrated in their own lives and works, the utility as well as the delight of reading. The four master builders, Hamilton, John Adams, Jefferson, and Madison, were probably the four most widely read men of their age." We do not know whether these leaders were great because they were well-read or were well-read because they were great. But there is no question that reading helped them to build and guide our nation in its early years.

Whether people achieve greatness or not, they can become better persons through reading. Both their present and future depend, at least in part, upon what they read and how they read.

If you are a poor reader, you read very slowly and get very little from what you read. You spend most of your reading time trying to cover what you are required to read—your textbook assignments, for example. As a result, you miss out on the wealth of reading materials that could enrich your life. Because your reading is limited, you as a person are limited. And you are only to a degree the person you might become.

But if you are a good reader, you read many things efficiently. You do your necessary reading within a short period of time and with good understanding. In the time left over, you read widely in fields that interest you—biography, travel, fiction, science, and so forth. You tap books,

magazines, and newspapers as sources of information and enjoyment. You do more reading and get more from it. You become a "person unlimited," and there is real satisfaction in that.

What have you learned about the benefits of better reading?

Mark a + at the left of each *true* statement. Mark a O at the left of each *false* statement.

1. If you learn to read faster and better, you can do many of your jobs better.

2. If you read faster, you will probably get fewer correct ideas during an hour of reading time.

3. Reading is required in only about half of the things you do in high school and college subjects.

4. Good readers are usually good students, but many good students are poor readers.

5. Good students who have the same intelligence as poor students are better in both reading and vocabulary abilities.

6. If you are employed, better reading can help you do your job better.

7. Most business executives do not have time to improve their reading abilities.

8. If you read better, you will probably get more enjoyment from reading.

9. Through improving your reading, you can learn to understand yourself and to get along with other people.

10. The well-read man is seldom popular or successful.

Here are the correct answers to this test: (o-o1 ;+-6
;+-8 ;o-7 ;+-6 ;o-5 ;o-4 ;o-3 ;o-2 ;+-1)

Do general reading exercise 2 (page 191)

The article in this exercise is of average difficulty for persons who have graduated from the eighth grade. Therefore, high school students or high school graduates should be able to read this selection at a rate of at least 275 words per minute. They should also be able to make a comprehension score of at least 14 and a vocabulary score of at least 7. That is 70 percent right of all the items in each of the two tests.

If your rate is above 275 and your comprehension and vocabulary scores are 70 percent or higher, you may be fairly well satisfied. Yet, you will want to raise your rate and your comprehension to even higher levels to obtain the important benefits that this better reading will bring.

If your rate on the article is below 275 words per minute, you will certainly want to increase it. As you push yourself to do so, you should be sure that your comprehension does not go down.

If your comprehension is 70 percent or below, you will surely want to concentrate upon improving your understanding. To do this, you may have to slow down your reading rate for a time.

If your rate is below 150 words per minute and if your comprehension is below 50 percent, you may need special help in a reading class or reading center.

With these points in mind, go ahead now and do General Reading Exercise 2.

In this lesson, you have looked into some of the many benefits that better reading can bring you. In Lesson 3, you will find answers to the question: How much can you improve your reading?

How much can you improve your reading?

IF SOMEONE SAYS, "You can improve your reading by 50 percent within two months," you will probably reply, "I can't believe that!"

Whether or not you believe you can make great gains in your reading in the coming weeks, you will be interested in finding out what other people have done. Like yourself, these people had their own reading improvement programs. Through these programs, they systematically tried to improve their reading abilities over a period of time—and made surprisingly good progress, as the examples given next show.

Groups have stepped up their reading power

By taking a reading course, many groups of people have improved their reading abilities. And this was true whether the persons in the group were poor, average, or good readers at the start of the training period.

1. *From non-readers to readers.* During World War I the Army had thousands of enlisted men who could not read even a grade school primer. Through a reading program that lasted about eight weeks, 90 percent of these men learned to read well enough to take the basic training required of all soldiers.

2. *High school students.* At the California (Missouri) High School, 50 ninth-grade students improved their rate 58 percent and their comprehension 25 percent in just four months. At the Medford (Massachusetts) High School, 15 juniors and seniors raised their rate 108 percent and their comprehension 15 percent during a 20-week training program. In one-half year, 56 students in the Concord (Massachusetts) High School made a three-year gain in reading rate and a 1¼-year gain in reading comprehension, according to the norms of standardized reading tests.

3. *College students.* At the Mechanical and Agricultural College of Texas, 172 freshmen gained 116 percent in rate and 14 percent in comprehension during one semester.

4. *Adult readers.* At the Racine (Wisconsin) public library 24 adults took an 18-session reading improvement course. They increased their rate by 152 words

per minute without loss in understanding.

5. *Military officers.* In the Air Forces, a group of officers attended special reading classes for six weeks. At the beginning of the training period, a typical class read at an average rate of 294 words a minute. At the end, it read at an average rate of 488 words a minute—a gain of 66 percent. Even though the class read two-thirds faster than at the start, it did not lose in comprehension.

6. *Office workers.* Fifty top-level employees of the Mutual Life Insurance Company of New York took part in a 15-hour reading program distributed over a ten-day period. They changed from 275 to 420 words a minute—a 53 percent gain. Before training, these employees, on the average, spent about 4½ hours a day in reading. After training, they could do this same amount of reading in about 3 hours. They used the 1½ hours saved to do other worth-while jobs. Through training all its employees to read faster and better, the company expects to boost its production by 25 per cent.

7. *Librarians.* Forty-one staff members of the Enoch Pratt Free Library, Baltimore, took a reading course that met twice a week for eight weeks. These librarians increased their reading rate by 147 words a minute—a gain of 61 percent. Their comprehension continued at a high level. Even these librarians, the professional people who know reading materials best, proved that they could learn to read much faster and better.

Individuals have streamlined their reading

As the examples just given showed, many people have improved their reading by attending a reading class where an instructor worked with a group. Others have increased their reading abilities by going to a reading center where a specialist helped them individually. Their reading progress and its benefits are illustrated in the cases presented next.

1. *Nancy's case.* Nancy, the tenth-grade student quoted in Lesson 2, received individual assistance in the reading center of a college. She took a seven weeks' course, three hours per week. During her 21 hours of training, Nancy increased her reading rate from 240 to 433 words a minute, a gain of 80 percent. She also kept her comprehension at 90 percent, a very high level.

2. *Bill's case.* While Bill was a senior in high school he was planning to go to college and to specialize in engineering. But Bill ran into trouble, serious trouble.

Bill had the mental ability needed to succeed in college. And he worked hard on high school subjects, spending long hours on homework. Even so, his school marks were only fair.

Reading was Bill's main problem. He read his assignments so slowly that he was seldom able to finish them. Because he could not keep up with the rest of his class, he was nearly ready to abandon his plans for college.

Bill took his problem to the school counselor. The counselor gave him several reading tests. According to these tests, Bill understood very well what he read; however, he read all types of material at a rate of only 150 words a minute.

The counselor helped Bill to plan and carry out a reading improvement program. By the end of his senior year, Bill had *doubled* his reading speed, without reducing his comprehension. He read his assignments much faster, much better, and much more easily than before. Because of this, Bill raised his marks; he was able to go ahead with his plans for an engineering degree.

3. *Mary's case.* As a college freshman, Mary read so poorly that she was in serious danger of "flunking out" before the end of her first year. Because of eyestrain while reading, Mary went to an optician. He found that she had a visual defect. After her defect was corrected by glasses, she began a program of daily reading exercises. Within six months, Mary was reading easily and efficiently. She also was succeeding in all her college studies.

4. *Mr. Jones's case.* A senior business executive, whom we shall call "Mr. Jones," went to an adult reading center in a Chicago college for aid in improving his reading. He was a college graduate and an above-average reader. Yet he believed that he could become a much better reader.

Mr. Jones took five one-hour lessons a week over a period of eight weeks—a total of 40 hours of training. During this training, he tripled his reading rate. He also kept his comprehension at a high level. After this training, Mr. Jones found that he could read an entire book on Sunday, and that he could do this reading with ease and with a sense of accomplishment.

An exercise in reading a letter

Here is a copy of the letter that Mr. Jones wrote to the director of the reading center. Read this letter and then take the short test that follows it.

In the time box, write down your starting time. Then start reading the letter.

Time Box

Finishing time	
Starting time	
Reading time	
Reading rate	

March 5, 1953

Dr. Harold K. Smith
Director, Reading Improvement Center
Chicago City College
315 North Central Ave., Chicago, Ill.

Dear Dr. Smith:

Only yesterday I completed my reading course and am so full of enthusiasm about what you have done for me that I am compelled to write you and try to give you an idea of what reading means to me.

Ever since I was a child, reading has been one of those necessary drudgeries. Yes, I completed my school assignments not without success, but practically never did I read a book for myself and only the headlines of newspapers. After a half-hour's reading I always felt so tired that my mind began to wander and it was never difficult to find excuses to do something else. But always in the back of my mind lurked the idea that I was missing something really worth-while.

Certain experiences kept bringing me back to this subject. About twenty-four years ago I was working on my first job and living temporarily with my sister in New York. One Sunday I watched my young nephew pick up a normal sized novel and only about two hours later put it down finished. It is not possible, I said to myself, that he knows more than vaguely what is in that book and I resolved to find out. It took me every night for a week to read the book my way, but by the next week end I had prepared mentally almost one hundred detailed questions about the book. With no apparent effort this boy answered every question correctly. Now, I am rarely jealous about other people's skills or possessions, but on this occasion was green with jealousy. But what to do about it?

Nobody enjoys doing things which he does badly, so in the years that followed I tried to minimize the importance of reading skill and this was not difficult at a time when I was so engrossed in making a place for myself in the business world. When, however, I joined the Great Books courses two years ago, the biweekly assignments reminded me continually not only of the effort which my reading required but of the real pleasure I was missing through my deficiency.

Then one day I had a talk with a friend whose son was in college. He told me how an accelerated reading course had changed both the boy's achievement and enjoyment of college from night to day. I had never before heard of such a course, but this was the clue I needed. Next day I telephoned a school teacher friend and asked her to inquire for me whether there was such a reading clinic for adults. The day I received her information was the same day on which I first appeared in your office.

All you told me made sense except one thing—How could one expect better comprehension as a companion to faster reading? Yes, your theoretical explanation sounded feasible, but practically I was most dubious. Now that I have completed the course, I realize that even this part is true. Every Sunday since I began

the training I have read an entire book. In the beginning this was quite a task but there were two big compensations. First, I discovered that no longer did I feel fatigue from reading and secondly, there was a great thrill of accomplishment in doing something which had heretofore been impossible for me. By now, this Sunday reading session has become a real source of happiness and satisfaction. A vote of thanks is due you for giving me the opportunity of catching up now on so much that I have missed these many years.

Sincerely yours,
Robert A. Jones

Write your finishing time in the time box. Then take this test on the letter you have just read.

Mark a + at the left of each *true* statement. Mark a O at the left of each *false* statement.

1. When Mr. Jones was a child, his reading was slow, difficult, and tiring, and he did very little reading.

2. Mr. Jones's nephew read a novel in two hours and understood thoroughly what he read, while Mr. Jones required seven evenings to finish the same book.

3. For years Mr. Jones minimized the importance of reading mainly because he read so poorly and did not enjoy reading.

4. Mr. Jones became acutely aware of what he was missing because of poor reading when he took a Great Books course.

5. Mr. Jones went to the office of the reading center soon after he found that an accelerated reading course had helped the son of a friend.

6. At first, Mr. Jones thought that if he read faster, his comprehension would go down.

7. Mr. Jones now reads an entire book every Sunday with ease and a sense of accomplishment.

8. In greater reading power, Mr. Jones finds a source of happiness and satisfaction.

9. Mr. Jones's letter shows that a person is never too old to learn to read faster and better.

10. Mr. Jones's experience indicates that if you very much want to improve your reading, you can greatly increase your reading power.

Now figure out your reading time for the letter. Change your reading time into your reading rate; use the table given here. Write your reading rate in the time box.

Time-to-Rate Table for the Letter
(621 Words)

Reading time	Reading rate
1:00-1:14	556
1:15-1:29	454
1:30-1:44	384
1:45-1:59	333
2:00-2:14	293
2:15-2:29	262
2:30-2:44	237
2:45-2:59	217
3:00-3:14	199
3:15-3:29	184
3:30-3:44	172
3:45-3:59	161
4:00-4:14	151
4:15-4:29	142
4:30-4:44	135
4:45-4:59	128
5:00-5:14	121
5:15-5:29	116

Here are the correct answers to the test: (Each of the statements is true and therefore should be marked +.)

You, too, can read much better

As the examples given in this lesson show, many young people and adults have greatly improved their reading. What they have done, you also can do.

If you are determined to make real progress in reading, you must pursue the better reading program that appears, lesson by lesson, in this book. In this program, as you will note, you will take these steps:

First—Find out how well you can read. Discover your reading strengths and weaknesses. List the reading skills, habits, and areas in which you need to improve.

Second—Plan your reading program so that you will replace poor skills and habits with good ones.

Third—Continue your reading program long enough to be sure that you develop and maintain good skills and habits.

Fourth—Regularly, say once a week, check to see if you are reading more and more efficiently than before.

Your better reading program will not take much of your time—and it will not take years to complete. But this program will require you to work hard and efficiently during the weeks ahead.

Do general reading exercise 3 (page 197)

The article in this exercise requires you to read instructions on "How to Handle an Outdoor Cook Fire." This is the kind of reading that you often have to do in school, at home, or on the job.

In doing this exercise, try to increase your reading rate. At the same time, try to make sure that you understand reasonably well what you are reading. Keep in mind, too, that you can apply what you learn from this article.

Go ahead and do General Reading Exercise 3.

If you are to work as effectively as possible in improving your reading, you must determine what your reading needs are. You will do this in Lesson 4.

LESSON 4

What are your reading needs?

AS YOU RECALL, there was a time in your life when you systematically learned to read and tried to improve your reading. While you were in elementary school, you undoubtedly had a reading lesson every day. You may have had some help in reading in the seventh and eighth grades. If you are in high school or college, you may be taking a special course in reading or you may be receiving instruction in reading from your subject-matter teachers.

No matter where you are or last were on the school or college ladder, you may have had much reading practice. Yet, if from time to time you fall down on the job in school, at work, or elsewhere, your trouble may be reading. Then, to get ahead, you will have to do more than just practice reading. You will have to gear your training in reading to your reading needs.

Are you a good reader or a poor one?

You can determine your reading needs in a general way by comparing the skills and habits of a good reader with those of a poor reader. This comparison appears in the table given here.

TABLE 1

A COMPARISON BETWEEN A GOOD READER AND A POOR READER

If you are *a good reader*, you read rapidly and you understand well what you read. This means that you have such skills and habits as these:	If you are *a poor reader*, you read slowly and understand poorly what you read. This means that you have such skills and habits as these:
1. *You read for a purpose.* Your purpose is always clear-cut—to get the general story, to remember details, or to answer questions.	1. *You read without a purpose.* You seldom know why you are reading something. As a result, your reading is often aimless.

21

TABLE 1 *(Cont.)*

A COMPARISON BETWEEN A GOOD READER AND A POOR READER

---

2. *You read thought units.* You grasp the meaning of a group of words at a glance. You quickly relate these meanings to get the idea presented in a sentence or a paragraph.

3. *You have many reading rates.* You adjust your reading rate to the materials you are reading and to your reasons for reading them. If you are reading a novel to enjoy the story, you read at a rapid rate. But, if you are reading a scientific book to remember details, you read at a slower rate, for thorough understanding.

4. *You evaluate what you read.* You often ask yourself: "Does what I am reading make good sense to me? Is the author qualified to write on this particular topic? Is he presenting only one point of view of the problem being considered?"

5. *You have a good vocabulary.* You already know what many words mean. You are skilled at getting the meanings of new words from their context—that is, from the words around them or from the sentences or paragraphs in which these words appear. You know how to use the dictionary, and you often use it to clarify the meanings of words.

6. *You read varied materials.* You read books, magazines, and newspapers. You read in many different fields—fiction, science, and history, for example. At times, you may do most of your reading in the field of your special interest, but you also do some reading in other fields.

7. *You read widely and enjoy reading.* You find that reading brings information and pleasure. You read whenever you can.

2. *You read word by word.* You get the meaning of each word in turn. Then you try to put these meanings together to understand each sentence. You often have to reread words.

3. *You have only one reading rate.* No matter what you are reading or why you are reading, you read at the same plodding rate. You read a novel for enjoyment at the same slow rate that you read a scientific book. You cannot skim something to get the general idea or to answer a particular question.

4. *You believe everything you read.* You believe that what you see in print is always true. You seldom check what you are reading with your own experience or with other sources. You never think critically about the writer and his point of view.

5. *You have a limited vocabulary.* You know the meanings of very few words. You never reread a sentence to get the meaning of a hard word. You seldom look up a word in the dictionary. When you do, you may have trouble in finding the word. And you have difficulty in understanding the word's definition and in selecting the right meaning for the word.

6. *You usually read the same kind of materials.* When you do read, you may choose the comics, love stories, mysteries, or sport news. Because you are a one-track reader, you miss the many interesting things that you could get from different kinds of books, magazines, and newspapers.

7. *You read little and dislike reading.* You find that reading is both a chore and a bore. You read only when you have to.

What factors affect your reading?

By studying Table 1, you learned *in general* what your reading needs are. You will next want to find out more precisely what your needs are and what you can do about them. To find your specific needs, you will have to consider the seven main factors connected with reading success or failure. These are:

A. Physical conditions
B. Speed of reading
C. Oral reading
D. Vocabulary
E. Reading comprehension
F. Ability to use reference materials
G. Pattern of reading

All these factors relate to your success in developing the skills, habits, and attitudes that contribute to efficient reading.

FACTOR A—PHYSICAL CONDITIONS

Have your eyes and ears checked. Make certain that your vision and hearing are reasonably good. If either is poor, you may be having difficulty in recognizing or pronouncing words. This, of course, interferes with your reading progress.

If print looks blurred to you, your vision is probably not as good as it should be. If you have frequent headaches, you may have eyestrain. This eyestrain may be due to the fact that you need properly-fitted glasses.

You may have to listen intently to hear what is being said. You may confuse words spoken to you. You may frequently have to ask a person to repeat what he has just said.

If you have any of these troubles, consult a specialist. He can test your vision or hearing. If you have defects, he may be able to correct them. As soon as you have thus made sure that your eyes and ears are all right, you are ready to go ahead with your reading improvement program.

Read at the same time every day. If possible, you should schedule a certain hour of the day to work on your reading improvement.

Make sure that your reading light is right. When you are reading, the light should not be too bright or too dim for your eyes. It should not shine directly into your eyes. When the light is right, you read comfortably and conserve your eyesight.

Read in a quiet place. You should do your reading in a place that is reasonably free from interruptions or distractions. This, of course, means that you should turn off the radio or television set so that you can give full attention to your reading.

FACTOR B—SPEED OF READING

Your reading speed depends both upon your reading habits and your reading skills. If you move your lips while reading, this slows down your rate. But if you read a group of words instead of a single word at a glance, this steps up your reading speed.

FACTOR C—ORAL READING

If you are a good reader, you are able to read aloud with clarity and expression. You don't stumble over words or read in a monotone. Rather, you read so that your listeners understand and enjoy what you are reading.

FACTOR D—VOCABULARY

The better your vocabulary the better your reading. Whether your vocabulary is now good or poor, you should keep on trying to learn the meanings of new words.

When you come across a word you do not know, do not stop reading. Keep on reading until you finish a chapter or a magazine article. Then reread the sentence in which the new word appears. Try to get the word's meaning from the words around it. If you still are not sure what the word means, look it up in a dictionary. Always compare the different meanings and select the one that fits your reading.

FACTOR E—READING COMPREHENSION

Reading comprehension is not just one ability; it is many different abilities. These abilities include a long and varied list of reading skills and habits.

If you have good comprehension, you give close attention to what you are reading. You read to meet your own well-defined purpose. You relate what you read to your own experience. You have a critical attitude toward what you read. And you are able to organize the information you get from reading.

FACTOR F—ABILITY TO USE REFERENCES

If you are a good reader, you are familiar with reference materials such as dictionaries, encyclopedias, yearbooks, atlases, and the library's card catalog. You know where to find these references and how to use them.

FACTOR G—PATTERN OF READING

If you are an effective reader, you have a pattern of reading that covers a wide variety of interests. You read magazine articles and books on different subjects. You read both fiction and nonfiction. You skim a newspaper and read carefully the most important parts. And you probably make good use of the public library.

Check upon your reading needs

To find your reading needs, answer the questions appearing in Table 2.

TABLE 2
USE THIS CHECK LIST TO FIND YOUR READING NEEDS

DIRECTIONS: Read Question 1. Write your answer, "Yes" or "No," at the right of the question. Answer each of the other questions in the same way. If you are not sure about your answer, do not answer the question.

A. Physical conditions

1. Is my general health good?
2. Is my vision satisfactory?
3. Is my hearing satisfactory?
4. Do I set aside a certain time each day for reading?
5. Do I have good lighting when I read?
6. Do I read in a fairly quiet place, free from distracting noises?

B. Speed of Reading

7. Do I read silently without moving my lips?
8. Do I read groups of words rather than one word at a time?
9. Do I usually read forward from left to right and down the page without looking back to words I have already read?
10. Do I fit my speed of reading to my reading purpose and to the type of material I am reading?
11. Do I read easy materials rapidly but with understanding?

C. Oral Reading

12. Do I pronounce words clearly and accurately?
13. Do I know how to work out the pronunciation of words?
14. Do I read aloud without embarrassment or discomfort?

15. Do I observe punctuation marks as I read aloud?

16. Do I read aloud in such a way that my listeners understand and enjoy what I am reading?

17. Can I make an oral summary of what I have just read aloud?

D. Vocabulary

18. Do I have a good general vocabulary?

19. Do I have the technical vocabularies necessary to understand the subjects or fields that I am now studying?

20. Do I know how to work out the meaning of new words from their context—that is, from the sentence or paragraph?

21. Do I know how to obtain the meanings of new words from the dictionary?

22. Do I keep a list of the new words I find in reading and do I review these words until I have made them my own?

E. Reading Comprehension

23. Do I have a well-defined purpose for reading a particular book, magazine article, or newspaper story?

24. Do I read with undivided attention?

25. Do I think about what I am reading?

26. Do I remember what I have read?

27. Do I know how to find the words that tell the central thought of a paragraph?

28. Do I know how to skim in finding answers to specific questions?

29. Do I know how to read quickly and accurately for details?

30. Do I check on the author's qualifications to write on a special subject?

31. Do I question statements that are illogical or inaccurate?

32. Can I make a satisfactory outline or summary of a book chapter or magazine article?

33. Can I make a satisfactory outline or summary of an entire book?

34. Am I able to understand and follow written directions?

35. Can I read maps, graphs, pictures, and other illustrations with understanding?

36. Can I read and interpret figures and tables of figures correctly?

F. Ability to Use Reference Materials

37. Do I know how to use the card catalog at the library?

38. Do I know how to find books and other reference materials?

39. Do I know where to find the magazine articles I want?

40. Do I know how to use the table of contents, the index, and the appendix in a reference book?

41. Do I know how to use aids such as dictionaries, encyclopedias, and yearbooks?

G. Pattern of Reading

42. Do I read both fiction and non-fiction stories and books?

43. Do I read books, magazine articles, and newspaper stories in many different fields?

44. Do I read only a moderate number of mystery stories or comic books?

45. Do I read stories that give me a true picture of life?

46. Do I read books or other publications that help me solve my personal problems?

47. Do I read newspapers and magazines regularly?

48. Do I read poetry with understanding and enjoyment?

49. Do I read and enjoy plays?

50. Do I find real enjoyment in reading different kinds of materials?

TABLE 3
A Summary of My Reading Needs and How to Meet Them
(An Example)

Physical Conditions

While reading, I've noticed lately that the print is sometimes blurred. I must get my glasses checked.

Speed of Reading

I often look back at words I have already read. And I read everything at about the same slow rate. I must push myself to read faster by timing myself. I must also improve my comprehension.

Oral Reading

Pronunciation is my biggest problem here. I must look up in the dictionary the pronunciation of the words that I may be saying incorrectly.

Vocabulary

I never remember the new words I find in the dictionary. Therefore, I have to look up these words again and again.

I must write down these new words in a notebook. I must learn to use them correctly in writing and speaking.

Reading Comprehension

I need to practice skimming to save time when looking up information. Also, I need help in finding the main ideas of paragraphs, articles, and chapters.

Ability to Use Reference Materials

I must find out which reference guides are worth knowing about, especially for reading biographies and books about music.

Pattern of Reading

I haven't much range or variety in my reading. In newspapers, books, and magazines, I must read more about current events, business, and perhaps science.

Summarize your reading needs and indicate how you can meet them

To get full value from this check list, you should quickly reread the questions and your answers. Examine those you have answered "Yes." Next, reread carefully the questions that you answered "No" as well as those you omitted. These answers indicate your reading weaknesses or your reading needs. Study these needs carefully. Then write a summary that gives your main reading needs and suggests the ways that you plan to meet them. An example of such a summary appears in Table 3.

During your better reading program, use the summary that you have just prepared. In this way you can check upon

your progress in satisfying your specific reading needs. Have your reading abilities tested and get the help you need.

Whatever your summary shows about your reading needs, you will probably find it desirable to take a standardized reading test. You can usually take such a test at a school or college. Or you can obtain the test from a publisher. The test results will help you determine your needs more accurately.

If your test shows that you are a very poor reader, you may want to seek the assistance of a specialist in reading. Or you may enroll in a reading class if one is offered in your community.

If you are like most people, however, you can improve your reading by independent effort. Whether your reading needs are serious or not, you can employ this book to become a better reader.

Do general reading exercise 4 (page 202)

Perhaps one of your needs is to read more good short stories. One such story appears in Article 4. It was written by O. Henry, an American author who was noted for the excellence of his style and for the surprise endings of his stories.

Go ahead and do General Reading Exercise 4. After you finish it, reread the article for further enjoyment. Then you will probably want to read other O. Henry stories.

In this lesson you studied your reading needs and found out how to meet them. In the next lesson you will learn how your eyes move while you are reading.

LESSON 5

How do your eyes behave while reading?

HERE IS A MESSAGE in International Code. Can you read it?

.—. . .— —.. .. —. —-. —.—.
.— —. —... . ..—. ..— —.

Each of these code symbols stands for a letter; the first symbol ".—." is the letter "R." Together these symbols spell out a simple sentence, which is the message.

If you don't know the code, you, of course, cannot read the message. If you are learning the code, you may be able slowly to read the letters in this way: R . . . E . . . A . . . D, and so on until you spell out the message. But if you are skilled in using the code, you get the message instantly: *Reading can be fun.*

You may never have to learn the International Code or read messages in it. Yet the facts about learning the code apply to learning to read. And they suggest one of the differences between a poor reader and a good reader. The very poorest reader reads letter by letter, and the poor reader reads word by word. But the good reader reads word group by word group.

Here is a comparison between two kinds of readers

To see how the reading skill of a poor reader compares with that of a good reader, look at Figure 1, "Slow Versus Fast Reading."

The column at the left shows how a slow reader reads. His eyes focus or fixate just above each dot; they take in only one word at a glance. In reading the column, they make a total of 123 fixations.

The column at the right indicates how a fast reader reads. His eyes fixate just above each dash. They take in a group of words at a glance. In reading the column, they make only 43 fixations—about a third as many fixations as are made by the eyes of the slow reader.

If you want to try an interesting experiment, have someone time you while you read the left-hand column as the slow reader reads it. Write down the number of seconds you required. Then have him time you while you read the right-hand column as the fast reader reads it. Again write down the number of seconds. Next, compare the two time periods that you

FIGURE I

Slow Versus Fast Reading[1]

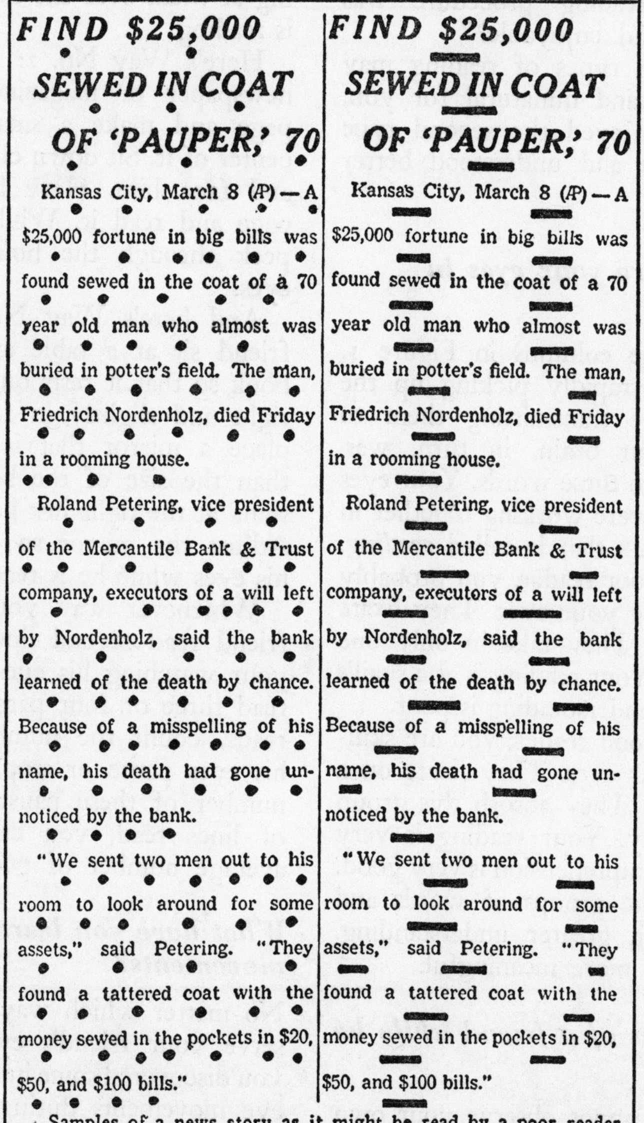

FIND $25,000 SEWED IN COAT OF 'PAUPER,' 70	FIND $25,000 SEWED IN COAT OF 'PAUPER,' 70
Kansas City, March 8 (Æ) — A $25,000 fortune in big bills was found sewed in the coat of a 70 year old man who almost was buried in potter's field. The man, Friedrich Nordenholz, died Friday in a rooming house.	Kansas City, March 8 (Æ) — A $25,000 fortune in big bills was found sewed in the coat of a 70 year old man who almost was buried in potter's field. The man, Friedrich Nordenholz, died Friday in a rooming house.
Roland Petering, vice president of the Mercantile Bank & Trust company, executors of a will left by Nordenholz, said the bank learned of the death by chance. Because of a misspelling of his name, his death had gone unnoticed by the bank.	Roland Petering, vice president of the Mercantile Bank & Trust company, executors of a will left by Nordenholz, said the bank learned of the death by chance. Because of a misspelling of his name, his death had gone unnoticed by the bank.
"We sent two men out to his room to look around for some assets," said Petering. "They found a tattered coat with the money sewed in the pockets in $20, $50, and $100 bills."	"We sent two men out to his room to look around for some assets," said Petering. "They found a tattered coat with the money sewed in the pockets in $20, $50, and $100 bills."

Samples of a news story as it might be read by a poor reader (left) and skilful reader (right). The less than average reader stops for each word. The skilled reader takes in groups of words which make sense. This takes less time, causes less eye fatigue, and increases understanding.

[1]From the *Chicago Daily Tribune,* March 29, 1951. Reprinted with permission of the publisher.

have recorded. Then, ask: "Did I understand the story better when I read slowly or when I read fast? Did I read more comfortably the first or the second time? Which reading procedure was more pleasant and enjoyable?"

Although both types of reading may have been new and unnatural for you, you probably enjoyed the second type of reading more and understood better what you read.

How skillful are your eyes in reading?

As you read the columns in Figure 1, your eyes were rapidly picking up the words and were transmitting them to your brain. Your brain, in turn, was giving meaning to these words. Your eyes and your brain were working together in the mental process that is called *reading*.

If you are a poor reader, you probably lack skill in using your eyes. They fixate on every word. They take in only one word at a time. Your reading is at a snail's pace, and your understanding is poor.

If you are a good reader, you are skillful in using your eyes. They fixate on a group of words. They absorb this group of words rapidly. Your reading is very fast, and your comprehension is very good. You react to the groups of words and hence read with greater understanding. Your reading is more meaningful.

Watch the eyes of a friend while he is reading

You obviously cannot observe your own eyes while you are reading, but you can learn much about the way your eyes behave by observing the eyes of a friend. You can first observe your friend's eyes as he reads. You can then have him observe your eyes as you read.

You can make these eye-to-eye observations in a number of simple ways. Here's Way No. 1: Sit in front of your friend. Watch his eyes directly by looking at them over the top of the book he is reading.

Here's Way No. 2: Find a story in a newspaper or magazine. Tear out the page and make a small hole near the center of it. Sit down close to your friend and face him. Have him hold up the page and read it. While he is doing so, peek through the hole and watch his eyes.

And here's Way No. 3: Have your friend sit at a table and hold an open book so that it rests on the table. At the right and slightly in front of the book place a mirror that is somewhat larger than the size of the book's page. Then stand at the right just behind your friend. Adjust the mirror so that you can see his eyes while he is reading.

Whichever way you use, have your friend read several lines to get used to your watching his eyes. Then have him read three or four paragraphs. While he reads, count the number of times that his eyes pause or stop. By dividing the number of these pauses by the number of lines read, you can figure out his average number of pauses per line.

What have you learned about eye movements?

No matter which way you used to observe your friend's eyes while reading, you discovered some important facts about eye movements during the act of reading. These facts deal with:
1. Fixation pause
2. Fixation point
3. Recognition-span
4. Return sweep
5. Regressive movement

When you watched your friend's eyes in reading, you noticed that they did *not* move in a continuous sweep from the beginning to the end of a line. Instead, his eyes moved along the line in a series of interrupted movements that can be described as: *Stop—Go—Stop—Go—Stop—Go. When* his eyes stopped for an instant, that instant was a *fixation pause. Where* his eyes stopped during that instant was a *fixation point. The number of words* his eyes took in at that fixation point was his *recognition-span.*

After your friend's eyes completed one line of print, you noticed that they quickly moved to the beginning of the next line. This movement was the *return sweep.* Then you observed that his eyes moved along the line as they had moved along the line before—that is, in a *Stop—Go—Stop—Go* movement.

Sometimes your friend's eyes moved back to reread something. They did this when he did not understand a word or phrase. This movement is called a *regressive movement.* Such movements are frequently made by the poor reader.

You get the meaning only when your eyes pause

Let your eyes sweep across each of the two lines below without pausing:

A $25,000 fortune in big bills was found sewed in the coat of a 70 year old man.

If your eyes moved without a stop you probably did not get any meaning from what you saw.

Now read the two lines at your usual speed:

A $25,000 fortune in big bills was found sewed in the coat of a 70 year old man.

This time your eyes had a *Stop—Go—Stop—Go* movement. During each stop, your eyes paused for an instant on a word or word group, and you obtained the meaning of the words. Only during the brief stop in your eye movements do you get the meaning of the word or words that you see. While your eyes are on the go, they are not taking in the meanings of the words.

The shorter the pause the better the reading

If you are a poor reader, your fixation pauses are too long. During such a long pause, you are having difficulty in recognizing a word. This slows down your reading; this also interferes with your understanding.

If you are a good reader, your fixation pauses are very short. During such a pause, you quickly and easily recognize a word or a group of words—and get the meaning, too. Because your eye pause is short, you read rapidly. You also read with understanding.

The fewer the fixations the better the reading

If you are a poor reader, your eyes stop on nearly every word that you read. In a line of print made up of 10 words, you may make as many as 10 fixations.

If you are a good reader, however, your eyes stop and take in a group of words. In reading 10 words, you may make only three fixations. For example, at the first fixation, your eyes take in three words; at the second, four words; and at the third, three words.

The wider the recognition-span the better the reading

The number of words that your eyes absorb at a single fixation is known as your *recognition-span.* This span includes the word on which your eyes are focusing; it also includes the word or words your eyes are seeing immediately at the left and at the right of that focal word.

If you are a poor reader, your recognition-span is narrow. At a single fixation, your eyes take in only one word—the word on which they are focusing. And your mind gets the meaning of that one word only.

You may be reading these three words: *A $25,000 fortune.* Your eyes see the first word *A*, then the second word *$25,000*, and finally the third word *fortune.* As your mind gets the meaning of each word in turn, it has to relate that meaning to the meanings of the words that went before. As a result, your reading is slow and difficult, and your understanding is poor.

But if you are a good reader, your recognition-span is broad. When your eyes focus at a point on a line of print, they see a group of words and your mind takes in its meaning instantly.

You may say to yourself: "I can read only one word at a time." If so, consider these three words again:

A $25,000 fortune

Focus your eyes steadily on the center word *$25,000*. Without moving your eyes, what word do you see at the left? What word do you see at the right?

It is probable that you are now seeing all three words at almost the same time—the word group *A $25,000 fortune.*

The fewer the regressions the better the reading

If you are a poor reader, your eyes make many regressive movements. They often go back to see again what they have already seen in the line or in the previous line.

Take, for example, the sentence already presented:

A $25,000 fortune in big bills was found sewed in the coat of a 70 year old man.

If your eyes go back to reread, the message that they send to your mind is something like this:

A $25,000 fortune in big fortune bills was found sewed $25,000 found in the coat of a coat of a 70 year old 70 year old man.

If that was the message your eyes brought, no wonder that you had trouble understanding what the sentence meant!

If you are a good reader, your eyes seldom backtrack along a line or jump back and forth from one line to a line seen before. Rather, your eyes have a *Stop—Go—Stop—Go* movement from left to right along a line. And they also have a smooth, fast movement from right to left in returning from the end of one line to the beginning of the next line, just below it. Your eyes do not regress. Instead, they bring a fast-moving and free-flowing message to your mind.

Here is a summary of good and poor eye movements

Your study of eye movements has shown you four important differences between poor readers and good readers. These differences are:

1. Poor readers have long eye pauses; good readers have short ones.

2. Poor readers make many eye fixations; good readers make few.

3. Poor readers have a narrow recognition-span; good readers have a broad recognition-span.

4. Poor readers make many eye regressions; good readers make few or none.

How can you improve your eye movements?

You can read faster and better by shortening your eye pauses, by reducing the number of your fixations, by broadening your recognition-span, and by getting rid of the tendency to make frequent regressions.

You can train your eyes for better reading at the reading center of a school or college. This reading center may have different kinds of testing and training devices.

You may use special reading devices

The opthalmograph. If the reading center has this device, you can use it to check upon your eye movements while reading. In using this machine, you read a paragraph appearing on a small card. As you read, your eye movements are photographed on motion picture film. The jagged lines on this film show you the number of fixations your eyes made in reading the paragraph. From these fixations you can determine your recognition-span—the average number of words you took in during each eye fixation.

A tachistoscope. The reading center may have one of these devices, too. Used as a part of a reading program, it may help you to broaden your eye-span and to decrease your regressive movements.

In one kind of tachistoscope, you put in cards that have numbers, letters, or words on them. You move one of these cards into place before your eyes. You then press a button. The card lights up for an instant—from one-tenth to one-hundredth of a second. During the flash of light, you try to read all that is on the card.

As you use this device, you may im-prove your skills in two ways: First, you may come to recognize three words instead of only one during the flash. And second, you may recognize three words with increasing speed.

The reading film. At the center, you may watch a reading film that is projected on a large screen. In this moving picture, you see one word group, then the next word group, and so on until your eyes have seen, in turn, all the word groups making up a story. Afterward, you take a comprehension test on the story. The film aims to help you to read rapidly word groups instead of single words.

The reading pacer.[2] The reading center may have a simple machine that is called a *reading pacer*. This machine is used to assist you to read faster and to concentrate better on what you are reading.

On the sloping platform of the reading pacer, you place an open book or magazine so that you can read one of the pages. You then set the pacer at a rate of so many words a minute. When you start the machine, a shutter like a window shade descends over the page you are reading. The descending shutter prevents your eyes from rereading or regressing.

By setting the pacer at faster and faster rates, you may increase your reading speed and improve your ability to concentrate.

The mechanical devices just described may prove helpful. They are, however, not required for better reading.

On your own, you can train your eyes to read better

You may be unable to go to a reading

---

[2]One kind of pacer is the *SRA Reading Accelerator*, available from Science Research Associates, Chicago.

center at a school or college to get eye training. But you can improve your eye movements without this training by using this book. Through reading practice, you can get the necessary eye training.

For example, you can increase your recognition-span. If you are an efficient reader, as said before, your recognition-span covers a group of words that make a natural thought unit. For example, one such thought unit was the phrase *A $25,-000 fortune.*

In the first two sentences of the story in Figure 1, the natural thought units are presented in the order of their appearance. Read these units by fixing your eyes for a fraction of a second at the middle of each unit. Glance at the first unit, then at the second unit, and so on.

A $25,000 fortune
in big bills
was found sewed
in the coat
of a 70 year old man
who almost was buried
in potter's field.
The man, Friedrich Nordenholz,
died Friday
in a rooming house.

Try to read these same thought units faster by placing a 3 x 5-inch card just above the first thought unit. Then move the card down the column of thought units so that you read each unit rapidly.

You may want to make yourself a set of *flash cards.* To do this, get a package of 3 x 5-inch cards. On each card, print or type a group of words that is a thought unit.

Some groups may be short—only two words; others may be long—three to six words. Make up a set of cards containing word groups from the sentences that appear on one page of a textbook, novel, magazine, or newspaper.

After you have made approximately 50 cards, you are ready to begin your practice. Ask a friend to assist you. Have him flash each card as rapidly as you can successfully read aloud each phrase.

After you have gone through the deck, shuffle the cards. Have your friend flash the cards again, one by one, as he did before. Then ask him to re-shuffle the cards and show them again increasing the speed of showing them. Continue this practice until you quickly recognize every word group. Then go back and reread the page. You will undoubtedly find that your rate of reading that page has increased greatly.

Concentrate on thought units

The best way to train your eyes and your mind to grasp word groups instead of single words is to use thought units in all your reading. To get a clearer idea of what this means, you might practice reading the thought units that appear in the next reading exercise. Notice that each thought unit is marked off by the slanting lines. In reading each unit, glance at or near the middle of the word group. Then glance at the middle of the next word group, and so until you finish the selection.

It was / with some difficulty /
he found the way / to his own house, /
which he approached / with silent awe, /
expecting every moment / to hear /
the shrill voice / of Dame Van Winkle. /
He found the house / gone to decay— /
the roof fallen in, / the windows shattered, /
and the doors / off the hinges. /
A half-starved dog, / that looked like Wolf, /
was skulking about it. / Rip called him /
by name, / but the cur snarled, /
showed his teeth, / and passed on. /
This was / an unkind cut, indeed— /

"My very dog," / sighed poor Rip, / "has forgotten me!"[3]/

Try to read faster without regressions

To improve your eye movements, you can select something that is very interesting and fairly easy to read. You may, for example, read a newspaper story. Its single column is usually narrow. Therefore, with practice you can often get the meaning of a whole line of type by letting your eyes glance only once at the middle of that line.

As you go through the story, *try to read ahead*. Do not look back to reread. After you finish, ask yourself, "What have I read?" Then try to summarize the main points.

If you are doubtful about certain points in the story, go back and reread the parts where these points appear. This kind of rereading will help you to clarify the meaning of what you have just read. If you first read the passage or story as a whole, this rereading will not slow down your reading rate or interfere with your understanding.

Get rid of lip movements and other bad habits

Perhaps you have heard the joke about the fellow who was applying for a driver's license. He passed the eye test and driving test but failed the written test on traffic laws. In the last test he had to give oral answers to ten true-false statements. Afterward a friend asked him why he had failed. He said: "I just bought a new set of teeth. Because I couldn't pronounce the words with them, I couldn't read the questions."

Some poor readers, like this unfortu-

[3]From "Rip Van Winkle," *The Sketch Book*, by Washington Irving.

nate fellow, have developed poor habits of silent reading. As they read, they move their lips or use their throat muscles as if they were pronouncing the words aloud. Other poor readers move their heads or move their fingers along a line of print. All these practices make reading slow.

If you have any such habits, you should try to get rid of them. They are carry-overs from the oral reading you did during your early school days. To determine whether you have these poor habits, ask yourself each of these questions:

1. While reading silently, do I move my lips? (If you do, you are speaking the words to yourself whether you are conscious of it or not.)

2. Do I move my head from left to right along a line and from the end of one line to the beginning of the next line? (If you do, your head is doing what your eyes should do.)

3. Do I move my finger along a line of print as I read it? (If you do, your eyes are following the slow pace set by your finger.)

If you have any of these poor habits, your speed of silent reading is being hindered. These habits are definite obstacles to rapid reading, for your eyes can move much faster than your lips can form words, than your head can move, or than your finger can point. In fact, the hand is never quicker than the eye in silent reading.

Suppose that you have one of these poor habits and want to overcome it. If you are *a lip mover*, you can do this: Place a finger on your lips. Then you will notice if and when your lips move. If you have all three poor habits, put your finger (the one you usually point with) on your lips. Then practice reading rapidly some very easy, highly interesting materials. Try to read rapidly and to avoid lip movements.

You can improve your reading habits, however, by reading for ideas and by reading so rapidly that you do not have time to whisper words, turn your head, or point with your finger. These habits usually will disappear as you learn to read rapidly. Begin with very easy materials. Increase your speed gradually as you increase the amount and difficulty of your reading.

How can you improve your eye movements?

Up to now in this lesson, you have learned a great deal about the mechanics of eye movements in reading. You have also learned certain ways to improve them.

As you work toward improvement, you should keep in mind what the experts have discovered about eye movements. On the basis of many studies, they believe that poor eye movements are a symptom rather than a cause of poor reading ability. This means that, *if you make a determined effort to read faster and better, your eye movements are likely to improve automatically.* And your lip movements and other poor habits are likely to disappear.

If you concentrate on improving your eye movements, you will give all or most of your attention to them instead of to the meaning of what you are reading. As a result, you will almost surely decrease your understanding. But if you concentrate on getting meanings rapidly from the printed page, you will find that you will usually improve your reading rate. You will raise your comprehension, shorten your fixation pauses, reduce the number of your fixation points, broaden your recognition-span, cut down your regres-

sions, and eliminate both lip and throat movements.

What have you learned about better reading?

Mark a + at the left of each *true* statement. Mark a O at the left of each *false* statement.

1. In reading a story, the good reader makes many more fixations than the poor reader makes.
2. The word-by-word reader understands better what he is reading than does the reader who reads by word groups or thought units.
3. In reading, the eyes of every person have a *stop-go-stop-go* movement.
4. A person is getting meaning only when his eyes fixate or pause on a word or word group.
5. Your recognition-span is the number of words you see and understand at a single glance.
6. While reading something for the first time, the good reader often goes back to reread words or word groups.
7. One machine that assists you to read faster is called the *reading pacer.*
8. Through using the tachistoscope, you may learn to read more words faster, at a single glance.
9. If you pronounce words to yourself while reading, you slow down your rate.
10. The best way to improve your eye movements is to give your full attention to these movements while you read.

Here are the correct answers to this test: (10-o; 9-+; 8-+; 7-+; 6-o; 5-+; 4-+; 3-+; 2-o; 1-o)

Do general reading exercise 5 (page 208)

In doing this exercise, make an effort

to increase your reading rate, comprehension, and vocabulary. As you read the article, try to apply what you have learned in Lesson 5. For example, try to grasp groups of words that are thought units instead of single words.

After you finish this general reading exercise, compare your scores with those you made in the first such exercise. How much has your reading rate increased?

Has your comprehension improved? Has your vocabulary improved?

In this lesson you have learned much about your eye movements while you are reading. In the next lesson you will find out why and how you should read for a purpose.

LESSON 6

How can you read for a purpose?

AS YOU ARE DOING each lesson in this book, you have a definite purpose in mind. That purpose is to improve yourself in one or more reading abilities. In this lesson, you will develop the skills you need to fit your reading to your reading purpose.

Learn to read for different purposes

Nearly every day you probably do some reading. Today you may read a newspaper, a magazine article, or a chapter in a book. Yet you may not have a clear idea of your reading purpose. Even if you do, you may not use the best methods for meeting that purpose. As a result, your reading may not be nearly as efficient as it could be.

Your purpose may be mainly to enjoy what you are reading. It may be to get the facts that you want. Or it may be to follow the instructions for doing something or for making something.

Whatever your purpose, you should fit your methods of reading to it. How you do this is illustrated in Table 4. Study carefully the examples given. The first example deals with the purchasing of groceries. It points out: To locate good food buys, you should read the advertisements in your local newspaper. You should read these ads quickly, writing down the names of the stores and the best buys in them. The other examples show other reading purposes, materials, and methods that are important to use in your daily life.

TABLE 4

EXAMPLES OF READING PURPOSES, READING MATERIALS, AND READING METHODS

WHY YOU ARE READING	WHAT YOU ARE READING	HOW YOU SHOULD READ
1. To locate good food buys	1. Advertisements in your local newspapers	1. Read through the ads quickly; write down the names of the stores and the best buys.
2. To see what is happening in your own community	2. Your local newspaper	2. Skim the newspaper, reading the headlines. Stop to read carefully the stories you are most interested in.

TABLE 4 (*Cont.*)

WHY YOU ARE READING	WHAT YOU ARE READING	HOW YOU SHOULD READ
3. To keep posted on what is going on in the United States and in other nations	3. A metropolitan newspaper or national news magazine	3. Skim the newspaper or magazine. Read carefully the stories that are most important.
4. To enjoy stories during leisure time	4. A popular magazine	4. Turn through the entire magazine. Read the table of contents. Select some articles or stories to read. You may want to skim some articles and to read others carefully.
5. To make a written or oral book report	5. A fiction or non-fiction book	5. Read the table of contents. Then turn through the book quickly to see what is in it. Read the whole book rapidly. Makes notes as you go along. Reread carefully the parts that appeal to you.
6. To answer a question that comes up in a discussion at home or at school	6. A yearbook or an encyclopedia	6. Use the index to find the page that answers the question. Read that page carefully and make notes on it.
7. To build storage shelves	7. A book chapter, booklet, or magazine article on simple carpentry	7. Read the material through quickly. Then read it carefully, paying close attention to all instructions.
8. To do a homework assignment in English	8. English textbook and workbook	8. Read the entire chapter rapidly. Then reread it carefully. Do what the workbook tells you to do. In the textbook, reread each part that you do not understand.
9. To get ready for an examination in general science	9. Science textbook and science notebook	9. Read the section in the textbook and notebook that the test is to cover. Concentrate on careful reading and remembering. Reread parts that are not clear to you.
10. To learn to get along better with others	10. A magazine or newspaper article, or a book chapter or booklet on this subject	10. Read the material rapidly and then more carefully. Compare what you are reading with your own experience. Apply what you have learned.

Fit your reading to your purpose

If you are a poor reader, you may not adapt your reading to your purpose. You read a novel and a serious book at the same slow rate. You read the table of contents of a magazine or the index of a book as though you were trying to memorize it. In a newspaper, you take as much time to read the comics page as the editorial page.

But if you are a good reader, you always fit your reading methods to your reading purpose. When reading a novel for enjoyment, you read at a rapid rate. When reading a serious book to answer your questions, you read carefully and at times slowly. You have trained yourself in a variety of reading skills. And you know how, where, and when to use the skill that best serves your reading purpose.

An exercise in reading for different purposes

According to reading experts, you should learn to read skillfully for such purposes as these:

A. To get the main idea
B. To get the important details
C. To answer a specific question
D. To evaluate what you are reading
E. To apply what you are reading

To test yourself on your abilities to read for different purposes, read the magazine article that appears next. You will read the article several times, each time for a different purpose.

Read to get the main idea of the article

Skim this article to find out what it is about. Don't stop to read the details.

HOW LONG WILL YOU LIVE?[1]
by Paul D. Green

FEW OF US are such optimists that we don't worry about how long we'll live, and even fewer are such pessimists as not to care. Therefore, the latest figures on life and death in America should give pleasure to practically everyone in the nation.

For instance, according to the annual report issued by the U.S. Public Health Service, based on 1949 vital statistics, we are in the best state of health of all time. We can expect to live longer than any of our ancestors—an average of 68 years. This means almost 66 for men and better than 71 for women.

This average is a full five years better than the record of a decade ago, 10 years better than in 1930; 13 better than in 1921; 16 better than in 1911; 21 better than in 1901; and almost twice as good as in 1880 or earlier.

It's so good, in fact, that if we continue to improve at the same rate—100 percent in 70 years—within a century we'll be the oldest living mammals, outlasting even the turtle.

Your own life-expectancy figure depends a great deal on the year and place you were born; your marital status; the kind of food you eat; whether you are too thin or too fat; the kind of work you do; your temperament and many other factors.

The following personal test is based on statistics from many sources—the before-mentioned U.S. Public Health Service, the Institute of Life Insurance, and compilations of various individual

[1]Reprinted from *This Week* Magazine. Copyright 1952, by United Newspapers Magazine Corporation.

insurance companies. It is not guaranteed to be accurate for every reader. After all, who knows when a safe is going to fall on him? But statistically it is accurate.

It's true that Mark Twain once said, "There are lies and there are damn lies, and then there are statistics," but most of us still like to fool around with figures and predict the future.

So let's go, and, first of all, remember that the statisticians are presuming that you are in moderately good health. But be sure you have a pencil in hand—you're going to come in need of it.

1. Year of Birth. Select from the following columns the number of years you were expected to live the year you were born:

Period	Men	Women
1880-1900	35-40 yrs.	37-42 yrs.
1901-1904	46 yr. 6 mo.	48 yr. 8 mo.
1905-1908	48 yr. 8 mo.	51 yr. 5 mo.
1909-1912	50 yr. 7 mo.	54 yr. 4 mo.
1913-1916	51 yr. 8 mo.	56 yr. 6 mo.
1917-1920	52 yr. 6 mo.	56 yr. 5 mo.
1921-1924	59 yr. 2 mo.	61 yr. 10 mo.
1925-1928	58 yr. 5 mo.	61 yr. 6 mo.
1929-1932	59 yr. 10 mo.	63 yr. 2 mo.
1933-1936	60 yr. 6 mo.	64 yr. 5 mo.
1937-1940	62 yr.	66 yr.
1941-1944	64 yr. 6 mo.	68 yr.
1945-1948	65 yr.	70 yr. 4 mo.
1949-1952	65 yr. 11 mo.	71 yr. 6 mo.

Write down your basic life expectancy.

_____yrs. _____mos.

2. Place of birth. The longevity records vary somewhat in different parts of the U.S. and greatly in foreign countries. (Skip this question if you were born in a foreign country.) Make the following adjustments according to where you were born in the U.S.:

New England   add 6 months
Middle Atlantic States subtract 1 month
South Atlantic States subtract 1 year
North Central States   add 7 months
South Central States   subtract 7 months
Mountain & Western   subtract 10 months
New Total _____yrs. _____mos.

3. Present age: No matter what the estimate of your life expectancy was at birth, it improves the longer you live. So add the following based on the number of years you have already lived:

Age	Add	Age	Add
1-10	. . . . 1 yr.	41-45	. . . . 6 yrs.
11-15	. . . . 2 yrs.	46-50	. . . . 6½ yrs.
16-20	. . . . 3½ yrs.	51-55	. . . . 8 yrs.
21-25	. . . . 4 yrs.	56-65	. . . . 9 yrs.
26-30	. . . . 4½ yrs.	66-80	. . . 10 yrs.
31-35	. . . . 5 yrs.	81-90	. . . . 6 yrs.
36-40	. . . . 5½ yrs.	91 up	. . . . 5 yrs.

New Total _____yrs. _____mos.

4. Wonder drugs: In addition to these adjustments, you are entitled to still another for having survived the early decades of this century and entered the era of better medicine, sanitation and wonder drugs.

So, add 6 months for every year you have lived until 1946, when wonder drugs were made generally available.

New Total _____yrs. _____mos.

So much for the basic factors. Now we come to the human factors, or things that you have done or have happened to you which affect your life expectancy. Many experts think that how long you live depends somewhat on your parents' age at death. Actually this is very hard to prove—there are too many factors involved. So let's go on to more predictable matters.

5. Marital status: Married folks generally live longer than unmarried people, statistics show and psychiatrists affirm. So if you're over 25 and not yet married,

for every unwedded decade, deduct 1 year. Or if you are married, ADD 5 years.

New Total _____yrs. _____mos.

6. Occupation: A recent survey shows that U.S. clergymen, surprisingly, live at least one year less than most people. And doctors, despite their medical knowledge, generally have a shorter life than the people they try to keep alive. So, if you're a doctor or clergyman, deduct four months to a year, depending on how harassed you feel. Teachers, trained nurses, lawyers and clerical workers should add three years.

Industrial workers have improved considerably in the last few decades. If you were working at an industrial occupation before 1940, deduct 1 year for each 5 that you were working. After 1940, add 1 year because you're now a healthier specimen than white-collar workers. Farmers, despite a high accident rate, should add two years because of their healthy outdoor life.

People with certain types of hazardous occupations are rated by insurance companies as having a lower expectancy than the average person. Some companies will not insure certain types of workers, others charge extra premiums for people engaged in hazardous occupations, and some advance the age of insured persons in certain occupations. For example, they consider a 35-year-old dishwasher or cook as having a life expectancy only of a man of 40. Other age advances used by the New York Life Insurance Company are brewery process workers, eight years, laborers in iron and steel smelting plants, 12 years, actors and actresses, stage managers, theatrical workers, musicians, generally five years.

Airline pilots, house wreckers, electric linemen, cable splicers, tower erectors, bridge builders, submarine workers, merchant marine crewmen (not officers), railroad brakemen on freight trains, outside painters who work on scaffolding are all charged extra premiums from $2.50 to $10 a year.

Steeplejacks and tunnel workers entering caissons and drivers of trucks carrying explosives are non-insurable by N.Y. Life.

New Total _____yrs. _____mos.

7. Where you live: Small-town folks outlive city dwellers, all other things being equal. If you're a non-farmer, live in a small town, add four years. City folks subtract two.

New Total _____yrs. _____mos.

8. Economic status: Paradoxically, rich people die just as fast if not faster than poor people because they tend to eat and drink too much and expire early from diseases due to overindulgence. Poor people lead shorter lives due to malnutrition, bad environment and being more subject to disease. Therefore, if you have been either wealthy or poor for the most part of your life, deduct four years.

New Total _____yrs. _____mos.

9. Your figure: A Metropolitan Life Insurance Company study on the effects of obesity on health, for example, showed that 50 per cent more overweight men died before their time than normal men, and 47 per cent more obese women.

The reason for premature deaths due to obesity is that overweight causes such killers as hypertension, heart disease, diabetes, cancer and gall bladder trouble.

Accordingly, if you are over 40, you should deduct 1 year for every 5 pounds you are overweight.

New Total _____yrs. _____mos.

10. Alcoholism: To date, there have been no comprehensive surveys which arrive at any definite conclusions about the effects of alcohol on longevity. There

are many cases, in fact, of heavy drinkers or downright alcoholics living past the seventies.

Heavy drinkers (who consume a pint a day on the average and are drunk once a week or so) are likely to suffer from diabetes, high blood pressure, cirrhosis of the liver, neuritis, gout and Bright's disease, all of which may shorten life.

Confirmed alcoholics (drunk almost daily, and regularly insensibly drunk), invite early demise because of malnutrition which makes them susceptible to disease (particularly pneumonia) and less able to cope with operations. They are also accident prone and subject to delirium tremens.

So, on the side of temperance or moderation, if you're a heavy drinker, deduct 5 years; if an alcoholic, deduct 10. If you just take a drink now and then, forget it.

New Total _____yrs. _____mos.

11. Disposition: This has a bearing on how long you will live, too. A perpetual crank, worry-wart, neurotic or pessimist invites bodily or mental disturbances which make for an unhappy and shorter life. So, if you're one of these people, deduct five years. If you are good-natured and placid, however, add up to five years.

New Total _____yrs. _____mos.

12. Family and environment: A British survey of life expectancy for children of large families turned up this interesting conclusion:

A. Children from large families live longer than those from small families, except when the large families number more than ten.

B. Children in large families vary, too. Those born between the fourth and eighth years of their parents' marriage usually live longer than those born before and after them.

If you can place yourself here, give or take two years.

New Total _____yrs. _____mos.

This last figure is how long you should normally be expected to live, barring an invasion from other planets, a rain of atomic bombs, earthquakes, epidemics or geological upheavals.

There may be other factors influencing your life-expectancy figure, however. It may make a difference whether you're a vegetarian or meat-eater. In Western North Carolina, for example, there are natives who swear that chewing a certain weed known as ramp insures living to be 100.

Then there are such factors as whether you were born with innate vitality of the nervous or circulatory systems, which may offset a lot of the foregoing derogatory influences.

It might make a difference whether you were brought up in crowded city tenements or in the wide open spaces; whether you go to sea (mariners generally outlive landlubbers). Your I.Q., your romantic life, and even your morals have a bearing on your length of life. Gamblers, for example, have a low rating because of the hazards of their profession.

Also, as I pointed out in the beginning, the above is at best a conjecture, and depends a lot on your state of health. If you are already in poor health, you will have to make allowances for that.

In any case, it may make you feel better to compare your final life-expectancy figure with that of people in certain foreign countries. Here are some comparisons according to latest available studies:

	Men	Women
United States	67	71
Australia	67	71
France	62	68
Denmark	66	68
Netherlands	69	71
Canada	65	69
Japan	56	60
Chile	38	40
Scotland	64	68
Egypt	36	41
Portugal	49	53

Now that you have skimmed the article for its main idea, do the test item below. Mark a check (✔) at the left of the correct choice.

1. The main idea of the article was that you will probably
   (A) live through the next world war
   (B) lose your life in an accident
   (C) live longer than you now expect
   (D) die from a disease of old age
   (E) live happily for many more years

Read to get the important details

Read the article a second time, this time more carefully. However, try to read at a reasonably fast rate. Concentrate upon getting the main facts presented in the article. During this reading, do not write down the figures that apply to your own life expectancy.

After you finish the article, take the following test to find out whether you understood the important ideas.

2. According to the U.S. Public Health Service, the average American can now expect to live to the age of about
   (A) 58 years
   (B) 68 years
   (C) 78 years

Here are the main factors that affect your life expectancy. Mark a check (✔) at the left of each choice that will help lengthen your life span.

3. Sex:
   (A) Male
   (B) Female
4. Year of birth:
   (A) 1937-1940
   (B) 1917-1920
5. Place of birth:
   (A) North Central States
   (B) South Central States
6. Kind of drugs:
   (A) Old-fashioned
   (B) Wonder
7. Marital status:
   (A) Single
   (B) Married
8. Occupation:
   (A) Farmer
   (B) Doctor
9. Where you live:
   (A) City
   (B) Small town
10. Economic status:
    (A) Wealthy or poor
    (B) Middle income
11. Your figure:
    (A) Fat
    (B) Thin
12. Alcohol:
    (A) Nondrinker
    (B) Heavy drinker
13. Disposition:
    (A) Happy
    (B) Worried
14. Family:
    (A) Large
    (B) Small
15. Health:
    (A) Poor
    (B) Good
16. Nation of residence:
    (A) Egypt
    (B) United States

Read to answer a specific question

Here are three specific questions that are answered in the article. First, read the question. Then skim the article and find the answer. In each blank space, mark a check (✔) at the right of the correct answer, or write in the correct answer.

17. In the United States, which person can expect, on the average, to live longer? The male? _____ The female? _____ How many years longer? _____years.

18. Which worker has the longer life expectancy today? An industrial worker? _____ A white-collar worker? _____

19. What is the life expectancy of a man who lives in Japan? _____years.

Read to evaluate what you are reading

Reread the article to answer this test. If a statement is *true*, mark a + at the left of it. If a statement is *false*, mark a O at the left of it.

20. The facts and figures given in the article appear to come from reliable sources.

21. You are almost certain to live as long as the life expectancy you worked out for yourself.

22. Mark Twain was right when he implied that statistics are worse than "damn lies."

23. The author gave sound interpretations of the information he presented, not just pleasant interpretations.

Read to apply what you are reading

Here is the question: How long will you live? Reread the article carefully. As you do so, fill in the blanks in this table.

Table of Your Life Expectancy

	Years	Months
1. Year of birth:		
2. Place of birth:		
3. Present age:		
4. Wonder drugs:		
5. Marital status:		
6. Occupation:		
7. Where you live:		
8. Economic status:		
9. Your figure:		
10. Alcohol:		
11. Disposition:		
12. Family:		
13. Other:		
Total:		

Add the years and months you have recorded. The total gives you an estimated answer to the question: How long can you expect to live?

Here are the correct answers to all the test items: (1-C; 2-B; 3-B; 4-A; 5-A; 6-B; 7-B; 8-A; 9-B; 10-B; 11-B; 12-A; 13-A; 14-A; 15-B; 16-B; 17-Female, 5 years; 18-An industrial worker, 19-56 years; 20-+; 21-0; 22-0; 23-+.)

Do general reading exercise 6 (page 214)

Through this exercise, you will again check upon your reading rate, your reading comprehension, and your reading vocabulary.

After you complete this exercise, examine your rate and comprehension graphs. Remember that you should expect certain ups and downs to appear in these graphs. The main thing to notice is whether these lines show upward trends for the first six general reading exercises.

In the next lesson, you will concentrate upon ways by which you can read faster and faster.

LESSON 7

How can you read faster?

"WELL, IN OUR COUNTRY," said Alice, still panting a little, "you'd generally get to somewhere else—if you ran very fast for a long time, as we've been doing."

"A slow sort of country!" said the Queen. "Now, *here*, you see, it takes all the running *you* can do to keep in the same place. If you want to get somewhere else, you must run twice as fast as that!"[1]

You do not need to go through the looking glass with Alice to realize that you are living in a fast sort of country. Now, here, you must read faster, perhaps twice as fast, to get to the places you must go. If you read at a horse-and-buggy rate, you'll be left far behind in this jet-propelled age.

Why should you learn to read faster?

In the modern world there is so much to read and so little time in which to read. And that is true whether you are a young person who is trying to finish a school assignment or an adult who is trying to do a job better.

To be successful at school, at work, at home, or elsewhere, you must be able

[1]Lewis Carroll, *Through the Looking Glass.*

to read rapidly and skillfully many kinds of materials—newspapers, magazines, books, pamphlets, and letters, for example.

If you are a slow reader, you are unable to read a daily newspaper or to complete your reading work within a reasonable period of time. If you increase your rate by 50 percent, you will be able to get your required reading done in one-third less time than before. Then you will have time to read other things. To help you speed up your reading, previous lessons gave you a number of practical suggestions. This lesson will give you additional help.

Does fast reading mean poor reading?

"Slow but sure"—you may have heard that saying before. But is this true of reading? The answer is: "Not in many kinds of reading." In general, the slow reader is less sure about the meaning of what he is reading than is the fast reader.

You may also have heard that the more slowly a person reads the better he understands, or that the more rapidly he reads the poorer his comprehension. But

46

is what you have heard really true? Again the answer is: "Not in many kinds of reading." The typical person finds that when he speeds up his reading he also may improve his comprehension.

Fast readers are usually good readers

Experiments show that rapid readers are efficient readers. They often understand and remember what they read as well as, if not better than, slow readers.

The skills—speed and comprehension —tend to go together. As you raise your speed of reading, you can also improve your comprehension. And as you improve your comprehension, you can also speed up your reading. With greater reading speed, you are able to cover more material, to get more ideas, and to gain a broader understanding—all in a given amount of time.

Understanding is always most important

What has just been said does *not* mean that if you try to read faster, you will automatically understand better what you read. It does *not* mean that you should read all materials at the same rate of speed. It does *not* mean that you should consider speed more important than comprehension.

Although you will find many advantages in reading more rapidly, you must always keep in mind the importance of understanding what you read. That is why each of the general reading exercises in this book has the direction: Read the article as fast as you can, but make sure you understand what you are reading. That also is why each exercise is followed by a test through which you can check upon your comprehension of what you have read.

Follow these suggestions for faster reading

With the foregoing facts in mind, you will want to follow these suggestions for becoming a faster and better reader.

Suggestion Number 1—Try to read faster

You can read faster if you wish to, but you will have to push yourself to do it. If you just coast along while reading, you will make little or no increase in your rate. If you keep trying day by day to step up your reading speed, however, you'll be surprised and pleased to discover that you are making progress.

There are several ways you can accelerate your reading from low into high gear. For example, every time you do one of the reading exercises in this book, you should make a real effort to read faster than before. When you read other books, magazines, or newspapers, you should also try to read more rapidly. If you try and try again, you are likely to succeed in your attempt to read faster.

You may be reading a chapter in a novel, for example, so fast that you think you are not understanding it. Because of this, you may feel that you should slow down your reading rate or reread certain parts of the chapter. But do not give in to this feeling. Rather, keep up your reading speed until you have finished the chapter.

After you have completed the chapter, make an oral or written summary of what you have read. Then check your understanding by rereading the chapter from start to finish. This time read a little faster than you read before. Because you are familiar with the chapter, you should now be able to read it faster and with greater understanding.

Suggestion Number 2—Adjust your rate to your purpose and your materials

In certain ways, driving a car is like reading. If you are a good driver, you adjust your speed to your driving purpose and to driving conditions. If you want to get somewhere in a hurry on a clear highway, you step on the gas. If you want to enjoy the countryside, you drive at a moderate speed. If you want to avoid an accident in heavy downtown traffic, you drive slowly and carefully.

In reading, you should adjust your reading speed to your reading purpose and to the material you are reading. You can easily do this if you are a good reader. The good reader has a number of reading speeds, not just one; he uses the speed that best fits his reading purpose and his reading material.

In deciding how fast you should read, ask yourself these questions: "Why am I reading this material? What exactly do I want to get from it?" Your answers will help you determine which reading speed you should use.

Suppose that you are going to read a chapter in a history book that is of average difficulty. Suppose also that you want to get a general idea of what is in the chapter. Then you should read that chapter rapidly.

Suppose, however, that you want to read to remember exact details such as the names, places, and dates given in the chapter. Then you should probably use a relatively slow reading rate so that you can pay attention to these details. When you reread the chapter, you may wish to write down these details for later reference.

Now, suppose that you are reading a novel to make a written or oral book report. You will probably want to read this book at a moderate speed. Then re-read the chapter or book rapidly, perhaps making notes of important points. These notes may be in outline form. You may reread certain parts carefully to fill in the details of your outline. If you are reading a novel for recreation or enjoyment, however, you will want to read it at a fairly rapid rate.

When you skim, you read at your fastest rate. You skim when your purpose is to find the book you want in a library or bookstore, or to locate the word you want in a dictionary.

No matter what you are reading, always try to fit your reading rate to your reading purpose and to the material you are reading. Keep trying to do this until this skill becomes a habit. You will then be able to adjust your rate automatically.

Use Table 5 to guide your reading rate. It shows three kinds of reading purposes, three types of reading, and three different reading rates. For each purpose and type, the table suggests the rate that you will find most suitable. As you study this table, note that it emphasizes one main idea: *Fit your reading rate to your reading purpose.*

As Table 5 suggests, you will want to read slowly and carefully the directions for each of these activities:

1. Making a dress
2. Baking a cake
3. Caring for a pet
4. Repairing a faucet
5. Filling out a job application
6. Filling out an income tax form
7. Driving safely on streets and highways
8. Solving a mathematics problem
9. Conducting a scientific experiment
10. Using this better reading book

In general, you will read slowly not only the directions that you must follow but also the materials that you find difficult to understand. For example, you may have to look up an article in the *Encyclopaedia Britannica*. If that article is hard for you, you will read it slowly for thorough understanding.

You will read at a moderate rate those materials that are of average difficulty for you and that you are reading to get enjoyment or general information. And you will read at a rapid rate when you are skimming materials to find a specific fact.

As just mentioned, you will find that, at times, you should read slowly. But if you read slowly *all the time*, you will be handicapped. You will fail to complete all your necessary reading.

Whatever you are reading, here's a good rule to follow: *Always adjust your reading rate to your purpose and to your materials.* Remember that you should *not* do all your reading at the same rate.

TABLE 5

HERE'S HOW TO FIT YOUR TYPE OF READING AND YOUR READING RATE TO YOUR READING PURPOSE

READING PURPOSE	TYPE OF READING	SUITABLE RATE
To find out how to do or to make something To get detailed information, especially from unfamiliar material To judge or criticize ideas	*Intensive:* thorough, work-type or study-type of reading	Slow rate, from 150 to about 250 words per minute, depending on how unfamiliar and how difficult the material is
To obtain pleasure and appreciation To broaden your general knowledge and experience	*Extensive:* fairly careful, recreational type of reading	Moderate rate, from about 250 words per minute up, depending on the difficulty of the reading matter
To find key sentence, phrase, or word To find answers to specific questions To locate information To get trend or organization of thought as it appears in an article, chapter, or book	*Skimming:* rapid information-getting type of reading	Fast rate, often several pages a minute

SUGGESTION NUMBER 3—At first, read easy and interesting materials

In your efforts to read faster, you should start with books, magazine articles, or newspaper stories that are relatively low in difficulty and relatively high in interest.

If you are reading materials that are fairly easy for you, you are likely to increase your reading rate. And if these materials are interesting, you are likely to enjoy reading them. If you get pleasure from your reading, you will probably read faster and faster.

You will find easy and interesting reading materials in the Sunday editions of large city newspapers, in popular magazines, and in some best-seller books. You can get help in locating these materials from the librarian of your school, college, or public library.

As you learn to read faster and with better understanding, you can take on more difficult reading materials. By consistent effort, you can read these harder materials faster and faster.

Practice reading with a reading pacer

You yourself can speed up your reading. By continuing efforts to read faster, you can increase your reading rate and keep your comprehension high. The proof of this is the record of your scores on the general reading exercises in this book.

But you probably can make even larger gains in your reading rate if you use a reading pacer.[2] You set this machine so that a shutter descends at a reading rate that is comfortable to you. You read several pages at this rate. Then you set the machine at a rate that is 10 percent faster. You practice a half hour at this new rate or until you feel that you are

[2]This pacer, such as the SRA Reading Accelerator, was described in Lesson 5, page 33.

reading efficiently and easily. At the next practice, you again set the machine at a 10 percent faster rate, and practice a half hour as you did before. After 10 to 20 such practices, you will probably find that your reading rate has increased considerably—and that your understanding has not gone down. Note, however, that you can make gains in rate of reading without the help of such machines.

An exercise in faster reading

To test your reading rate at its very fastest, read the magazine story that appears next. As you read it, try to read as rapidly as possible. Keep in mind also that your reading purpose is to get the few main points of the story. This means that you will *not* read details carefully or try to remember them exactly.

You will probably be able to read this story very quickly because it is both easy and interesting.

In the time box, write your starting time. Then read the story.

Time Box

Finishing time	
Starting time	
Reading time	
Reading rate	

HE CARRIED THE MESSAGE TO GARCIA[3]
by Richard Aston

ONE EVENING IN February, 1899, an obscure publisher and job printer in East

[3]Condensed from *Coronet*, May, 1952. Copyright 1952, by Esquire, Inc. Reprinted with permission of the publisher and the author.

Aurora, New York, sat talking with his son. Like many other Americans, they were discussing the Spanish-American War, the last shot of which had been fired only a few months before.

"I don't know how you feel, Dad," said Bert, "but I think the real hero of the war was Rowan. You remember—the man who found Garcia."

Elbert Hubbard slowly put down his teacup. Yes, he mused, the hero in any human endeavor is the man who does his work—who carries the message to Garcia! Hubbard rushed over to his desk and in an hour dashed off an editorial for *The Philistine*, a crusading monthly which he published.

Hubbard's editorial touched the heart of America. And when it was reprinted by the New York Central Railroad in an advertising brochure, it was titled: "A Message to Garcia."

But what of Rowan, the man who actually carried the message to Garcia? Not until a quarter-century after his courageous deed was Col. Andrew Summers Rowan, then retired to his modest home in San Francisco, lifted from obscurity to receive the Distinguished Service Cross. When he died in a California military hospital in January, 1943, at 85, newspapers printed brief obituaries of the forgotten man who had carried the message to Garcia. Few had heard of Rowan, still fewer knew the story behind his heroic exploit . . .

At midnight on April 24, 1898, a tiny fishing boat, its lights extinguished, slipped quietly into a small bay on Cuba's south coast and anchored. Soon afterward, the bow grated onto the sand of a half-moon beach separating black jungle from black water. From the cabin amidships, a dark figure emerged, mumbled a few words to

the pilot, then leaped ashore. Four more dark figures followed at his heels.

As the little party walked hesitantly across the sand, a second group of men emerged from the jungle. The visitors halted apprehensively.

"Who are you?" one whispered in Spanish.

"Friends," a voice replied. "Where is the man?"

A figure stepped forward and bowed low, military fashion. "I am First Lieutenant Andrew S. Rowan, U. S. Army."

The groups mingled, exchanged muffled introductions. Then the leader of the reception committee said: "We are Cuban patriots assigned to bring you to General Garcia's headquarters."

For the first time since he had left Jamaica, 100 miles away, Rowan breathed a quiet sigh. It had been a rough, dangerous voyage. The waters between Jamaica and Cuba were crisscrossed by Spanish patrol boats. One had even intercepted the rebel-manned fishing sloop, but Rowan and his companions escaped capture when the skipper plaintively explained that his craft was off course. Now the Lieutenant shivered as a cold ocean breeze swept the beach.

"If you are ready, we will go," the Cuban guide whispered.

Shouldering their packs, the five men moved off single file into the black jungle. Machetes swinging, the Cubans cleared a rough path as they walked. Rowan, pushing vines and branches from his face, followed closely behind. The tropical night was filled with the screeches of birds awakened from sleep and the singsong buzzing of countless insects.

Only 18 days before, Rowan recalled, he had been just another anonymous junior officer in a peace-time army. His single claim to fame—and Rowan chuckled grimly as he thought of it—was a little book called *The Island of Cuba* which he had written two years before. Not that he knew very much about Cuba: in fact, he had never been there before this night. But he had always been intrigued by the little island, so had compiled a book about its geography and topography after a study of other authors' works.

Then one day in April, Rowan was asked to lunch with his superior officer. War with Spain was imminent. The United States had a potential ally in an almost-legendary Cuban rebel leader, Gen. Calixto Garcia y Iniguez. But he was fighting somewhere in the remote vastness of the Cuban mountains. No one knew where.

Col. Arthur Wagner gave Rowan his orders. Go to Cuba. Locate Garcia—somehow. Find out from him what the Spanish are doing. Ask him what he needs. Get his reaction on our sending an American invasion force to Cuba. Then return to Washington.

Rowan listened intently. He had no idea where Garcia was. His knowledge of Cuba was strictly academic, his Spanish was faulty. Moreover, he was almost 41 years old and not very robust. But an order was an order. On April 8, he left Washington.

Now, as the sun began to burn down through matted jungle trees, Rowan cursed the day he wrote that fool book. But there could be no turning back. Silently he plodded along behind his silent escort.

Then Rowan and his men were accosted by a band of tattered, bearded soldiers. Claiming to be Spanish deserters, they begged to join the expedition.

Their story is fantastic, Rowan warned himself. I've got to be careful—very careful. So when the motley group pitched camp that night, Rowan had a guard placed over them. Before daybreak, one of the men tried to escape and was killed.

When Rowan had finally fallen into a fatigue-drugged sleep, he was awakened by a shot. As he jumped up, one of the deserters lunged at him. In his hand was a shining knife, aimed at Rowan's throat. Before it could move, however, there was a swish in the night and the glint of a second blade. A watchful Cuban rebel had cut down the deserter with a machete.

On April 28, the unshaven and tattered Rowan stumbled into the camp of one of Garcia's lieutenants. There the haggard party was given an escort of cavalry. Then they rode off toward the Sierra Maestra mountains in the distance.

Three days later, on May 1, a rebel sentry near the town of Bayamo raised his musket. A burlesque military unit confronted him. Surrounded by sweat-stained troopers was a civilian horseman, his face burned and swollen, his cheeks covered with stubble.

"I am Lieutenant Rowan of the U. S. Army," the stranger gasped. "Take me to General Garcia."

Garcia, a burly 58-year-old revolutionary veteran, received Rowan. The American presented his credentials identifying him as "a man in whom we have confidence."

After breakfast, Rowan shot all his questions at the General, who listened in silence. Then Garcia got up and walked away, leaving his son to entertain the American. Several hours later, he returned and announced that three officers would go back to the United States with Rowan to answer the War Department's questions. He himself had no time to answer questions. He had a war to fight.

As soon as Rowan's escort arrived, the four men set off on horseback for the north coast. Again the jungle sent mosquitoes, a blazing sun, a humid heat to harass the American. But after five grueling days, he and his party reached the coast. There they were crowded into a fishing boat even smaller than the one which had brought Rowan to Cuba. Yet the unseaworthy craft carried him past Spanish gunboats to Hog Island in the Bahamas—where a cold reception awaited him.

He and his crew were ignominiously marched off to a yellow-fever quarantine camp. Tears of desperation flooded Rowan's eyes. This was the last straw! But two days later, the American consul secured Rowan's release to catch a vessel bound for Key West, Florida.

On May 15, five weeks after he had left on the first lap of his journey, Lieutenant Rowan limped into the office of Russell A. Alger, Secretary of War. Mission accomplished, sir!

The War Department was pleased, even grateful. But there were no headlines, no White House receptions, no parades with banners flying. True, Rowan was promoted to the temporary rank of lieutenant colonel. But the nation-wide acclaim he so richly deserved went to a man Rowan had never heard of—an obscure pamphleteer of East Aurora who knew how to write words that inspired a nation's heart.

Write your finishing time in the time box. Then take the following test. If you believe a statement is *true*, mark a + at the left of it. If you believe the statement is *false*, mark a O at the left of it.

1. In carrying the message to Garcia, Rowan did his duty and did it exceedingly well.

2. When Rowan died, all America mourned.

3. Rowan was selected to carry the message to Garcia because he had written a book about Cuba.

4. Before Rowan sailed for Cuba, he had been there once before.

5. Rowan made the trip to Cuba mainly to find out how the United States could help Garcia's rebels fight the Spaniards.

6. Before Rowan left for Cuba, he had a fairly good idea of where he could find Garcia.

7. Because Rowan knew the Cuban jungles and mountains, he had an easy time going through them.

8. Several times Rowan was nearly captured or killed.

9. When Rowan returned to Washington, D.C., he was received as a great hero.

10. The message to Garcia brought much more fame to Editor Hubbard than it did to Lieutenant Rowan.

In the time box, figure out your reading time. Then change your reading time into your reading rate; use the table at the end of this book. Write this rate in your time box. How does this rate compare with your usual rate: Is it higher? Is it lower? Is it about the same?

Next correct and score your test. Here are the correct answers: (+-01 ;o-6 ;+-8 ;o-7 ;o-9 ;+-5 ;o-4 ;+-3 ;o-2 ;+-1)

Do general reading exercise 7 (page 219)

In doing this reading exercise, try to read faster than you have been reading. As you read, however, keep in mind that after you finish the article, you will take a comprehension test and a vocabulary test on the article. Next, do General Reading Exercise 7.

After you complete the exercise, look again at your rate and comprehension scores. Perhaps on some exercises they have gone down or have stayed about the same. If so, don't let this worry you. You may be on a plateau in your reading; while on such a plateau you are learning certain new skills and combining them. After a time, these new combinations will enable you to lift your rate and your comprehension to even higher levels than before.

In the next lesson, you will learn to skim—that is, to read at a very fast rate.

How can you

learn to skim?

He'd fly through the air
  with the greatest of ease,
This handsome young man
  on the flying trapeze;
His movements were graceful,
  all girls he could please,
And my love he purloined away!

George Leybourne

WHAT THE YOUNG MAN did in the field of acrobatics, you can do in the field of reading. By learning to skim, you can fly through books and other reading matter with the greatest of ease. And, you can quickly get the information or enjoyment that you are seeking.

What is skimming?

Skimming, as you already know, is your very fastest rate of reading. If you have the ability to skim, you can quickly cover reading material and find what you are looking for.

If you are a good reader, you can skim the pages of a telephone book and locate within a few seconds the name and number of the person you want to call. Within a few minutes, you can skim an entire book and get a general idea of what is in that book.

When you skim, your eyes do not look at every word, sentence, or paragraph. Rather they move swiftly across and down one page. They then do the same on the next page. Your eyes do this, page after page, until they spot the part that you want. You then read carefully that particular part.

Why is skimming important?

If you can skim effectively, you can find quickly what you want—and this is valuable. You can also go over many pages of reading matter within a relatively short period of time. And this is valuable.

If you cannot skim, you are handicapped in many different ways. You spend too much time trying to find what you want —and you are unable to finish all the reading that you have to do.

The businessman who cannot skim is unable to read many of the important papers, magazines, and books that come to his desk. The doctor who cannot skim is unable to keep up with the latest and best information in his field. And the same is true of persons engaged in teaching and in many other occupations.

Students who cannot skim often have trouble with their academic work. Howard, for example, had never learned to read rapidly even though he graduated from high school with honors. In his freshman year at college, he took courses in literature and history. In these courses, each student had to read a large number of reference books and magazines.

Because Howard read so slowly and laboriously, he was unable to cover the required references. He did read a few of these references, but this reading took so much time that he could not organize and write up the information obtained. As a result, Howard failed both the literature and the history courses.

Because of these failures, Howard decided early in the second semester that his job was to learn to skim. He realized that he needed this skill to do the reading that was required in many college courses. By learning to skim certain references and to read other references carefully, Howard was able to do satisfactory work in all his courses.

How do you skim for a particular detail?

You can skim reading materials to find the detail that you want, as these examples show:

1. You want to know the meaning of a word. You *skim* the dictionary to locate that word.

2. You want to know certain facts about the background of China. You *skim* the index volume of an encyclopedia to find the number of the volume and the pages that give you these facts.

3. You want to locate a magazine article on how to prevent and treat a common cold. You *skim* the "Health" section of the *Reader's Guide to Periodical Lit-*

erature. In that section you find the title of an article that appeared in an issue of the magazine, *Today's Health*.

4. You want to find a reliable book on the most important geographical discoveries in history. In the public library, you *skim* through the card catalog. There you find a card for the book, *Great Adventures and Explorations*, edited by Vilhjalmur Stefansson. You use the call number on this card to get the book.

5. You want to learn more about the discovery of the South Pole. In *Great Adventures and Explorations*, you *skim* the table of contents. You note that Chapter 18 entitled "The Attainment of the South Pole" begins on page 757.

6. You want to know when and where Ferdinand Magellan died. In the reference book just mentioned, you *skim* the index. There you find the entry: "Magellan, Ferdinand, death of, 261-262, 263-264." You *skim* all these pages. On page 262, you find that Magellan was killed on April 27, 1521, in a battle on the shore of Mactan Island in the Philippines.

In each of the examples given, you had to use the alphabet. If you know the alphabet backward as well as forward, you are better able to skim efficiently when you are looking for a specific detail in your reading. You also are able to locate quickly a name appearing in a telephone book, a product listed in a mail order catalog, and an entry presented in an almanac, yearbook, or atlas.

To practice skimming for a detail, get a recent copy of a large city newspaper. Skim the newspaper to find a "help wanted" ad for the kind of job in which you are interested. Next skim the paper to find these things—a radio or television program to tune in, a movie to go to, a bargain to buy, and a home to rent.

Next, get a book that will probably

answer your question about a hobby or an interest. In that book, skim the table of contents and then examine the index. There you may locate the page or pages that will answer your question. If the book does not have an index, turn rapidly through the pages skimming as you go. If this book does not yield the answer, find another promising book to skim for the answer.

In skimming for a detail, you of course do not pay close attention to every word that appears before your eyes. Rather, you skip quickly over many parts until you find the part that you want.

How do you skim for a general impression?

You can skim a newspaper, a magazine, or a book to get a general idea of its contents. If the publication does not have a table of contents, you can turn through it quickly, reading only the headlines, the titles of articles, or the headings of chapters. Through this skimming, you can decide which story, article, or chapter you want to read.

If you are looking for a novel to read for enjoyment, you may find such a book at a library or bookstore. By skimming, you can get a general impression of the book. In skimming, as said before, you read certain parts carefully and skip over other parts. If you like the samples that you read carefully, you may decide to read the book from cover to cover.

If you are examining a historical or a scientific volume for the first time, you can skim it in this way: Read rapidly the table of contents; it gives the titles of chapters and usually the main headings within each chapter. Then go quickly through the pages of the book. As you

skim, read headings and sentences here and there and glance at the pictures. From the general impression you thus get through skimming, you can decide whether to read the book carefully.

How good a skimmer are you?

Good readers are so expert in skimming that they can get a specific fact from a reference book within a few seconds or a sound general impression of a novel or nonfiction book within a few minutes. Whether you are a good reader or not, you can probably become more skillful in skimming for various purposes. To test your skimming power and to increase it, do the skimming exercises that follow:

SKIMMING EXERCISE 1

If you are a good skimmer, you can find information quickly and accurately in reference books such as an almanac.

Suppose that you and your friends are talking about actors and actresses and raise these questions:

1. In what year was Judith Anderson born? _____

2. Where was Don Ameche born? _____

3. In what year was Walter Abel born? _____

4. Where was Maude Adams born? _____

5. Where was Gracie Allen born? _____

6. Who is older—Brian Aherne or Richard Ainley? _____

You will find the answers to these questions in Table 6; it was reprinted from an almanac. Read the first question, "In what year was Judith Anderson born?" Skim Table 6 to find the answer. Write the answer on the blank that follows the question. In the same way, answer each of the other questions.

TABLE 6
PERSONALITIES OF STAGE, SCREEN, RADIO, TELEVISION.[1]

NAME	BIRTHPLACE	BORN
Abba, Marta	Rome, Italy	1907
Abbott, Bud (Wm.)	Asbury Park, N. J.	1898
Abbott, George	Salamanca, N.Y.	1887
Abel, Walter	St. Paul, Minn.	1898
Adams, Maude	Salt Lake City, Utah	1872
Adler, Larry	Baltimore, Md.	1914
Adler, Stella	New York, N.Y.	1902
Adrian, Iris	Los Angeles, Calif.	1913
Aherne, Brian	Worcestershire, Eng.	1902
Ainley, Richard	Stanmore, Eng.	1910
Albert, Eddie	Rock Island, Ill.	1908
Albertson, Frank	Fergus Falls, Minn.	1909
Albright, Hardie	Charleroi, Pa.	1905
Alda, Francis	Christchurch, N.Z.	1883
Alda, Robert	New York, N.Y.	1914
Alexander, Ben	Goldfield, Nev.	1911
Alexander, John	Newport, Ky.	1897
Alexander, Katherine	Arkansas	1901
Allan, Elizabeth	Skegness, Eng.	1910
Allen, Fred	Cambridge, Mass.	1894
Allen, Gracie	San Francisco, Calif.	—
Allen, Robert	Mt. Vernon, N.Y.	1906
Albritton, Louise	Oklahoma City, Okla.	1920
Algood, Sara	Dublin, Ireland	1883
Allister, Claud	London, England	1893
Alper, Murray	New York, N.Y.	1904
Alvarado, Don	Albuquerque, N. M.	1904
Ameche, Don	Kenosha, Wis.	1908
Amos, F. F. Gosden	Richmond, Va.	1899
Anders, Glenn	Los Angeles, Calif.	1890
Anderson, Judith	Adelaide, Australia	1898

Here are the correct answers:

(1—1898; 2—Kenosha, Wis.; 3—1898; 4—Salt Lake City; 5—San Francisco; 6—Brian Aherne.)

SKIMMING EXERCISE 2

The Readers' Guide to Periodical Literature[2] lists magazine articles soon after they first appear in print. The selection from the *Readers' Guide* that follows has 22 entries, each for a particular article.

[1]*The World Almanac and Book of Facts*, 1950. Copyright 1950, by the New York World-Telegram. Reprinted with permission of the publisher. Sources: Latest authentic records: as of June 1, 1949.

[2]Reprinted with permission of the publisher—The H. W. Wilson Company, New York, N. Y.

For test purposes, each entry is numbered.

Skim the selection to find the answers to each of the questions. On the lines, write the numbers of the articles.

A. What articles tell about the life of a person who has cancer? No._____; No._____; No._____

B. What articles deal with smoking as a possible cause of cancer? No._____; No._____; No._____

C. What article describes the gains that have been made in the fight against cancer? No._____

No.

CANCER

1   Cells can transform into cancer in at least 6 ways. Sci N L 62:121 Ag 23 '52
2   Cigarettes and cancer. Newsweek 40:102 N 3 '52
3   Diagnose cancer cells. Sci N L 62:196 S 27 '52
4   Drive to chain smoke possible cancer cause. Sci N L 62:216 O 4 '52
5   Effect of prior injection of non-mouse tissues on growth of tumor homoiografts in mice. N. Kaliss. bibliog tab Science 116:279-80 S 12 '52
6   I am living with cancer; excerpt from Living with cancer. E. Kaehele. Womans Home C 79:30-1+ S '52
7   I speak without a voice; cancer of the vocal cords; ed. by S. Brott. R. Greer. Coronet 33:131-5 N '52
8   In my case it was cancer. E. R. Bills. il Sat Eve Post 225:45+ O 25 '52
9   Unsuspected cancer. Time 60:80+ O 20 '52

Prevention and control

10 Your skin and cancer. S. G. Mullins and R. P. Little. Todays Health 30:26-7 N '52

Therapy

11 Anti-cancer atoms. il Newsweek 40:66 O 27 '52
12 Atomic weapons against cancer. E. N. Lockard. Smithson Rep 1951:263-72
13 Cobalt 60. L. M. Miller and J. Monahan. Read Digest 61:19-22 O '52
14 Rx atoms for cancer. J. Lear. il Colliers 130:13-15 O 11 '52
15 There's hope in some hopeless cancers. P. De Kruif. Todays Health 30:28-9 O '52; Same abr. with title New attack on cancer of prostate and breast. Read Digest 61:224+ N '52

CANCER research

16 Atomic weapons against cancer. E. N. Lockard. Smithson Rep 1951:263-72
17 Fear of cancer saves; lung cancer-smoking question. Sci N L 62:287 N 1 '52
18 In mice, at least, work prevents cancer. Sci N L 62:136 Ag 30 '52
19 Mortality and regression of sarcoma 180. J. Patti. tab Science 116:400 O 10 '52
20 Nucleic acid content of the squamous cancer cell. R. C. Mellors and others. bibliog tabs Science 116:265-9 S 12 '52
21 Of important mice and men. J. D. Ratcliff. il Colliers 130:13-15 N 8 '52
22 Progress report on the war against cancer. B. Merson. il Colliers 130:24-6+ O 4 '52

Here are the correct answers:

(A—6, 7, 8; B—2, 4, 17; C—22.)

SKIMMING EXERCISE 3

Say that you and a friend get into an argument as to whether the snapping turtle's vision is good or poor. To settle the argument, you get *Speaking of Animals*, a book by Alan Devoe.

In Devoe's book, you find the paragraph that follows. This paragraph gives many facts about snapping turtles. For the moment, however, you are interested in the answer to only one question: What kind of vision does the snapping turtle have?

With this question in mind, skim the paragraph. Don't read every word. Let your eyes move rapidly through the paragraph, searching only for the answer. Look for words like *eyes, vision, sight;* ignore words describing the turtle's size, weight, shape, and shell.

Now find the answer to the question about the snapping turtle's vision. Write your answer here: The snapping turtle's vision is _____

Snapping turtles are the biggest fresh-water turtles in the country. The hugest of them, the alligator snapping turtles of the Mississippi and the Gulf, attain to 140 pounds. Even a specimen of the common species, found everywhere east of the Rockies, may attain in old age to seventy or eighty pounds or more, and almost any grown individual will weigh twenty. Squat, chunky, massive, the snapping turtle has a dull-colored carapace, roughened and ridged, with a series of broken, sawtoothed indentations at the rear of the shell. Past these projects a long, heavy-fleshed tail, scaly and serrated, like a dragon's. From the sides of the shell protrude the powerful legs, with great, broad feet, heavily webbed, bearing strong, coarse nails. From under the fore edge of the carapace is perpetually extruded the snapper's oversized snake-necked head, too big ever to be withdrawn inside the inadequate shell. The

reptilian eyes are tiny, but the power of vision in them is exceptionally keen. The jaws of the great head are heavy and hooked, and in both upper and lower are bony cutting edges that make the snapper's beak an instrument comparable to a pair of powerful shears with jagged blades.[3]

Here is the correct answer:

(The snapping turtle's vision is exceptionally keen.)

SKIMMING EXERCISE 4

In this exercise, try to skim even more rapidly than you did before. In one or two seconds, go through the story about New Salem and find the answer to this question: (A) How many years did Abraham Lincoln live in New Salem, Illinois? _____years. Write your answer on the blank that follows the question.

NEW SALEM[4]

AS THE PASSING years add to the stature of Lincoln among the figures of men in history, so do they change the significance and importance of New Salem State Park among the historic shrines of America.

Infinite labor and endless research characterize the re-creation of this village where young Lincoln clerked in a store, chopped wood, enlisted in the Black Hawk War, served as postmaster, deputy surveyor and legislator, failed in business, and courted Ann Rutledge.

The Park, situated on a hill one hundred feet high, overlooks the Sangamon River Valley. It was on this bluff in 1828 that James Rutledge and John Camron erected their homes and the following

---

[3]From *Speaking of Animals,* by Alan Devoe, Copyright, 1947. A Creative Age Press Book, Farrar, Straus & Young, Inc. publishers. Reprinted with permission of the publisher.
[4]From *New Salem State Park — The Lincoln Country.* Issued by the Division of Parks and Memorials, State of Illinois, Springfield.

year, after building their grist and saw mill on the river below, laid out the town of New Salem and started selling lots.

Strangely, the six years that Lincoln spent in New Salem almost completely encompass the town's brief history. The community was growing and thriving when Lincoln reached there in 1831, but in 1839, just two years after he had left for Springfield to practice law and advance himself in the fascinating maze of politics, the county seat was established at nearby Petersburg. Thereafter, New Salem declined rapidly.

Next, answer this question: (B) Who laid out the town of New Salem? _____

If you do not know the answer, skim the story again, this time more rapidly than before.

Here are the correct answers: (ˑuoɹɹɐƆ uɥoſ puɐ ǝᵷpǝlʇnᴚ sǝɯɐſ-ᗺ ʼsɹɐǝʎ xᴉS-∀)

SKIMMING EXERCISE 5

Skim the paragraph that follows to get a general impression or idea of what is in it. Then answer the test item that follows the paragraph.

POLIOMYELITIS[5]

AT THE MENTION of "polio," you probably have a mental picture of someone severely crippled. While polio, or infantile paralysis, is a disease no one wants to have, the fear that people have of it is neither justified nor helpful. It is a fact that more

---

[5]From *You and Your Health*, by J. Roswell Gallagher, M.D. Copyright, 1950, by Science Research Associates, Inc., Chicago.

than half the people who have had polio recover completely and have no after-effects. This is not a disease to be careless about, but you can help, should an epidemic hit your community, by being calm and going about your business as usual. Gossip and scare stories breed fear and anxiety, which in turn do no one any good.

Mark a check (✔) at the left of the correct choice.

(A) You should be calm and do things as usual if polio hits your town.

(B) You should think about how dangerous polio is.

(C) You should tell others about bad cases of polio.

(∀ :sᴉ ɹǝʍsuɐ ʇɔǝɹɹoɔ ǝɥʇ)

Do general reading exercise 8 (page 225)

When you do this exercise, try to shift your reading speed into high gear. By continuous efforts to read faster and better, you will almost surely increase your reading scores. Now do the exercise.

After you finish this exercise, give yourself more practice in skimming. First, skim a newspaper to find something you want to know. Second, skim a magazine to locate an article you wish to read. And third, skim a book to get a general impression of what is in it.

Now that you have worked to improve your skimming ability, you are ready to consider ways to find the main idea while reading. These ways are presented in Lesson 9.

LESSON 9

How do you find the
main idea in reading?

"WHAT'S THE MAIN idea?" That is the question you should always ask yourself and try to answer while you are reading.

If you are a skillful reader, you are able to read a paragraph rapidly and locate the main idea with accuracy. You are also able quickly and surely to get the main idea of an entire story, article, chapter, or book. But if you are a poor reader, you have difficulty in finding the main idea of even a single paragraph.

Where can you find the main idea?

In a paragraph, the main idea usually appears in the *topic sentence*. This sentence, of course, gives the central thought that the paragraph develops. All the other sentences help to explain this thought. The main idea may appear in part of a sentence—that is, in a clause or in a phrase. However the main idea appears, you should be able to locate it quickly.

The topic sentence frequently appears first in a paragraph, as it did in the paragraph you just read. Occasionally, this sentence is in the middle of the paragraph. It may even be the last sentence

in a paragraph, as here. In short, the topic sentence may appear at any place in a paragraph.

No matter where the main idea of a paragraph is located, you will want to be able to find it. If you can get the main idea quickly and accurately, you have the key to understanding the whole paragraph.

How can you learn to find the main idea in a paragraph?

The best way to build your skill in locating the main idea is to practice doing it. During this practice, you will at first be conscious of the fact that you are reading a paragraph to find the main idea. As a result, you will probably read the paragraph slowly and carefully.

As you develop this skill, however, you will be less and less conscious of your purpose. You will automatically read most paragraphs for their main ideas. You will then find that this skill contributes greatly to efficient reading.

You will next try to improve your skill in getting the main idea through doing the exercises that follow.

EXERCISE 1—Finding the main idea in a paragraph

To test yourself on your ability to locate the main idea, read this paragraph. Then take the test that follows the paragraph.

There was a man on board this boat, with a light fresh-colored face, and a pepper-and-salt suit of clothes, who was the most inquisitive fellow that can possibly be imagined. He never spoke otherwise than interrogatively. He was an embodied inquiry. Sitting down or standing up, still or moving, walking the deck or taking his meals, there he was, with a great note of interrogation in each eye, two in his cocked ears, two more in his turned-up nose and chin, at least half a dozen more about the corners of his mouth, and the largest one of all in his hair, which was brushed pertly off his forehead in a flaxen clump. Every button in his clothes said, "Eh? What's that? Did you speak? Say that again, will you?" He was always wide awake, like the enchanted bride who drove her husband frantic; perpetually seeking and never finding. There never was such a curious man.[1]

Mark a check (✔) at the left of the statement that gives the main idea about the man described in the paragraph.
(A) He had a fresh-colored face and wore a pepper-and-salt suit of clothes.
(B) He was the strangest man ever seen.
(C) Every button in his clothes said, "Eh? What's that? Did you speak?"
(D) He was the most inquisitive fellow that can possibly be imagined.
(E) He was always thirsting for answers; perpetually seeking and never finding.

---

[1] From *American Notes*, by Charles Dickens.

Look again at the paragraph. The main idea about the man described is given in the last clause of the first sentence. That clause tells you, the reader, that he "was the most inquisitive man that can possibly be imagined." The first clause of the first sentence and the other sentences in the paragraph do not introduce any really important ideas about the man. Rather, these sentences give details that *support* the main idea.

EXERCISE 2—Finding the main idea in a paragraph

In the next paragraph, the main idea is some common sense advice on what you should do in using the telephone. Read this paragraph somewhat faster than you read the paragraph in Exercise 1.

Face the telephone problem squarely. Other people have as much right to the phone's use as you do and if you monopolize it, that's inconsiderate. And if the line is not private, your thoughtlessness spreads out and touches dozens of people. If you have the telephone tied up for an hour and a half while you daydream with Ginny, no one else can put through calls, no one else can receive them—and that may put a great many people to a lot of inconvenience. There's nothing right about that, and if you stubbornly hold out, you're plain selfish. Why not time-limit your conversations? Keep an eye on the clock and when you've consumed five minutes, give someone else a break. After all, if you haven't finished the chatter, you can always call back again in an hour or so. Better still, pay a face to face visit. Unfortunately, the things you chatter about, while they are terrifically important to you, do not seem to add up to much to a person who's anxious to use the phone. Of course, you know what is and is not important in your life, but if you mind your manners, you won't discuss it for hours over the phone![2]

Mark a check (✓) at the left of the statement that gives the main idea of the paragraph.
(A) Other people have as much right to the phone's use as you do.
(B) If you mind your manners, you won't talk for hours over the phone.
(C) What is important to you isn't important to others who want to use the same phone line.
(D) While you are talking over a party line, others on the line can't receive phone calls.
(E) Limit your phone call to five minutes—give someone else a break.

In the paragraph on telephone manners, the main idea appears in the sentence, "Keep an eye on the clock and when you've consumed five minutes, give someone else a break." This topic sentence appears at about the middle of the paragraph.

EXERCISE 3—Finding the main idea in a paragraph

Find the main idea in the following paragraph. Read it faster than you read the other paragraphs.

If you don't enjoy taking a chance, if you aren't fascinated by the unknown, if you don't like to make new friends and discover people, blind dates are not for you. When you agree to fly blind, you make an unspoken bargain —that you'll be a gentleman, that you'll show the girl a good time and that you expect to have fun yourself. That's the contract. There is no clause which de-

mands a repeat. You never have to date this girl again and you won't if she isn't your type, but the time you spend with her can be fun for the moment and pleasant to remember. You don't want to be on any girl's black list because you upstaged her.[3]

Mark a check (✓) at the left of the choice that gives the main idea of the paragraph.

A blind date is an unspoken agreement
(A) to behave as you please
(B) to go steady
(C) to share good clean fun
(D) to take a chance
(E) to blacklist someone

(The correct answer is: C.)

EXERCISE 4—Finding the main idea in a paragraph

In the following paragraph, concentrate on finding the main idea, but read as fast as you can.

Peanuts are not normal food for squirrels. They are one reason why squirrels in parks grow scraggly and luster-less. What the wild, natural Shadow-Tail especially esteems are hickories. Now, in the autumn, he can hardly wait for them. He strips them, green from shagbarks, in a fury of appetite. Every sunup, every evening, he patters incessantly up and down the nut trees, harvesting, inspecting, eating, storing. His way is to take the nut in his small, adroit forepaws and turn it carefully over and over, licking it. His sign and seal on it, he scampers off with it a little way and digs a hole in the earth, perhaps three inches deep. The nut is inserted, point

---

[2]Judith Unger Scott, *Manners for Moderns*. Philadelphia: Macrae Smith Company, 1949, p. 25.

[3]Judith Unger Scott, *Manners for Moderns*. Philadelphia: Macrae Smith Company, 1949, p. 183.

downward, the soil scooped back over it, the disturbed fallen leaves raked and smoothed to look as they did before. Shadow-Tail is back up the tree again, detaching another morsel. He eats hardly more than two or three nuts of each dozen harvested. The number of his cached ones, as the autumn rolls on, may mount eventually to thousands.[4]

Mark a check (✔) at the left of the choice that gives the main idea of the paragraph.

The food that is best for squirrels and that they like best is:
(A) peanuts
(B) hickory nuts
(C) walnuts
(D) bark
(E) popcorn

(The correct answer is: B.)

EXERCISE 5—Finding the main idea in a paragraph

Now locate the main idea in the following paragraph. As you read it, try to increase your reading rate.

Volunteer fire fighting has become a serious business without glamor or glory. Hardship and danger and backbreaking toil await every volunteer when the alarm siren blows. There is something in the fire call that stirs within the fireman an irresistible urge to be up and at it. A red glow in the night over the housetops beckons him on as a flame attracts a moth. And well he knows that danger lurks in every fire, no matter how small. Recently a volunteer fireman, in putting out a simple brush blaze, was seriously wounded by an exploding shot-gun shell dropped by some careless hunter.[5]

[4]Alan Devoe, *Speaking of Animals*. New York: Creative Age Press, 1947, p. 95.
[5]John J. Floherty, *Five Alarm*. Philadelphia and New York: J. B. Lippincott Co., 1949, pp. 24-25.

Mark a check (✔) at the left of the choice that gives the main idea of the paragraph.

Volunteer fire fighting is usually
(A) challenging and attractive work
(B) glorious and glamorous work
(C) easy and safe work
(D) dirty and unpleasant work
(E) hard and dangerous work

(The correct answer is: E.)

EXERCISE 6—Finding the main idea in a paragraph

Locate the main idea in the following paragraph. Read it rapidly, but make sure you understand what you are reading.

The nurse in industry is a modern development which grew out of the fact that industrialists began to realize that healthy employees are the most efficient ones. Then liability insurance came into being, and the nurse became more important to employers than ever. For nurses could reduce accidents and illness in factories by developing good health and safety conditions, by supervising the cafeterias to see that employees got nourishing, balanced food. Nurses in the plants give first-aid immediately an accident occurs, and so make comparatively mild cases out of many that might be serious if the patient had to wait until a doctor could be called.[6]

Mark a check (✔) at the left of the choice that gives the main idea of the paragraph.

The employment of nurses in industry has increased mainly because employers found that
(A) the healthier employees are the more efficient they are

[6]Irmengarde Eberle, *Nurse*. New York: Thomas Y. Crowell Company, 1944, p. 133.

(B) employees are glad to contribute to the salaries of nurses

(C) the more accidents among employees, the more liability insurance costs

(D) nurses could give employees first-aid right away

(E) the provision of nurses' services was a modern development

(The correct answer is: A.)

EXERCISE 7—Finding the main idea in a paragraph

Locate the main idea in the following paragraph. Read it very thoughtfully and rapidly.

When the complete history of the twentieth century comes to be written, it will tell how the diets of millions of people were changed by science. The old idea was to fill the belly with as much food as possible, regardless of its chemical composition. The new idea is to supply the body with only the essential factors necessary for healthy growth. One hundred years ago the Association for the Improvement of the Condition of the Poor fed its unfortunates on a diet of Indian meal, hominy, beans, peas, salt pork and dried fish. Today the Bureau of Home Economics of the United States Department of Agriculture advises for minimum relief equally inexpensive meals comprising, however, one pint of milk, one vegetable or fruit, bread and cereals daily, with the addition of codliver oil for those under the age of two.[7]

Mark a check (✔) at the left of the choice that gives the main idea of the paragraph.

According to twentieth century science,

[7]Reprinted from *Men of Science in America* by permission of Simon and Schuster, Publishers. Copyright, 1944, by Bernard Jaffe.

the most important question you should ask yourself about the food you eat is:

(A) Does my stomach feel full after meals?

(B) Am I spending too much for food?

(C) Does the food I eat give me the chemicals my body needs?

(D) For my body needs, is my diet better than that of my ancestors?

(E) Can I buy inexpensive foods that are nutritious?

(The correct answer is: C.)

How can you learn to find the main idea in a story?

To become an efficient reader, you must gain skill in finding the main idea not only in a paragraph but also in an entire story.

A well-written story like a well-written paragraph often has one main idea. This idea may appear anywhere in the story. In a well-written newspaper story, this idea usually is in the first paragraph; it tells *who, what, when,* and *where*. In Lesson 1, for example, the story "Saves Boy From Third Rail" begins with this short paragraph: "A 22-year-old Korean war veteran saved a 13-year-old boy from death by electrocution Monday." In General Reading Exercise 8, the magazine article "The Man Who Rode A Shark" presents the main idea in the first paragraph. In each of these stories, moreover, the writer stated the main idea in such an interesting way that you probably wanted to read the rest of the story to get the details.

To give yourself practice in finding the main idea of a story, refer again to the articles appearing in the first four general reading exercises. Skim each of these articles to find the paragraph in which the main idea appears.

Now answer each of these questions.

Write your answers on a separate sheet of paper.

1. Skim Article 1, "Last Warning." Which paragraph has the main idea?

2. Skim Article 2, "They Ask To Be Killed." Which paragraph has the main idea?

3. Skim Article 3, "How To Handle An Outdoor Cook Fire." Which two paragraphs have the main idea?

4. Skim Article 4, "The Romance Of A Busy Broker." Which paragraph has the main idea?

Here are the correct answers:

(Article 1—The paragraph: " 'Don't go crazy with the heat, you junkhead.' Durbin warned. 'I've offered to buy. Last chance, Muir.' ")

(Article 2—The last sentence of the first paragraph.)

(Article 3—This article has two main ideas: The paragraph beginning, "The fire you want is the Indian fire," and the paragraph beginning, "Now that you have no further use for the fire, put it out.")

(Article 4—The last paragraph.)

Do general reading exercise 9 (page 230)

In doing this exercise, apply what you have learned in this lesson. As you read the article try to find the main idea of each paragraph and of the story as a whole. This should not slow down your reading rate because you will almost unconsciously look for the main ideas as you read.

After you finish this exercise, look again at the rate, comprehension, and vocabulary scores that you have recorded for the general reading exercises. Look also at your rate and comprehension graphs. How do your scores on Exercise 9 compare with your scores on Exercise 1? Have your scores improved? Do you feel that you are becoming a better reader? Are you getting more information and enjoyment from your reading than you did when you started this book?

You have learned and used many new and better reading skills. In Lesson 10, you will develop another skill—that of learning to read carefully.

LESSON 10

How can you do careful detailed reading?

THERE ARE MANY times when you have to read something carefully to remember details and to use them.

If you are a high school or college student, you often have to do this kind of reading. For example, you have to read thoroughly a textbook chapter for the next day's assignment, test, or class discussion.

In everyday life, you frequently have to read carefully to make sure that you understand details. For example, you may need to read carefully the instructions for filling out an income tax form or a business report. Then too you may want to read carefully a magazine article that gives ideas on budgeting your income. To do this type of reading effectively, you must be skilled in reading for details.

You will be able to understand, recall, and use the facts that you get from reading if you learn to concentrate. The suggestions that follow will help you to concentrate better on your reading. Some of these suggestions will be familiar to you; others will be new—but all will help you to concentrate more efficiently while you are reading for details.

1. Have a definite purpose for your reading. Keep this purpose in mind as you read.

2. Give your full attention to what you are reading. Do not permit your mind to wander. Do not interrupt your reading by conversation. Turn off the radio or television set.

3. Try to get the greatest good from your reading. Read actively, not passively. If you are reading to answer questions, keep these questions in mind as you read. When you complete your reading, try to recall the answers to your questions.

4. Read in a place that is quiet, comfortable, and well-lighted.

5. Set a time limit and try to complete a given reading job within that limit.

6. While you are reading, try to be calm and relaxed. If you avoid excitement or anxiety, you will be able to concentrate better. Do not read for too long a period of time. If you become restless after a half hour or more of sustained effort, take a rest. Then return to your reading.

Practice careful reading in a book

For this practice, select any book, preferably one that appears to be very interesting. In this book, pick out a chapter that you would like to read carefully for details.

Read the chapter quickly to get the main ideas. These ideas may appear in the center or side headings within the chapter. Or they may appear as the topic sentences of paragraphs, as mentioned in Lesson 9.

After you have read the chapter rapidly, reread it to find important details. Your reading should be at a fairly rapid rate. However, if you read the chapter too rapidly, you may fail to understand some of the important details, and you may miss other such details altogether. Yet if you read the chapter too slowly, your attention may wander, and you may fail to note the important details. In short, adjust your rate so that you grasp all the important details. Then you may want to read again certain sentences or paragraphs. Through this rereading, you can make sure that you have comprehended the chapter's details as thoroughly as possible.

Learn to read carefully by doing these exercises

You can increase your ability to do careful reading by doing the practice exercises that follow.

In the exercises, you will try to understand thoroughly what you are reading and to get this understanding at faster and faster reading rates.

Careful reading exercise 1

Read the selection here for thorough understanding. After you finish the selection, you will take a short test on it.

GETTING ALONG WITH OTHERS[1]
by Helen Schacter

THERE ARE CERTAIN characteristics toward which to aim for good social relationships —self-confidence, serenity, and cheerfulness. Making friends will be simplified if you achieve these qualities. Establishing and maintaining good relationships will be possible. And perhaps most important of all, a happy marriage will be easier to achieve.

It would be convenient if a formula could be learned to bring them about. Unfortunately, there is none. But it helps to consider yourself critically and honestly. Try to—

Be dependable. If you say you'll do something, do it.

Be interested in others. Show a real, sincere interest, not just superficial or polite attention.

Make the most of your appearance. Then forget about it.

Find something pleasant to say if you talk about a person. If you can't, don't say anything about him.

Be agreeable when a plan other than yours is adopted. You can't have your own way all of the time.

Be a good sport. If a party stunt seems silly to you, don't spoil the fun for the others.

Plan a party yourself now and then. People love to be invited out. If you occasionally give an invitation, more will come your way.

Look for balance—in your interests, in your friends, in your time for work and play and rest, in your personality.

Every one of us enjoys people who make

[1]From *Getting Along with Others*, by Helen Schacter. Copyright, 1949, by Science Research Associates, Inc.

us feel interesting and worth while. No one enjoys hurt feelings. The warm, friendly personality is the personality people seek out. Cultivate it. You will get along better with the people in your life today. You will broaden your social contacts. And you will be building toward successful social relationships for your future.

Now take the test that appears next. If a statement is *true*, mark a + at the left of it. If a statement is *false*, mark a O at the left of it.

If you want to get along *better* with others, you should:

1. Be self-confident, cheerful, and friendly.
2. Look at yourself critically and honestly.
3. Work out a formula and follow it.
4. Do what you say you are going to do.
5. Be interested mainly in yourself.
6. Never forget your appearance.
7. Have your own way at a party.
8. Invite your friends to your own party.
9. Have many different friends.
10. Criticize others.

Here are the correct answers:

(6+; 10-0)
(1+; 2+; 3-0; 4+; 5-0; 6-0; 7-0; 8-;

To apply what you have learned from reading the selection carefully, make a short list of the things you can do to get along better with other people.

Careful reading exercise 2

To do this exercise, you should read the newspaper story that follows. This time you should try to read carefully but faster than you did before. When you have finished reading, you will take a short test.

AT THE RISK OF LIFE AND LIMB[2]
by John Crosby

THAT NEWSREEL film of the presidential candidates you see on "Camel Caravan" and "Today" is brought to you at the risk of life and limb.

In this campaign, NBC has found that the fastest way to get film from place to place is by a two-wheel motorcycle ridden by a hell-for-leather driver named Scotty McLeod.

These messengers with packs of film strapped to their backs and wearing goggles are known in the trade as Space Cadets.

Sometimes, fairly frequently, they must drive at top speed, picking up and delivering film for 24 hours. McLeod has averaged 65 mph on a long trip which gives you some idea of their top speed.

When Eisenhower was in South Bend, Scotty left Chicago at 7 a.m., rode 100 miles to South Bend, picked up film and tape from the Eisenhower train, and drove the 100 miles back to Chicago, doing the last lap at 90 mph.

After dropping off the film at the lab, he drove back to meet the Eisenhower train again at the city limits, picked up more film, dropped it off at the lab and picked up the film he'd left earlier. It had been processed by then and he took it to the cutting room in time to make the Caravan show. He left immediately on another breakneck trip to Ottawa, Ill., about 125 miles away.

The awed NBC news staff swears he left Chicago at 6:45 p.m. and got to Ottawa at 8 p.m. Scotty picked up film and tape and left immediately for Chicago again. His day ended at 5:45 a.m., just

[2]From the Chicago *Sun-Times*, October 23, 1952. Reprinted with permission of the publishers and the author.

22 3/4 hours after it began. That's not even an unusual day for Scotty.

Filming the story is another headache. Frank Bourgholtzer, who is in charge of the NBC coverage on the Stevenson train, has wired the following description.

"To film a whistle stop speech means leaping from the train with a box containing camera and amplifier, cable and microphone weighing eighty to 100 pounds, plus a power unit, plus a silent camera. You run three cars back to set up the equipment. By this time the crowd has surged in tight against the rear platform and there is a fierce fight to wedge through the crowd into position.

"There is never enough room to get a decent picture. There is a frantic unloading of equipment, hooking this cable into that piece of gear, getting a microphone up, checking to see if sound and film are operating properly and by that time the candidate is speaking.

"You shoot the speech until your film runs out, then gather your equipment together, fight back through the crowd and run like the dickens to the door of your car. By this time, likely as not, the train is moving. After all, it stopped only for five or 10 minutes altogether. This goes on all day, varied with interviews and whatever else can be thought up to tell the story."

Actually, these whistle stop speeches are pretty repetitious. But they don't dare miss filming any of them because the candidate might uncork something hot which everyone would then have except NBC.

Stevenson's speech on Labor Day in Detroit was filmed at 12:30 p.m. and was to have been flown to Chicago for processing directly afterwards.

The one-hour plane trip took five hours with seven emergency landings. Wind and rain pitched the plane around so badly the equipment had to be lashed down. At the Chicago airport, Scotty picked up the film and rushed it to the laboratory, then to the studio for the Caravan. He got there just 60 seconds too late for the show.

Take this test. If a statement is *true*, mark a + at the left of it. If a statement is *false*, mark a O at the left of it.

1. The man who delivered motion picture films during the presidential campaign had to drive so fast that he risked his life.

2. The messengers who delivered movie films on motorcycles were called *Time Demons*.

3. The messenger, Scotty McLeod, was delayed five hours in taking a newsreel film from Detroit to Chicago.

4. Although Scotty had to deliver film in a hurry, he always drove safely.

5. The NBC news staff swore that Scotty made the 125-mile trip from Chicago to Ottawa in an hour and a quarter.

6. In filming a whistle stop speech, the cameraman had to get his equipment out and in place within a few minutes' time.

7. The crowd at a whistle stop usually kept a path clear for the cameraman.

8. On a number of occasions, the cameraman almost missed the train while he was trying to get his equipment back into a car.

9. The sound cameraman never worried too much about taking pictures at whistle stops because the candidate often said the same thing again and again.

10. The plane had to take much more time than usual in flying from Detroit to Chicago because of engine trouble.

Here are the correct answers:

(9-o; 10-o)
(1--+; 2-o; 3-o; 4-o; 5-+-; 6-+-; 7-o; 8-+-;

Careful reading exercise 3

The selection appearing next is somewhat harder reading than the selections that you have just read. Even so, try to speed up your reading. At the same time, read carefully so that you understand the important details.

In the time box, write down your starting time. Then start to read the story.

Time Box

Finishing time	
Starting time	
Reading time	
Reading rate	

CUSTER'S LAST BATTLE[3]

GENERAL GEORGE A. CUSTER had started up the Rosebud Creek with about 600 soldiers, 44 Indian Scouts, and 20 or more packers, guides, and civilians. They moved cautiously along the creek, crossing it several times as they sought the most advantageous marching and camping ground.

The afternoon of the third day, June 24, 1876, the scouts reported that the Indian trail they were following turned abruptly to the right and went westward toward the Little Bighorn River Valley. After darkness set in and the men and horses had rested, Custer broke camp

[3] Adapted from *Custer Battlefield National Monument—Montana*, by Edward S. and Evelyn S. Luce. National Park Service, Washington, D.C., 1949.

and continued to follow the trail. During the night the cavalrymen moved several miles nearer the high divide between the Little Bighorn and Rosebud Valleys. Then they halted to await daylight so that a more careful reconnaissance of the surrounding country might be made.

At daybreak, from a high point on the divide, the scouts observed smoke in the Little Bighorn Valley, implying that the Indians were encamped there. This information was carried to Custer, but by the time he reached the point a haze obscured the view.

About noon on June 25, Custer set up three battalions, commanded respectively by Maj. Marcus A. Reno, Capt. Frederick W. Benteen, and Custer himself. Benteen was sent immediately to make a scout to the left of the trail, while Custer and Reno followed on opposite banks of a small creek toward the Little Bighorn Valley.

About two miles from the Little Bighorn River, portions of the Indian encampment were viewed lying on the west bank of the river and extending farther down-stream. Reno was told to move on down, cross the river, and charge this camp. Custer turned to the right, evidently planning to support Reno's attack in the river bottom by suddenly appearing in the lower end of the Indian camp and attacking their flank and rear.

At about 2:30 p.m., Major Reno crossed the Little Bighorn River to its west side and advanced down the valley toward the Indian camps. He had not gone far when it became evident that there were a great many more tepees and Indians in the valley than had been observed from the hills prior to his separation from Custer. Bluffs and the foliage of tall cottonwood trees had hidden the camps from their view.

The Indian warriors swarmed into the

open view as Reno and his men rode down the valley. Shortly after the battle between Reno's troops and the Indians began, Reno had his men dismount and deploy in a skirmish line to fight on foot. This move tended to check the onrush of the Indians. After almost half an hour, the increasing number of Indians forced the soldiers into a timber thicket. A defensive stand was made here until Reno ordered his men to mount and retreat to the bluffs.

The retreat of the soldiers became a panicky flight, with every man for himself, while the Indians continued their attack until the troops crossed the river. About a third of the whites dropped out, either having been killed, wounded, or forced to seek cover in the brush. The others crossed the river and reached the top of the hill on the east side. Here they took a defensive position.

Custer's route after he was last seen with Company E on a high promontory overlooking the river bottom where Reno was engaging the Indians, is still shrouded in mystery. As Custer looked down from the bluffs at the battle between Reno's troops and the Indians, he was seen by some of these troops to wave his hat as in encouragement.

During the time Custer disappeared from the bluffs and descended for a short distance, probably down the deep ravine near Medicine Tail Coulee, Reno had started his retreat from his position on the river flat to seek higher ground for defensive purposes. Perhaps about the time Reno left the river bottom, Custer and his troops reached a point across the Little Bighorn River from the main Indian camp. The attack against Reno's troops had eased off, and the mass of Indians immediately started after the Custer column. There were only about 225

cavalrymen against warriors numbering possibly up to 5,000. This was more than the small body of troopers could withstand, and the cavalrymen were gradually pushed to the positions now indicated by the silent white markers that dot Custer Hill.

Custer and his two-hundred-odd troopers on this hill fought one of the bloodiest battles with the Indians in the annals of American history. Many of the horses that had brought these troopers nearly 1,000 miles were shot to make breastworks against the deadly bullets and arrows from the Sioux and Cheyenne warriors.

It is thought that not long after the Indians began to show a strong force in Custer's front, he turned his column to the left and advanced in the direction of the Indian village to the junction of two ravines just below a spring. Here he probably dismounted two companies, under command of Keogh and Calhoun, to fight on foot. It is quite possible that the companies advanced to a knoll, now marked by Crittenden's marker, while the remaining three mounted companies continued along the ridge to Custer Hill.

The line occupied by Custer's battalion was the first considerable ridge back of the river. His front was extended about three-fourths of a mile. Most of the Indian village was in view. A few hundred yards from his line was another, but lower, ridge, the further slope of which was not commanded by his line. It was from here that the Indians, under Crazy Horse, from the lower part of the encampment, part of whom were Cheyennes, moved on Custer and cut off all access to the village. Gall and his warriors had been the first to meet Custer.

Many of the participants on both sides were on foot and doing much fighting from prone positions on the ground. The warriors outnumbered Custer's men possibly as much as 20 to 1. The horde of Indians were wriggling along gullies and hiding behind knolls on all sides of the troops. One need only to walk over the battlefield today and observe the terrain to understand how well they could hide themselves from the fire of the soldiers.

The only accounts of the battle have come from the Indians, since there were no surviving whites; but, because of the circumstances, much of what happened may never be solved conclusively. The fighting may have lasted about an hour, although the exact duration will never be known. The Indians managed to start the troopers' horses into a stampede, and many were caught by the Indian women in the valley. Some of these horses carried extra ammunition in their saddlebags. It is thought that Custer's men had some of the extra ammunition in their possession before the stampede occurred, but the loss may have seriously affected others.

The horse stampede was followed quickly by a concerted attack by the Indians which was so successful and so swiftly carried out that not a Custer trooper remained alive. The Indians stated that not one prisoner was taken alive and that they were not trying to capture any of them as prisoners. They also stated that there was no final charge on horseback such as often has been represented in writings and paintings. The only semblance to such culminating action was a "charge" by the mounted Indian youths and old men in a rush to seize and plunder from the dead bodies of Custer's men.

Benteen's and Reno's troops fought the Indians throughout the forenoon and into the afternoon of the 26th. Late that day the Indians fired the grass in the valley. When the cloud of smoke lifted, the troops watched with relief the departure of the entire Indian encampment.

The Custer Battlefield National Monument is located in southeastern Montana. Over the graves of most of the battle's victims is a large granite shaft. White markers, scattered over the hillsides, show as nearly as possible where the dead were found after their struggle was over.

Write your finishing time in the time box. Then take this test on careful reading. In each test item, mark a check (✔) at the left of the correct choice.

1. Custer's last battle was fought in the territory that later became the state of
   (A) North Dakota
   (B) Wyoming
   (C) Montana

2. Custer sent scouts ahead
   (A) to find the Indian trail
   (B) to fool the Indians
   (C) to capture Indian patrols

3. Custer halted his troops and waited for daylight because he wanted
   (A) to give his men a good night's rest
   (B) to see exactly where the Indians were
   (C) to wait for the ammunition pack train to come

4. Custer was unable to find out how many Indians there were because
   (A) his scouts were killed by Indians
   (B) the valley was covered by a mist
   (C) the Indians were hiding in a forest

5. According to Custer's plan of battle, Reno's group of soldiers was to make a frontal attack on the Indian camp while Custer's group was
   (A) to make a side and rear attack
   (B) to wait to re-enforce Reno's group
   (C) to surround the Indian camp

6. Reno's troops retreated because they
   (A) preferred to attack at night
   (B) ran out of ammunition
   (C) were attacked by so many Indians
7. Reno's troops last saw Custer alive when he was
   (A) waving to them from a bluff
   (B) riding down from the bluff toward the Indians
   (C) calling to Reno to join him
8. Custer and all of his 225 men were killed mainly because his troops
   (A) had to kill all their horses for breastworks
   (B) were attacked by up to 5,000 Indians
   (C) did not have enough ammunition with them
9. The Indians were greatly helped in their attack on Custer's group on the ridge mainly because
   (A) the many small hills and gullies gave them protection
   (B) the wide river cut off Custer's attempt to retreat
   (C) the many tepees in the camp provided good hiding places
10. The chief reason why Custer and his men lost both the battle and their lives was that Custer did *not*
   (A) prevent the Indians from stampeding their horses
   (B) order Reno to come to his aid soon enough
   (C) find out in advance how many Indians there were

Next, figure out your reading time for the story. Change your reading time into your reading rate; use the table on the last page of this book. Write your rate in the time box.

Correct your test and count your score. Here are the correct answers: (1-C; 2-A; 3-B; 4-B; 5-A; 6-C; 7-A; 8-B; 9-A; 10-C).

In reading this story carefully, what was your reading rate? What was your comprehension score? If your rate was 300 or more words a minute and if your score was 8 or more correct, your performance on this exercise was excellent.

Do general reading exercise 10 (page 236)

You can apply what you have learned in this lesson to General Reading Exercise 10. In reading the article in that exercise, pay close attention to what you are reading. Try to make sure that you understand the important details. Then take the test that covers these details.

If you are a good reader, you not only understand the important details of a story. You also grasp the main idea of that story, as mentioned in the previous lesson.

Next, find out whether you got the main idea in Article 10 by taking this test. Mark a check (✔) at the left of the correct choice.

The main idea of "What Makes A Hero?" is this:
(A) In facing danger, a boy may have as much "X" stuff of courage as a man.
(B) The untrained persons who have the most "X" stuff of courage are firemen and policemen.
(C) In an emergency, an ordinary person may show the "X" stuff of courage.
(D) An ounce of prevention is worth a pound of cure.
(E) The "X" stuff of courage depends upon the secretions of certain glands.

(The correct choice is: C.)

You may now be able to read a story for the main idea or for the important details. But can you read it and at the same time evaluate what you are reading? This is the subject of the next lesson.

How can you evaluate what you read?

IF YOU ARE A good reader, you are able to evaluate what you read. Because your mind is on the alert, you often ask yourself: "Is this statement true or false?" You then answer the question by comparing the statement with the facts that you have already acquired. On the basis of this comparison, you decide whether or not the statement is true.

In previous lessons, you have learned many things about reading. Therefore, you now have a store of information that you can draw upon to evaluate the statements that appear next.

Read each statement. If you believe that a statement is *true*, mark a + at the left of it. If you believe that a statement is *false*, mark a O at the left of it.

1. You can learn to read faster and better—much better than you are reading now.

2. By becoming an efficient reader, you will get A's in all your school subjects; or you will be given a better job.

3. If you are an adult, you can improve your reading very little because "you can't teach an old dog new tricks."

4. Within a week or two from now, you can probably double your reading rate and comprehension.

5. To read much better, you will have to practice reading systematically day by day.

6. You should read everything at about the same rate.

7. You should seldom read fast because the faster you read the more poorly you understand.

8. If you have a clear-cut reading purpose, you will get more from what you are reading.

9. Sometimes you should skim to get a specific fact or a general impression.

10. At other times you should read carefully to understand all the important details.

Here are the correct answers:

(+-01 ;+-6
;+-8 ;o-𝘓 ;o-9 ;+-𝘚 ;o-4 ;o-3 ;o-z ;+-1)

In deciding whether each statement was true or false, you were comparing what you were reading with what you already knew. In short, you were evaluating each statement.

75

Learn to evaluate better what you are reading

You may know someone who believes the statement: "If you see it in print, it's true." When he reads a false or misleading statement, he accepts it uncritically. He never thinks about whether or not the statement is true.

If you learn to evaluate what you are reading, you will read not only to get information but also to judge the soundness of what you read. You will ask yourself such questions as: Is the statement on this matter true? Does it make sense? Who is the author? What is he trying to do? You will try to answer these questions as best you can, by drawing upon your own experience and upon the experiences of others. You will also read statements on the same matter by other authors.

Newspapers, magazines, and books often contain reading matter that deals with controversial issues, such as taxation, governmental expenditures, candidates for public office, national defense, and foreign relations.

Sometimes this reading matter is in the form of a newspaper or magazine story that is decidedly for or against a point of view. You should always read such a story critically. You should weigh the facts given by the writer. And you should decide for yourself whether the writer's conclusions are justified.

At other times, this reading matter is in the form of an editorial. In a newspaper editorial, the writer frankly states his point of view on a controversial issue. He may give you both sides of the issue and then tell you which side he favors. Or, he may present one side only, making no mention of the opposing side.

In reading an editorial, you should recognize that the writer is trying to win you over to his point of view. Or he is trying to strengthen your belief in the opinion that he is expressing.

In studying an editorial or any other reading matter on a controversial issue, you should be alert to identify devices that the writer may use to influence your thinking. These devices include the appeal to prejudice or vanity, the omission of important facts, and the slanting or loading of statements so that they point in one direction only. To spot such devices, ask yourself: Does the writer have "an ax to grind"? "A bone to pick"? Is the writer appealing to reason or to emotion? Does he give the important facts? Are his conclusions justified by the facts he presents or by the facts you know?

You will find that questions like these are easier to ask than to answer. Yet you should make a real effort to answer them. In this effort, you may want to read something written by a person who expresses a different point of view.

If you are a critical reader, you read materials by authors who hold opposing opinions on a controversial issue. You can do this, for example, in your newspaper reading. Read an editorial in Newspaper A that vigorously favors one point of view on an important controversial issue. Then read an editorial in Newspaper B that strongly favors the opposing point of view. After comparing the two editorials, make up your own mind about the controversial issue. If possible, read other materials that deal with this issue.

You can do a similar kind of reading to evaluate magazine articles and books that discuss controversial issues. You can, for instance, read two books on the same subject by authors who present opposing points of view. Two such books on the atom bomb are *No Place to Hide*, by David Bradley, and *Why Must We*

Hide, by Ralph Lapp. After you read these books, compare the authors' statements and conclusions. Then decide which author you believe is more nearly right.

Use good sources to help evaluate what you are reading

Your main source for evaluating your reading matter is and should be you yourself. If you read actively and critically, you will increase your ability to compare what you read with what you already know about a subject. You will also learn which reading sources are reliable and which are not.

To guide your evaluation of newspapers, you can get a great deal of help from such books as *How to Read a Newspaper*, by Edgar Dale (Scott, Foresman and Company), or *Keeping Up With The News*, by Per G. Stensland and Larry Dennis (Science Research Associates).

In evaluating books either before or after reading them, you can read book reviews. The writers of these reviews are often recognized experts in their fields. They comment on the content, style, point of view, completeness, and reliability of a book. Their reviews appear in the book review sections of newspapers and magazines. They also appear in a magazine entitled the *Book Review Digest*, which is found in many libraries.

Whatever your sources for evaluating reading materials, the best one, as said before, is you yourself. By drawing on your experience and by using common sense, you will find yourself growing in the power to evaluate intelligently what you are reading.

Do the following exercises in careful reading and in evaluation

If you are to have a sound basis for judg-ing an editorial, you must be informed about the subject of that editorial. If you have little or no knowledge of the subject, then your opinion of the editorial is almost certain to be superficial—no more reliable than a prejudice.

Presented next are two reading exercises —one is a newspaper story to be read for information; the other, a newspaper editorial to be read critically.

Start by reading the news story headed "Truman Approves Draft Deferment for Best Students." This story appeared in the New York *Times*, April 1, 1951. Read the whole story rapidly. Then re-read carefully those parts that you did not understand.

An exercise in careful reading for information

TRUMAN APPROVES DRAFT DEFERMENT FOR BEST STUDENTS [1]

HE REVISES RULES SO NATIONAL TEST OR CLASS STANDING WILL FIX COLLEGIANS' STATUS

High School Boys Barred

Excluded from examinations which will be held on May 26, June 16 and 30, over U.S.

WASHINGTON, March 31, 1951—President Truman today approved draft deferment for college students of superior scholastic standing or those achieving a high score in a national aptitude test to be given in May and June.

In an executive order amending the Selective Service regulations, the President authorized Maj. Gen. Lewis B. Hershey, Selective Service Director, to prescribe the levels of college grades or the scores of the aptitude test that may qualify a college student's activity as "necessary to the maintenance of the national health, safety or interest."

---

[1]From the New York *Times*, April 1, 1951. Reprinted with permission of the publisher.

General Hershey, in an accompanying statement, said that the new deferment policy would apply to a total of about a million male, nonveteran students now in college but he added that "it would be impossible at this time to estimate how many will be deferred."

The Government is currently unable to make that estimate because the level of college standing or the score on the aptitude tests that may qualify a student for deferment have not yet been determined.

HIGH SCHOOL STUDENTS EXCLUDED

Immediately eligible for consideration under the new deferment criteria are students now in college expecting to continue their college work and college seniors and others planning to enter graduate or professional schools.

The first qualification tests will be given at about 1,000 examination centers in the United States and its Territories on May 26, June 16 and June 30. High school seniors or others planning to enter college this fall are not yet eligible for the tests. But students who have begun their first year of college and expressed their intention to continue will be allowed to take them.

Draft officials have indicated that the aptitude test might have a conventionally maximum score of 100 and that "passing"—qualifying the applicant for deferment—might initially be 70.

The only basis for student deferment at the present time is a draft bulletin advising local boards to "consider" the possibility of deferment for college students in the upper half of the classes. The present practice is to enable all students, however, to complete their current year before being inducted.

The procedure authorized by President Truman today will give local draft officials a relatively hard-and-fast yardstick for offering or rejecting student deferment.

Students will not be eligible to take the test if they are 26 years of age or older. There will be no second chance for students who fail in the examinations.

NEEDS OF THE ECONOMY NOTED

General Hershey said that high-grade students would be deferred because of the needs of the economy for trained and qualified scientists, technicians and other specialists of superior education. He added that military officials had recently told Congress that "since we cannot hope to match the Iron Curtain countries in manpower, our advantage lies in our superiority in scientific and technical know how."

"Congress took advantage of this," General Hershey continued, "and made provisions to permit the deferment of college and university students in such numbers as may be necessary to the maintenance of the national health, safety or interest."

He described the new student deferment plan as one "based upon either capacity to learn as demonstrated by the results of a nationwide test or upon scholastic performance as evidenced by class standing."

The Selective Service Director said the standards of the two criteria would be raised or lowered to either increase or diminish the number of students in training, as the national interest may require.

To check on how well you understand the New York *Times* story, take the following comprehension test. In each test item, mark a check (✔) at the left of the correct choice.

1. The President's executive order provided that male college students who had high grades or who made high scores on an aptitude test would be
   (A) eligible for draft deferment
   (B) exempt from draft registration
   (C) given officer training in the Armed Services
   (D) drafted after college graduation
   (E) offered government scholarships
2. The only persons eligible to take the national aptitude examination were
   (A) high school seniors who had high marks
   (B) college graduates who were physically fit
   (C) students who were in college
   (D) students who were 26 years of age or older
   (E) college students who had high marks
3. The policy described in this story provided a new yardstick according to which college students would be inducted into military service or deferred by
   (A) college presidents
   (B) draft boards

(C) the Selective Service Director

(D) the President of the United States

(E) the Veterans Administration

4. General Hershey, Selective Service Director, said that high-grade students would be deferred because the United States needed

(A) fewer men in military service than did Iron Curtain nations

(B) more men in colleges and universities than ever before

(C) better-educated men in civilian jobs than in military service

(D) more intelligent and well-trained men in the fields of health and safety

(E) more able and well-trained scientists and technicians

5. General Hershey pointed out that the standards for deferment based on students' grades or students' aptitude test scores would be set according to

(A) Congressional laws

(B) the Iron Curtain

(C) local draft boards

(D) the chances of an atomic bomb attack

(E) the national interest

Here are the correct answers:

(1-A; 2-C; 3-B; 4-E; 5-E)

An exercise in critical reading for evaluation

Next, read the editorial headed "Setting Up an Elite Class." This editorial appeared in the Chicago *Sun-Times*, April 3, 1951.

Setting up an Elite Class[2]

WE BELIEVE President Truman made a mistake when he authorized the draft deferment of college students with high marks or who score high in a special intelligence test.

---

[2]From the Chicago *Sun-Times*, April 3, 1951. Reprinted with permission of the publisher.

The scheme is one devised by educators to keep colleges from being emptied by the draft. The ostensible justification for it is the nation's need for technicians, scientists and other specialists. But the new system will exempt any youngster with a bright mind whose parents have enough money to send him to college.

Boys whose parents can send them to college can escape military service. Boys who might be just as bright but must go to work after high school will be put into uniform. Sen. Paul Douglas (D. Ill.) says: "It's very dangerous to protect an elite class from fighting and dying for their country."

Moreover, the elite system undercuts the very men who should be leaders of their generation. The intellectuals will not share the experience of their contemporaries in military service. They will not be able to understand the minds of men who have served in the armed forces. And the vets will reject the leadership of men whose brains entitle them to be leaders.

We repeat our earlier proposal: Let the armed services take in all young men on an equal basis. Let those who have special aptitudes continue in college as part of their training.

But let us not have an elite class of youngsters who are spared from serving their country because they have the money to go to college and the brains to get high marks.

If you wish to compare the statements in the editorial with those in the news story, reread the news statements. Notice that the news story presents the point of view of General Hershey, Selective Service Director; also that the editorial gives the point of view of a newspaper.

Next, take the evaluation test. In this test, indicate your opinions of the editorial. There are no correct answers to this opinion test. In each item, mark a check (✔) at the left of the choice that you believe is correct.

1. What is your opinion of the editorial?

(A) I agree with it.

(B) I disagree with it.

(C) I am uncertain.

2. I believe that the editorial gives

(A) arguments on one side only

(B) arguments on both sides

(C) no good arguments

3. I feel that the editorial states the newspaper's position
    (A) weakly
    (B) moderately
    (C) strongly

4. The editorial writer uses two key words to influence the reader's opinion. These words are:
    (A) scheme and deferment
    (B) ostensible and elite
    (C) brains and intellectuals

5. The editorial clearly implies that
    (A) only bright young men should be taken into the military services
    (B) only non-college young men should be taken into the military services
    (C) all young men should be taken into the military services on an equal basis

Now that you have read the newspaper story and evaluated the newspaper editorial on it, you will be interested to know that the federal government went ahead with the plan authorized by the President. According to this plan, thousands of college students took a scholastic aptitude test. The scores made by students on this test and their college marks were used as a basis for determining whether or not they should be deferred from military service.

Do general reading exercise 11 (page 241)

You have completed half of the 20 general reading exercises that are in this book. Your scores on these exercises have probably shown that you have made real gains in your reading power. Yet you can make even more gains in the reading exercises ahead.

Next, do General Reading Exercise 11. Try even harder than before to raise your rate, comprehension, and vocabulary scores.

After you finish this reading exercise, evaluate what you have read. Did the author's presentation make good sense to you? Did he include important facts? And did he interpret the facts correctly?

To develop further your skill in reading to evaluate materials, you will want to read critically the editorials that are appearing in your local newspapers. During this reading, you must read carefully and thoughtfully, as suggested in this lesson.

In the next lesson, you will learn to read better the type of material that is known as creative writing.

LESSON **12**

How can you appreciate creative writing?

GOOD LITERATURE, often referred to as *creative writing*, is available in many forms. When this type of writing is mentioned, most people think of poetry. Actually, creative writing includes not only poetry but also novels, biographies, short stories, plays, essays, and other forms of well-written prose.

Examples of creative writing at its best are *Alice in Wonderland* and *Through The Looking Glass*, by Lewis Carroll. If you have not read these books since childhood, you will want to read them again because now they will mean so much more to you.

An exercise in reading creative writing

Read the following selection from *Alice in Wonderland:*

The Mock Turtle sang this, very slowly and sadly:

" 'Will you walk a little faster?' said a whiting to a snail,

'There's a porpoise close behind us, and he's treading on my tail!"

"If I'd been the whiting," said Alice, whose thoughts were still running on the song, "I'd have said to the porpoise, 'Keep back, please; we don't want you with us!' "

"They were obliged to have him with them," the Mock Turtle said. "No wise fish would go anywhere without a porpoise."

"Wouldn't it really?" said Alice in a tone of great surprise.

"Of course not," said the Mock Turtle. "Why, if a fish came to *me*, and told me he was going on a journey, I should say, 'With what porpoise?' "

"Don't you mean 'purpose'?" said Alice.

"I mean what I say," the Mock Turtle replied in an offended tone.[1]

In reading this selection, you may have enjoyed the nonsense—the picture of the snail and whiting being pushed to walk faster and faster by the porpoise. You may have delighted in the pun—the Mock Turtle's use of the word "porpoise" to mean "purpose." Or, you may have observed some sense in the nonsense—the need to have a purpose when you are

---

[1]Condensed from *Alice in Wonderland*, by Lewis Carroll.

reading, traveling, or doing something else. If you read this selection with appreciation, you both laughed at and learned from what you read.

Because Lewis Carroll's books are so filled with humor and ideas, they are regarded as classics. These books are widely read and enjoyed by children, young people, and adults. In the stories in both books, you, in your imagination, can accompany Alice as she moves through a strange and amusing dreamlike world. Or, you can compare what happens in the stories with some of your own experiences. In these ways, you learn to appreciate Lewis Carroll's books.

Reading creative writing leads to appreciation of literature

As you read creative writing, you may use many of the skills that you have been learning. You may skim to find the main idea, read carefully to locate important details, or read thoughtfully to evaluate the soundness of what the author has written. But in reading to appreciate, you employ abilities that have not yet been mentioned.

According to the dictionary, to *appreciate* means to recognize the worth or quality of something. To appreciate a literary selection, you must, of course, be able to understand the literal meanings of the words, phrases, and sentences. In addition, you must be able to get other kinds of meanings—for instance, meanings that are less obvious.

Moreover, in reading creative expression, you involve your attitudes and feelings, not just your thoughts. You sense the beauty of what you are reading; or you feel the closeness of the author's expression to some experience you have had. Often, your emotions are deeply moved by your reading.

As an illustration of this form of creative expression, read the following verse from a poem by Robert Frost (1875-):[2]

> Some say the world will end in fire,
> Some say in ice.
> From what I've tasted of desire
> I hold with those who favor fire.
> But if it had to perish twice,
> I think I know enough of hate
> To say that for destruction ice
> Is also great
> And would suffice.

You probably found it difficult to indicate your reactions while you were reading this poem. That was because the poem's words carry more than their literal meanings; together these words arouse feelings that are distinctly your own.

Creative writing may be serious, as was the verse by Robert Frost. Or, it may be humorous, as was the selection from *Alice in Wonderland*. Whether such writing is serious or not, it is often subtle—the meanings are somewhat delicate and elusive. Yet this subtle writing may evoke emotional responses that are very satisfying to the appreciative reader.

As another example of writing that is subtly humorous, read the following short stanza by Emily Dickinson (1830-1886):[3]

> The pedigree of honey
> Does not concern the bee;
> A clover, anytime, to him
> Is aristocracy.

In writing this stanza, the poet expressed meanings that convey humor, imagination, and understanding. The person who appreciates creative writing gets most of the author's meanings and also supplies his own.

Creative writing often makes so deep

---

[2]From *New Hampshire* by Robert Frost. Copyright, 1923, by Henry Holt and Co., Inc. Copyright, 1951, by Robert Frost. Used by permission of the publisher. Also used by permission of Jonathan Cape Limited, London.

[3]From *Poems by Emily Dickinson*. Edited by Martha Dickinson Bianchi and Alfred Leete Hampson, Little, Brown and Co.

an impression on the reader that he recalls again and again a phrase or a sentence from his reading. From Shakespeare's *Romeo and Juliet*, you may remember: "What's in a name? That which we call a rose by any other name would smell as sweet." And from Carl Sandburg's *Chicago*, you may recall: "Hog butcher for the world, toolmaker, stacker of wheat."

In good literature, you may come across a passage of rare insight and humor. For example, in reviewing a Broadway play, one drama critic wrote: "The whole thing can't be a typographical error." To appreciate this comment, you must understand the literal meaning—that a typographical error is due to the typist, not to the author or playwright. You must also grasp the implied meaning—that the critic believed the play was not worth seeing.

If you wish to get the most out of reading a short story, a novel, or a play, you must try to understand the characters and to follow the plot. If you do, you may learn much about people and the situations they face. You may also learn many important things about yourself. This will be true especially if you compare your own reactions to certain situations with those of the characters depicted, for example, in good books. If you read good literature widely and thoughtfully, you will grow in your ability to appreciate and to enjoy creative writing.

How do you read poetry?

Perhaps you say, "I never read poetry because I don't understand it and because I don't like it." You, of course, have the privilege of making this decision. But if you do not learn to appreciate poetry, you will miss a reading experience that can enrich your life.

Whether or not you enjoy poetry, you will be interested in knowing the views of people who place a high value on this type of literature. Some of them are quoted here:

"Poetry is the record of the best and happiest moments of the happiest and best minds."—Percy Bysshe Shelley (1792-1822).

"Poetry is simply the most beautiful, impressive and effective mode of saying things and hence its importance."—Matthew Arnold (1822-1888).

"A vein of poetry exists in the hearts of all men."—Thomas Carlyle (1795-1881).

"Poetry—the *best* words in the best order."—Samuel T. Coleridge (1772-1834).

You may appreciate what Coleridge meant when you read "God's World," by Edna St. Vincent Millay. This gifted poetess had what Edwin Arlington Robinson (1869-1935) called the power "to shake the tree of life itself and bring down fruit unheard of."

An exercise in reading a poem

Edna St. Vincent Millay (1892-1950) was one of America's finest lyrical poets. Among her best creations was "God's World," reprinted here. Try to relive, in your imagination, what the poet may have experienced when she wrote this lyric:

GOD'S WORLD[4]
by Edna St. Vincent Millay

O WORLD, I cannot hold thee close enough!
   Thy winds, thy wide grey skies!
   Thy mists, that roll and rise!
Thy woods, this autumn day, that ache and sag
And all but cry with colour! That gaunt crag
To crush! To lift the lean of that black bluff!
World, World, I cannot get thee close enough!

[4]From *Renaissance and Other Poems*, published by Harper & Brothers. Copyright 1913, 1941, by Edna St. Vincent Millay.

Long have I known a glory in it all,
    But never knew I this;
    Here such a passion is
As stretcheth me apart,—Lord, I do fear
Thou'st made the world too beautiful this year;
My soul is all but out of me,—let fall
No burning leaf; prithee, let no bird call.

Did you enjoy the poem? Read the poem again. Try to imagine the author's thought as this poem was being written.

It is, of course, difficult to check your appreciation of a poem. However, the following exercise may stimulate you to consider some of the ideas expressed.

In each item, mark a check (✔) at the left of the choice that you believe is correct.

1. The author wanted
    (A) to escape from the world
    (B) to die for the world
    (C) to get nearer to the world
2. The poem mainly describes the author's feelings about
    (A) the beauty of the autumn woods
    (B) the pleasantness of the autumn winds
    (C) the glory of the gray skies and rolling mists
3. When the author wrote that the colour of the woods seems to crush a gaunt crag and to lift the lean of a black bluff, she meant that this colour appeared
    (A) to increase the size of the world
    (B) to lessen the ugliness of the world
    (C) to make the world more sorrowful
4. According to the author, she was so moved to take in all the glory of the scene that her emotions seemed to
    (A) stretch her apart
    (B) make her sad
    (C) pull her together

5. The author wanted no leaf to fall and no bird to call because she wished
    (A) to continue her feeling of oneness with the world
    (B) to write a poem about the glory of autumn
    (C) to prolong her feeling of ecstasy

Here are some answers to compare with your own: (1-C; 2-A; 3-B; 4-A; 5-C)

An exercise in reading a spiritual essay

Sometimes in your reading you come across an essay which moves you much as a great poem does. Such an essay was written years ago by John Donne (1573-1631), an English poet.

During his mature years Donne became a minister whose sermons were noted for their deep and stirring nature. Late in life, Donne's health was very poor and much of his writing was concerned with sickness and death. At that time, he wrote his collection of "Devotions." One of these is reprinted here in part and in modern form.

In reading the selection, picture Donne lying gravely ill on his bed and listening intently to the bell of a near-by church. As you read, try to get the meanings of the author's statements. Try also to discover his attitude toward death, religion, and mankind. Note particularly his vivid figures of speech, for example, his comparison of a man to a chapter in a book and to a part of the continent of Europe. Next, read the selection.

A DEVOTION
by **John Donne**

NOW THIS BELL tolling softly for another, says to me, Thou must die.

Perchance he for whom this bell tolls, may be so ill, as that he knows not it tolls for him. And perchance I may think myself so much better than I am, as that they who are about me, and see my state, may have caused it to toll for me, and I know not that.

The Church is catholic, universal, so are all her actions. All that she does, belongs to all. When she baptizes a child, that action concerns me; for that child is thereby connected to that head which is my head too, and engrafted into that body, whereof I am a member. And when she buries a man, that action concerns me.

All mankind is of one Author, and is one volume; when one man dies, one chapter is not torn out of the book, but translated into a better language; and every chapter must be so translated. God employs several translators; some pieces are translated by age, some by sickness, some by war, some by justice; but God's hand is in every translation; and his hand shall bind up all our scattered leaves again, for that library where every book shall lie open to one another. As therefore the bell that rings to a sermon, calls not upon the preacher only, but upon the congregation to come. So this bell calls us all; but how much more, who am brought so near the door by this sickness. . . .

The bell doth toll for him that thinks it doth; and though it intermit again, yet from that minute, that occasion wrought upon him he is united to God. Who casts not up his eye to the sun when it rises? But who takes off his eye from a comet when that breaks out? Who bends not his ear to any bell, which upon any occasion rings? But who can remove it from that bell, which is passing a piece of himself out of this world?

No man is an island, entire of itself; every man is a piece of the continent, a part of the main. If a clod be washed away by the sea, Europe is the less, as well as if a promontory were, as well as if a manor of thy friends or of thine own were. And therefore never send to know for whom the bell tolls. It tolls for thee.

Reread "A Devotion" to appreciate its deeper meanings. Read the essay aloud to someone and then discuss it. Next, write a paragraph telling what this essay means to you. You may want to write about yourself, your dearest relative, or your best friend—or even about all mankind. But try as best you can to put your own feelings on paper.

How do you read a play?

The play's the thing which you often enjoy on screen or stage but which you may seldom read. Yet, you can add to your appreciation of a play by reading it before or after you see it performed.

You may, for example, have seen the motion pictures, *Henry the Fifth* and *Hamlet*, in which Laurence Olivier, the British actor, starred. And you may have liked both pictures very much. But, if you had read each play in advance, you would probably have derived greater understanding and enjoyment when you saw it. And, if you had read the play afterward, your appreciation of it would have been heightened.

You can, of course, get real pleasure from reading plays even if you do not see them. In reading a play, you can permit your imagination to supply the settings and the characters. You can also make the play come to life by projecting yourself into it. Thus, by reading a play with thought and imagination, you can appreciate it better than in any other way.

An exercise in reading a part of a play

In any play, of course, the conversation is very important. Sometimes there is a rapid-fire give-and-take between the characters. At other times a character makes a fairly long speech. In the speech he may express in detail his thoughts and feelings.

Such a speech, from Shakespeare's *As You Like It*, appears next. Read this speech through rapidly, to enjoy it and to get its general flow. Then reread the speech more slowly, and think carefully about the different ideas that are presented.

> All the world's a stage,
> And all the men and women merely players.
> They have their exits and their entrances;
> And one man in his time plays many parts,
> His acts being seven ages. At first the infant,
> Mewling and puking in the nurse's arms.
> And then the whining schoolboy, with his satchel
> And shining morning face, creeping like snail
> Unwillingly to school. And then the lover,
> Sighing like furnace, with a woeful ballad
> Made to his mistress' eyebrow. Then a soldier,
> Full of strange oaths, and bearded like the pard;
> Jealous in honour, sudden and quick in quarrel,
> Seeking the bubble reputation
> Even in the cannon's mouth. And then the justice,
> In fair round belly with good capon lined,
> With eyes severe and beard of formal cut,
> Full of wise saws and modern instances;
> And so he plays his part. The sixth age shifts
> Into the lean and slipper'd pantaloon,
> With spectacles on nose and pouch on side;
> His youthful hose, well saved, a world too wide
> For his shrunk shank; and his big manly voice,
> Turning again toward childish treble, pipes
> And whistles in his sound. Last scene of all,
> That ends this strange eventful history,
> Is second childishness, and mere oblivion,
> Sans teeth, sans eyes, sans taste, sans everything.[5]

---

[5]William Shakespeare (1564-1616), *As You Like It*. Act II, Scene 7.

Now that you have carefully read this quotation from *As You Like It*, do you understand and appreciate it? You may recall that, according to Shakespeare's speaker, the seven ages through which a man passes are as follows: (1) an infant; (2) a schoolboy; (3) a lover; (4) a soldier; (5) a judge; (6) a middle-aged man; and (7) an old man. Do you agree with this classification? Why?

You may have noticed the colorful language used in this play. Does the reference to the schoolboy seem true today? What do such expressions as "with good capon lined" and "full of wise saws" mean?

If you enjoyed this selection, you may wish to read all of Shakespeare's comedy, *As You Like It*, and other plays by him. In these plays, you may discover that the play's the thing that can bring you reading satisfactions that are available from no other source.

An exercise in reading an imaginative essay

Perhaps when you were very young, someone asked you the riddle: "When is a door not a door?" He then gave the answer, "When it's ajar"—and laughed loudly at his own joke.

Since then, you, of course, have seen many doors. You have opened doors, walked through them, and shut them, never thinking twice about them.

But to a creative writer like Christopher Morley, a door is much more than simply a door. You will discover this when you read his essay, "On Doors," given next.

In reading this essay, check upon your reading rate and comprehension. In the time box, write your starting time. Then read the essay. Although you may come across some hard words, try to read at a fast rate. After you finish the essay, you will take a short test on it.

Time Box

Finishing time	
Starting time	
Reading time	
Reading rate	

ON DOORS[6]
by Christopher Morley

THE OPENING AND closing of doors are the most significant actions of a man's life. What a mystery lies in doors!

No man knows what awaits him when he opens a door. Even the most familiar room, where the clock ticks and the hearth grows red at dusk, may harbor surprises. The plumber may actually have called (while you were out) and fixed that leaking faucet. The cook may have had a fit of the vapors and demanded her passports. The wise man opens his front door with humility and a spirit of acceptance.

Which one of us has not sat in some anteroom and watched the inscrutable panels of a door that was full of meaning? Perhaps you were waiting to apply for a job; perhaps you had some "deal" you were ambitious to put over. You watched the confidential stenographer flit in and out, carelessly turning that mystic portal which, to you, revolved on hinges of fate. And then the young woman said, "Mr. Cranberry will see you now." As you

[6]From *Mince Pie*. Copyright, 1919, 1947, by Christopher Morley. Published by J. B. Lippincott Company. Reprinted with permission of the author and the publisher.

grasped the knob the thought flashed, "When I open this door again, what will have happened?"

There are many kinds of doors. Revolving doors for hotels, shops, and public buildings. These are typical of the brisk, bustling ways of modern life. Can you imagine John Milton or William Penn skipping through a revolving door? Then there are the curious little slatted doors that still swing outside denatured barrooms, and extend only from shoulder to knee. There are trapdoors, sliding doors, double doors, stage doors, prison doors, glass doors. But the symbol and mystery of a door resides in its quality of concealment. A glass door is not a door at all, but a window. The meaning of a door is to hide what lies inside; to keep the heart in suspense.

Also, there are many ways of opening doors. There is the cheery push of elbow with which the waiter shoves open the kitchen door when he bears in your tray of supper. There is the suspicious and tentative withdrawal of a door before the unhappy book agent or peddler. There is the genteel and carefully modulated recession with which footmen swing wide the oaken barriers of the great. There is the sympathetic and awful silence of the dentist's maid who opens the door into the operating room and, without speaking, implies that the doctor is ready for you. There is the brisk cataclysmic opening of a door when the nurse comes in, very early in the morning—"It's a boy!"

Doors are the symbol of privacy, of retreat, of the mind's escape into blissful quietude or sad secret struggle. A room without doors is not a room, but a hallway. No matter where he is, a man can make himself at home behind a closed door. The mind works best behind closed doors. Men are not horses to be herded together.

Dogs know the meaning and anguish of doors. Have you ever noticed a puppy yearning at a shut portal? It is a symbol of human life.

The opening of doors is a mystic act: it has in it some flavor of the unknown, some sense of moving into a new moment, a new pattern of the human rigmarole. It includes the highest glimpses of mortal gladness: reunions, reconciliations, the bliss of lovers long parted. Even in sadness, the opening of a door may bring relief: it changes and redistributes human forces. But the closing of doors is far more terrible. It is a confession of finality. Every door closed brings something to an end. And there are degrees of sadness in the closing of doors. A door slammed is a confession of weakness. A door gently shut is often the most tragic gesture in life. Every one knows the seizure of anguish that comes just after the closing of a door, when the loved one is still near, within sound of voice, and yet already far away.

The opening and closing of doors is a part of the stern fluency of life. Life will not stay still and let us alone. We are continually opening doors with hope, closing them with despair. Life lasts not much longer than a pipe of tobacco, and destiny knocks us out like the ashes.

The closing of a door is irrevocable. It snaps the pack-thread of the heart. It is no avail to reopen, to go back. Pinero spoke nonsense when he made Paula Tanqueray say, "The future is only the past entered through another gate." Alas, there is no other gate. When the door is shut, it is shut forever. There is no other entrance to that vanished pulse of time. "The moving finger writes, and having writ—"

There is a certain kind of door-shutting that will come to us all. The kind of door-shutting that is done very quietly, with the sharp click of the latch to break the stillness. They will think then, one hopes, of our unfulfilled decencies rather than of our pluperfected misdemeanors. Then they will go out and close the door.

Write your finishing time in the time box. Then take this test. In each item, mark a check (✔) at the left of the correct choice.

1. According to the author, the opening and closing of doors are
   (A) the most mysterious actions of a man's life
   (B) the most troublesome actions of a man's life
   (C) the most significant actions of a man's life
2. Because surprising things may have happened while a person was away from home, the wise man opens his front door with a spirit of
   (A) humility and acceptance
   (B) pride and rejection
   (C) modesty and wonder
3. Nearly everyone of us has sat in an outer office and watched the panels of the main office's door because it was full of
   (A) questions
   (B) shadows
   (C) meanings
4. Revolving doors are symbols of
   (A) the merry-go-round of modern life
   (B) the hustle and bustle of modern life
   (C) the smooth efficiency of modern life
5. The meaning of a barroom door, a stage door, a prison door, or any other kind of door is
   (A) to show what lies inside

(B) to hide what lies inside
(C) to lead to what lies inside

6. According to the author, there are many ways of opening doors. To prove this, he gives examples that show that the way a door is opened depends upon
   (A) who is waiting outside and why he is waiting outside
   (B) who is opening it and why he is opening it
   (C) what is happening both inside and outside the door

7. To a man, doors are a symbol of
   (A) privacy, retreat, and escape
   (B) yearning, frustration, and anguish
   (C) publicity, attack, and victory

8. The opening of doors is a mystic act that has in it
   (A) some flavor of the known
   (B) a new pattern of human life
   (C) some sense of reliving an old moment

9. The closing of doors is more terrible than the opening of doors, even in sadness, because every closed door
   (A) brings something to an end
   (B) is a confession of weakness
   (C) means a loved one is still near and yet already far away

10. In a certain kind of quiet door-shutting that will come to us all, we hope that our visitors before leaving will think of
    (A) the nice things they might have done rather than the bad things they did
    (B) the wrong things we did rather than the right things we might have done
    (C) the nice things we might have done rather than the bad things we did

---

Now figure out your reading time for the essay. Change your reading time into your reading rate; use the table given here. Write your reading rate in the time box.

Time-to-Rate Table for the Essay (848 words)

Reading time	Reading rate
1:00-1:14	759
1:15-1:29	620
1:30-1:44	525
1:45-1:59	454
2:00-2:14	401
2:15-2:29	358
2:30-2:44	324
2:45-2:59	296
3:00-3:14	272
3:15-3:29	252
3:30-3:44	234
3:45-3:59	219
4:00-4:14	206
4:15-4:29	194
4:30-4:44	184
4:45-4:59	174
5:00-5:14	166
5:15-5:29	158
5:30-5:44	151
5:45-5:59	145

Next, correct and score your answers to the test. Here are the correct answers:

(1-C; 2-A; 3-C; 4-B; 5-B; 6-B; 7-A; 8-B; 9-A; 10-C)

Do general reading exercise 12 (page 247)

You can find creative writing in a poem, a novel, a play, and an essay. You can also find it in a short story like the magazine article of General Reading Exercise 12. That article, "The Divine Story of Handel's Messiah," is a fine example of creative writing about a creative genius in the field of music.

As you do this general reading exercise, push yourself to read faster and to raise your comprehension and your vocabulary scores.

After you finish this general reading exercise, answer these questions: How did Handel show that he was a musical genius? Why did he compose *The Messiah?* What words, phrases, or sentences in the story indicate the creative writing ability of the author?

You may want to find out more about Handel and his compositions. If so, look up the facts about his life in an encyclopedia or in a longer biography. You may also want to hear *The Messiah.* If so, listen to phonograph records of this oratorio or of selections from it. After get-

ting more facts about Handel's life and after hearing some of his music, you will want to reread "The Divine Story of Handel's Messiah." During this final reading, you will appreciate more than ever before the literary qualities of this story.

In this lesson you learned not only to appreciate creative writing but also to do one kind of study-type reading. In the next lesson, you will learn about other kinds of such reading and about how best to do them.

LESSON 13

How can you do study-type reading?

WHETHER YOU ARE now in school or are working full time, you probably have tasks that require study-type reading. If you can do this kind of reading effectively, you will perform these tasks with greater success.

In study-type reading, you read for a serious purpose. You have a definite goal in mind. And you apply many of the reading skills and habits that you have already acquired. As you worked on the previous lessons in this book, much of your reading was the study-type.

If you are in school or college, you must do much study-type reading. You study the chapter that was assigned for the next day's class; you may have to answer questions on the chapter or take a test on it. You study reference books to prepare an oral or a written report.

You frequently do study-type reading at home, at work, and elsewhere. In many tasks, you have to read carefully a book, a magazine article, a pamphlet, or other printed materials; you then apply what

you have read to your work. Here are examples of such tasks:

1. Baking a cake
2. Making a dress
3. Building, repairing, or refinishing furniture
4. Doing simple household repairs
5. Planting and caring for a garden
6. Filling out an income tax return
7. Buying an insurance policy
8. Renting or purchasing a home
9. Rearing children
10. Improving your health or appearance

If you are in military service, you have to read carefully such materials as the *Manual of Arms, Soldier's Handbook,* and *General Orders.* If you are a civilian, you may want to study books and other materials that will help you do your work better or to get a better job.

If you are a farmer, you must study bulletins that deal with soil conservation, crop raising, livestock production, and prevention of diseases. If you are a skilled worker, you must read carefully the instructions and directions that relate to your work.

If you are a businessman, you must study many kinds of printed matter—important letters, financial statements, and trade magazines.

If you are a professional person such as a physician, nurse, teacher, lawyer, engineer, or writer, you must often do study-type reading. To illustrate, the physician must read the journals and bulletins of the medical associations to which he belongs. And the teacher must read many publications to keep informed in his field.

You can improve your study-type reading

You can develop the skills and habits that you need for study-type reading. In the selections that follow, you will find practical suggestions on how to do this kind of reading more efficiently.

HOW TO READ FOR AN EXAMINATION

If you are a student, you will find that the best way to get ready for an examination in any subject is to keep your reading and other work up-to-date and of high quality every day. If you do so, you will have little to worry about when you take a test.

Several days before a test, you may find it valuable to review thoroughly what the test is to cover. This intensive review, sometimes called "cramming," will help you to recall important facts during the test.

While reviewing for an examination, you can take these steps:
1. Skim the textbook or the part of it on which you will be tested.

2. Read carefully for important details, especially those that are difficult for you.

3. Take notes on what you are reading. Make these notes in outline form so that you can easily see the main topics and subtopics and their relationships.

4. Use your notebook. If you have kept good notes during the course, these notes will be very helpful, too.

5. Have a classmate ask you questions. Give the answers orally; then check your answers by referring to your textbook or notebook.

If you are an adult, you can use the steps just given in a number of important situations. For example, you can follow these steps in preparing for a written examination or for an interview about a job. You can also take the same steps in preparing a talk before a club or study group. If you read and review carefully what you must know about the problem or the topic to be considered, you are most likely to be successful.

An exercise in reading for a test

If you are getting ready to take an examination for a driver's license, you will have to read carefully the booklet issued by the state department of motor vehicles. This booklet tells you the state laws that you must obey in driving an automobile; it also gives you information on how to drive safely.

The selection that follows is from a booklet published by the State of Illinois. Read the selection only once, rapidly and carefully. Afterward, you will take a short test on it.

Write down your starting time in the time box. Then start reading the selection.

Time Box

Finishing time	
Starting time	
Reading time	
Reading rate	

SHARING THE ROAD WITH OTHERS[1]

YOU ARE ENTITLED to half the road—don't take your half out of the middle. Courtesy on the road will bring about a remarkable reduction in highway accidents.

It is one thing to drive safely when there are no other cars or pedestrians near, but quite another and more difficult matter to avoid accidents in traffic. Certain rules are important in sharing the road with others.

KEEP TO THE RIGHT. You should drive as far to the right side of the road as possible, except when passing another vehicle or when preparing to make a left turn.

NEVER DRIVE ON THE LEFT SIDE OF THE ROAD in the following places:
- Nearing a bridge or viaduct, tunnel or underpass.
- At street crossings or highway intersections.
- At a railroad crossing.
- On a hill or curve, or any other section of roadway where you cannot see clearly ahead.
- When you are meeting another vehicle.
- When there is a yellow line on your side of the center line.

[1]Edward J. Barrett (comp.), *Rules of the Road.* (Springfield: State of Illinois, 1951.)

- When there are two or more traffic lanes in each direction.

WHEN OVERTAKING AND PASSING another vehicle, pass on the left and do not come back to the right lane until you have put a safe distance between your vehicle and the vehicle you have passed. You may pass on the right when the car you are passing has pulled to the left to make a left turn.

Never pass a driver on the left when he has signaled his intention of making a left turn.

When you wish to overtake and pass a car going in the same direction, take these steps:

Before you cross to the left-hand side of the center line, make sure there is ample time to pass and get back into the right-hand lane before meeting any car coming from the opposite direction.

Sound your horn so the driver ahead will know what you intend to do.

Give a left-turn signal for the information of the driver behind you.

After passing and before returning to the right-hand lane, be sure there is ample clearance. Avoid "cutting in" too quickly. A general safety rule is to wait until you can see the car you have just passed in your rear vision mirror.

Get back on the right-hand side of the roadway before you come within 100 feet of any vehicle approaching from the opposite direction.

Never overtake and pass a car stopped at an intersection to let a pedestrian cross.

When a driver behind you sounds his horn to pass, keep to the right and slow down.

Courteous Driving and Safe Driving Are Synonymous.

Write your finishing time in the time

box. Then take the test. In each item, mark a check (✔) at the left of the correct choice.

1. While you are driving, your car always has the right to
   (A) the left side of the road
   (B) the middle of the road
   (C) the right side of the road
   (D) both sides of the road
   (E) the left shoulder of the road

2. You are more likely to avoid accidents with other cars if you are always
   (A) a rude driver
   (B) a carefree driver
   (C) a courteous driver
   (D) a slow driver
   (E) a tense driver

3. If you drive safely, the law allows you to drive on the left side of the road when you are
   (A) nearing a bridge, tunnel, or under-pass
   (B) going up a hill or rounding a curve
   (C) crossing a railroad track or road intersection
   (D) overtaking and passing another car
   (E) seeing a yellow line on your side of the road

4. In overtaking and passing another car, you should always do each of these four things:
   (A) Make sure that you have enough time to pass and get back into the right-hand lane.
   (B) Make sure that your car can stop more quickly than the other car.
   (C) Turn on your lights so that the driver ahead knows you want to pass.
   (D) Sound your horn so that the driver ahead knows you want to pass.
   (E) Give a left-turn signal to inform the driver behind you.

   (F) Give a right-turn signal to inform the driver behind you.
   (G) Wait until you see the overtaken car in your rear vision mirror before you get back into the right-hand lane.
   (H) Get back into the right-hand lane just as soon as your car is slightly ahead of the overtaken car.

5. When a driver behind you sounds his horn to pass, you should
   (A) keep to the right and speed up
   (B) drive off the highway and stop
   (C) keep to the left and slow down
   (D) keep to the right and sound your horn
   (E) keep to the right and slow down

Time-to-Rate Table for
"Sharing the Road With Others"
(442 words)

Reading time	Reading rate
1:00-1:14	396
1:15-1:29	323
1:30-1:44	273
1:45-1:59	237
2:00-2:14	209
2:15-2:29	187
2:30-2:44	169
2:45-2:59	154
3:00-3:14	142
3:15-3:29	131
3:30-3:44	122
3:45-3:59	114
4:00-4:14	107
4:15-4:29	101

Here are the correct answers to the test:
(1-C; 2-C; 3-D; 4-A, D, E, G; 5-E)

HOW TO READ FOR THOROUGH UNDERSTANDING

In study-type reading, you must be sure that you understand thoroughly what you are reading because you will need to apply what you are learning. The material you thus plan to read carefully may be a chapter in a social studies textbook, a newspaper story, or a magazine article.

In reading a selection for thorough understanding, you should take these steps:

1. Read the selection rapidly from beginning to end to get a general idea of what it is about.

2. Read the selection again, carefully this time to understand the main points.

3. If necessary, make notes on the main points. Refer to these notes to recall what is in the selection.

An exercise in reading for thorough understanding

You will now apply the first two steps just given to the selection presented next. It contains a clause of the United States Constitution and an explanation of that clause.

Step 1. Read the selection to get its general idea.

A SELECTION ON THE UNITED STATES CONSTITUTION[2]

ARTICLE 1
Section 2
Clause 3

"REPRESENTATIVES AND direct taxes shall be apportioned among the several states which may be included within the Union, according to their respective numbers. The actual enumeration shall be made within three years after the first meeting of the Congress of the United States, and within every subsequent term of ten years, in such manner as they shall by law direct. The number of Representatives shall not exceed one for every thirty thousand, but each state shall have at least one Representative."

[2]B. A. Findlay and E. B. Findlay, *Your Rugged Constitution* (Chicago: Science Research Associates, Inc., 1952), pp. 20-23.

This clause was put into the Constitution as a result of the "Great Compromise" of the Constitutional Convention, held in 1787. Delegates from the larger states, led by Virginia, wanted the total number of members of Congress to be divided among the states according to their populations. That is, they wanted a state with twice as many people as another state to have twice as many members in Congress. But the delegates from the smaller states, led by New Jersey, wanted every state to have the same number of members.

After long and bitter arguments in the Constitutional Convention, the large states and the small states finally worked out the "Great Compromise." They agreed that the more people any state had, the more members that state could send to the House of Representatives. But they also agreed that each state should send two members, and two only, to the Senate.

This compromise satisfied both the larger and the smaller states. The state with the largest population had the most Representatives in the House; the smallest state, however, had as many members in the Senate as the largest state. And no bill could become a law unless it was passed by both the House and the Senate.

To avoid arguments over the number of Representatives from any state, the Constitution ordered that a census—an official count of the number of people—should be taken in each state every ten years. A national law now requires that after every census each state must be told how many Representatives it may have in Congress.

The men who wrote the Constitution intended that there should be no more than one Representative for every thirty thousand people. But as the population increased, people saw that the House might have too many members to do its work well. For this reason a law was passed in 1929 limiting the total number of Representatives to 435. But each state, no matter how small its population, must still have at least one member in the House of Representatives.

In the first part of the clause dealing with Representatives, the Constitution also says that the payment of direct taxes must be divided among the states in the same way the total number of Representatives is divided. (Direct taxes are those which individuals pay directly to the government.)

Mark a check (✔) at the left of the choice that gives the general idea of the selection.
1. According to the Constitution, Congress must distribute Representatives and assess direct taxes on the basis of
   (A) the total population of the United States
   (B) the population of the several states
   (C) the areas of the several states
   (D) the wealth of the several states
   (E) the dates when the several states entered the Union

Step 2. Reread the selection to understand the main points.

Take this test that covers the main points. If a statement is *true*, mark a + at the left of it. If a statement is *false*, mark a O at the left of it.
2. Nevada has two Senators but no Representatives because its population is so small.
3. At the Constitutional Convention, the states with large populations wanted a state with twice as many people as another state to have twice as many members in Congress.

4. According to the "Great Compromise," each state was given about the same number of Representatives in both the Senate and the House of Representatives.
5. A bill for the raising of money has to be passed only by the House of Representatives.
6. The census is an official count every ten years of the number of persons living within the several states.
7. The census figures are used to determine the numbers of Senators each state may have.
8. In Congress today, there is one Representative for each 30,000 persons in the United States.
9. The Constitution states that the number of Representatives shall be no more than 435.
10. Every state is guaranteed at least one Representative.
11. Direct taxes must be divided among the states according to their populations.

Here are the correct answers:

(1-B; 2-o; 3-+; 4-o; 5-o; 6-+; 7-o; 8-o; 9-o; 10-+; 11-+)

How to read for problem-solving

In the field of mathematics, you have to read words, numbers, and symbols. You then have to put them together in solving problems. Some are computational problems; they require mainly the reading of numbers. Others are reasoning problems; they require the reading of both numbers and sentences.

When you are doing a computational or a reasoning problem, you should make sure that you have copied the numbers correctly. You can do this by checking the numbers you have written down with the numbers given in the book.

When solving a reasoning problem, you

should first read the problem quickly from beginning to end. You should then reread the problem slowly and carefully, making sure you know the meaning of all the words. During this second reading, you should ask yourself such questions as these: Do I know the meaning of the words used? What is called for? What is given? And, how can I get from the given to the called for?

Exercise 1. Reading a reasoning problem

Read this problem quickly and then carefully.

Out of your savings, you buy a $25 United States Savings Bond (Series E) every month, January through December, during one year. You pay $18.75 for each bond. You hold each bond until it matures, ten years later. How much total cash will you receive for all these bonds?

Cover up the problem. Then write your answer to these questions on the blank lines.

1. What kind of bond is named in the problem? _____
2. How much do you pay for each bond? _____
3. How many years do you have to hold each bond until it matures? _____
4. How much cash is each matured bond worth? _____

Here are the correct answers:

(1–United States Savings Bonds, Series E; 2–$18.75; 3–10 years; 4–$25.00)

Exercise 2. Reading a reasoning problem

Read this problem quickly and then carefully.

You are planning to drive from Chicago to Cincinnati, a distance of 294 miles. According to your highway map, you will average about 35 miles an hour. This average takes into account the fact that you will drive slowly through cities and towns and that you will stop for rests and one meal. You leave Chicago at 11:00 A.M. Central Standard Time. At what time (Eastern Standard Time) will you arrive in Cincinnati?

Cover up the problem. Then write your answers to these questions on the blank lines.

1. Between what two cities are you driving? _____ and _____
2. What is the distance between these cities? _____ miles.
3. How many miles per hour will you average for the trip? _____ miles per hour.
4. Does this average include time out for rests and a meal? _____
5. At what time do you expect to leave? _____
6. When you arrive at your destination, your watch will read 7:24. What is the correct time (Eastern Standard Time)? 6:24 A.M.; 7:24 A.M.; 8:24 A.M.; 6:24 P.M.; 7:24 P.M.; or 8:24 P.M.? _____

Here are the correct answers:

(1–Chicago and Cincinnati; 2–294 or about 300 miles; 3–35 miles per hour; 4–Yes; 5–11 A.M.; 6–8:24 P.M. EST.)

Here is the solution to this problem:

1. Your driving distance is 294 miles. Your average rate of speed is 35 miles an hour. Dividing 294 by 35, the quotient is 8.4. You will take 8.4 hours, or 8 hours 24 minutes to make the trip.
2. You leave Chicago at 11 A.M. You will arrive in Cincinnati 8.4 hours later, or at about 7:24 P.M. Central Standard Time. This is 8:24 P.M. Eastern Standard Time.

Exercise 3. Reading a reasoning problem

Read this problem quickly and carefully.

The price of a bottle and a cork together is $1.10. The bottle is worth a dollar more than the cork. What is the price of the cork?

Cover up the problem. Then take this test. In each item, mark a check (✔) at the left of the correct choice.

1. What is the price of the bottle and cork together?
   (A) 11 cents
   (B) 95 cents
   (C) $1.00
   (D) $1.05
   (E) $1.10
2. How much is the bottle worth?
   (A) A dollar more than the cork
   (B) Ten times the price of the cork
   (C) $1.00
   (D) 10 cents
3. The problem asks you to figure out the price of the
   (A) bottle
   (B) cork
   (C) bottle and cork together

Here are the correct answers:

(1-E; 2-A; 3-B)

Here is the solution to this problem, using simple algebra:

Let X = the price of the cork
$X + \$1.00$ = the price of the bottle
Adding the two: $X + X + \$1.00 = \$1.10$

$$2X + \$1.00 = \$1.10$$
$$-1.00 = -1.00$$
$$2X = .10$$
$$X = .05$$

How to read in preparing a report

From time to time you may have to read a book, magazine article, or newspaper story in order to make a report on it. You may give this report orally or you may write it. Whichever you do, you can follow the suggestions given in the example that appears next. This example shows how to prepare a report on a novel.

1. Read the entire book rapidly but with understanding. Then, reread the book. As you reread, make notes on the important points that you want to remember.

2. Using your notes prepare an outline of the book. Your outline may include such information as this:

   a. The title of the book; the name of its author; the name of the publisher; and the date of publication

   b. The story or plot of the book; the main characters—who they were, where they lived, and what they did

   c. Your reactions to the book—whether you enjoyed it; why you liked or disliked it

In reading a novel to make a report, you should try not only to read rapidly but also to understand the book's content. If you reread and make notes about the book, these notes will come in handy when you draw up your outline.

If you spend an hour or two every day reading the book, you will probably finish it within a few days. If you take too much time to read a book or if you let days go by without reading it, you will forget much of what you have read.

Just as soon as you finish the book, prepare your outline on it. Refer to your notes in making this outline. You can use the outline in developing an oral or written report of the book. Keep this outline before you while you are giving an oral book report. Refer to this outline while you are preparing a written book report. If you use an outline, you are more likely to give a talk or write a report that is well organized and interesting.

An exercise in reading to prepare a report

Read this story rapidly to find out what it is about. Then read the story carefully.

ARE FISH COLOR BLIND?[3]
by Tom Farley

CAN YOU FOOL a fish with color? This reasonable question has provoked one of the longest drawn out controversies in angling. No one knows who brought the question up for the first time—or when; it has been kicked around for at least a century, and perhaps since the inception of sport fishing.

Some anglers maintain that fish are so sensitive to colors that you can put down a trout rise, for example, simply by switching to a different shade of the same fly pattern you had been using with success. And they'll point to a mass of reports based on scientific experiments which show that fish have excellent color-perception.

Other scientists, however, have muddied up the question thoroughly by proving—to themselves and to a great many others—that all fish are color-blind!

Who is right?

Well, back in the 1880's the German scientist Graber ran exhaustive tests on several species and concluded that fish were definitely attracted by certain colored lights and food. Another German, Bauer, conducted similar experiments in 1910 and 1911 and came to the same conclusion.

At about the time Bauer was backing up Graber's theory a scientist named Hess was making some tests of his own.

---

[3]Tom Farley, "Are Fish Color Blind?," *Michigan Conservation*, XXI (July-August, 1952), pp. 13-14. Reprinted from *Iowa Conservationist* of May 15, 1951.

When he completed them, in 1914, he announced that his findings disagreed sharply with those of Graber and Bauer. Hess concluded that a fish's vision was similar to that of a color-blind man; that its response to colors depended upon the color's intensity—not its hue.

Two more scientists, Schiemenz and Wolff, looked into the squabble over fishes' color-perception in the mid-20's and stated after a time that a minnow could distinguish among about 20 colors of the visible spectrum.

Dr. Frank A. Brown, working with the Illinois Natural History Survey, made nearly 15,000 experiments with the color-perception of largemouth bass. In one of the tests he lowered a glass tube, wrapped with a colored band, into a tank of the fish. When a bass swam near it he was rewarded with food. Then other colors were wrapped around tubes which were placed in the tank—but when a bass investigated these he was given a small electric shock. After a few experiences with this treatment most of the fish could distinguish between strong shades of red, yellow, green, and blue.

Dr. Brown decided: "It is probable that largemouth bass are able to distinguish among colors in about the same manner as would a human being with perfectly normal vision—if he were looking through a yellowish filter."

One of the most devastating arguments in favor of fishes' ability to recognize colors came out of tests conducted by the scientists Kottgen and Abelsdorf. In all eyes —human, fish, and other animal—the only identified substance which permits color perception is a chemical known as rhodopsin; by comparative tests of rhodopsin from human and fish eyes, these scientists found that each had virtually the same qualities.

The fishing tackle business has reacted to the color argument with enthusiasm. Anglers can buy lures in practically any color of the spectrum for the purpose of attracting fish. A whole lot less attention has been paid to another important color angle, however—the use of color in lines to hide their presence in the water.

Many dry-fly fishermen will use only light colors in their lines. They believe that since a fish normally sees a dry-fly line as it lies on top of the water—silhouetted against the sky—light colors are less noticeable and thus less likely to spook the quarry.

Bait-casting lines are, of course, a different story. They have no floating qualities and they are much more finely calibrated than fly lines. Therefore the possibility of their casting a shadow in the water is considerably lessened. However, the color of a bait-casting line may very well be of far greater importance than that of a fly line. This is because a sunken bait-line comes directly into a fish's view.

By far the most commonly used color in bait-lines is, at present, black. There is no apparent explanation for this; black is certainly not a shade calculated to blend in with all types of water. Nor is it a shade which fish can't see. If bass, for example, were totally oblivious to black, there would be small point indeed to fishing for them with black plugs—which actually are notable bass killers under some conditions.

One fishing tackle manufacturer, The Horton Bristol Co., has engaged in extensive research and brought out a line which they say will match water colors and conditions—the variations which are encountered among lake, creek, river, pond, and ocean fishing. The idea behind the blended colors is, of course, to disguise the fact that the lure is connected to a line

which in turn is connected to a fisherman —circumstances which fish regard with understandable concern.

A good many fishermen will embrace the idea of blended lines because it agrees exactly with what they have been saying all along.

The others—the ones who scout the notion that fish can be fooled with color? They'll wait and see. After all, this squabble has been going on for generations.

Now take this test. In each item, mark a check (✔) at the left of the correct choice.

1. Fishermen have been talking about whether you can fool a fish with color for at least
   (A) one year
   (B) 10 years
   (C) 100 years
2. On the question, "Are fish color blind?" scientists
   (A) disagree with one another
   (B) have no good information
   (C) agree with one another
3. The scientists who did many of the early experiments on the ability of fish to distinguish colors were
   (A) Englishmen
   (B) Germans
   (C) Americans
4. In 1914 Hess concluded that a fish's vision was similar to that of a color-blind man; in other words, a fish distinguishes colors by their
   (A) shade or intensity
   (B) hue or kind
   (C) size or shape
5. Dr. Frank A. Brown of the Illinois Natural History Survey found that a largemouth bass could learn to distinguish between strong shades of red, yellow, green, and blue. To the

bass these colors looked as they would to a human being who was looking through
(A) a reddish filter
(B) a greenish filter
(C) a yellowish filter

6. Two scientists believe that a fish can see colors because its eyes, like those of a human being, have the following that is needed for color perception:
(A) Rhodopsin
(B) Filter
(C) Intensity

7. On the basis of the studies by scientists, fishing tackle businesses now sell lures (flies and plugs) that are
(A) deep colors only
(B) light colors only
(C) all colors of the rainbow

8. Many fishermen are now using thin, light-colored lines because they believe that these lines are
(A) harder for fish to see
(B) less likely to break
(C) cheaper than black lines

9. The proof that fish can see the color black is that fishermen often catch bass when they use black
(A) flies
(B) plugs
(C) worms

10. One fishing tackle manufacturer has brought out lines that blend with
(A) water bobs and lures
(B) water plugs and flies
(C) water colors and conditions

Correct your answers to the test. Here are the correct answers:

(1-C; 2-A; 3-B; 4-A; 5-C; 6-A; 7-C; 8-A; 9-B; 10-C)

Next, make an outline of this story so that you can make an oral or written report on it. Your outline might look like this:

Outline of the Story
"Are Fish Color Blind?"

1. Arguments about this carried on by anglers for many years
   a. Some anglers successful when color of fly is changed
2. Scientists disagree—some say fish have color-perception; others, fish are color-blind
   a. Between 1880 and 1911 two German scientists found fish attracted by certain colored lights and foods
   b. Later another scientist found that fish are color-blind—can distinguish between intensities of colors but not between colors themselves
   c. Still later, scientists found minnows could distinguish 20 different colors
   d. Dr. Frank A. Brown found a bass could learn to distinguish strong shades of red, yellow, green, and blue—appearing to bass as seen through yellowish filter (like yellowish sun glasses)
      (1) Bass approaching one color was rewarded with food
      (2) Bass going near another color was punished with electric shock
   e. Other scientists found that fish eyes, like human eyes, have substance called rhodopsin, necessary for color-perception
3. Results of experiments used by fishing tackle business
   a. Lures of same pattern made in different colors
   b. Light instead of dark lines made—purpose to make lines harder for fish to see
   c. Thinner lines made to reduce line shadows in water
4. Black fish lines vs. light-colored fish lines

a. Fish can see black—example, bass caught on black plugs

b. One company making lines that blend with water colors and conditions—purpose to conceal lines from fish

Next, write a summary of the story. In this summary give your main conclusions. Your summary might look like this:

[*Summary:* All anglers do not agree on whether fish are color-blind. And neither do all scientists. But several scientific studies indicate that fish can distinguish different shades of the same color and different colors. These findings are being used by fishing tackle manufacturers who are making many different colored lures (flies and plugs) and many different colored lines.]

How to read to follow directions

You often have to do study-type reading in order to follow directions. You do this kind of reading in preparing school or college assignments. You also do this kind of reading in jobs at home and at work; some of these jobs were mentioned earlier in this lesson.

If you are reading to follow directions, you will find that these suggestions are helpful:

1. Read the directions quickly from beginning to end. By doing so, you get a good idea of the directions as a whole and their relationships.

2. Read the first direction carefully; then carry it out. Next, read the second direction and follow it. Continue until you have read and carried out all of the directions.

3. If a direction gives a number for measurement, always reread that direction to make sure you are using the correct number.

Whatever the project, in reading to fol-

low directions, you should always read with extreme care. In a woodworking project, for example, the first direction may tell you to measure off exactly 6 feet 11½ inches on a plank. Here is how you should make the measurement:

1. Read the distance (6 feet 11½ inches).
2. Measure that distance on the plank.
3. Reread the number.
4. Measure again that distance on the plank.

By checking and double-checking each direction as you read it and carry it out, you are more likely to follow that direction exactly. You are less likely to make mistakes that cost you time and money, and you have a better chance to succeed in what you are doing.

Do general reading exercise 13 (page 252)

In this exercise, the article, "Our Plundered Planet," is much like a chapter in a serious book in the field of social studies or general science. Therefore, to understand this article, you must do study-type reading. To make this reading as meaningful as possible, here briefly is the background of the main ideas presented in the article.

Dr. Fairfield Osborn, the author, discusses an important theory developed by the Reverend T. R. Malthus (1766-1834), a noted political economist. On the basis of the knowledge then available, Malthus stated that the population of the world tended to multiply faster than its production of food. For this reason, he predicted, more and more of the world's people were doomed to hunger and starvation.

With the Malthusian theory in mind, do General Reading Exercise 13. After you complete the exercise, answer these study-type questions:

1. Since Malthus died in 1834, has his

prediction come true? Why do you think so?

2. Does Dr. Osborn agree with Malthus? Give evidence to support your answer.

3. According to Dr. Osborn, what is the main problem? Why did the problem arise? How can it best be solved?

4. Do you agree with Dr. Osborn? Why?

Because study-type reading often requires you to do research on a subject, read about Malthus in an encyclopedia. Read at least one chapter in Dr. Osborn's book, *Our Plundered Planet*.

While improving your study-type reading, you should pay more and more attention to the vocabulary of what you read. Building vocabulary power is the subject of the next two lessons.

LESSON 14

How can you build your vocabulary?

YOUR VOCABULARY plays an important role in your reading. If your vocabulary is good, you probably have little difficulty in understanding most of the books or articles that you read. Moreover, you have a good basis on which to build better reading skills and habits.

If your vocabulary is limited, you undoubtedly have trouble in understanding many of the things that you read. You also have difficulty in improving your reading abilities.

Words can be stumbling blocks to reading progress or they can be wings to better reading. If you know the exact meanings of words, you are able to read with greater ease and fluency. For this reason, you must continually strive to develop and to improve your vocabulary.

A vocabulary-building exercise

You can see for yourself how important your vocabulary is by reading again this selection from Article 13:

> Man has injured vast fertile areas in various parts of the earth, many of them so ruined that they have become deserts and uninhabitable. In such places, flourishing civilizations have disappeared, their cities buried under wastes

of sand, their inhabitants scattered to new lands. But now, with isolated and inconsequential exceptions, there are no fresh lands, anywhere. Human civilization has permeated virtually every living area of the earth's surface.

This paragraph contains a number of hard words. To find out whether you know their meanings, take this matching test. Match the words in List I with the words in List II. Read the first word in List I. In List II, find the word or phrase that has the same meaning. Write its letter at the left of number 1 in List I. Match the other words in the same way.

List I		List II
1. vast	7	A. not important
2. fertile	3	B. different
3. various	2	C. able to produce much
4. uninhabitable	1	D. really
5. flourishing	5	E. thriving
6. isolated	8	F. unusual
7. inconsequential	4	G. not fit to live in
8. exceptional	1	H. very great
9. permeated	6	I. separated from others
10. virtually	9	J. spread through the whole of

Correct and score your answers to the test. The correct answers are: (9-J; 10-D) (1-H; 2-C; 3-B; 4-G; 5-F; 6-I; 7-A; 8-F;

If your score is 9 or 10, you probably understood the paragraph very well. But if it is 2 or 3, you probably got little meaning from what you read. In a dictionary, look up the meanings of the words you missed. Then reread the paragraph. You will now find your reading easier and your understanding greater. After you have done this, you will appreciate the importance of vocabulary in determining how well you read. And you will probably have a greater respect for words and a stronger desire to improve your vocabulary.

What are words, anyway?

Before you attempt to build your vocabulary, consider for a moment what words really are. Words are similar to money, as the following comparison shows.

You may have heard someone say that money is "a medium of exchange." Money itself—the paper and metal out of which bills and coins are made—has only a small actual value. The real value of money is in what it stands for. And that *what* includes among other things groceries, clothing, shelter, automobiles, movies, and medical care.

Words, like money, have little value in and of themselves. They are important because they stand for real things—objects, actions, sounds, thoughts, and feelings. They are also important because they are a medium for the exchange of ideas.

If you want to get a clearer notion of what words mean to you every day, try getting along without them. When you sit down to dinner this evening, "tell" your family something you did today. Instead of using words, try to use sign language only. You will find it difficult if not impossible to exchange many ideas. Then, tell your story in words. You will quickly decide that, as a medium of communication, words are truly wonderful.

Words promote better living

If you are short on words, you may also be short on ideas. This will handicap you in school or college, on the job, at home, or elsewhere. But if you know many words, you are likely to have a wealth of ideas. You are better able to understand what you read or hear. You are also better able to express yourself when you talk or write.

Studies of successful people clearly show that they usually have large vocabularies. They know the exact meanings of words. And they use the right word in the right place at the right time.

Because words are an aid to good living, you will want to build your vocabulary. As you do so, you will improve your reading.

Words can be walls or gateways to understanding

Assume that you have a very small vocabulary. Also assume that you do not know how to get the meanings of new words. When you come across an unfamiliar word, that word may block, like a wall, your understanding of the material. Your eyes pause too long on the word as you try to get its meaning. You go back and read the word again trying to obtain its meaning from the context—the words in the sentence where the word appears. As a result, you read much more slowly than you should—and you find that the hard word is a wall to your comprehension.

Suppose, however, that you know many words and that you are skilled in finding the meanings of new words. Then, your eyes move quickly and you read rapidly. You comprehend instantly what you are reading. To you, words are gateways which lead to better understanding.

If you have a good vocabulary, moreover, you are more likely to read for ideas. As your eyes move along a line of print, you do not think of words as words. When you see a word group, you think an idea—the idea for which the word group stands.

You can master new words

No matter how good your vocabulary may be, you can always improve it. To strengthen your word power, you should set up your own program. This lesson will suggest ways to do it.

After you finish this lesson, you will want to continue your word-building program. If you do, you will maintain your interest in vocabulary growth. You will expand your vocabulary. And this will challenge your thinking, broaden your ideas, and increase the information and enjoyment that you get from reading.

Your bigger and better vocabulary will also help you to increase the speed and accuracy of your reading. New and hard words will no longer master you, for you will have become their master.

What are the main types of vocabulary?

If you take a close look at the words you use, you will find that you really have *two* main types of vocabulary. The first type is your *general vocabulary;* the second type is made up of your *technical vocabularies.*

Your general vocabulary includes the words you commonly use in conversa-

tion and correspondence, and the words you read in newspapers, books, and magazines. Your technical vocabularies include the words you find in specialized subjects or fields such as English, history, chemistry, engineering, medicine, farming, auto repair, and cooking.

You can build your general vocabulary *indirectly* through extensive reading—that is, through reading widely in different fields. You can also increase your general vocabulary *directly* through studying words.

Through your reading and your other experiences, you can develop your technical vocabularies. You, of course, do not want to master the technical vocabularies of all the different professions or trades, for example. In fact, you could not learn all these vocabularies even though you spent a lifetime trying to do so. Yet, you will need to acquire a technical vocabulary in each subject or field in which you are especially interested.

How can you best learn the meanings of new words?

As mentioned before, you use words in four main ways:

1. You read what other people have written.
2. You listen to other people.
3. You talk to other people.
4. You write to other people.

In each of these ways, you can increase your word power. With this greater word power, you can improve your reading, your conversation, and your writing.

Because you are using this book to become a better reader, this lesson tells you how you can build your vocabulary through reading and for reading. To increase your word knowledge, here are some suggestions:

1. *Look and listen for new words.* Keep your eyes and ears open for words that you do not know. You will see them in reading. You will hear them in talking with other people, in watching movies, and in listening to radio or television programs.

2. *Write down your new words.* Get yourself a pocket notebook and label it, "My Vocabulary Notebook." Carry this notebook with you. In it, write down every new word that you see or hear. Do this immediately. If you wait, you may forget the new word.

3. *Find the meanings of new words.* In the dictionary, look up the meanings of the new words that you have written in your vocabulary notebook. At the right of each word, write the dictionary definition or meaning that applies to the word as it was used in what you read or heard.

4. *Make the new words your own.* Use each new word in talking with your family or friends. Pronounce the word accurately. Also, use this word in what you are writing. Spell the word correctly. In speaking or writing, be sure that you use the word as it should be used.

5. *Enter several new words in your vocabulary notebook each day.* Keep building your word power. At the end of the week, quickly review the new words you entered during the seven-day period just ended. This review will help you remember the meanings of these words.

Build your vocabulary while you read

When you meet a new word in your reading, guess its meaning. Using your pencil, mark a check near the word so that you can find it later. Then keep on reading until you finish the entire story or part of the story. In this way, you do not allow a new word to slow down your reading speed or to interrupt your understanding of the flow of the story.

After you finish the story or part of it, go back and find the new words that you did not know. Write each word in your vocabulary notebook. Then take these steps:

1. Try to guess the meaning of the word. Write down your guess.

2. Try to get the word's meaning by reading again the sentence in which the word appears. Copy the sentence.

3. Look up the word in the dictionary. Find the definition or meaning that applies to the sentence in which the word appears. Write down this meaning.

4. Write your own sentence that includes this word.

Here, except for the explanations given in parentheses, is how your word entry may look:

disguise—
1. Funny clothes (your guess)
2. Words are living things; they even wear disguises. (the sentence)
3. Use of a changed or unusual dress and appearance in order not to be known. (dictionary definition)
4. On Halloween my disguise will be a devil's costume. (your own sentence)

Get the dictionary habit

Because the dictionary can be one of your most valuable books, you should have one in your home. Have the dictionary near you while you are reading. If the dictionary is near-by, you are likely to use it as you read.

Develop the dictionary habit. Look up a new word soon after you first meet it. This will help you to build your word power.

Some people seldom if ever use a dictionary. These people may be just plain lazy. Or they may not have the skills needed to handle a dictionary efficiently.

Sharpen your dictionary skills

While you are getting the dictionary habit, you can increase your skills in using the dictionary. These skills will help you to find a new word quickly. They also will help you to get the word's exact meaning in place of the hazy meaning that you may have had before.

If you wish to sharpen your dictionary skills, take the steps given next. Suppose that you are looking up the meaning of the word *perseverance*.

First, use the thumb index to turn to the first page of words beginning with the letter "P." If your dictionary does not have a thumb index, turn through the pages until you come to words starting with "P."

Second, watch the guide words at the top of each column on a page. The guide word at the left shows the first word on the page. The guide word at the right shows the last word on the page.

Third, find the page on which the word *perseverance* appears. That page will have such guide words as *perplexity* and *perspective*. Somewhere between these words, you will find the word *perseverance*.

Fourth, skim down the left-hand column, and then the right-hand column, if necessary, until you come to the word *perseverance*.

Fifth, read the meanings given there for the word *perseverance*. For this word, the *Thorndike Barnhart Comprehensive Dictionary*[1] gives these meanings:

perseverance. A sticking to a purpose or an aim; never giving up what one

[1]From: *Thorndike Barnhart Comprehensive Dictionary*. Copyright 1951 by Scott, Foresman and Company, Inc. Reprinted by permission of Doubleday & Company, Inc.

has set out to do—Syn. persistence, tenacity, diligence, pertinacity.

Next, see how quickly you can find each of these words in your dictionary: *xylophone, massacre, psychology, banal*, and *frivolous*. Also, for each word, write down the first meaning given in the dictionary.

As you sharpen your dictionary skills, you will make more use of the dictionary and you will thus strengthen your dictionary habits.

Get both facts and fun from your dictionary

You can use your dictionary in many ways to get information and enjoyment from it. For example, skim your dictionary as you skim any other book. Find some interesting words that you do not know. Read the definitions or meanings of these words. Try out some of the new words on your friends.

Arrange a dictionary quiz. You can enlarge and improve your vocabulary through a dictionary quiz; two or more persons can take part in this quiz. Select one person as the quizzer. He must have a dictionary, preferably a large unabridged one. He looks through the dictionary for a hard word—a word that he thinks the others do not know. He pronounces and spells the word and then asks what it means.

Each person tries to be first in giving the correct meaning of the word. He does not have to give the exact words appearing in the dictionary definition. He has only to give an explanation that is reasonably correct and that is in his own words. If this person gives the correct meaning of the word, he takes over the dictionary and becomes the quizzer.

Before the quiz starts, a person may make up a list of words that he believes to be hard. On his list he might have such unusual words as these: *aggravate, gesture, prudent, syzygy, vole,* and *waif.*

During the quiz, all those playing the game will learn many new words. They will also get a clearer understanding of the hard words they already know.

Devise other word games. You can also increase your word power through such games as crossword puzzles and anagrams. In these games, you should always refer to the dictionary when you need its help.

An exercise in vocabulary building

In your vocabulary notebook, enter each of the ten words listed next. Then look up the meaning of each word in your dictionary.

acrimonious   diminutive
cajolery   expedient
contemporaries   ebullient
cryptic   equanimity
derelict   inane

Read carefully the first sentence, below. On the blank line, write the word from the list that belongs there. Do each of the other sentences in the same way.

1. I did not understand what he was saying because his words were _____ *cryptic* .

2. I chose the number by the simple *expedient* of closing my eyes and placing my finger on a number.

3. The princess was a *diminutive* edition of her stately mother.

4. Without self respect you may soon become a *derelict* .

5. Often the sessions of the club were rather *acrimonious* but in time the members learned to conduct the meetings with temperate points of view.

6. Few of my *contemporaries* in high school were still living in the old home town.

7. _____ *inane* _____ remarks about the weather always irritated him.

8. She was usually a serene person. But on this day something happened that almost upset her *equanimity* .

9. The soldiers on leave behaved like *ebullient* youngsters driven by high spirits.

10. In spite of her husband's *cajolery* _____, she would not change her plans for the holiday.

Here are the correct answers:

(1—cryptic; 2—expedient; 3—diminutive; 4—derelict; 5—acrimonious; 6—contemporaries; 7—inane; 8—equanimity; 9—ebullient, 10—cajolery)

Do general reading exercise 14 (page 258)

In doing this exercise, read the article rapidly and for good understanding. Do not allow the hard words to slow down your reading.

After you complete the exercise, reread Article 14 and make a list of the technical words that appear in it. Some of these words are: *radarman, parachute, deceleration, hangar, gear, robot,* and *missiles.* Look up each word that you do not know in your dictionary; make sure that you understand what it means.

In this lesson, you have started a program of vocabulary building. You have observed the importance of a good vocabulary in effective reading. And you have made a beginning toward improving your vocabulary by learning how to use the dictionary effectively. But there are other habits and skills that must be improved if you are to develop and extend your vocabulary. Some of these will be presented in the next lesson.

LESSON 15

How can you improve your vocabulary?

"WHEN I USE A WORD," Humpty Dumpty said in rather a scornful tone, "it means just what I choose it to mean—neither more nor less."

"The question is," said Alice, "whether you can make words mean so many different things."

"The question is," said Humpty Dumpty, "which is to be master—that's all."[1]

When you are looking for the meaning of a word, the dictionary becomes the "master." For a particular word, the dictionary presents meanings that are accepted by people generally as well as by scholars. For each word, the dictionary usually gives several different meanings —all sensible and useful, too. You must decide which of these meanings applies best to what you are reading.

As you work to improve your reading, you will find that the dictionary is a highly valuable aid. No other book is probably as helpful in your efforts to get the exact meanings of words. For this reason, you should have a dictionary at hand while you are carrying out the suggestions given next.

[1]Lewis Carroll, *Through the Looking Glass.*

Here are suggestions for improving your vocabulary

1. Pay attention to the different meanings of words.

Even a simple word may have many meanings. For example, take the word *run.* Make a list of all the meanings you can think of for this word. Then look up *run* in a large dictionary. Check your list of meanings with those given in the dictionary. Are you surprised at the large number of meanings that the word has? You probably wrote down only a small percentage of the total number of meanings for this word. As a matter of fact, *run,* with its compounds like *home run,* has about 800 different meanings!

Now consider the longer word, *constitution.* Look it up in a dictionary. There you will find several definitions. The word may mean the document that provides for a system of government—the *Constitution* of the United States of America, for example. Or it may refer to a person's nature or make-up—his physical *constitution.* There are many other meanings, too.

110

If you are a good reader, you will carefully notice the different meanings or definitions of a word. And you will try to choose the meaning that best fits into what you are reading. To check upon your ability to select the correct meanings, consider the following words that occur frequently in books and articles on history. Look up the meanings of each of these words. Select the meaning that is most often used in a history book.[2]

appropriation	excise	patent
caucus	extradition	quorum
convene	jeopardy	revolution
democracy	jurisdiction	suffrage

2. *Study the roots of interesting or difficult words.*

In building your understanding of words, you will find it worth-while to look up the roots of words. Consider, for example, the following words that may appear often in your reading:

manufacture	equivalent	rectangle
telegraph	modify	century

Take the first word *manufacture*. According to the dictionary, this English word has two roots. These roots are two Latin words—*manus* (hand)—*factura* (a making).

Although you may know the root that is common to two words, you will have to be careful in using these words. For example, consider the words, *amiable* and *amicable*. Their root is the Latin word, *amicabilis*. *Amiable* means "good-natured" or "agreeable," but *amicable* means "peaceable." If you are a good reader, you will observe differences as well as likenesses in words that have a common root.

[2]See "Words You Should Understand" in *Your Rugged Constitution* (Textbook Edition). Chicago: Science Research Associates, 1952. pp. 293-298.

In your dictionary, look up the meanings of each of the words in this list:

1. amiable amicable	4. envious invidious
2. censor censure	5. human humane
3. construct construe	

Read the first sentence, 1a, which follows. For the blank in this sentence, decide whether the word *amiable* or *amicable* is correct. Write that word in sentence 1a. Do each of the other sentences in the same way.

1a. He seemed disposed to please those persons associated with him. In fact he was the most *amiable* gentleman I have ever known.

1b. The company and the union came to an *amicable* settlement of their dispute.

2a. The majority party in Parliament was barely able to defeat the latest vote of *censure*.

2b. Before a war correspondent sends a story to his newspaper, he must have that story approved by a military *censor*.

3a. Sometimes the citizen finds it hard to *construe* what the candidate is saying.

3b. The company plans to *construct* a large addition to its present plant.

4a. The man was *envious* of his neighbor's wealth.

4b. The mother made an *invidious* comparison between her daughter and her daughter's friends.

5a. If you are kind to dumb animals, you have a *humane* attitude.

5b. Let me plead, with the poet: To err is *human*; to forgive, divine.

Correct and score the test. Here are the correct answers: (5b—human; 5a—humane; 4b—invidious; 4a—envious; 3b—construct; 3a—construe; 2b—censor; 2a—censure; 1b—amicable; 1a—amiable)

3. Learn the meanings of the common prefixes and suffixes of words.

If you know the meaning of prefixes and suffixes, you are better able to work out the meanings of many words. To see how you do this, consider one prefix and one suffix. The prefix *in* usually means *not*. Inconvenient, therefore, means *not* convenient. One meaning of the suffix *ive* is *likely to*. Active therefore means *likely to act*.

On one page of your vocabulary notebook, write this heading, *Common Prefixes and Suffixes*. Under this heading write down the prefixes and suffixes that are given in the following list:

Prefixes		Suffixes	
ab-	in-	-able	-ing
bi-	non-	-al	-ive
co-	pre-	-ent	-ize
con-	post-	-est	-less
de-	re-	-ful	-ment
dis-	un-	-ible	-ous

At the right of each prefix and suffix write what it means, as here.

The prefix	What it means	The word	What it means
bi	two	bicycle	A two-wheeled vehicle
The suffix			
al	belonging to	personal	Belonging to a person

4. Learn the synonyms and antonyms of words.

Synonyms are words that have nearly the same meanings. For example, the words *cold, icy, frigid, freezing,* and *chilly* are synonyms. Although synonyms are similar in meaning, they are not always *identical* in meaning. By studying synonyms, you can learn the exact meanings of these related words. You can then choose the synonym that is best for the word you are reading. Through mastering synonyms, you develop preciseness in your thinking. You improve your reading comprehension; you also improve the quality of your speaking and writing vocabularies.

As an example of the value of synonym study, take the word *erase*. Here is the entry for this word as it appears in Webster's *New Collegiate Dictionary*.

e·rase′ (ê·rās′; *esp. Brit.,* -rāz′), *v. t.* [L. *erasus,* past part. of *eradere* to erase, fr. *e* out + *radere* to scrape.] To rub or scrape out, as letters or characters written, engraved, or painted; to efface; expunge. — **e·ras′a·ble** (-rās′à·b'l; -rāz′à·b'l), *adj.*
Syn. Erase, expunge, cancel, efface, obliterate, blot out, delete mean to strike out something. Erase implies action such as or like rubbing or scraping out; expunge now implies so thoroughgoing an erasure that the thing affected is wiped out; cancel implies some action, such as marking, rescinding, or neutralizing, that makes a thing no longer useful or effective; efface implies removal of every sign of a thing's identity or of its existence; obliterate and blot out both imply a smearing with or as if with ink that removes all traces of a thing's existence; delete now suggests a marking, an obliteration, etc., that means the elimination of the thing.
By permission. From Webster's New Collegiate Dictionary
Copyright, 1949, 1951
by G. & C. Merriam Co.

Consider the synonyms just given: *erase, expunge, cancel, efface,* and *obliterate.* Read the first sentence below. Then on the blank line, write in the correct synonym. Do each of the other sentences in the same way.

1. The mischievous boys _____ advertisements that are posted in buses.
2. When supervisors find that they have wrongly given typists unsatisfactory ratings, they _____ these ratings from employment records.
3. The atom bomb can _____ a city.
4. Post offices always _____ the stamps on all letters.
5. Typists _____ the words that they have misspelled.

Here are the correct answers:

(4—cancel; 5—erase.)

(1—efface; 2—expunge; 3—obliterate;

Again test your power to pick the correct synonym. Read the first sentence and the two synonyms that appear in parentheses. On the blank line, write in the correct synonym. Do each of the other sentences in the same way.

1. By evening the breadwinner was exhausted. His daily work was so _____ _____. (difficult, arduous)

2. By fair means and foul, the young woman seized the estate and ignored the claims of others. Her _____ _____ was overbearing. (pride, arrogance)

3. Because of starvation and other mistreatment as a prisoner of war, the soldier appeared _____. (thin, haggard)

4. Abraham Lincoln rose from an obscure to a (an) _____ station in life. (exalted, pompous)

5. The widow found that she could _____ her grief by doing good deeds for her neighbors. (pacify, alleviate)

Here are the correct answers:

(4—exalted; 5—alleviate.)

(1—arduous; 2—arrogance; 3—haggard;

Antonyms are words that have opposite meanings. For example, the words *frigid* and *torrid* are antonyms. If you learn the antonyms of words, you will understand better the meanings of these words. You will thus improve your vocabulary and reading power.

Test your antonym power by matching the words in List I with the words in List II. Consider the first word, *decry*, in List I. In List II find the antonym of *decry*. It is *applaud*. At the right of the word, *decry*, write the word *applaud*. Do each of the other words in the same way.

List I		List II
decry	_applaud_	unwary
concede	_deny_	doubt
fusion	_fission_	satisfaction
relinquish	_retain_	honest
generous	_greedy_	loss
believe	_doubt_	applaud
chagrin	_satisfaction_	fission
deceitful	_honest_	retain
gain	_loss_	greedy
vigilant	_unwary_	deny

Here are the correct answers:

(decry-applaud; concede-deny; fusion-fission; relinquish-retain; generous-greedy; believe-doubt; chagrin-satisfaction; deceitful-honest; gain-loss; vigilant-unwary)

5. *Watch out for homonyms.*

Homonyms are words that are pronounced the same but have different spellings and meanings. A common example is: *to, two,* and *too*. You probably have little trouble with homonyms in speaking or listening; but in reading or writing, homonyms may be a real problem to you.

To test your homonym power, here are two short lists. One list gives pairs of words; the other list gives pairs of sentences. Read the first sentence, below. Then on the blank line, write in the correct homonym. Do each of the other sentences in the same way.

List of Homonyms

1. to	3. pour	5. principal
too	pore	principle
2. bear	4. faint	6. discreet
bare	feint	discrete

List of Sentences

1a. _____ be, or not _____ be: that is the question.

1b. Aid came _____ little and _____ late.

2a. Please give me the _____ facts about your hunting trip.

2b. The hunter followed the trail of _____ tracks.

3a. During floods, river waters _____ over the dikes.

3b. Good students _____ over their textbooks.

4a. _____heart never won fair lady.

4b. Skilled boxers often _____.

5a. The _____ of our school understands young people.

5b. The _____ of tolerance helps people to live together peacefully and happily.

6a. Animals and plants are _____ forms of life.

6b. Wise persons are _____ about the personal lives of their friends.

Here are the correct answers:

(1a. to   3a. pour   5a. principal
1b. too   3b. pore   5b. principle
2a. bare   4a. faint   6a. discrete
2b. bear   4b. feint   6b. discreet)

6. Look up the origins of words.

Every word has a history. And that history may be interesting and well worth your study. Take, for example, the word *bunkum* or *bunk*. You have heard and used the expression, "That's a lot of bunk."

Here is the entry for this word as it appears in Webster's dictionary.

bun'combe, bun'kum (bŭng′kŭm), *n.* [From *Buncombe*, a county of North Carolina.] *Colloq.* Speechmaking to please constituents, or gain applause; anything said or done for mere show; hence, nonsense.
By permission. From Webster's New Collegiate Dictionary
Copyright, 1949, 1951
by G. & C. Merriam Co.

According to Dr. Joseph T. Shipley, expert in word origins, *bunkum* first came from the French, "C'est bon comme ca." That means "It's good enough the way it is."

As this example suggests, you can increase your appreciation of a word by studying its origin. Through this study, you can discover where a word came

from and how its meanings and uses have changed with the passing of time.

In a large unabridged dictionary, you can find the background of many of the important words that you use. If you want to study further the origin of a particular word, read the books *Wordlore*, by Duane Clayton Barnes (E. P. Dutton and Company), and *Picturesque Word Origins* (G. and C. Merriam Company). By discovering a word's past, you may get a better understanding of its present meaning. And you may learn to interpret that word with greater accuracy when you see it in print.

To show how the origins of words can help improve your vocabulary, consider the word *glamour*. *Glamour* comes from an old Scotch word meaning the study of Latin grammar. In the Middle Ages the educated clergy could read, write, or speak Latin, but the common people could not. As a result, the common people came to regard Latin grammar spelled *grammerye* as something mysterious or magical. Later, the word *grammerye* became *glamour* with the meaning of magic, charm, or enchantment.[3]

Consider next the Latin word *cappa* meaning cloak. *Cappa* is the root of a large and interesting family of words including these: *cap, caparison, cape, chapel, chaperone, chaplain, escape.* From this list, select the correct word for each item in the following test. Write the word on the blank line. Then answer the question: What does it mean today? If you are not sure about the meaning of a word, look it up in the dictionary.

1. It originally meant a hooded cloak. It later referred to the hood only. Finally it came to mean an older woman who wore the hood. What is

[3]Duane C. Barnes, *Wordlore* (New York: E. P. Dutton and Company, 1948).

the word? _____ What does it mean today? _____
_____

2. It originally meant a shrine in France where St. Martin's cloak was preserved. What is the word? _____ What does it mean today? _____

3. It originally meant the custodian of St. Francis' cloak. What is the word? _____ What does it mean today? _____

4. It came to mean the cloak itself. What is the word? _____ What does it mean today? _____
_____

5. It came to mean the hood of the cloak. What is the word? _____ What does it mean today? _____

6. It originally meant "to slip out of a coat and run away." What is the word? _____ What does it mean today? _____

7. It refers to a richly decorated covering for a horse. What is the word? _____ What does it mean today? _____

The correct answers are:

(1-chaperone; 2-chapel; 3-chaplain; 4-cape; 5-cap; 6-escape; 7-caparison.)

7. *Develop lists of words that belong to special fields.*

You are probably reading certain books, magazine articles, and newspaper stories that deal with fields in which you are very much interested. If so, you should make sure that you understand the important words in these special fields.

On separate pages of your vocabulary notebook, enter the headings of these fields —fiction, history, science, poetry, and hobbies, for example. Then, under the proper heading, list each word that belongs there.

Next to the word, write its meaning or definition. Be sure to write the meaning that best fits the setting or context in which that word appeared. Next, copy the sentence in which you found the word. Also write your own sentence using the word correctly.

Build your science vocabulary. Suppose that you wish to develop your technical vocabulary in the field of science. On the "Science" page of your vocabulary notebook, make a list of the technical terms (words or word groups) that appear in italics in the following sentences.[4]

1. On August 6, 1945, the first *atomic bomb* ever used in warfare killed 78,000 people, in the Japanese city of Hiroshima.

2. Destructive as *atomic energy* is when used for purposes of war, it can be a force that is of real benefit to man.

3. The number of *protons* in any particular atom determines what that atom is.

4. Up to the present time, 98 *elements* have been discovered in nature or created in the laboratory.

5. The atomic number of an element is the number of protons in the *nucleus* of the atom of that element.

6. When scientists were trying to start a *chain reaction*, they looked for elements that would split easily.

7. When an atom splits, part of the great forces that held its protons and *neutrons* together in the nucleus is released.

8. If the nucleus of an atom were the size of a baseball in the pitcher's hand and the *electrons* were in the outfield, the outfielders would be half a mile away from the pitcher's mound; an atom that size would be one mile across.

9. When an atomic bomb explodes, it

[4]The sentences given are adapted from *Primer of Atomic Energy*, John Lewellen. Chicago: Science Research Associates, 1952.

produces heat and an expansion of gases; it also produces *radiation*.

10. The atomic bomb (A-bomb) works through the *fission*, or the splitting of atoms; the hydrogen bomb (H-bomb) works through the *fusion*, or the building up of atoms.

Now go over the list of the technical terms that you have just written in your notebook. Then try to write a good definition of each term.

Add to your vocabulary of descriptive words. Poetry is especially rich in colorful words. These words often evoke sensory images. On a page in your vocabulary notebook, write these words and their meanings:

dulcet	grotesque	stentorian
brusque	sarcastic	rococo
abstemious	limpid	bedlam
effervescence	pomposity	murmur

From time to time, add other words to this list.

List the words related to your hobby. Whatever your hobby is, it has a special vocabulary. The hobby of stamp collecting, for example, includes these special words: *philatelist, commemorative, mint, watermark,* and *imperforated*.

On the hobby page of your vocabulary notebook, list the special words belonging to that hobby. Also, write the meanings of the words.

The words you learn can help your reading

You will improve your vocabulary through the ways already suggested in this lesson. *How much* you improve will also depend on these things:

1. How carefully you select your reading materials

2. How varied your interests and experiences are

3. How conscientious you are about your reading

In an effort to get the greatest vocabulary improvement possible, keep a sharp lookout for new words—in conversation, newspapers, magazines, radio and television broadcasts, movies, and so forth.

As you improve your vocabulary, you will also improve your reading. If your vocabulary power is strengthened, you will be able to read more rapidly and with greater understanding.

Do general reading exercise 15 (page 264)

In reading the article in this exercise, you will probably come across some hard words. Do not let these words slow down your reading.

After you complete this exercise, skim the article. Make a list of the words you do not understand. This list may include such words as: *exclusively, tragically, vaguely, uniformity, tinsel, spectacular, tights, alternate, demented, perishable, rehearsal, incarnation, abundant, technique, superb,* and *xylophone*. Then read carefully the sentence in which the difficult word appears. Finally look up the word in your dictionary.

You can continue to build and improve your vocabulary by reading more and better books. How you can do this is suggested in the next lesson.

LESSON 16

How can you find the reading materials you want?

YOU HAVE NOW completed 15 of the 20 lessons in this book. Lesson by lesson, you have grown in your reading power. You have developed more effective reading skills—and these have helped you to read faster and to understand better what you read.

If you are like most persons who have learned to read more efficiently, you are now doing much more reading than ever before. Because you are able to get more information and enjoyment from reading, you are probably spending a larger share of your leisure time in reading.

Your desire to read is undoubtedly much greater than it was when you started this book. Yet you still face the problem of deciding which materials will best satisfy your needs.

What reading materials do you want?

To answer this question, you may need a clearer idea of the values that reading can bring to you. The values of books, for example, were described by John Denham, an Englishman. Some 300 years ago, Denham wrote:

"Books should to one of these four
    ends conduce,
  For wisdom, piety, delight, or use."

Denham's couplet suggests that you may read for one of four different values. How you can do so is illustrated next, by the titles of books.

For a kind of *wisdom*, you might read such nonfiction books as *Crusade in Europe*, by Dwight D. Eisenhower; *The Sea Around Us*, by Rachel Carson; *The Mature Mind*, by Harry Overstreet; or *A Study of History*, by Arnold Toynbee.

For *piety*, you might read such books as the *Bible*, the world's best selling book; or *The Greatest Story Ever Told*, by Fulton Oursler.

For *delight*, you might read such books as *The Caine Mutiny*, by Herman Wouk; *Melville Goodwin*, by John P. Marquand; *Return to Paradise*, by James Michener; *Gone with the Wind*, by Margaret Mitchell; *Cheaper by the Dozen*, by Frank B. Gilbreth, Jr., and Ernestine Gilbreth Cary; or *Kon-Tiki*, by Thor Hayerdahl.

For *use*, you might read one or more of these books: *Look Younger, Live*

Longer, by Gayelord Hauser; *Betty Crocker's Cook Book;* or *Better Homes and Gardens Handyman's Book.*

A book, of course, may provide more than one of these values. Some books indeed may supply all of them. In reading *The Sea Around Us*, by Rachel Carson, for instance, you will gain in *wisdom*— that is, you will acquire important information about the world's oceans. You will get real *delight* from the author's style of writing and from the many interesting facts presented. And you will learn much that you can *use* in your discussions at school, at home, or elsewhere.

In magazines and newspapers, you will find a variety of reading materials—articles that will add to your knowledge of yourself and the world about you, articles that will give you religious understanding and inspiration, articles that will bring you rich enjoyment, and articles that will show you how to make and do things.

You can browse to find what you want

Many books, magazine articles, and newspaper accounts are available on nearly every subject you can think of. And on any subject from *aardvark* to *zymurgy*, you can find reading materials.

Because there are so many materials to choose from, you will want to learn to browse. According to the dictionary, to *browse* means to read here and there in a newspaper, magazine, or book. In browsing, you make use of the skimming skills that you have been developing.

In looking for a magazine, you may go to a store that has many different magazines on display. After you pick up a magazine, you should turn through its pages rapidly. You may look at the titles of articles and at the pictures. You may skim the table of contents that usually appears near the front of the magazine; if you do, you are a wise browser, for this is the best way to learn what is in a magazine. After you have looked at one magazine, you quickly examine another, then another, and so on until you locate the one that you want to buy. You can take the same steps in selecting a magazine to read from the different magazines available in a library.

In looking for a book, you may browse among the books that are available in a bookstore or in the library. After you select a book, you should go through it rapidly. You may read carefully the first page or two and the last page. Or you may turn through the book stopping to read a paragraph or two here and there. Thus you will read samples of what is in the book. If you like these samples, you buy or borrow the book to read perhaps from cover to cover.

An exercise in browsing in a book

You will next read a selection from a highly interesting book—*People of the Deer*, by Farley Mowat. The selection is a sample of the paragraphs that you might read while browsing through this book in a library or a bookstore.

In the time box, write your starting time. Then read the selection as rapidly as possible. Afterward, you will take a short test on it.

Time Box

Finishing time	
Starting time	
Reading time	
Reading rate	

PEOPLE OF THE DEER[1]

by Farley Mowat

THE PORT OF Churchill in Canada was a miserable conglomeration of cowering shacks half-buried under great drifts. In May 1947 that "ocean port" was the ultimate desolation of man's contriving.

On the morning after the day I arrived, Johnny, my pilot, and I hurriedly loaded my gear and slogged through the already softening drifts to Landing Lake, where the Anson plane stood waiting.

After a startled look at the looming bulk of the load, Johnny turned quickly away and started up the engines. As the overburdened plane lumbered down the lake, the homemade skis flung driving slush outward and upward, enveloping us in chill spray. Then we were air-borne and turned northward up the icebound coast.

The Anson grumbled forward on her arctic quest. When we left the coast we also left the sun behind us—obscured by a thick overcast of snow-laden clouds.

The overcast had been steadily lowering, and as we turned eastward we were flying at less than 500 feet. At this slim height we suddenly saw the land gape wide beneath us to expose a great valley walled in by rocky cliffs and snow-free hills. And in that instant I caught a fleeting glimpse of something. "Johnny!" I yelled. "Cabin . . . down there!"

He wasted no precious gas on a preliminary circuit. The sound of the engines dulled abruptly and we sank heavily between the valley walls. Before us stood a twisted, stunted little stand of spruce; a river mouth, still frozen; and the top foot or so of what was certainly a shanty

roof, protruding slyly from the drifts. We jumped stiffly down to the ice and shook hands, for there was no doubt about this being my destination.

The leaden skies were closing in and the wind was still rising; there was time only to dump my gear onto the ice. Johnny stood for a long moment in the doorway of the plane, then waved his hand and vanished into the fuselage. In a moment the Anson was bumping down the bay and I was alone.

I made for the half-hidden cabin. The doorway was snowed in to a depth of several feet, and when I had dug my way through, I found only a log cavern in the drifts—dank and murky and foul-smelling. Against one wall was a massive stove.

The walls of the cabin were finished in fur. Wolf and arctic fox pelts, all as white as the snow of early winter, were spread over the log walls to dry, and by their simple presence showed that the place was not completely deserted after all.

Some days later, on June 4, I climbed a long, rocky slope behind the cabin for a glimpse of the lands that lay behind the camp. I was sitting in the lee of a great boulder, avoiding the hot glare of the sun, when I heard the cries of dogs from far up the half-frozen river. I listened until the dogs came into view—nine immense beasts hauling a sled that dwarfed them, for it was 20 feet in length. Two massive runners with sparse crossbars supported a pile of deerskins, and on the skins was the figure of a man.

It was a tense and uneasy meeting. I set about explaining myself and my presence at the cabin as best I could, and the words sounded rather lame.

Oddly enough Franz asked no questions and betrayed no curiosity about me after the initial explanations had been made. Instead he talked of the long trip he had

---

[1]From *People of the Deer* by Farley Mowat, by permission of Little, Brown and Co., and the Atlantic Monthly Press. Copyright 1951, 1952 by Farley Mowat.

just completed, and from that point his talk worked backward through the winter, into the years before.

His father, Karl, had come to Canada from Germany, three decades earlier. The immigrant brought with him some of the memories of a cultivated man, but for reasons of his own he shunned the semi-civilized South of Canada and wandered to the North. Here, in due time, he found a wife among the mission-trained Cree Indians who live on the south verges of the high northern forests.

About 1930, the trading company at Nueltin Lake asked Karl to be their manager there. He accepted, and after a three weeks' canoe trip north from Broehet, the family arrived at Windy Bay.

In the thirties the People of the Barrens were still numerous enough so that nearly forty hunters—all heads of families —could come to trade their fox pelts at the little post. But as the years passed, so passed the hunters. The price of pelts on the world's markets fell and so the profits of the post fell off. At last the company decided to withdraw, and in due course that message came to Karl.

When spring came, Karl prepared to leave the land forever. His two sons, Franz and Hans, were unwilling to go south, and in the end he left them behind, confident that they would continue to make a good catch of foxes every year.

Once each year the boys loaded their canoe and traveled as far south as the nearest outpost of trade; and here, quickly, they disposed of their furs, bought what they needed for the year, and fled back through the forests to the arctic plains. For the rest of the year they roamed the Barrens, by dog team in winter, and on foot or with pack dogs in summer. Each had his own trap line in a different area.

Some 60 miles due north of Windy Bay, across the sodden plains and gravel ridges, there is a nest of Little Lakes huddled close up against the banks of the river which we call the Kazan but which the Eskimos, who call themselves *Innuit*, named *Innuit Ku*. This little group of lakes has for some centuries been the center of the inland culture. It was from this place that the people spread up and down the river until their camps stood on each lake and river in the rolling plains. And it is from the mounded hills which lie about the Little Lakes that this branch of the Innuit took their local name— *Ihalmiut*, the people of the Little Hills.

In all the time that the Ihalmiut have known the land and roamed its endless spaces, they have had no ties to any plot of ground for long. And yet the Little Lakes that lie beside the wide Kazan have exercised a hold upon the People, for it was from these lakes that men set out to permeate the plains with human life. So it was natural enough, when the tide was turned against them by powers greater than even those the Barrens know, when plague and starvation struck their blows against the camps, that as the Ihalmiut retreated, they should fall back upon the place from which they had once eddied out over the land.

On the day following the arrival of Hans and his two children, I was awakened by the sound of heavy firing. I hurriedly pulled on my clothes and went out into the June morning. Franz, Antoeelik, and Hans were sitting on the ridge above the cabin and they were steadily firing their rifles across the river. On the sloping southern bank nearly a hundred deer, all does, were milling in stupid anxiety. I could see the gray bursts of dust as bullets sang off the rocks, and I could hear the flat thud of bullets going home in living flesh.

That night I sat for a long time on the ridge behind the cabin, smoking and thinking. I knew little of the People of the Deer as yet; and now that I had seen the herds, I was aware that I knew nothing of the deer themselves. The People and the deer fused in my mind, an entity. I found I could not think of one without the other, and so by accident I stumbled on the secret of the Ihalmiut before I had even met them. I believe it was this vague awareness of the indivisibility of the Barrens People and the caribou that made my later attempts to understand the Eskimos yield fruit.

Write your finishing time in the time box. Then take this test. In each test item, mark a check (✔) at the left of the correct choice.

1. The People of the Deer lived and hunted in this part of northern Canada:
   (A) The high barren plains
   (B) The deep forested valleys
   (C) The tree-covered mountains

2. The author and his pilot almost missed finding the cabin at Windy Bay mainly because
   (A) the plane nearly ran out of gasoline
   (B) the map showed the wrong location
   (C) the land had a low overcast of clouds

3. The author immediately knew that someone was living in the cabin when he saw
   (A) a large stove with firewood nearby
   (B) furs hanging on the walls to dry
   (C) the tracks of a man and dogs leading up to the door

4. Soon after Franz arrived, he told the author mainly about
   (A) his five-dog team
   (B) his life and family
   (C) the People of the Deer

5. The parents of Franz and Hans were as follows:
   (A) Their father was a Canadian; their mother, a Cree Indian.
   (B) Their father was a German; their mother, an Ihalmiut Indian.
   (C) Their father was a German; their mother, a Cree Indian.

6. In the Barrens, the fur trade suffered mainly because
   (A) the world prices of fox pelts went down
   (B) the numbers of wild foxes decreased
   (C) the only fur trading post was shut down

7. Franz and Hans spent most of their time every year in
   (A) delivering fox pelts to the nearest post
   (B) trapping foxes in the Barrens
   (C) selling ammunition and food to the Eskimos

8. After years of hardship and suffering, the Ihalmiut returned to their original home, which was
   (A) the hilly country near a group of little lakes
   (B) the rolling high country called the Barrens
   (C) the heavily forested land in the Kazan River Valley

9. The Ihalmiut were destroyed mainly by
   (A) unusually cold and long winters
   (B) the guns of many white men
   (C) starvation and diseases

10. After the author watched Franz and Hans firing at the herd of deer, he

for the first time discovered that the Ihalmiut and the deer were

(A) invisible
(B) indivisible
(C) invincible

Next, figure out your reading time. Change your reading time into your reading rate; use the table at the end of this book. Write your rate in the time box.

Correct and score your test. Here are the correct answers: (9-C; 10-B)
(1-A; 2-C; 3-B; 4-B; 5-C; 6-A; 7-B; 8-A;

If you liked the selection, get the book *People of the Deer*, and read it for both information and enjoyment.

You can learn to use the library efficiently

You can find the titles of books and magazine articles that you want to read by talking with other people. Friends will tell you about what they have enjoyed reading. And teachers will suggest things that you might like to read.

Because a reader's best friend is the librarian, you should go to him for help in finding the reading materials you want. The librarian will be glad to talk with you about books and magazines and to show you how to use the library more effectively.

When you go to the library, you will find it worth-while to spend a few minutes discussing your reading needs with the librarian. He may take you on a "conducted tour" of the library, pointing out the location of the card catalog, reference books, and other reader's aids.

In many libraries, you will find that reference books are placed on shelves or on tables in the general reading room. These references usually include encyclopedias, dictionaries, almanacs, yearbooks, and atlases. You may look through these reference materials in the reading room,

but you may not check them out to take home.

In the general reading room or in the periodical room, you will find current and back issues of newspapers and magazines. Some of the older back issues are bound in large volumes. You, of course, can read any of these periodicals without having to check them out at the librarian's desk.

HOW TO FIND MAGAZINE ARTICLES

On the shelves or on the tables near where magazines are displayed in the library, you will often see copies of the *Readers' Guide to Periodical Literature*.[2] This is your best source for finding magazine articles.

The *Readers' Guide* is an index to articles that appear in more than 100 magazines. The entries in this index, arranged alphabetically, cover a wide variety of subjects—*cancer, espionage, ice, Michigan, music, skin, toads, wolves,* and *Yukon,* to mention a few. Other entries refer to article authors by name.

The *Readers' Guide* is issued twice a month except during July and August. For the latest available articles on a subject, the most recent issues of the guide should be used. The *Readers' Guide* also appears in annual and two-year volumes that alphabetize all entries for the year or years covered.

In using an issue of the *Readers' Guide*, you should first look up the subject in which you are interested. If that subject is *cancer,* you will find that it appears alphabetically in the guide. Under the subject heading *Cancer,* you should skim all the entries; you skimmed these entries on page 58 of this book. If you want a popular article about or by a person who has

[2]Published by The H. W. Wilson Company, New York.

cancer, you may come across this guide entry:

In my case it was cancer. E. R. Bills. il Sat Eve Post 225:45 + O 25 '52.

This entry gives the following information: title of the article (In my case it was cancer); author's name (E. R. Bills); illustrations (il); name of magazine (Saturday Evening Post); volume number (225); the first page of the article (45); and the publication date (October 25, 1952).

You next copy the entry on a 3 x 5-inch card. You use this card to obtain the issue of the magazine in which the article appeared and to locate the article within that issue.

HOW BOOKS ARE CATALOGED

In the typical library, books are arranged according to subjects and are placed on the shelves of bookcases which are called "the stacks." If the library has "open stacks," you can wander through these stacks and choose your own book.

In cataloging books, the library classifies fiction books alphabetically by the author's last name. For example, *Gone With The Wind*, by Margaret Mitchell, has a call number that begins with "Mi," the first two letters of the author's surname. This book is placed on a shelf that holds other novels whose authors' names start with the letters "Mi."

In classifying nonfiction books, the library uses the Dewey Decimal System. The system is called *decimal* because it provides ten large subject groups, as follows:

000 General Works	500 Science
100 Philosophy	600 Useful Arts
200 Religion	700 Fine Arts
300 Social Sciences	800 Literature
400 Languages	900 History

Each of the ten large groups is broken down into smaller groups. For example, the large 600 group entitled "Useful Arts" contains such collections as: 608—radio; 655—printing; and 680—handicrafts.

According to the Dewey Decimal System, each nonfiction book has a call number. This number is written or printed inside the cover and on the backbone —the part of the book that shows when it is on a shelf.

The call number of *4-Square Planning For Your Career*, by S. A. Hamrin, for example, may look like this:

371.4
Ha
Cop.3

Here is what the 371.4 stands for:

300 represents the *Social Sciences*.

370 represents *Education*, a part of the social sciences.

371 represents *Teachers, Methods, Discipline*, a part of education.

371.4 represents systems of education including vocational guidance.

The *Ha* stands for "Hamrin," the author.

Cop.3 stands for the third copy of this book that the library has.

HOW TO USE THE CARD CATALOG

To help you find the book you want, the library has a card catalog. It is made up of 3 x 5-inch cards that are kept in file drawers. All the cards are arranged alphabetically.

For each book in the library, the catalog has at least two cards. One card (the main entry card) is *the author's card*. The other card is *the title card*. For some books, the catalog has *subject cards* with such headings as "aviation" and "electronics."

Perhaps you want a book on television. In the card catalog drawer labeled "T," turn through the cards until you find a subject card marked *Television*. This card may read: See *Electronics*. If so, look in the drawer labeled "E" until you find the subject card that reads *Electronics*. Following this subject card you will find a number of other subject cards; each card headed *Electronics* gives the title of a book and the name of its author. One of these cards may read *Electronics—Electronics for Young People*, by Jeanne Bendick.

You may know the title of the book you want—for example, *Electronics for Young People*. Look through the card catalog drawer labeled "E" for the title card of that book. Or, you may know the name of the author whose books you like to read. Suppose that this author is Jeanne Bendick. Look through the card catalog drawer labeled "B" until you come to the name: *Bendick, Jeanne*. Her name appears on the author card for *Electronics for Young People* and also on author cards for other books she has written.

After you have located the title card or the author card of the book you want, fill out a request slip for the book. On this slip write the call number of the book, the name of its author, the book's title, and your name. Then hand this slip to the librarian. The librarian will get the book for you. If the book is in the open stacks, you yourself can get it. To find the book quickly on the shelves, use the book's call number as your guide.

What are some good sources of books?

If you want to build up your library at home, you may wish to join one of these book clubs — Book-of-the-Month Club; Literary Guild of America; Peoples Book Club; Book Find Club; History Book Club; American History Publication Society; Natural History Book Club; or Condensed Book Club (Reader's Digest Book Club). Each club selects and distributes interesting and timely books to its members.

Still other sources of good books are the College Entrance Book Company and the Globe Book Company. Both companies publish classics in an inexpensive and readable form. The titles of some of these classics are *Les Miserables*, *The Count of Monte Cristo*, *The Black Arrow*, *Moby Dick*, and *A Tale of Two Cities*.

A source of valuable booklets is the Public Affairs Committee, New York. This committee publishes *Public Affairs Pamphlets* on a wide range of subjects mainly in the field of current affairs. Another source of booklets is Science Research Associates, Chicago. It issues *Life Adjustment Booklets* that deal with many of the problems that are vital to young people.

Where can you get good inexpensive books?

At the nearest store, you may find on display a wide variety of paper-bound books. These books range in quality from good to poor, but you can try to pick the good ones. Also, these books are pocket-sized, easy to carry and convenient to handle. They are priced as low as 25 cents each. And together they sell in the millions.

For the story of these little books and how they grew, read next the following selection from an article by David Dempsey. He is one of the editors of the *New York Times Book Review*.

THE REVOLUTION IN BOOKS[3]

by David Dempsey

UNTIL THE WAR, we Americans who bought books—and there were not many of us—constituted a fairly cohesive and civilized community, operating from a common set of literary values. We did not necessarily read the same books, but we agreed that books were necessary; and by our support of the book clubs and patronage of bookshops, by our approval of the titles stocked in public libraries, and by the occasional expensive set of classics that we installed in our living rooms we dominated literary taste.

Today we are being invaded by a multitude of people whose frantic appetite for books in paper covers accounted for the sale of 257 million copies in 1952 alone. Over the past few years these men and women, the majority of whom did not buy books at all before the reprint craze, purchased 40 million copies of Erle Stanley Gardner's mysteries, 6 million copies of Erskine Caldwell's *God's Little Acre*, over 3 million copies of *How to Win Friends and Influence People*, 1.6 million copies of *The Pocket Book of Verse*, a million copies of Shakespeare's *Tragedies*, 750,000 copies of George Orwell's *1984*, 300,000 copies of *The Dialogues of Plato*, and 200,000 copies of Susanne Langer's *Philosophy in a New Key*.

The success of the reprints is a logical expression of our times. These books are small, and adapted to the marsupial habits of a nation that does much of its reading on the jump. They are easy to buy (many are now sold in vending machines, like chewing gum), alluringly packaged, and available to millions of persons who live outside the range of a bookstore or are afraid to enter one.

There are today about twenty paperback houses in the field. Seven of these—The New American Library, Pocket Books, Bantam, Gold Medal, Popular, Avon, and Dell, in approximately that pecking order—account for about 85 per cent of the total business. Their product is a highly competitive and indiscriminate melange of serious literature and trash, of self-help and pseudo science, of sex and inspiration—never before has American publishing put forth such a nicely homogenized product, with the cream of letters so palatably disseminated in the total output. This explains why such books as Edith Hamilton's *The Greek Way to Western Civilization* and the novels of Kathleen Winsor can be sold bust by jowl on drug counters. It accounts for the fact that Faulkner's *The Wild Palms* has been made available, if not necessarily comprehensible, to a million rank-and-file buyers. It has suddenly made the books of Flaubert, Hawthorne, and D. H. Lawrence contemporary with Marquand and Steinbeck. If the reprints have done nothing else, they have taken the classics away from the protective custody of the pedants.

Who buys them? At present, a million high school students use reprints through their membership in the Teen Age Book Club. Some 172 titles on the New American Library's list, mostly from its excellent *Mentor* nonfiction series, are required reading in schools and colleges. The United Automobile Workers, CIO, operating its own book club, uses reprints exclusively. The Armed Services buy millions of copies for distribution to troops, the State Department distributes them by the hundreds of thousands in countries such

---

as India, and an estimated 20 million copies last year were sold abroad.

But the bulk of 1952's astronomical total was sold to a hard core of 10 million "regular" buyers. In a survey for Bantam Books a few years ago, the George Gallup organization discovered that only one in every three of these people bought trade editions of books, and a high proportion of these sales could be attributed to interest stimulated by reprints. The fact, too, that quarter-book fans attended the movies more frequently than the population as a whole and spent more time viewing TV is evidence that they are not conventional book buyers—that the reprints, in fact, have created a new public for books.

One of the characteristics of this audience is that it comes to literature with a kind of healthy ignorance, willing to take the good with the bad, hardly aware of Faulkner's reputation among professional littérateurs but profoundly affected by the vitality of his storytelling. But more than this, these readers are democratic in their allegiances—an "unknown" may do as well as or better than an established writer since, in a sense, to the new audience most authors are unknown. Richard Bissell's *A Stretch on the River*, that lusty book which first saw the light of day in the *Atlantic*, was an indifferent success in the trade but rolled up a sale of 750,000 at 25 cents. And the same thing happens to the established author who has never had a "hit"—the man who has lived on the admiration of a small group of critics and suddenly finds himself with a reading public.

What are good sources of book titles?

You can locate the titles of new books that you may want by reading the book reviews in current newspapers and magazines. These reviews, written by book critics, appear in such periodicals as these: *The Saturday Review; The Horn Book; The New York Times Book Review; The New York Herald Tribune Book Review; The Chicago Sun-Times Book Week; The Chicago Sunday Tribune Magazine of Books; Harper's Magazine; The Atlantic; Time;* and *Newsweek.*

At a library, you will find a number of good sources of book titles. Among these sources are the book lists published by the American Library Association and by the National Council of Teachers of English. Reviews of new books appear in *The Booklist*, published monthly by the American Library Association, Chicago; *The Book Review Digest*, published monthly by the H. W. Wilson Company, New York; and *Current Biography*, also published by the H. W. Wilson Company.

You should keep in mind that many books published in the past as well as many new books are worth while. A good source for finding such books is *What Shall We Read Next?* by Jean C. Roos; it was published by the H. W. Wilson Company. This reference suggests books to read in this way: "If You Like This, You Will Like These."

A good list of books of fiction and biography appears in *Lenrow's Reader's Guide to Prose Fiction*, published by D. Appleton-Century, New York. This guide classifies book titles according to different subject fields. For this reason, you can easily and quickly locate the titles of the books in which you are most interested. Still another reference is the *Kuder Book List*, available free from Science Research Associates, Chicago. This list arranges book titles according to different fields of vocational interest.

For a selected list of good book titles, see the bibliography that begins on page 174 of this book.

How can you select materials to improve your reading?

To give yourself practice in finding the reading materials you want, go to a store that sells both magazines and inexpensive paper-bound books. Browse until you locate a magazine and a novel that you like. After you buy them, see how quickly you can read them.

In one evening, say, within two hours, read the entire magazine from cover to cover. Skim some articles but read others carefully. In two evenings totaling six hours of reading time, try to complete the novel.

Now ask yourself: Did I select a magazine or book that gave me pleasure? Did I select one that gave me information?

What do you know about finding the reading materials you want?

Take the test that follows. If a statement is *true*, mark a + at the left of it. If a statement is *false*, mark a O at the left of it.

1. You now read better than you did when you started this book.

2. John Denham wrote that books provide four main values—wisdom, piety, delight, or use.

3. Sometimes while reading a given book, you get enjoyment as well as information.

4. In browsing, you usually read an entire book as carefully as possible.

5. Before you start reading a book or magazine, you should read the table of contents.

6. The person who can help you most in selecting good reading materials is the librarian.

7. In looking for the title of a book on a certain subject, you should use the *Reader's Guide to Periodical Literature.*

8. In a typical library, fiction books are classified into ten main groups according to the Dewey Decimal System.

9. In a library's card catalog, the cards for books are arranged alphabetically by author, title, or subject.

10. Among good sources of information about books are the reviews that appear in newspapers and magazines.

Correct and score your test. Here are the correct answers: (1-+; 2-+; 3-+; 4-O; 5-+; 6-O; 7-O; 8-O; 9-+; 10-+)

Do general reading exercise 16 (page 269)

In reading the article in this exercise, concentrate upon reading rapidly. After you complete the exercise, you may want to read the book from which it was taken. This book is *Lives of the Hunted*, by Ernest Thompson Seton.

Seton is well-known for his animal stories. Although his stories are fictional, they are based upon the many years that he spent in observing wild animals in the Yellowstone Park area and elsewhere.

In this lesson you have learned how to find reading materials. In the next lesson you will consider how you can best read a book.

LESSON 17

How can you best read a book?

NEARLY 400 YEARS AGO, Francis Bacon, an English philosopher, made this comment about books:

"Some books are to be tasted, others to be swallowed, and some few to be chewed and digested."

As you already know, books can serve a variety of your needs. The best way to read a book, therefore, depends upon your purpose for reading and upon the kind of material you have chosen.

If you are reading a light novel for enjoyment, you may "taste" that book— that is, you may skim it. You may read certain parts only, to get the book's flavor.

If you are reading a scientific book for information, you may "swallow" the facts given. If the author is an expert in his field and if he presents reliable information, you may accept what he writes without reservation. Critical reading will probably not be needed.

If you are reading a book of Shakespeare's plays for thorough understanding, you may "chew and digest" what you are reading. You may, for example, read "Hamlet" thoughtfully to understand what each character means by what he says.

You may apply what you are reading to your own experience—to the people you know—to the situations you face.

You may "chew" a historical book that deals with a debatable issue. You will want to read each important statement carefully to determine whether it is supported by facts.

How should you read a nonfiction book?

When you want to read a book on a subject of great interest to you, your first problem is to find the right book. To do so, you can follow the suggestions given in Lesson 16. Your second problem, of course, is to read that book so as to obtain the most from it. To help you in solving both these problems, read and study the example given next.

An example of how to read a book about newspapers

As you were reading your local newspaper last night, you may have asked yourself this question: How is the newspaper's staff able to gather news and put it into print within a period of 24 hours?

To answer the question, you might visit the newspaper's office and go through its plant. Whether or not you make this visit, you might read a good book on newspaper publishing. Such a book is *How to Read a Newspaper*, by Edgar Dale. You gain the most from reading this book by following these suggestions:

1. *Read the title page.* It gives the book's title and author: "How to Read a Newspaper, by Edgar Dale." You notice that the author is on the staff of the "Bureau of Educational Research, Ohio State University," and that he is a "Member, Committee on Standards for Motion Pictures and Newspapers, National Council of Teachers of English." These facts indicate that the author is well-qualified to write about the subject of newspapers. You then observe that the publisher is "Scott, Foresman and Company."

2. *Look at the copyright date.* It usually appears on the back of the title page. In the Dale book you read: "Copyright, 1941, by Scott, Foresman and Company. Printed in the United States of America." Although this book was published more than ten years ago, it has much information that is still up to date. (Note that if you had been looking for a technical book in a field such as radar, atomic energy, or television, you would have selected a book with a more recent copyright date. In each of these fields, there have been many important developments during the past few years.)

3. *Read the foreword.* In the Dale book, the foreword is headed, "Explanation For Students." There the author points out that "this book is intended to help you and other young people answer your questions about newspapers." He then presents the four main purposes of the book.

4. *Skim the acknowledgments.* The author gives the names of all the persons and newspapers who helped in the preparation of his book. Because these helpers were experts in their respective fields, they aided in making the book as accurate and interesting as possible.

5. *Read the contents.* In the Dale book, the contents appear on pages vii through ix. The contents are divided into three parts and thirteen chapters. The main headings within a chapter are listed. Except for these headings, the contents of this book are reprinted here:

Contents

By reading the contents quickly but carefully, you get an over-all picture of what is in this book. You also get the number of the page on which each chapter begins. This is helpful if, for example, you want information such as that found in Chapter 6, "Readers Can Improve Their Reading"; this chapter starts on page 53. But if you wish to get a clearer picture of the contents of *How To Read A Newspaper*, you should examine the entire book.

6. *Skim the whole book.* Turn through the pages quickly, glancing at the chapter titles and the pictures. This will give you an idea of what is in the book and of how it is presented. Near the back of the book you will notice a "Glossary of Newspaper Terms." Here is one item from it: "*Cub*—A beginning, inexperienced reporter." You will also observe an "Index"; one of its items is: "Freedom of the press, 23, 117-124; and advertising, 120; and government, 121-122; in wartime, 118, 122; reader's responsibility toward, 123." Each figure, of course, is the number of a page in the book.

7. *Read each chapter rapidly and then carefully.* As suggested before, read a whole chapter quickly to get a general idea of it. Then reread parts of the chapter thoughtfully for important details. You may have to read some of these parts more than twice in order to understand and remember them.

8. *Guess the meaning of a new word— then look it up.* When you come across a new word during your first reading of a chapter, try to get the word's meaning from the other words in the sentence in which it appeared. Try not to slow down your reading. Keep on reading the chapter until you finish it. Then go back and find the new word or words. Reread each sentence. If you cannot get the word's meaning in this way, look up the word in your dictionary.

Because the Dale book contains many technical terms, it provides two valuable aids for understanding these terms. Before you start reading the book, study the "Glossary of Newspaper Terms." Before you begin a chapter, you might read the footnotes that explain the technical terms. By using these two aids, you will be able to get all the important meanings that the book offers.

9. *Study each of the pictures.* In this book every picture tells part of the author's story. If you study a picture and read its legend, you will usually be helped in getting meaning from what you read.

10. *Evaluate what you read.* As you read a chapter, ask yourself such questions as these: Is the author presenting facts or opinions? Is he interpreting these facts correctly? Do his conclusions make sense?

Chapter 11, "You're the Judge of Newspapers," will help you learn to evaluate the newspaper. That chapter has suggestions that will aid you in thinking straight while you are reading a news story or an editorial. You can apply these suggestions in evaluating any book as well as any newspaper.

11. *Follow up your reading.* Every chapter in this book has a section entitled, "Inquiry and Action: Assignment Sheet." If you do the things suggested in this section, you will understand the chapter better. You will also be able to apply what you have learned to your newspaper reading.

12. *Make a report or a summary of what you have read.* After you finish a chapter, tell somebody else what you have just read. Or, write a short summary covering the chapter's main points.

How should you read fiction?

Novels and other kinds of fiction are read for a variety of purposes. For example, you may read *Main Street*, by Sinclair Lewis, to get a picture of small-town life in the Middle West during the 1920's. You may read *The Snake Pit*, by Mary Jane Ward, to gain an understanding of the experiences of a patient in a mental hospital. Or, you may read *Tales of The South Pacific*, by James A. Michener, to find out the thoughts, feelings, and actions of the men who fought the Japanese in the Pacific theatre of operations during World War II. But, in reading most books of fiction, your main purpose is to gain enjoyment. And the more such books you read, the more enjoyment you can get from this type of reading.

When you started this better reading book, you may have been reading from one to five novels a year. You probably read few novels because your reading was slow and laborious. Now that you have increased your reading power, you should be able to read many more novels than you did. To do so, you should set a goal such as this: *Read two or more novels each month.*

Although you have become a better reader, you may say, "I like to take my time in reading a novel. If I try to speed up, I don't enjoy the book as much." You have a good point here. Certainly you should not read a novel so fast that you fail to get understanding and pleasure from it. But while you are reading such a book, do you read at too leisurely a pace? Do you let your mind wander? Do you get as much satisfaction as possible from the book?

If you try to read novels more rapidly, you may be surprised and pleased with the added enjoyment you get. As you try to read faster, you should give your full attention to your reading. In this way, you will gain a richer understanding. And this will increase your appreciation of what you read.

To speed up your reading of fiction, do this experiment:

1. Get a book of fiction that is highly interesting and that is fairly easy to read. This book may be a novel, a mystery story, or a collection of short stories.

2. During an evening, spend two to three hours in reading the book. Try to finish it in that time. If you don't, try to complete the book the next evening.

When you start this experiment, you will probably feel uncomfortable. This feeling may interfere with the enjoyment that you usually get from reading. But as you read other books at even faster rates, you will find that your feelings of discomfort will tend to disappear. And you will discover that your reading will bring you greater satisfaction and enjoyment.

An exercise in reading a short story

To practice the reading of fiction at a fast rate, read the short story given next. Write down your starting time in the time box. Then start reading the story. After finishing the story, you will take a short test on it.

Time Box

Finishing time	
Starting time	
Reading time	
Reading rate	

THE ADVENTURE OF THE MAZARIN STONE[1]

by Sir Arthur Conan Doyle

IT WAS PLEASANT to Dr. Watson to find himself once more in the untidy room of the first floor in Baker Street which had been the starting-point of so many remarkable adventures. He looked round him at the scientific charts upon the wall, the acid-charred bench of chemicals, the violin-case leaning in the corner, the coal-scuttle, which contained of old the pipes and tobacco. Finally, his eyes came round to the fresh and smiling face of Billy, the young but very wise and tactful page, who had helped a little to fill up the gap of loneliness and isolation which surrounded the saturnine figure of the great detective.

"It all seems very unchanged, Billy. You don't change, either. I hope the same can be said of him?"

Billy glanced, with some solicitude, at the closed door of the bedroom.

"I think he's in bed and asleep," he said.

It was seven in the evening of a lovely summer's day, but Dr. Watson was sufficiently familiar with the irregularity of his old friend's hours to feel no surprise at the idea.

"That means a case, I suppose?"

"Yes, sir; he is very hard at it just now. I'm frightened for his health. He gets paler and thinner, and he eats nothing. 'When will you be pleased to dine, Mr. Holmes?' Mrs. Hudson asked. 'Seven-thirty, the day after to-morrow,' said he. You know his way when he is keen on a case."

"Yes, Billy, I know."

"He's following someone. Yesterday

he was out as a workman looking for a job. To-day he was an old woman. Fairly took me in, he did, and I ought to know his ways by now." Billy pointed with a grin to a very baggy parasol which leaned against the sofa. "That's part of the old woman's outfit," he said.

"But what is it all about, Billy?"

Billy sank his voice, as one who discusses great secrets of State. "I don't mind telling you, sir, but it should go no farther. It's this case of the Crown diamond."

"What—the hundred-thousand-pound burglary?"

"Yes, sir. They must get it back, sir. Why, we had the Prime Minister and the Home Secretary both sitting on that very sofa. Mr. Holmes was very nice to them. He soon put them at their ease and promised he would do all he could. Then there is Lord Cantlemere—"

"Ah!"

"Yes, sir; you know what that means. He's a stiff 'un, sir, if I may say so. I can get along with the Prime Minister, and I've nothing against the Home Secretary, who seemed a civil, obliging sort of man, but I can't stand his lordship. Neither can Mr. Holmes, sir. You see, he don't believe in Mr. Holmes and he was against employing him. He'd *rather* he failed."

"And Mr. Holmes knows it?"

"Mr. Holmes always knows whatever there is to know."

"Well, we'll hope he won't fail and that Lord Cantlemere will be confounded. But I say, Billy, what is that curtain for across the window?"

"Mr. Holmes had it put up there three days ago. We've got something funny behind it."

Billy advanced and drew away the drapery which screened the alcove of the bow window.

[1]Published by arrangement with the Estate of the late Sir Arthur Conan Doyle.

Dr. Watson could not restrain a cry of amazement. There was a facsimile of his old friend, dressing-gown and all, the face turned three-quarters toward the window and downwards, as though reading an invisible book, while the body was sunk deep in an arm-chair. Billy detached the head and held it in the air.

"We put it at different angles, so that it may seem more life-like. I wouldn't dare touch it if the blind were not down. But when it's up you can see this from across the way."

"We used something of the sort once before."

"Before my time," said Billy. He drew the window curtains apart and looked out into the street. "There are folk who watch us from over yonder. I can see a fellow now at the window. Have a look for yourself."

Watson had taken a step forward when the bedroom door opened, and the long, thin form of Holmes emerged, his face pale and drawn, but his step and bearing as active as ever. With a single spring he was at the window, and had drawn the blind once more.

"That will do, Billy," said he. "You were in danger of your life then, my boy, and I can't do without you just yet. Well, Watson, it is good to see you in your old quarters once again. You come at a critical moment."

"So I gather."

"You can go, Billy. That boy is a problem, Watson. How far am I justified in allowing him to be in danger?"

"Danger of what, Holmes?"

"Of sudden death. I'm expecting something this evening."

"Expecting what?"

"To be murdered, Watson."

"No, no; you are joking, Holmes!"

"Even my limited sense of humour could evolve a better joke than that. But we may be comfortable in the meantime, may we not? Is alcohol permitted? The gasogene and cigars are in the old place. Let me see you once more in the customary arm-chair. You have not, I hope, learned to despise my pipe and my lamentable tobacco? It has to take the place of food these days."

"But why not eat?"

"Because the faculties become refined when you starve them. Why, surely, as a doctor, my dear Watson, you must admit that what your digestion gains in the way of blood supply is so much lost to the brain. I am a brain, Watson. The rest of me is a mere appendix. Therefore, it is the brain I must consider."

"But this danger, Holmes?"

"Ah, yes; in case it should come off, it would perhaps be as well that you should burden your memory with the name and address of the murderer. You can give it to Scotland Yard, with my love and a parting blessing. Sylvius is the name—Count Negretto Sylvius. Write it down, man, write it down! 136 Moorside Gardens, N.W. Got it?"

Watson's honest face was twitching with anxiety. He knew only too well the immense risks taken by Holmes, and was well aware that what he said was more likely to be under-statement than exaggeration. Watson was always the man of action, and he rose to the occasion.

"Count me in, Holmes. I have nothing to do for a day or two."

"Your morals don't improve, Watson. You have added fibbing to your other vices. You bear every sign of the busy medical man, with calls on him every hour."

"Not such important ones. But can't you have this fellow arrested?"

"Yes, Watson, I could. That's what worries him so."

"But why don't you?"

"Because I don't know where the diamond is."

"Ah! Billy told me—the missing Crown jewel!"

"Yes, the great yellow Mazarin stone. I've cast my net and I have my fish. But I have not got the stone. What is the use of taking *them?* We can make the world a better place by laying them by the heels. But that is not what I am out for. It's the stone I want."

"And is this Count Sylvius one of your fish?"

"Yes, and he's a shark. He bites. The other is Sam Merton, the boxer. Not a bad fellow, Sam, but the Count has used him. Sam's not a shark. He is a great big silly bull-headed gudgeon. But he is flopping about in my net all the same."

"Where is this Count Sylvius?"

"I've been at his very elbow all the morning. You've seen me as an old lady, Watson. I was never more convincing. He actually picked up my parasol for me once. 'By your leave, madame,' said he—half-Italian, you know, and with the Southern graces of manner when in the mood, but a devil incarnate in the other mood. Life is full of whimsical happenings, Watson."

"It might have been tragedy."

"Well, perhaps it might. I followed him to an old Straubenzee's workshop in the Minories. Straubenzee made the air-gun —a very pretty bit of work, as I understand, and I rather fancy it is in the opposite window at the present moment. Have you seen the dummy? Of course, Billy showed it to you. Well, it may get a bullet through its beautiful head at any moment. Ah, Billy, what is it?"

The boy had reappeared in the room with a card upon a tray. Holmes glanced at it with raised eyebrows and an amused smile.

"The man himself. I had hardly expected this. Grasp the nettle, Watson! A man of nerve. Possibly you have heard of his reputation as a shooter of big game. It would indeed be a triumphant ending to his excellent sporting record if he added me to his bag. This is a proof that he feels my toe very close behind his heel."

"Send for the police."

"I probably shall. But not just yet. Would you glance carefully out of the window, Watson, and see if anyone is hanging about in the street?"

Watson looked warily round the edge of the curtain.

"Yes, there is one rough fellow near the door."

"That will be Sam Merton—the faithful but rather fatuous Sam. Where is this gentleman, Billy?"

"In the waiting-room, sir."

"Show him up when I ring."

"Yes, sir."

"If I am not in the room, show him in all the same."

"Yes, sir."

Watson waited until the door was closed, and then he turned earnestly to his companion.

"Look, here, Holmes, this is simply impossible. This is a desperate man, who sticks at nothing. He may have come to murder you."

"I should not be surprised."

"I insist upon staying with you."

"You would be horribly in the way."

"In *his* way?"

"No, my dear fellow—in my way."

"Well, I can't possibly leave you."

"Yes, you can, Watson. And you will, for you have never failed to play the game.

I am sure you will play it to the end. This man has come for his own purpose, but he may stay for mine." Holmes took out his notebook and scribbled a few lines. "Take a cab to Scotland Yard and give this to Youghal of the C.I.D. Come back with the police. The fellow's arrest will follow."

"I'll do that with joy."

"Before you return I may have just time enough to find out where the stone is." He touched the bell. "I think we will go out through the bedroom. This second exit is exceedingly useful. I rather want to see my shark without his seeing me, and I have, as you will remember, my own way of doing it."

It was, therefore, an empty room into which Billy, a minute later, ushered Count Sylvius. The famous gameshot, sportsman, and man-about-town was a big, swarthy fellow, with a formidable dark moustache, shading a cruel, thin-lipped mouth, and surmounted by a long, curved nose, like the beak of an eagle. He was well dressed, but his brilliant necktie, shining pin, and glittering rings were flamboyant in their effect. As the door closed behind him he looked round him with fierce, startled eyes, like one who suspects a trap at every turn. Then he gave a violent start as he saw the impassive head and the collar of the dressing gown which projected above the arm-chair in the window. At first his expression was one of pure amazement. Then the light of a horrible hope gleamed in his dark, murderous eyes. He took one more glance round to see that there were no witnesses, and then, on tiptoe, his thick stick half raised, he approached the silent figure. He was crouching for his final spring and blow when a cool, sardonic voice greeted him from the open bedroom door:

"Don't break it, Count! Don't break it!"

The assassin staggered back, amazement in his convulsed face. For an instant he half raised his loaded cane once more, as if he would turn his violence from the effigy to the original; but there was something in that steady grey eye and mocking smile which caused his hand to sink to his side.

"It's a pretty little thing," said Holmes, advancing towards the image. "Tavernier, the French modeller, made it. He is as good at waxworks as your friend Straubenzee is at air-guns."

"Air-guns, sir! What do you mean?"

"Put your hat and stick on the side-table. Thank you! Pray take a seat. Would you care to put your revolver out also? Oh, very good, if you prefer to sit upon it. Your visit is really most opportune, for I wanted badly to have a few minutes' chat with you."

The Count scowled, with heavy threatening eyebrows.

"I, too, wished to have some words with you, Holmes. That is why I am here. I won't deny that I intended to assault you just now."

Holmes swung his leg on the edge of the table.

"I rather gathered that you had some idea of the sort in your head," said he. "But why these personal attentions?"

"Because you have gone out of your way to annoy me. Because you have put your creatures upon my track."

"My creatures! I assure you no!"

"Nonsense! I have had them followed. Two can play at that game, Holmes."

"It is a small point, Count Sylvius, but perhaps you would kindly give me my prefix when you address me. You can understand that, with my routine of work, I should find myself on familiar terms with half the rogues' gallery, and you will agree that exceptions are invidious."

"Well, *Mr.* Holmes, then."

"Excellent! But I assure you you are mistaken about my alleged agents."

Count Sylvius laughed contemptuously.

"Other people can observe as well as you. Yesterday there was an old sporting man. To-day it was an elderly woman. They held me in view all day."

"Really, sir, you compliment me. Old Baron Dowson said the night before he was hanged that in my case what the law had gained the stage had lost. And now you give my little impersonations your kindly praise!"

"It was you—you yourself?"

Holmes shrugged his shoulders. "You can see in the corner the parasol which you so politely handed to me in the Minories before you began to suspect."

"If I had known, you might never—"

"Have seen this humble home again. I was well aware of it. We all have neglected opportunities to deplore. As it happens, you did not know, so here we are!"

The Count's knotted brows gathered more heavily over his menacing eyes. "What you say only makes the matter worse. It was not your agents, but your play acting, busybody self! You admit that you have dogged me. Why?"

"Come now, Count. You used to shoot lions in Algeria."

"Well?"

"But why?"

"Why? The sport—the excitement—the danger!"

"And, no doubt, to free the country from a pest?"

"Exactly!"

"My reasons in a nutshell!"

The Count sprang to his feet, and his hand involuntarily moved back to his hip-pocket.

"Sit down, sir, sit down! There was another, more practical, reason. I want that yellow diamond!"

Count Sylvius lay back in his chair with an evil smile.

"Upon my word!" said he.

"You knew that I was after you for that. The real reason why you are here to-night is to find out how much I know about the matter and how far my removal is absolutely essential. Well, I should say that, from your point of view, it *is* absolutely essential, for I know all about it, save only one thing, which you are about to tell me."

"Oh, indeed! And, pray, what is this missing fact?"

"Where the Crown diamond now is."

The Count looked sharply at his companion. "Oh, you want to know that, do you? How the devil should I be able to tell you where it is?"

"You can, and you will."

"Indeed!"

"You can't bluff me, Count Sylvius." Holmes's eyes, as he gazed at him, contracted and lightened until they were like two menacing points of steel. "You are absolute plate-glass. I see to the very back of your mind."

"Then, of course, you see where the diamond is!"

Holmes clapped his hands with amusement, and then pointed a derisive finger. "Then you do know. You have admitted it!"

"I admit nothing."

"Now, Count, if you will be reasonable, we can do business. If not, you will get hurt."

Count Sylvius threw up his eyes to the ceiling. "And you talk about bluff!" said he.

Holmes looked at him thoughtfully, like a master chess-player who meditates his crowning move. Then he threw open the table drawer and drew out a squat notebook.

"Do you know what I keep in this book?"

"No, sir, I do not!"

"You!"

"Me?"

"Yes, sir, *you!* You are all here—every action of your vile and dangerous life."

"Damn you, Holmes!" cried the Count, with blazing eyes. "There are limits to my patience!"

"It's all here, Count. The real facts as to the death of old Mrs. Harold, who left you the Blymer estate, which you so rapidly gambled away."

"You are dreaming!"

"And the complete life history of Miss Minnie Warrender."

"Tut! You will make nothing of that!"

"Plenty more here, Count. Here is the robbery in the train-de-luxe to the Riviera on February 13, 1892. Here is the forged cheque in the same year on the Crédit Lyonnais."

"No; you're wrong there."

"Then I am right on the others! Now, Count, you are a card-player. When the other fellow has all the trumps, it saves time to throw down your hand."

"What has all this talk to do with the jewel of which you spoke?"

"Gently, Count. Restrain that eager mind! Let me get to the points in my own humdrum fashion. I have all this against you; but, above all, I have a clear case against both you and your fighting bully in the case of the Crown diamond."

"Indeed!"

"I have the cabman who took you to Whitehall and the cabman who brought you away. I have the Commissionaire who saw you near the case. I have Ikey Sanders, who refused to cut it up for you. Ikey has peached, and the game is up."

The veins stood out on the Count's forehead. His dark, hairy hands were clenched in a convulsion of restrained emotion. He tried to speak, but the words would not shape themselves.

"That's the hand I play from," said Holmes. "I put it all upon the table. But one card is missing. It's the King of Diamonds. I don't know where the stone is."

"You never shall know."

"No? Now, be reasonable, Count. Consider the situation. You are going to be locked up for twenty years. So is Sam Merton. What good are you going to get out of your diamond? None in the world. But if you hand it over—well, I'll compound a felony. We don't want you or Sam. We want the stone. Give that up, and so far as I am concerned you can go free so long as you behave yourself in the future. If you make another slip—well, it will be the last. But this time my commission is to get the stone, not you."

"But if I refuse?"

"Why, then—alas!—it must be you and not the stone."

Billy had appeared in answer to a ring.

"I think, Count, that it would be as well to have your friend Sam at this conference. After all, his interests should be represented. Billy, you will see a large and ugly gentleman outside the front door. Ask him to come up."

"If he won't come, sir?"

"No violence, Billy. Don't be rough with him. If you tell him that Count Sylvius wants him he will certainly come."

"What are you going to do now?" asked the Count, as Billy disappeared.

"My friend Watson was with me just now. I told him that I had a shark and a gudgeon in my net; now I am drawing the net and up they come together."

The Count had risen from his chair, and his hand was behind his back. Holmes held something half protruding from the pocket of his dressing-gown.

"You won't die in your bed, Holmes."

"I have often had the same idea. Does it matter very much? After all, Count, your own exit is more likely to be perpendicular than horizontal. But these anticipations of the future are morbid. Why not give ourselves up to the unrestrained enjoyment of the present?"

A sudden wild-beast light sprang up in the dark, menacing eyes of the master criminal. Holmes's figure seemed to grow taller as he grew tense and ready.

"It is no use your fingering your revolver, my friend," he said, in a quiet voice. "You know perfectly well that you dare not use it, even if I gave you time to draw it. Nasty, noisy things, revolvers, Count. Better stick to air-guns. Ah! I think I hear the fairy footstep of your estimable partner. Good day, Mr. Merton. Rather dull in the street, is it not?"

The prize-fighter, a heavily built young man with a stupid, obstinate, slab-sided face, stood awkwardly at the door, looking about him with a puzzled expression. Holmes's debonair manner was a new experience, and though he vaguely felt that it was hostile, he did not know how to counter it. He turned to his more astute comrade for help.

"What's the game now, Count? What's this fellow want? What's up?" His voice was deep and raucous.

The Count shrugged his shoulders, and it was Holmes who answered.

"If I may put it in a nutshell, Mr. Merton, I should say it was *all* up."

The boxer still addressed his remarks to his associate.

"Is this cove trying to be funny, or what? I'm not in the funny mood myself."

"No, I expect not," said Holmes. "I think I can promise you that you will feel even less humorous as the evening advances. Now, look here, Count Sylvius. I'm a busy man and I can't waste time. I'm going into that bedroom. Pray make yourselves quite at home in my absence. You can explain to your friend how the matter lies without the restraint of my presence. I shall try over the Hoffmann *Barcarole* upon my violin. In five minutes I shall return for your final answer. You quite grasp the alternative, do you not? Shall we take you, or shall we have the stone?"

Holmes withdrew, picking up his violin from the corner as he passed. A few moments later the long-drawn, wailing notes of that most haunting of tunes came faintly through the closed door of the bedroom.

"What is it, then?" asked Merton anxiously, as his companion turned to him. "Does he know about the stone?"

"He knows a damned sight too much about it. I'm not sure that he doesn't know all about it."

"Good Lord!" The boxer's sallow face turned a shade whiter.

"Ikey Sanders has split on us."

"He has, has he? I'll do him down a thick 'un for that if I swing for it."

"That won't help us much. We've got to make up our minds what to do."

"Half a mo'," said the boxer, looking suspiciously at the bedroom door. "He's a leary cove that wants watching. I suppose he's not listening?"

"How can he be listening with that music going?"

"That's right. Maybe somebody's behind a curtain. Too many curtains in this room." As he looked round he suddenly saw for the first time the effigy in the window, and stood staring and pointing, too amazed for words.

"Tut! it's only a dummy," said the Count.

"A fake, is it? Well, strike me! Madame Tussaud ain't in it. It's the living spit of him, gown and all. But them curtains, Count!"

"Oh, confound the curtains! We are wasting our time, and there is none too much. He can lag us over this stone."

"The deuce he can!"

"But he'll let us slip if we only tell him where the swag is."

"What! Give it up? Give up a hundred thousand quid?"

"It's one or the other."

Merton scratched his short-cropped pate.

"He's alone in there. Let's do him in. If his light were out we should have nothing to fear."

The Count shook his head.

"He is armed and ready. If we shot him we could hardly get away in a place like this. Besides, it's likely enough that the police know whatever evidence he has got. Hallo! What was that?"

There was a vague sound which seemed to come from the window. Both men sprang round, but all was quiet. Save for the one strange figure seated in the chair, the room was certainly empty.

"Something in the street," said Merton. "Now look here, guv'nor, you've got the brains. Surely you can think a way out of it. If slugging is no use then it's up to you."

"I've fooled better men than he," the Count answered. "The stone is here in my secret pocket. I take no chances leaving it about. It can be out of England tonight and cut into four pieces in Am-sterdam before Sunday. He knows nothing of Van Seddar."

"I thought Van Seddar was going next week."

"He *was*. But now he must get off by the next boat. One or other of us must slip round with the stone to Lime Street and tell him."

"But the false bottom ain't ready."

"Well, he must take it as it is and chance it. There's not a moment to lose." Again, with the sense of danger which becomes an instinct with the sportsman, he paused and looked hard at the window. Yes, it was surely from the street that the faint sound had come.

"As to Holmes," he continued, "we can fool him easily enough. You see, the damned fool won't arrest us if he can get the stone. Well, we'll promise him the stone. We'll put him on the wrong track about it, and before he finds that it *is* the wrong track it will be in Holland and we out of the country."

"That sounds good to me!" cried Sam Merton, with a grin.

"You go on and tell the Dutchman to get a move on him. I'll see this sucker and fill him up with a bogus confession. I'll tell him that the stone is in Liverpool. Confound that whining music; it gets on my nerves! By the time he finds it isn't in Liverpool it will be in quarters and we on the blue water. Come back here, out of a line with that keyhole. Here is the stone."

"I wonder you dare carry it."

"Where could I have it safer? If we could take it out of Whitehall someone else could surely take it out of my lodgings."

"Let's have a look at it."

Count Sylvius cast a somewhat unflattering glance at his associate, and disregarded the unwashed hand which was extended towards him.

"What—d'ye think I'm going to snatch it off you? See here, mister, I'm getting a bit tired of your ways."

"Well, well; no offense, Sam. We can't afford to quarrel. Come over to the window, if you want to see the beauty properly. Now hold it to the light! Here!"

"Thank you!"

With a single spring Holmes had leaped from the dummy's chair and had grasped the precious jewel. He held it now in one hand, while his other pointed a revolver at the Count's head. The two villains staggered back in utter amazement. Before they had recovered, Holmes had pressed the electric bell.

"No violence, gentlemen—no violence, I beg of you! Consider the furniture! It must be very clear to you that your position is an impossible one. The police are waiting below."

The count's bewilderment overmastered his rage and fear.

"But how the deuce—?" he gasped.

"Your surprise is very natural. You are not aware that a second door from my bedroom leads behind that curtain. I fancied that you must have heard me when I displaced the figure, but luck was on my side. It gave me a chance of listening to your racy conversation which would have been painfully constrained had you been aware of my presence."

The Count gave a gesture of resignation.

"We give you best, Holmes. I believe you are the devil himself."

"Not far from him, at any rate," Holmes answered, with a polite smile.

Sam Merton's slow intellect had only gradually appreciated the situation. Now, as the sound of heavy steps came from the stairs outside, he broke silence at last.

"A fair cop!" said he. "But, I say, what about that bloomin' fiddle! I hear it yet."

"Tut, tut!" Holmes answered. "You are perfectly right. Let it play! These modern gramophones are a remarkable invention."

There was an inrush of police, the handcuffs clicked and the criminals were led to the waiting cab. Watson lingered with Holmes, congratulating him upon this fresh leaf to his laurels. Once more their conversation was interrupted by the imperturbable Billy with his card-tray.

"Lord Cantlemere, sir."

"Show him up, Billy. This is the eminent peer who represents the very highest interests," said Holmes. "He is an excellent and loyal person, but rather of the old regime. Shall we make him unbend? Dare we venture upon a slight liberty? He knows, we may conjecture, nothing of what has occurred."

The door opened to admit a thin, austere figure with a hatchet face and drooping mid-Victorian whiskers of a glossy blackness which hardly corresponded with the rounded shoulders and feeble gait. Holmes advanced affably, and shook an unresponsive hand.

"How-do-you-do, Lord Cantlemere? It is chilly, for the time of year, but rather warm indoors. May I take your overcoat?"

"No, I thank you; I will not take it off."

Holmes laid his hand insistently upon the sleeve.

"Pray allow me! My friend Dr. Watson would assure you that these changes of temperature are most insidious."

His lordship shook himself free with some impatience.

"I am quite comfortable, sir. I have no need to stay. I have simply looked in to know how your self-appointed task was progressing."

"It is difficult—very difficult."

"I feared that you would find it so."

There was a distinct sneer in the old courtier's words and manner.

"Every man finds his limitations, Mr. Holmes, but at least it cures us of the weakness of self-satisfaction."

"Yes, sir, I have been much perplexed."

"No doubt."

"Especially upon one point. Possibly you could help me upon it?"

"You apply for my advice rather late in the day. I thought that you had your own all-sufficient methods. Still, I am ready to help you."

"You see, Lord Cantlemere, we can no doubt frame a case against the actual thieves."

"When you have caught them."

"Exactly. But the question is—how shall we proceed against the receiver?"

"Is this not rather premature?"

"It is as well to have our plans ready. Now, what would you regard as final evidence against the receiver?"

"The actual possession of the stone."

"You would arrest him upon that?"

"Most undoubtedly."

Holmes seldom laughed, but he got as near it as his old friend Watson could remember.

"In that case, my dear sir, I shall be under the painful necessity of advising your arrest."

Lord Cantlemere was very angry. Some of the ancient fires flickered up into his sallow cheeks.

"You take a great liberty, Mr. Holmes. In fifty years of official life I cannot recall such a case. I am a busy man, sir, engaged upon important affairs, and I have no time or taste for foolish jokes. I may tell you frankly, sir, that I have never been a believer in your powers, and that I have always been of the opinion that the matter was far safer in the hands of the regular police force. Your conduct confirms all my conclusions. I have the honour, sir, to wish you good evening."

Holmes had swiftly changed his position and was between the peer and the door.

"One moment, sir," said he. "To actually go off with the Mazarin stone would be a more serious offence than to be found in temporary possession of it."

"Sir, this is intolerable! Let me pass."

"Put your hand in the right-hand pocket of your overcoat."

"What do you mean, sir?"

"Come—come; do what I ask."

An instant later the amazed peer was standing, blinking and stammering, with the great yellow stone on his shaking palm.

"What! What! How is this, Mr. Holmes?"

"Too bad, Lord Cantlemere, too bad!" cried Holmes. "My old friend here will tell you that I have an impish habit of practical joking. Also that I can never resist a dramatic situation. I took the liberty—the very great liberty, I admit—of putting the stone into your pocket at the beginning of our interview."

The old peer stared from the stone to the smiling face before him.

"Sir, I am bewildered. But—yes—it is indeed the Mazarin stone. We are greatly your debtors, Mr. Holmes. Your sense of humour may, as you admit, be somewhat perverted, and its exhibition remarkably untimely, but at least I withdraw any reflection I have made upon your amazing professional powers. But how—"

"The case is but half finished; the details can wait. No doubt, Lord Cantlemere, your pleasure in telling of this successful result in the exalted circle to which you return will be some small atonement for my practical joke. Billy, you will show his lordship out, and tell Mrs. Hudson that I should be glad if she would send up dinner for two as soon as possible."

Write your finishing time in the time box. Then take this test. In each item, mark a check (✔) at the left of the correct choice.

1. In this story Sherlock Holmes was mainly interested in
   (A) arresting Count Sylvius, a notorious thief
   (B) saving the lives of Dr. Watson, Billy, and himself
   (C) getting back the stolen Crown diamond

2. When Holmes was following Count Sylvius all morning, he was disguised as
   (A) an old lady
   (B) an elderly gentleman
   (C) a jewel thief

3. Holmes, Dr. Watson, and Billy were most afraid that Count Sylvius would
   (A) shoot at them through the window from across the street
   (B) stab them from behind as they walked onto the sidewalk
   (C) slip into the house to surprise and kill them

4. When Count Sylvius first entered Holmes's living room, he saw the figure (a dummy) sitting near the window. He then started
   (A) to stab the figure with a knife
   (B) to strangle the figure with a sash cord
   (C) to hit the figure with his thick stick

5. Count Sylvius said he had come to see Holmes because he wanted
   (A) to be friendly with Holmes
   (B) Holmes to stop following him
   (C) to find out how much Holmes knew about the diamond

6. Holmes told Count Sylvius about many crimes charged against the Count and the punishments for these crimes. Holmes did this because he wished the Count
   (A) to deny having stolen the diamond
   (B) to give up the diamond voluntarily
   (C) to delay long enough so that the police could arrive

7. Holmes sent for Sam Merton, the Count's thug, because Holmes thought that the Count and Merton would talk about
   (A) where the diamond was
   (B) how they stole the diamond
   (C) why they should kill Holmes

8. While the Count and Merton were whispering, Holmes
   (A) played loudly on his violin in the bedroom
   (B) whispered to Dr. Watson to get the police
   (C) took the place of the dummy near the window

9. When Holmes jumped from behind the curtains and seized the jewel, he kept the Count and Merton from attacking him by telling them that
   (A) the police were waiting below
   (B) he would kill them if they moved
   (C) the police knew they had stolen the diamond

10. As a practical joke, Holmes slipped the diamond into the pocket of Lord Cantlemere's overcoat. Holmes did this because Cantlemere had indicated that he
    (A) should get credit for finding the diamond
    (B) did not believe in Holmes as a detective
    (C) was guilty of stealing the diamond

Time-to-Rate Table (5,663 words)

Reading time	Reading rate	Reading time	Reading rate	Reading time	Reading rate	Reading time	Reading rate
10:00-10:29	552	17:30-17:59	319	25:00-25:29	224	32:30-32:59	173
10:30-10:59	527	18:00-18:29	310	25:30-25:59	220	33:00-33:29	170
11:00-11:29	503	18:30-18:59	302	26:00-26:29	216	33:30-33:59	168
11:30-11:59	482	19:00-19:29	294	26:30-26:59	212	34:00-34:29	165
12:00-12:29	462	19:30-19:59	287	27:00-27:29	208	34:30-34:59	163
12:30-12:59	444	20:00-20:29	280	27:30-27:59	204	35:00-35:29	161
13:00-13:29	427	20:30-20:59	273	28:00-28:29	200	35:30-35:59	158
13:30-13:59	412	21:00-21:29	266	28:30-28:59	197	36:00-36:29	156
14:00-14:29	397	21:30-21:59	260	29:00-29:29	194	36:30-36:59	154
14:30-14:59	384	22:00-22:29	255	29:30-29:59	190	37:00-37:29	152
15:00-15:29	371	22:30-22:59	249	30:00-30:29	187	37:30-37:59	150
15:30-15:59	360	23:00-23:29	244	30:30-30:59	184	38:00-38:29	148
16:00-16:29	348	23:30-23:59	238	31:00-31:29	181	38:30-38:59	146
16:30-16:59	338	24:00-24:29	234	31:30-31:59	178	39:00-39:29	144
17:00-17:29	328	24:30-24:59	229	32:00-32:29	176	39:30-39:59	142

Now figure out your reading time for the story. Change your reading time into your reading rate; use the table given here. Write your reading rate in the time box.

Correct and score your answers to the test. Here are the correct answers:

(1-C; 2-A; 3-A; 4-C; 5-B; 6-B; 7-A; 8-C; 9-A; 10-B)

Do general reading exercise 17 (page 275)

In this reading exercise, make a special effort to increase your reading rate, comprehension score, and vocabulary score.

After you complete this general reading exercise, answer these questions: Did I enjoy the story? Do I know children like those described? Do I know a person who is like the aunt? According to the story-teller, was Bertha "a good girl" or "a goody-goody girl"?

If you liked Article 17, "The Story-Teller," you may wish to read other short stories by Saki. This was the pen name of H. H. Munro, an Englishman who was noted for the fine quality and delicate humor of his writing.

In this lesson, you have learned many of the ways to read a book with efficiency, understanding, and enjoyment. In the next lesson, you will study what you can do to have a well-balanced reading program.

LESSON 18

How can you balance your reading?

> All that mankind has done, thought, gained or been: it is lying as in magic preservation in the pages of books.
> *Thomas Carlyle* (1795-1845)

WHAT CARLYLE WROTE years ago is still true. Most of the worth-while activities of mankind are recorded in books and other printed materials. These materials deal with as many different subjects as people are or were interested in. They are of various types. Some are novels. Others are biographies. Still others are straight factual accounts.

What is balanced reading?

If you wish to learn what mankind has done through the ages and is doing today, you will want to develop a balanced reading program. In such a program, you will read a variety of books, magazine articles, newspaper presentations, and other written materials. You also will apply all of the different reading skills that you have been learning from this book.

If your reading program is balanced, you not only have a strong interest that leads you to read intensively in one field, but you also read extensively in other fields. You recognize that you, like every other person, have many interests that can be satisfied mainly through reading.

Unfortunately, many people are too limited or narrow in their reading. You may be one of them. For example, you may read only certain pages in newspapers. You may read only love stories or adventure stories in magazines. You may restrict your leisure reading to murder mysteries or light novels. Or you may be so concerned with one vocation that your reading is almost entirely in this single field.

If your reading is thus limited, it tends to make you a narrow person, a person who is uninteresting and uninformed. As such, your greatest loss is in the satisfactions that you yourself might obtain from a better balanced reading program.

Whether your reading is now narrow or wide, you should work to develop a balanced pattern of reading. You, of course, are the person who will design this pattern to fit all your own needs and wants.

144

Try to get a better balance in your reading

You can start at once toward building a reading program that is well-balanced. You can do this in your reading of newspapers, magazines, and books by following the suggestions given next.

Balance your reading of newspapers

A recent issue of the New York *Times* carried an interesting advertisement reprinted here in part:

Morning, noon, and night . . . nothing takes the place of the newspaper in the lives of the American people.

Other media may tell part of the story, but only the newspaper brings the people the full story, without which *knowledge* their lives would not be complete.

Knowledge of Local Affairs
Knowledge of National Affairs
Knowledge of International Affairs
Knowledge of Products Old and New

Newspapers are indispensable to the American people as proven by the fact that the people *buy* 54,017,938 newspapers every day for which they *pay* $2,589,000 per day, or over a billion dollars per year.

No other advertising media can match this record. No other advertising media has the selling power of the newspapers.

This advertisement clearly points out that newspapers inform us Americans about local, national, and international affairs, and about many products. It indicates, too, that most of us read newspapers. But it does not indicate what parts of newspapers we usually read.

If you are a typical reader of a city newspaper, you may glance at the headlines, the cartoons, and the photographs. You may turn to the comic pages where you read "Lil Abner," "Dick Tracy," and "Orphan Annie." Next, you may read the sports pages, or the women's pages. After that, you may read the most sensational stories, those about murders or airplane disasters, for example. You may then look quickly at the advertisements and read those that capture your attention.

If you are a really good reader, you read the important stories that appear throughout the paper. These accounts may include discussions of such matters as the explosion of the first H-bomb at Eniwetok, a statement by the President of the United States, a vote by Congress on a key bill, a strike settlement, the results of an election abroad, and an action by the United Nations. You also read and think about the editorials and the columns by news commentators. You then read the reviews of books, music, art, radio-TV, movies, or travel.

To give yourself practice in the balanced reading of a newspaper, get a copy of the Sunday edition of a metropolitan paper. Look through this newspaper quickly, noticing in general what is in each section. Then, in each section, skim one part and read another part carefully. These may be news stories, editorials, or advertisements, for example. Afterward, read your daily paper in the same balanced way.

Balance your reading of magazines

You can get a better balance in your reading of magazines in two ways. *First,* skim all the articles in an issue of your favorite magazine to get a general idea of what these articles contain. Then read carefully the most interesting articles. *Second*, read regularly at least several different magazines, not just one magazine. Choose magazines that best meet your interests or your needs.

If you are a typical magazine reader, you are probably reading regularly one or more of the magazines listed in Table 7. This table gives the names and the circulation figures of all the most popular American magazines except the comics.

TABLE 7[1]
CIRCULATION OF BEST-SELLING AMERICAN MAGAZINES

Magazine	Average Monthly or Weekly Circulation
Reader's Digest	10,000,000
Life	5,340,000
Ladies' Home Journal	4,575,000
Woman's Home Companion	4,259,000
McCall's	4,238,000
Saturday Evening Post	4,224,000
Woman's Day	3,840,000
Better Homes and Gardens	3,600,000
Family Circle Magazine	3,535,000
Look	3,302,000
Good Housekeeping	3,201,000
Collier's	3,120,000
American Home	2,951,000
American Legion Magazine	2,778,000
Coronet	2,763,000
American Magazine	2,565,000
True Story	2,221,000
National Geographic Magazine	2,066,000
Redbook	1,980,000
Cosmopolitan	1,866,000
True	1,776,000
Time	1,707,000
True Confessions	1,703,000
Photoplay	1,318,000

Table 7 may have the names of some magazines that you have never seen. If

---

[1]Except for the *Reader's Digest*, all the figures given are from *Consumer Magazine*, Jan. 15, 1953. Evanston, Ill.: Standard Rate and Data Service, Inc.

so, you may want to become familiar with these magazines. You can examine copies of many of them at a library. There you will also find other magazines that may interest you.

In addition, you may want to familiarize yourself with some magazines that have relatively small circulations but that have articles that are well worth your reading. Among such magazines are *The Atlantic Monthly, Harper's Magazine,* and *Saturday Review.*

To balance your magazine reading, you can read regularly at least one general magazine such as *Reader's Digest, Coronet, Saturday Evening Post, Collier's, American Magazine, Redbook,* or *Cosmopolitan;* and at least one weekly news magazine such as *Life, Look, Time,* or *Newsweek.* You can also read a monthly woman's magazine or a monthly men's magazine. And in your field of special interest, you can read at least one magazine such as *Scientific Monthly, Popular Mechanics, National Geographic, Holiday,* or *Natural History Magazine.*

You may enjoy some of the comics. These magazines are widely sold and read. Their total circulation is more than 60,000,000 per month. But you will want to be sure that you do not read these magazines in excess.

Balance your reading of books

You may want to examine your own reading pattern after first noting the books that are read most widely. Here, for example, are the national best-sellers of 1952, as reported by *Publishers' Weekly,* January 24, 1953. The titles are arranged according to sales in bookstores. The total sales of these books are given in parentheses.

NONFICTION BOOKS

The Holy Bible: Revised Standard Version. Nelson. (2,000,000)

Marshall, Catherine. *A Man Called Peter.* McGraw-Hill. (205,000)

Lait, Jack and Mortimer, Lee. *U. S. A. Confidential.* Crown. (163,961)

Carson, Rachel L. *The Sea Around Us.* Oxford Univ. Press. (105,795)

Bankhead, Tallulah. *Tallulah.* Harper. (No sales figure available)

Peale, Norman Vincent. *The Power of Positive Thinking.* Prentice-Hall. (102,340)

Morgan, Edward P., ed. *This I Believe.* Simon and Schuster. (98,500)

Hicks, Wilson, ed. *This Is Ike.* Holt. (90,000)

Chambers, Whittaker. *Witness.* Random House. (80,000)

Hillman, William. *Mr. President.* Farrar, Straus and Young. (77,246)

FICTION BOOKS

Costain, Thomas B. *The Silver Chalice.* Doubleday. (221,000)

Wouk, Herman. *The Caine Mutiny.* Doubleday. (189,000)

Steinbeck, John. *East of Eden.* Viking Press. (140,000)

du Maurier, Daphne. *My Cousin Rachel.* Doubleday. (130,000)

Keyes, Frances Parkinson. *Steamboat Gothic.* Messner. (120,000)

Ferber, Edna. *Giant.* Doubleday. (119,000)

Hemingway, Ernest. *The Old Man and the Sea.* Scribners. (No sales figure available)

Turnbull, Agnes Sligh. *Gown of Glory.* Houghton Mifflin. (62,500)

Yerby, Frank. *The Saracen Blade.* Dial Press. (55,000)

Spring, Howard. *The Houses in Between.* Harper. (No sales figure available)

How many of these books have *you* read? And how many of the current best-sellers do you know? You will find current lists of best-selling books in the book sections of metropolitan newspapers.

If you wish to have a well-balanced reading program, you will select some titles from current best-seller lists. You will also choose valuable books that were published months if not years in the past. For help in selecting good books consult your librarian.

Check on whether your reading is balanced

To determine whether your reading program is balanced, make a list of the books that you have read during the past four weeks. Classify these books according to fields—for example, fiction, biography, travel, science, and history. After studying this list, write down the names of the fields in which you need to do more reading.

To get the titles of books in these fields, go to the library. Consult the librarian or some of the book lists already mentioned in this book. After you list the titles, obtain the books and read them.

Six months from now, check again on whether your reading is becoming better balanced. Take the same steps that you did before to determine in what fields you should read more books. Through such a check-up, you will probably discover that you are doing more reading in different fields. And because variety, they say, is the spice of life, your varied reading is adding zest to your daily living.

Your reading program can be unique but still well-balanced

In your reading, you may concentrate in one field only. For example, you may read mostly science books and magazines. Or, you may spend much of your time on biographies. Or, you may read many novels. If you have a field of major interest, you should do much of your reading in that field. But you should also do some reading in other fields.

If your reading is both specialized and varied, your reading program will be surely unique—unlike that of any other person. Moreover, this program can be so well-balanced that it will help you to lead a better-balanced life.

A reading exercise to balance your reading program

In the busy world today, you may sometimes wish to read something that will carry you back to your childhood. You may recall such happy times as a picnic in the woods, a day at the zoo, the old swimming hole near your home, or your first automobile or airplane ride. Such memories are often pleasant and rewarding. Reading books others have written about their childhood may also give you great pleasure. That is why you will probably enjoy the following story.

Read the story twice—*first*, rapidly to get the author's flow of ideas; and *second*, carefully to enjoy the author's description. Then take the comprehension test and vocabulary test.

LEAVES FALLING, DEAD MEN CALLING[2]

by Bruce Hutchison

THE LEAVES AT home in Ontario used to turn yellow and then scarlet, and one morning a small boy would wake to see them fluttering down into the back yard. They were big, ragged maple leaves, the best kind for a boy's fire. When they lay thick upon the ground it was a delicious feeling to kick your feet through them as you walked and heard them rustle. If you pushed them with a long motion of the leg they sounded like the swish of

[2]From *The Unknown Country*, by Bruce Hutchison. Copyright, 1942, by Coward-McCann, Inc. Reprinted by permission.

a wave on a sandy beach. But the burning was the best of all.

Old William, our man-of-all-work, would rake them up with a wooden rake that he had made himself, and I would help him with a toy rake and toy wheelbarrow, demanding that we burn right away. But William would squint up at the trees and he would not burn until all the leaves were down. It was unlucky to burn twice, he said. "Leaves fallin', dead men callin'," William said. I never knew what it meant, but it had a fine sound of doom about it and I would repeat it over and over again —leaves falling, dead men calling. And after a week of raking, after the last leaf had torn itself loose from the naked trees, we would light our fire behind the stable, and now the sweet smoke of maple leaves would go up in the back yards all over town. All eastern Canada would be burning leaves then, an autumn custom, a universal rite.

Alas, there are no maple leaves where I live now on the western coast. There are oak leaves only—very superior in quality, of much better substance and fertilizing value when rotted down, but they lack the fragrance of the maple leaves and they contain no memories for me. We pile the oak leaves methodically but with none of the old pleasure. We watch them stream off the trees in October like a brown blizzard, while the white gulls beat in from the angry sea. We watch the leaves scampering across the fields, children who have just left their mother. We see them pouring down the rocks in torrents like molten bronze, and piling up in the ditches, imprisoned now, their brief flight over. We stride through them to hear them crackle, but they lack the perfect crisp sound, the whisper and chuckle of the maple leaves.

Slowly the oak leaves rot down, and

for two or three years in the great pile they still preserve their shape, closely packed together and thin now as tissue paper. Presently they have turned to dry powdery compost, the richest soil known, precious, every ounce of it, for growing plants, and the gardener rubs it thoughtfully between his fingers.

We dig down through the stratification of the leaf pile, through the new leaves, through the closely packed leaves of last year, the half-rotten leaves of the previous year, and finally into the black compost of antiquity. Each year has its own vintage. Each layer preserves some little relic of its passage. Near the top a baseball bat belonging to the little boy from next door, buried in the billows of October. Lower down, the wheel of a tricycle which was lost two years ago. In the next layer a toy canoe, with a wooden Indian in it, his feather war bonnet gone. In the last layer a little tin plate, diamond-shaped, which was used to mold cakes in the sandpile. All the history of those years when Robin was growing is written in the stratification of the leaf pile. We will remember oak leaves.

All the memories of Canadian childhood are thus held for most of us in autumn leaves. The sight of them fluttering down from the trees makes us think of the old days in Ontario, in Quebec, and the Maritimes. The maple leaf is Canada's emblem not by any official choice, not for its beauty of scarlet color, but for its memories, its place in our lives. We like to go back to the old provinces in the autumn and smell the leaf smoke and remember when we were young and awoke to see the leaves fluttering down in the back yard, on the village street. Leaves falling, dead men calling.

Comprehension Test. Take this test. In each item, mark a check (✔) at the left of the correct choice.

1. At the author's home in Ontario, the leaves that turned yellow and then scarlet in the autumn were
   (A) maple leaves
   (B) birch leaves
   (C) oak leaves

2. When the author as a boy saw autumn leaves thick upon the ground, he liked best
   (A) to kick his feet through them
   (B) to hear them rustle and swish
   (C) to roll in them

3. Old William would not set the leaves on fire until all the leaves had fallen because he believed that building more than one leaf fire might
   (A) damage the trees
   (B) bring bad luck
   (C) burn the children

4. When old William said, "Leaves fallin', dead men callin'," the author
   (A) hated to hear it because it meant nothing to him
   (B) liked to repeat it but never knew what it meant
   (C) liked to think about it because he knew what it meant

5. The author dislikes the oak leaves where he now lives because they
   (A) lack the fragrance and memories of maple leaves
   (B) make poorer fertilizer than did the maple leaves
   (C) are harder to rake and pile than are maple leaves

6. The oak leaves differ from the maple leaves because the oak leaves
   (A) fall from the trees in scarlet instead of brown torrents
   (B) scamper across the fields and pile up in ditches

(C) make a crackling instead of a whispering sound when walked through

7. After three years the rotting oak leaves in the great pile turn into a dry powdery compost that is
   (A) the richest soil known
   (B) the cheapest soil known
   (C) the longest-lasting soil known

8. As the author dug down through the many layers making up the leaf pile and found different parts of children's toys, he was most like
   (A) a geologist
   (B) an archeologist
   (C) an anthropologist

9. At the deepest layer of the leaf pile, the author found this "relic" of a toy:
   (A) A tricycle wheel
   (B) A baseball bat
   (C) A little tin plate

10. The author likes to return to the old provinces to see the autumn leaves and to smell them burning because they
    (A) bring back pleasant memories of his boyhood
    (B) make him wish he were a boy again
    (C) remind him of the years when his son was growing up

The correct answers are: (9-C; 10-A)
(1-A; 2-A; 3-B; 4-B; 5-A; 6-C; 7-A; 8-B;

Vocabulary Test. In each item read the first word. Then find the word at the right that has the same meaning. Draw a line under that word.

1. doom: (A) unhappy fate (B) uncertainty (C) sad past
2. universal: (A) unusual (B) civilized (C) general
3. rite: (A) correction (B) pleasure (C) ceremony

4. scampering: (A) running quickly (B) stealing slyly (C) skipping slowly
5. compost: (A) fence post (B) fertilizer (C) gravel
6. stratification: (A) many layers (B) many places (C) many satisfactions
7. antiquity: (A) old age (B) ancient times (C) modern days
8. relics: (A) rotting leaves (B) ruins (C) memories
9. billows: (A) large pillows (B) strong winds (C) great waves
10. emblem: (A) great honor (B) familiar sign (C) maple leaf

The correct answers are: (9-C; 10-B)
(1-A; 2-C; 3-C; 4-A; 5-B; 6-A; 7-B; 8-B;

Do general reading exercise 18 (page 281)

In the article in this exercise, concentrate closely on what you are reading. Try to lift your rate, comprehension, and vocabulary scores to the highest levels possible.

After you complete the general reading exercise, answer these questions: Did I like the story, "To Walk Alone"? Why? Have I ever had feelings like those expressed by the author? What were these feelings? How did the doctor help the author to get back on her feet?

"To Walk Alone" is from *Today's Health,* published by the American Medical Association, Chicago. You may want to read other articles that appear in this interesting and important monthly magazine.

You may also want to read such books as *You and Psychiatry,* by William C. Menninger and Munro Leaf; *Psychiatry in a Troubled World,* by William C. Menninger; *Fight Against Fear,* by Lucy Freeman; and *The Snake Pit,* by Mary Jane Ward. These books deal with the prevention and treatment of mental illness.

If you read magazine articles and books in the field of mental health, they will help you to get balance both in your read- ing and in your personal life. These materials will also aid you in becoming a mature reader, which is discussed next.

LESSON 19

How can you become a mature reader?

Are there not some pursuits that we practice because they are good in themselves, and some pleasures that are final? And is not this among them? I have sometimes dreamt, at least, that when the Day of Judgment dawns and the great conquerors and lawyers and statesmen come to receive their laurels, their names carved indelibly upon imperishable marble—the Almighty will turn to Peter and will say, not without a certain envy when He sees us coming with our books under our arms, "Look, these need no reward. We have nothing to give them here. They have loved reading."[1]

IN THIS SELECTION, Virginia Woolf pointed out one of the characteristics of the mature reader. He loves reading—and he finds that reading brings its own rich rewards.

As you have read more and more and with increasing effectiveness through using this book, you, too, have undoubtedly

[1]From *The Common Reader*, by Virginia Woolf. Copyright, 1925, by the author. Published by Harcourt, Brace, and Company, Inc., New York. Reprinted with permission of the publisher.

realized that reading yields great satisfactions—satisfactions that can come from no other source. And as you have developed your reading skills and have learned to balance your reading program, you have discovered that you were becoming a more mature reader.

To be a mature reader, you will have to continue your efforts to improve your reading skills and to read more widely. You will also have to acquire other important reading abilities including those that this lesson will emphasize. These abilities will contribute further to your personal and social growth. And they will add to the knowledge and enjoyment that you can get from reading.

Learn to "read between the lines"

A mature reader gets not only the direct meanings but also the indirect meanings of what he reads. This ability to obtain indirect or implied meanings is often referred to as "reading between the lines."

As an example, here are two lines from Shakespeare's play, *Hamlet:*

Polonius: What do you read, my lord?
Hamlet: Words, words, words.

To read between these lines, you will have to read the part of the play in which they occur. From that reading, you will find that, in his reply, Hamlet did not mean what he was saying. Rather, he was making fun of Polonius whom he did not respect. And he was probably going through the motions of reading while thinking of how to avenge the murder of his father.

You can develop the ability to read between the lines by thoughtful consideration of different kinds of reading materials —novels, plays, and poetry, for example. If you have and use this ability, you will get much more from your reading. You will understand better what the author is trying to tell you. You will project your own personal meanings into what he has written. And you will have "a residue of meanings"—ideas that you will recall again and again.

To obtain practice in reading for implied meanings, do the exercise given next.

An exercise in "reading between the lines"

The article, "To Walk Alone," on page 281, contains materials that provide an opportunity for you to read between the lines. Read the article again, looking for the implied meanings. Then take this test. In each item, mark a check (✔) at the left of the correct choice.

1. What did the author imply in the first three paragraphs?
   (A) She was trying to escape from an earthquake.
   (B) She was wishing to commit suicide.
   (C) She was having a nervous breakdown.

2. What did she imply by the next three paragraphs? With the doctor's help, she was able
   (A) to rebuild the foundations of her life
   (B) to clean out the basement of her house
   (C) to strengthen the foundations of her home

3. In the paragraphs dealing with the nursery, what did the author imply?
   (A) She had to imagine herself as a child before growing up.
   (B) She had to get rid of childish ways of thinking, feeling, and acting.
   (C) She had to throw away childhood toys and books.

4. In the paragraphs about her clothing and jewelry, what did the author imply?
   (A) She had to be herself and to develop her own talents.
   (B) She had to get a new dress and accessories before going out into the world.
   (C) She had to keep in mind what her friends thought of her.

5. In the last paragraphs of the story, what did the author imply?
   She was well mentally when she was able
   (A) to depend upon the doctor only once a year
   (B) to leave the city and start a new life
   (C) to manage her own life

Here are the answers that we believe the author implied. Compare them with your answers. (1-C; 2-A; 3-B; 4-A; 5-C)

Read challenging materials

Someone has said: "You are what you eat." In a way, this statement applies to what you read.

If you are a mature reader, you gain information and pleasure from books, magazine articles, and newspaper stories that challenge your thinking and broaden your horizons. You continue to grow through reading.

If you are an immature reader, you may find some pleasure in reading, but you continue to read materials that tend to limit both your thinking and your outlook. For example, if you are an immature reader, you read nothing but the comics, or you read only murder mysteries or love stories. In both cases, your reading adds little, if anything, to your growth.

There is, of course, nothing wrong with reading comics, mysteries, or similar kinds of materials. They are, in fact, sources of enjoyment to many people during their leisure. But if you restrict your reading to such materials, you will *not* become increasingly mature either as a reader or as a person.

To be a mature person, you must from time to time read books and magazines of good quality. In reading these challenging materials, you have an opportunity to examine new and important ideas, and to appreciate the best in writing style.

An exercise in reading challenging materials

You have probably heard the expression: "I'm just too old to learn." This statement is sometimes made by an adult who is no longer in school. But is such a person really too old to learn? The answer to this question is found in the following selection from a book by a well-known authority. Read the selection rapidly but with understanding. Then take the test that follows it.

CAN ADULTS LEARN?[2]

by H. A. Overstreet

IN 1928, EDWARD THORNDIKE published a book, *Adult Learning*, which reversed a long established assumption: namely, that childhood is the time of learning; that adulthood is the time of *having learned*.

Because of this ancient assumption the educational energies of the American people had been largely expended on the building of public schools for children and young people. The hope was that if all the young of America could be educated, the destinies of a democratic nation would be made secure. Where the young were not properly schooled, they were commonly taken to be "lost" so far as their education was concerned: adult minds were too old and stiff to be learning-minds. The accepted pronouncement was that you can't teach an old dog new tricks.

The establishment of adult education in America did not wait upon psychological research. Here, as in every other field, there were individuals of creative insight who saw in human nature much that was concealed from the average view. Even before Thorndike conducted his investigations and published his book, many pioneering ventures had grown up to independent strength and had federated into an American adult education movement. But again it was the psychologist who gave the scientific basis for what had already been done by trial and error; and it was the psychologist who so set forth facts regarding the *how* and *why* of adult learning that those facts could become naturalized in the common mind.

Based on an exhaustive examination of psychological data and on various specifically devised experiments with adult

[2]Reprinted from *The Mature Mind* by H. A. Overstreet. By permission of W. W. Norton and Co., Inc. Copyright 1949 by W. W. Norton and Co.

groups, Thorndike's book announced as its established conclusion the fact that adults can learn. "In general, nobody under forty-five should restrain himself from trying to learn anything because of a belief or fear that he is too old to be able to learn. Nor should he use that fear as an excuse for not learning anything which he ought to learn. If he fails in learning it, inability due directly to age will very rarely, if ever, be the reason."[3]

The actual reason why adults do not see themselves as learners, he pointed out, is that factors either *within themselves* or *within their culture* place certain obstacles in the way. The factors *within themselves* may be various: a lack of aptitude for learning the particular subject undertaken; a desire too weak to establish proper attention-habits where the habits are absent; ignorance of how to set about learning; habits, ideas, or emotional tendencies that block the learning experience. Obstacles *within the culture* arise from the *unusualness* of adult study: from the fact that the enterprise of organized learning lies outside the accustomed pattern of adult life. There is the possibility of ridicule; of being made conspicuous by "going to school" when grown ups are supposed to be through with school; loneliness in an experience that was a companionable one during the years of childhood; of being thought inferior or stupid by seeming to need to study at an age when study is presumed to have been accomplished. It is, Thorndike established once for all, factors like these—personal and cultural—that discourage adult learning. It is not adulthood itself.

For a people who had placidly accepted the immaturity of non-learning, this was a sharp alert. If adults did not learn, it was not the fault of nature. To justify the dying back of their brains by the fact that they were grown men and women would no longer do. Where there was aliveness of interest and purpose, "growing old" might mean growing wiser in mind and character. It might also mean growing more informed in matters relating to personal and common welfare.

As other psychologists and educators have carried further what Thorndike began, it has become increasingly apparent, not only that adults can learn, but that it is a threat to our whole society to have them stop learning, to have them become fixed in an unhappy or a complacent unchangeability in a world where they are constantly confronted by the problem of change. "This is an age . . . of rapid evolution and sometimes revolution in politics and economics as well as technology. Facts and ideas that were right yesterday may be wrong or completely irrelevant today. An adult who ceases after youth to unlearn and relearn his facts and to reconsider his opinions is like a blindfolded person walking into a familiar room where someone has moved the furniture. Furthermore he is a menace to a democratic community. One of the consequences of a rapidly changing world is that there is a much more important job for adult education than ever before. In fact, adult education in these days should rank in importance with elementary, secondary, and college education."[4]

Here, then, is a psychological contribution to the *maturity concept*. Whether or not old dogs can learn new tricks, old human beings can—and must—learn new facts and insights as long as they live.

---

[3]Edward L. Thorndike, *Adult Learning*, p. 177. New York: The Macmillan Company.

[4]Eugene Staley, "Knowledge for Survival," in *California Journal of Elementary Education*, November 1947, p. 96.

Take this test on the selection you have just read. In each item, mark a check (✔) at the left of the correct choice.

1. According to Edward Thorndike, a psychologist, nearly all adults
   (A) are too old to learn
   (B) can learn if they wish to
   (C) learn more slowly than young people

2. Through scientific studies, psychologists have discovered
   (A) *why* and *how* adults learn
   (B) *when* and *where* adults learn
   (C) *what* and *if* adults learn

3. Adults do not see themselves as learners because of personal factors and because of cultural factors. Mark a P before each *personal* factor; mark a C before each *cultural* factor.
   (A) Fear of ridicule for being "a student"
   (B) Lack of ability to learn a given subject
   (C) A weak desire to acquire new learning habits
   (D) Fear of being thought of as inferior or stupid
   (E) Ignorance of how to start learning something
   (F) Lack of companions about the same age

4. Adults should feel that, as they are growing older, they can
   (A) learn more and more from their children
   (B) understand more things without studying them
   (C) become better informed and wiser

5. According to the selection, an adult who stops learning is
   (A) a person who has had enough education
   (B) a menace to our democratic society

(C) a good student in the school of experience

Here are the correct answers:

(1-B; 2-A; 3-AC, BP, CP, DC, EP, FC; 4-C; 5-B)

Read to understand yourself and your world

By reading good books and magazine articles, you can learn to understand yourself better. This will help you to become a more mature person.

If you are a young person, you can read such booklets as *Understanding Yourself*, *How To Live With Parents*, and *Getting Along with Others*. These are among the *Life Adjustment Booklets* published by Science Research Associates.

Regardless of your age, you can get a better understanding of human behavior and history by reading such good books as these:

1. *A Study of History*, by Toynbee
2. *The Golden Bough*, by Frazer
3. *Leaves of Grass*, by Whitman
4. *Abraham Lincoln*, by Sandburg
5. *Moby Dick*, by Melville
6. *Don Quixote*, by Cervantes
7. *Rise of American Civilization*, by Beard
8. *Tom Jones*, by Fielding
9. *Crime and Punishment*, by Dostoevski
10. *Red Badge of Courage*, by Crane

You can obtain the titles of other good books by examining the lists on pages 174-181, by reading current book reviews, and by consulting your librarian.

An exercise in reading to understand yourself

To know yourself better, you should not only recognize your interests, abilities, and needs, but you should also see your-self in relation to the world about you—past and present. Sometimes this increased understanding comes from reading a novel like that from which the following selection was taken.

Read the selection quickly and thoughtfully. Then take the test on it.

THE LEFT HAND IS THE DREAMER[5]
by Nancy Wilson Ross

THE DAY AFTER CHRISTOPHER left for Washington to try for the Air Corps, Fredericka, at three o'clock in the afternoon, entered Room 21, Henley Hall, in Attica Center, and slid quietly into the nearest chair. The lecture had already begun. Before her was the man whom her father's old friend, Dr. Cooper, had recommended as a stimulating instructor in world history.

He was a thin man, handsome in a grave way, with dark skin, dark hair noticeably gray at the temples, and eyes concealed behind heavy-rimmed glasses. An Austrian, Dr. Cooper had told her. His name was Franz Allers. His hands, as he spoke, were clasped behind him, his head thrust forward, turning now toward his class, now away from it, as he paced the platform. He spoke clearly but with a pronounced foreign accent.

Studying him in those first moments Fredericka saw that he was serious about his lectures. There was a tenseness in his long, thin frame. The way he stood, it looked almost as if he hoped, by concentrating his muscles, by sheer physical force, to draw up from the well of his being the thought he now offered his students.

"And so," he was saying in a voice that managed, in spite of his posture, to

be casual, "as I told you at the beginning of this course, from time to time we shall digress and talk a little about man as he exists outside the present history books. For this is a class in history—but what is history?"

He stopped and looked hopefully at his students as though expecting some sudden illumination to break upon them. The girl seated beside Fredericka took advantage of this interval to draw out a pocket mirror, blow on it, look at herself critically, lick her lips, and return the mirror to her pocket, after which she hastily scribbled on a fresh page in her notebook: HISTORY: *what is it?* and then added her own name in large letters at the top.

"History," Dr. Allers repeated, pacing again. "What is history? Is it events, dates of statesmen and battles? Is it William of Orange, the Council of Trent, the years 1492 and 1776? Or is it cave paintings, test tubes, the visions of saints? Is it the quantum theory, the last words of Socrates, the martyrdom of Freud, Elizabethan lyrics? Is it Roman law?. . ."

He paused again. Was he actually waiting for them to answer? No one spoke. Looking around her nervously, with the feeling that the class must not fail the earnest man before them, Fredericka could see that the students were used to this type of rhetorical question from Dr. Franz Allers. They took it calmly, almost indifferently. Their pencils waited, like that of the girl beside her, poised in readiness for the ponderable fact.

"Today," he was now saying, "we go on a little journey with a postage stamp and a penny, thanks to the suggestion of Sir James Jeans."

Franz Allers took a penny and a stamp in either hand and held them up to the class to view. "With these we set out

[5]Adapted from *The Left Hand Is The Dreamer*, by Nancy Wilson Ross. Copyright, 1947, by Nancy Wilson Ross. Published by William Sloane Assoc., Inc., New York. Reprinted by permission of the author.

to climb Cleopatra's Needle where we lay the penny flat, with the postage stamp on top."

Fredericka observed for the first time on the blackboard a sketch of the Needle, beside a mountain drawn to scale. Allers half turned and nodded at the board.

"The height of this obelisk we are taking to represent the time that has elapsed since the earth was born. The thickness of the postage stamp represents the time man lived in an uncivilized state."

"Now we take postage stamp number two, and we lay it on top of the first. It now represents the next five thousand years of civilization. Then we just keep on sticking postage stamps on top of one another—which unfortunately I do not have—until we have built a pile as high as Mont Blanc." Again he nodded toward the drawings on the board.

"Even when the postage stamps reach the height of that great mountain, we are not near the length of the future which astronomy leads us to expect civilized humanity will enjoy. The penny and stamp together represent the time man has lived on earth. Postage stamp number one was the past of civilization. Postage stamp number two is the next five thousand years. The column of stamps higher than Mont Blanc is humanity's future."

He stopped, measuring their response, then went on: "Or, to put it another way, the first postage stamp is man's achievement so far; the pile higher than Mont Blanc represents what he may achieve if his future development is proportional to the time he presumably has on earth."

The pencils were flying automatically over the notebooks.

"Don't try to write this down," he said rather sternly as he looked over his glasses at the class. "It's all on the board. You can copy it down word for word later.

Just relax!" He grinned suddenly. "Relax and think!"

His grin was young, Fredericka decided. The front view, with the black shock of hair, was ten years the junior of the graying profile.

"I merely want to jolt you a little, if possible," he said, "into seeing your responsibility. I also want to give you hope—if you need hope."

Did they need hope? The jaws in front of Fredericka were moving rhythmically with gum. The hair of the girls was hidden under similar kerchiefs of bright color, their raincoats all the same cut and make. The girls were dressed with a monotonous uniformity and with a certain sloppy ease more pronounced than she remembered costumes from her own student days. . . There were also more men than she had expected to find in a war year. 4Fs, she supposed, though there was a sprinkling of boys in uniform who must be taking the course by special permission, for surely there was nothing here to help them in manning a PT boat, firing a machine gun, or making a beachhead over coral.

So here she was! And the grave dark foreigner whose wife had been murdered and who had gone to pieces and put himself together again was saying, "Yes, man is a dust speck measured against space and time." He stopped, while with his thumb and middle finger he measured man, the dust speck.

"A dust speck!" he repeated. "Yet when man sees this to be true, his faith and self-respect must increase, considering what he has achieved in only a breath of world time."

As he said the last words his voice dropped a little and he paused. He seemed to be running his mind over the achievements of man. Fredericka tried to summon her own list of human attainments. She saw the Sistine Chapel, sulfa drugs, the wheel, the arch, and a stratosphere plane. . . It was not a very convincing assemblage and she was about to try again when Franz Allers continued abruptly:

"But man, Western man, is what you Americans call a 'nervous wreck.' This is a danger signal. It is not just an outgrowth of war, this increasing tension. It was here well before the last two wars. It is a danger signal because it arises in part from man's placing the sensations of his own ego at the center of the universe. Perhaps we should try a displacement of some kind—old Chinese style, perhaps, where man is small against nature."

Up came the puzzled faces. The pencils hung again poised. *Chinese style: Nature vs. man*, wrote Fredericka's neighbor. She added a large firm question mark.

Dr. Allers dismissed his example of the Chinese with a quick impatient gesture, a gesture which had in it all his awareness of the gaps in his audience's knowledge.

"No matter," he said almost sharply, signifying, Don't, for goodness sake, make a note of it! Don't question me later! . . . "No matter!" he repeated. "Forget the Chinese for now."

He took a paper from the desk and began to read aloud:

" 'Man is the intermediary between the great world and the small world. On the one hand he can observe the planets, on the other the atoms. In time, without question, man will know the control of the atom, and even perhaps visit other planets. Your funny-paper heroes, your comic-strip dreams, your magazines of pseudo science on cheap paper are the prophets of these things to come. Man as observer brings into focus and meaning things as far apart as atoms and planets. In a sense he unites them in his own person because of the wonderful instruments of perception that he possesses with which to observe and evaluate them.' "

He put down the paper and stared straight at the class. "Instruments of perception . . ."

Fredericka's attention wandered once more. Then she brought herself firmly back to the man on the platform before her. She had apparently lost some important link while her thoughts dipped into the past, for he was saying: "The East, the Orient, has one great thing to teach us—that logic does not apply to life itself. The East can accept contradictions, or what we Westerners call contradictions, without even recognizing that that is what it does. It can, for instance, accept holy men who have miraculous powers of healing and prophecy and who yet live lives of nonmorality by our standards. To the East this is not necessarily a contradiction. To us in the West it is very baffling."

"Yes, it is baffling." His voice, his half-grin, recognized the bafflement on the faces before him. "Very baffling!" he repeated.

He went on to say how the West wants things cut and dried: the good are good, the bad are bad; Hitler is the Antichrist while every Allied soldier is an expression of the highest virtue. "Yet Hitler too is a man—one of us." He paused, faced the class, let it sink in. "From what did he spring? From us! And the Allied soldier, he too is what all men are—he is man, half way between ape and angel," he repeated.

He paused, a long pause, standing behind his desk, cupping one fist in the palm of the other hand, repeating the motion a half dozen times slowly, as though deciding whether to continue. Then abruptly, his tone stronger:

"If I were to read to you psychiatric reports about soldiers who have broken in battle, you would find human creatures —shocked into unconsciousness, into loss of memory by days of strafing without shelter, by too many scenes of horror— ceasing to act like men, in some cases reverting to an apelike state, the walk simian, shoulders down, arms hanging long and loose, wide shuffling gait. I have seen them."

Briefly he moved like an ape to illustrate. It was not humorous. No one laughed. It might have struck them as funny, but it didn't. The man was too earnest.

"Also they lose the power of speech." He was leaning on the desk now. (The preacher, Fredericka thought again.) "Fear and horror," he was saying, "have projected them back that small space of world time to the state of an apelike ancestor. Also, frequently, a traumatized soldier—shell-shocked, as we used to say —returns to infancy. He drools, blubbers, slobbers, loses control of his sphincter muscles, soils himself . . ."

He had now, at last, his class's full attention. This was something dramatic, a picture they could all understand, something that reached into all their lives— the effect of battle on a human being. The silence in the room was impressive.

"These examples," Allers continued— and now his accent was more marked, his placing of words a little foreign, as though the deeper he felt the less control he had of his speech—"do you know what they to me say? They say that this creature, this so-called animal, is in reality a being of the greatest delicacy and sensitivity. War is not natural to him, as always we are being told it is. Normal man has

an essential deep recoil from the act of murder. One proof—if proof you wish —is this: soldiers have been known to lose the entire use of the hand and arm with which they have killed another man. Yes, an enemy, to be sure, but still *another man*, at close range, looking into his frightened, equally reluctant eyes . . ."

His voice had grown thick. He stopped. There was a long pause. He had the class on his side now. Fredericka could sense it. But he did not let emotion mount. He resumed his former unimpassioned tone. His accent improved as he said quietly:

"Of course I hope I do not need to stress that there are times when man must fight. Obviously! We have not yet progressed beyond it. If we do not see danger in time to prevent the purchase of the gun, then we must strike when the gun is drawn on us."

He walked back to the desk, looked down for a moment at the papers in a nearsighted, abstracted way as though trying to remember where he had digressed.

"Logic, I have said, does not apply to life itself. Life is something else again."

He took off his glasses and held them out in front of him, revealing remarkable eyes, intense, remote, yet full of a desperate question: How can I say it, any of it, any of what I know so terribly to be true?

"It is here," he said aloud in a slow deliberate voice, "that man faces his greatest paradox—one of the great riddles. For the human mind has a passion for unification, for getting things neatly tagged and named, classified, filed away for handy reference under certain large simple labels. Nature, on the other hand, exhibits an equally ardent passion for multiplication, novelty, uniqueness, surprises, inconsistencies. . . . So, man, the poor devil . . ."

It's too much for me, Fredericka said

to herself. It's like concentrated food offered suddenly to a starving man. Now I realize how shut-off, how vacuumlike, my life has become. She looked around the class. The other students did not seem to find Franz Allers' remarks too much to swallow. Their minds, hitched to their pencils, moved along easily over what was to her totally unfamiliar and challenging material. Were their minds, being younger, more plastic, more agile? Or was it that, like all young people, ideas were just ideas to them and none seemed more important, more illuminating than any other? —whereas Fredericka knew she could ponder a single one of these statements for days: "Logic does not apply to life . . . . Life is something else again . . . . Accept contradictions . . ."

The ideas she had heard in the past hour began to go around in her head with uncomfortable dizzying speed.

I'm too old to begin this kind of course, she thought. It will exhaust me. I feel tired already. Why should I bother at my age? She deliberately closed her eyes and ears and rested.

When she listened again Franz Allers was winding to a finish, preparing to give the students something to take away that would not too greatly trouble or perplex them. She opened her eyes swiftly when he cried:

"Here one is!"

"Here one is!" he was saying, throwing out his arms, staring down at his legs in their dark trousers as though they were separate objects. "Here am I! A marvelously subtle and intricate mechanism with blood stream and lungs, cells and nerves, a face, hands, arms, ten toes and fingers, and all the rest of it, and we do not shout with amazement at the sight and thought of it. Instead we sit down with

the thing and grow heavy and die thirty years before we are buried."

"I am alive," he said solemnly. "You are alive. No, do not laugh. It is a sober thought. It carries grave responsibility. It is also a wonderful thought. To some of us—European—it is a thought of the greatest mystery and wonder. I am still alive! It makes us at once supremely elated and supremely sad. . . . Class is dismissed."

Take this test. In each item, mark a check (✔) at the left of the correct choice.

1. During his lecture, Dr. Allers was trying to get his students to think mainly about man and
   (A) his inhumanity to fellow man
   (B) his place in the universe
   (C) his greatness in time and space

2. Fredericka noticed that at first the other students in the class were doing
   (A) more note-taking than thinking
   (B) more whispering than listening
   (C) more thinking than note-taking

3. In Dr. Allers' talk he used each of the following things to represent a period in history or man's achievement during that period. To show how he used these things, match the items in List I with those in List II. There is one extra item in List I.

LIST I

(A) A height greater than that of Mont Blanc
(B) The thickness of the second stamp
(C) The thickness of the penny
(D) The thickness of the first stamp
(E) The height of Cleopatra's needle

LIST II

(1) The time since the world was born
(2) The time man lived in an uncivilized condition

(3) The time man lived in a civilized state

(4) The time ahead for mankind

4. Dr. Allers said that man's faith in and respect for himself was great and increasing mainly because he was able to

(A) see himself as a dust speck measured against space and time

(B) recover quickly and completely from a mental breakdown

(C) achieve so much in so short a time

5. Western man, stated Dr. Allers, has become a "nervous wreck" chiefly because he has

(A) placed his ego at the center of the universe

(B) gone through two world wars in 31 years

(C) invented the wheel, sulfa drugs, and so many other things

6. Man is able to understand the great world (the planets) and the small world (the atoms) because he has within himself

(A) the imagination required to create "superman" and science fiction

(B) the ability to see man as a part of nature

(C) the instruments needed to observe and evaluate

7. Dr. Allers pointed out that Eastern man accepted things that seemed to be

(A) contradictory to Western man

(B) distasteful to Western man

(C) harmonious to Western man

8. Dr. Allers said that psychiatrists reported that soldiers who broke down in battle often did *three* things:

(A) They remembered everything they had done as children.

(B) They shuffled along with their arms hanging loosely.

(C) They climbed trees and swung from the limbs.

(D) They lost their memories and their power of speech.

(E) They behaved like very young infants.

(F) They wanted to return to the battle right away.

9. According to Dr. Allers, a normal man

(A) likes to kill another man

(B) hates to kill another man

(C) should never fight

10. Man's greatest paradox is this:

(A) Man tries to unify things but nature does not.

(B) Man is always working against nature.

(C) Man attempts to master but not to enslave nature.

11. Fredericka found that she had to think for some time about what Dr. Allers had said mainly because

(A) she had not been in college for years

(B) the other students swallowed his ideas without question

(C) his ideas were so new and challenging

12. At the end of the lecture, Dr. Allers tried to make his students feel that man is

(A) a cruel, foolish, and dead creature

(B) a wonderful, mysterious, and alive creature

(C) a happy, go-lucky, intelligent creature

The correct answers are: (1-B; 2-A; 3-A(4), B(3), D(2), E(1); 4-C; 5-A; 6-C; 7-A; 8-B, D, E; 9-B; 10-A; 11-C; 12-B)

Read thoughtfully good materials

During this week and next, concentrate

on reading at least one good book and several good magazine articles. Select materials that are somewhat more difficult than those you usually read. In studying these materials, read between the lines to get the meanings implied by the author and to think about what you are reading. As you read these materials in a mature way, this will help you to grow both as a reader and as a person.

Do not be discouraged if you do not make rapid progress toward becoming a mature reader. But you can work toward this goal by carrying out the additional suggestions given next. First, talk with others about what you have read. And second, write out your own reactions to what you have read. Start by discussing with your friends the selections, "Can Adults Learn?" and "The Left Hand Is The Dreamer." Then write your comments on each of these selections.

When the mature person comes across a book that challenges his thinking, he not only reads it, but he usually wants to discuss it. And frequently he wants to write something about it. Thus, as Francis Bacon (1561-1626) said:

"Reading maketh a full man, conference a ready man, and writing an exact man."

Do general reading exercise 19 (page 286)

Try to read Article 19 at a much faster rate than you read previous articles. You should be able to do this because the article is both humorous and easy to read.

After you complete this reading exercise, study your rate, comprehension, and vocabulary scores. Were these scores higher than ever before? Was your rate at least 300 words a minute? Was your comprehension at least 17 (85 percent) of the 20 test items? Was your vocabulary at least 8 (80 percent)? If your answer to each of these questions is "Yes," you have reached a fairly high level of reading competence. But you should continue your efforts to improve your reading, as the next lesson will emphasize.

LESSON 20

How can you keep on reading better?

Read my little fable:
  He that runs may read.
Most can raise the flowers now,
  For all have got the seed.

THIS IS STANZA 5 of "The Flower" by the famous English poet, Alfred, Lord Tennyson (1809-1892). In it the author pointed out something that applies to your reading.

You have completed 19 lessons in this book. Through them, you "have got the seed"—better reading skills, habits, and attitudes. With these, you "can raise the flowers"—greater knowledge and enjoyment from reading.

You have become a better reader in many ways, as the information given next will indicate.

You have made progress in your reading

Since you started this book, you have developed many important reading abilities. For example, you have learned:

1. To determine what your reading needs are and how to meet them
2. To read for a purpose and to adapt your reading to that purpose

3. To read faster and faster without loss in comprehension
4. To skim for a general impression or for a specific fact
5. To find the main idea in what you are reading
6. To do careful detailed reading for understanding and for recall
7. To evaluate what you are reading
8. To appreciate many kinds of creative writing
9. To do study-type reading more effectively
10. To build and improve your vocabulary
11. To locate and use the reading materials you want
12. To become a better balanced and a more mature reader

You have measured many of your reading gains. For example, you have taken many tests of your reading speed and comprehension. And you have done the general reading exercises. Through these exercises, you tested your reading rate, comprehension, and vocabulary. You then recorded the scores that you made on the graphs in this book. These graphs showed you what some of your reading gains were.

You can learn to read even faster and better

No matter how great your reading progress has been, you can almost surely make further gains. To do so, you should work out a reading program, say for the next six months. In planning and carrying out this program, you may find the following suggestions helpful.

1. *Identify your reading needs and try to meet them.*

To determine your present reading needs, again answer the questions that appear in Lesson 4. Pay particular attention to a question that you answered "No." Keep that question in mind in planning your reading program for the weeks just ahead. Thus you will best fit your program to your reading needs.

2. *Set definite reading goals and work to reach them.*

Your reading goals may include such points as these:

a. Read at least one newspaper daily and at least one city newspaper every Sunday.

b. Read regularly at least one weekly magazine and one monthly magazine.

c. Read at least two books every month —one fiction and one nonfiction.

3. *Find and read the materials you want.*

In selecting books to read, refer again to the list of titles appearing on page 174 through page 181 of this book. You will find that the book titles are organized according to these headings or fields: you and other persons; home, family, and community life; animals; careers; history, government, and current affairs; science and mathematics; drama, poetry, art, music, and religion; entertainment, sports, and fun; interesting people; adventure and travel; how-to-do-it books; bibliographies of good books; and books on reading improvement.

Pick the field in which you are most interested. It may be one or more of the fields just mentioned. Then, in these fields, select the books that you want to read. If your field of interest is science, you may choose *The Sea Around Us*, by Carson. If it is home and family life, you may select *Cheaper By the Dozen*, by Gilbreth and Carey. If you need help in finding a book in your chosen field, a librarian will be glad to assist you.

After you select the titles of two books, get these books and read them. Try to finish these books during the next two weeks. Do this as part of your better reading program.

4. *Keep a record of what you have read.*

You have already made a record of the reading that you have done outside this book. You should continue to keep such a record, at least for several more months.

Instead of making a list of the materials that you have read, you can keep this record on 3x5-inch cards. Such cards are easy to handle and easy to file. As soon as you finish a book or magazine article, you may want to make out a card for it.

On the card, write information like that shown in Figure 2 or Figure 3 on the next page. Note that each card has a description of the content of what was read and a comment on it. In this comment the reader may evaluate the book or article.

FIGURE 2
AN EXAMPLE OF A BOOK CARD

Field: Home Life

Streeter, Edward   *Father of the Bride*

New York: Simon and Schuster, Inc., 1949. Illustrated by Gluyas Williams.

Source: Public Library

Content: This is a humorous account of what a doting father goes through when his daughter marries. The illustrations are just as funny as the story.

Comment: I enjoyed this book. I read it when I felt the need for relaxation. It will make a fine gift to the father of any girl engaged to be married.

FIGURE 3
AN EXAMPLE OF A CARD FOR A MAGAZINE ARTICLE

Field: Science

"Tuberculosis," by James E. Perkins, M.D. *Today's Health,* December 1950, page 22.

Source: School library

Content: Author reports on incidence of TB, yesterday and today; gives methods of diagnosis and treatment. "The death rate from tuberculosis in the United States was cut 85 percent in less than 50 years," he writes. But adds that efforts to control the disease must not be relaxed.

Comment: An interesting and important article.

You can use your book card or your article card to refer again, later, to what you have read. With this card in hand, you can quickly find the book or magazine, or you can help a friend to do so.

You should file your book cards and your magazine article cards according to fields. For example, the book card for *Father of the Bride* would be filed behind the field card marked *Home Life;* the article card for "Tuberculosis," behind the field card marked *Science.*

Because science is such a broad field, you may wish to have separate field cards on each important scientific branch, such as *Astronomy, Atomic Energy, Aviation, Flying Disks,* and *Health.* You would then file the article card for "Tuberculosis" behind the branch card *Health.*

5. *Balance your reading program.*

From time to time, perhaps once a month, look through your book cards and your article cards. Behind the field card that represents your special interest, you will probably have the largest number of book cards and article cards. And that's as it should be. But you should ask: Do the other field cards also have cards filed behind them? If not, you may want to do more reading in some of these fields.

If you read in such fields, you will help balance your reading program. You will make sure that you read books and magazine articles in a variety of fields, not in just one or two fields.

Because newspapers are an important part of a balanced program, you should, as said before, read at least one newspaper every day. In that newspaper, read not only the parts that are most interesting but also the parts that are most important—front-page news stories or editorials, for example.

6. *Get special help if you need or want it.*

You may have been studying this book without any outside help, or you may have been receiving assistance from a reading instructor. If you have studied this book on your own, you have probably improved your reading. But if you have used this book in a course to improve reading, you have probably made larger gains than you would have working alone.

If you have not taken a reading improvement course recently, you may wish to enroll in one. In such a course, you will be aided by the instructor. And you may take standardized reading tests and use modern reading devices and materials.[1]

Some of the main benefits from a reading improvement course are explained in the selection that follows.

A reading exercise about a better reading course

Read the newspaper story quickly and with understanding, and take the test

---

[1]You may, for example, take the *Diagnostic Reading Tests; Survey Section*, or the *SRA Reading Record*, to measure your standing in rate, comprehension, vocabulary, and other skills. You may use the *SRA Reading Accelerator* to help increase your rate and your comprehension. You may employ the *SRA Better Reading Books* to improve your speed and understanding.

that follows it. In the time box, write down your starting time. Then start reading the story.

Time Box

Finishing time	
Starting time	
Reading time	
Reading rate	

MUTUAL LIFE ASSISTING STAFF TO READ FASTER[2]

Hopes to Lift Productivity 25% in Average Work Day
by Thomas J. Costello

COURSES IN SPEED reading given by the management of Mutual Life Insurance Company of New York to its executives, supervisors, and other employees, are expected to be reflected in a 25 per cent increase in productivity in an average working day.

These courses in speed reading have been in session at Mutual for some two months and following completion of the course by fifty employees—five classes, each with ten students—results of the studies indicate strongly that they have considerable merit. The average reading speed of the students at the outset of their studies was 275 words a minute, and at the conclusion of the course their rate had jumped to 420 words a minute, and several students were absorbing as many as 800 words a minute. In addition, officials of Mutual Life have stated, comprehension actually improved as speed increased.

---

[2]From the New York *Herald Tribune*, August 10, 1952. Reprinted with permission of the publisher.

PAPER WORK CHORE CUT

What will such an acceleration in reading speed mean to the company? As far as management-level employees and executives are concerned, the faster rate of reading will cut sharply the time required daily by these top-level workers for reading of their vast amount of paper work. It has been estimated that most top personnel read four and a half hours a day, if they are to keep abreast of their office work, and often four and a half hours are insufficient for the reading of essential publications.

By teaching these workers to speed up their reading while improving their powers of absorption, say by 100 per cent, about two and a quarter hours of their time will be freed for wider reading or other activities. And based on an average working day, the boost in productivity would amount to 25 per cent.

Under the direction of E. Donald Hyer, assistant personnel director of Mutual, in charge of training, and George Ferguson, training specialist of the company's personnel department, the *speed reading course* takes *fifteen hours* over a *ten-day period*. Top-level employees of the insurance company are currently being offered the course because they have more reading to do in their daily work. However, Mutual feels that its entire organization will benefit by the course, both on the job and in leisure activities, so file clerks, statisticians, stenographers, secretaries, and other help will also be offered the course.

READ AGAINST STOP WATCH

Material from conventional books, magazines, and newspapers is used in the exercises and tests in the course. This material is read by students with the aid of a ma-chine known as the "accelerator." A shutter, whose speed can be set anywhere from 100 to more than 2,000 words a minute, moves automatically from the top to the bottom of a page, covering the page line by line, compelling the reader to keep ahead of the shutter and preventing him from regressing, which is a common fault among readers.

Prior to the use of the accelerator, however, students are taught that their eyes can grasp figures and words very rapidly. This is done by the use of another machine known as the "tachistoscope," or flashmeter, which projects numbers or phrases on a screen for 1/100th of a second. After ten minutes of exercise with the flashmeter, students are put to the test on the accelerator, and also read against a stop watch. Following the reading students measure their comprehension at the faster rate by answering questions based on the passages read.

Officials of Mutual feel that the courses will add to the firm's efficiency and that its experiences, with those of others in the field, can contribute importantly to American business as a whole. So enthusiastic is a female member of Mutual's research department, who is working on her doctorate, that she has purchased an accelerator machine to aid her in speeding up her required readings in her college work.

Write your finishing time in the time box. Then take this test. In each item, mark a check (✔) at the left of the correct choice.

1. The management of the life insurance company expects that its reading course will increase the productivity

of its executives and other top-level employees about

(A) 25 percent
(B) 50 percent
(C) 75 percent

2. The 50 employees who took the course increased their reading rate from 275 to 420 words a minute. This increase was about

(A) 25 percent
(B) 50 percent
(C) 100 percent
(D) 125 percent

3. The speed reading course required

(A) 15 hours over a 10-day period
(B) 20 hours over a 15-day period
(C) 30 hours over a 60-day period

4. After completing the reading course, top-level employees were able to do

(A) more and different reading during their limited leisure
(B) their necessary reading with better comprehension and in less time
(C) somewhat less reading than before

5. Students in the course learned to grasp figures and words more rapidly through training with

(A) a tachistoscope or flashmeter
(B) an accelerator or pacing machine
(C) a collection of popular books, magazines, and newspapers

6. The accelerator helped each student to read faster and better because its shutter could be set so that it

(A) hid a whole page of print within a period of 1/100th of a second
(B) presented question after question at an increasingly rapid rate
(C) covered a page at a certain number of words per minute

7. The students measured their gains in comprehension by

(A) counting the number of words or figures read at one flash
(B) reading many conventional books, magazines, and newspapers
(C) answering questions based on what they had just read

8. One employee bought a reading accelerator mainly because she wanted

(A) to do her required college work more efficiently
(B) to help other employees to learn to read faster and better
(C) to increase the effectiveness of her office work

Now figure out your reading time for the story. Change your reading time into your reading rate; use the table given here. Write your reading rate in the time box.

Time-to-Rate Table (636 words)	
Reading time	Reading rate
1:00-1:14	570
1:15-1:29	465
1:30-1:44	393
1:45-1:59	341
2:00-2:14	300
2:15-2:29	269
2:30-2:44	243
2:45-2:59	222
3:00-3:14	204
3:15-3:29	189
3:30-3:44	176
3:45-3:59	164
4:00-4:14	154
4:15-4:29	146
4:30-4:44	138
4:45-4:59	131
5:00-5:14	124
5:15-5:29	119
5:30-5:44	113
5:45-5:59	108
6:00-6:14	104
6:15-6:29	100

For the test, here are the correct answers:

(1-A; 2-B; 3-A; 4-B; 5-A; 6-C; 7-C; 8-A)

You have just read a newspaper story on how a life insurance company is training its employees to read more efficiently. You may now want to write a news story telling how you have improved your own reading since you started using this book.

Keep reading to read better

By doing the 20 lessons in this book, you have completed a reading course. Whether or not you had an instructor to help you, you have almost surely made many gains in your reading abilities. You have determined how rapidly you read and how well you understand what you read. You have acquired many valuable reading skills, habits, and attitudes.

Most important of all, you have learned the ways to improve your reading rate, your comprehension, your vocabulary, and your selection of reading materials.

You should continue to use these reading abilities. If you do *not* use them, you may lose them. Your reading rate may fall off—and so may your comprehension. But if you apply these abilities, you can develop and improve them. And these abilities, as mentioned in Lesson 2, will bring you many significant benefits in school, at home, on the job, and elsewhere.

Through studying this book, you have *become a better reader*. If you keep up your efforts, you can become a still better one—and also a still better person all around. This means that *the improvement of your reading and of yourself in the months and years ahead is mainly up to you.*

Do general reading exercise 20 (page 292)

Because this is the last reading exercise in the book, do your best to make the highest possible reading rate, comprehension score, and vocabulary score.

After you complete this reading exercise, answer these "thought" questions: According to the story, what characteristics did Daniel Boone and the other frontier men and women who were with him have? Do Americans today have the same or similar characteristics? Why do you think so?

If you enjoyed "The Attack on Boonesborough," you may want to read the book *Daniel Boone* from which this story was taken. Although the book combines fact and fiction, it is reasonably accurate historically; and it is well written and illustrated.

Check upon your progress as measured by the general reading exercises

To estimate your reading progress in this book, you can compare the scores you made in the first two exercises with those you made in the last two exercises. How you do this is explained by the example given next.

John finished all 20 of the general reading exercises in this book. He entered his scores, exercise by exercise, in the table at the bottom of page 2 and page 3 of his *Progress Folder*. He then prepared line graphs that pictured these scores. These tables and graphs are reproduced in Figure 4 and Figure 5. Furthermore, John kept a record of his vocabulary scores. John next prepared the worksheet shown in Figure 6.

In studying his reading rate graph (Figure 4), John noticed that although his rates for the articles went up and down, the trend was upward. As shown in John's

FIGURE 4
A TABLE AND GRAPH OF JOHN'S READING RATES

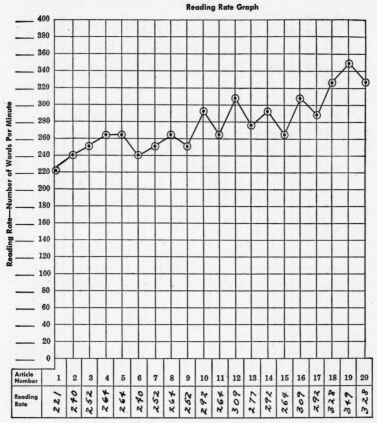

Reading Rate Graph

Article Number	1	2	3	4	5	6	7	8	9	10	11	12	13	14	15	16	17	18	19	20
Reading Rate	221	240	252	264	264	240	252	264	252	292	264	309	277	292	264	309	292	328	347	328

Reading Rate Table

worksheet, Figure 6, he computed his average rate for Article 1 and Article 2, the first two articles he read. This average was 461 divided by two, or 230.5 words per minute. In the same way, John figured out that his average rate for Article 19 and Article 20 was 338.5. His gain in words per minute was 108.0 (338.5 minus 230.5). Finally he computed his percentage gain. First, he divided 108.0 by 230.5; the result was .469. Then he changed this decimal into a percentage—about 47 percent.

In examining his reading comprehen-sion graph (Figure 5), John observed that his comprehension scores went up and down from test to test. He noted, however, that in all the tests his scores were relatively high. Next, he figured that his average score on Test 1 and Test 2 was 16.5; on Test 19 and Test 20, 18.5. His gain was 2.0 (18.5 minus 16.5). Di-viding 2.0 by 18.5, the result was .108, or about 11 percent.

Using his vocabulary scores, John fig-ured out that his average on Test 1 and Test 2 was 7.5; on Test 19 and Test 20,

FIGURE 5
A Table and Graph of John's Reading Comprehension Scores

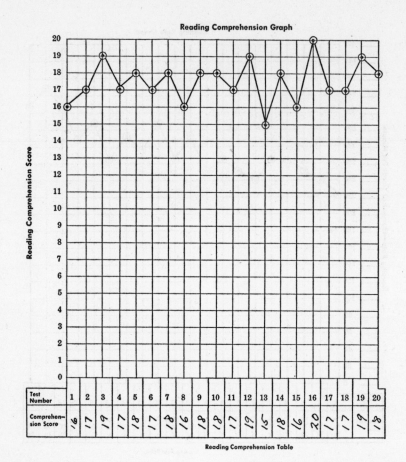

Reading Comprehension Graph

Test Number	1	2	3	4	5	6	7	8	9	10	11	12	13	14	15	16	17	18	19	20
Comprehension Score	16	17	19	17	18	17	18	16	18	18	17	19	15	18	16	20	17	17	19	18

Reading Comprehension Table

8.5. This represented a gain of 1.0, or about 13 percent.

John summed up his progress as determined by his scores on the first two general reading exercises and the last two such exercises. He concluded that he had:

1. Increased his reading rate by 47 percent
2. Increased his comprehension score by 11 percent
3. Increased his vocabulary score by 13 percent

John might have found that while his average rate went up 47 percent, his comprehension score, or his vocabulary score, or both went down slightly. If his average comprehension score was 16 or higher and if his average vocabulary score was 8 or higher as measured by the last two reading exercises, these scores were reasonably high. Therefore, John could rightly conclude that his large gain in reading rate represented a real increase in his ability to get ideas quickly and correctly from what he was reading.

As John did, use the worksheet in Figure 7 to find the average rate, comprehension, and vocabulary scores that you made in the first two general reading exercises and in the last two such exercises. Then figure the percentages of change in these rates and scores. If your percentages are like those obtained by John, they indicate that you have made good progress in your reading.

FIGURE 6
JOHN'S WORKSHEET FOR COMPUTING PERCENTAGE CHANGES BETWEEN EXERCISES 1 AND 2 AND EXERCISES 19 AND 20

Exercise	Rate	Comprehension	Vocabulary
1	221	16	8
2	240	17	7
Total	461	33	15
Average	230.5	16.5	7.5
19	349	19	9
20	328	18	8
Total	677	37	17
Average	338.5	18.5	8.5
Change: Amount	+108.0*	+2.0	+1.0
Change: Proportion	+0.469	+0.108	+0.133
Change: Percent	+47	+11	+13

*A positive change is indicated by a + sign. If a change had been negative, it would have been indicated by a — sign.

FIGURE 7
YOUR WORKSHEET FOR COMPUTING PERCENTAGE CHANGES

Exercise	Rate	Comprehension	Vocabulary
1			
2			
Total			
Average			
19			
20			
Total			
Average			
Change: Amount			
Change: Proportion			
Change: Percent			

BIBLIOGRAPHY

Here is a list of books that you may want to read

Books about you and other persons

Bailard, Virginia and Strang, Ruth M. Ways to Improve Your Personality. New York: McGraw-Hill Book Co., Inc., 1951.

Daly, Sheila J. Blondes Prefer Gentlemen. New York: Dodd, Mead and Co., 1949.

Gallagher, Roswell. You and Your Health. Chicago: Science Research Assoc., Inc., 1950.

Grabbe, Paul and Murphy, Gardner. We Call It Human Nature. New York: Harper and Bros., 1939.

Gumpert, Martin. You and Your Doctor. Indianapolis, Ind.: Bobbs-Merrill Co., 1952.

Lawton, George. How to be Happy Though Young. New York: Vanguard Press Inc., 1949.

Menninger, William C. and Leaf, Munro. You and Psychiatry. New York: Charles Scribner's Sons, 1948.

Overstreet, Harry. The Mature Mind. New York: W. W. Norton and Co., Inc., 1949.

Paulson, Blanche. World of My Making. Chicago: Chicago Board of Education, 1947.

Schacter, Helen. Getting Along With Others. Chicago: Science Research Assoc., Inc., 1949.

Scott, Judith Unger. Manners for Moderns. Philadelphia: Macrae Smith Co., 1949.

Tebbel, John W. Your Body, How to Keep It Healthy, with an Introduction by Morris Fishbein. New York: Harper and Bros., 1951.

Vanderbilt, Amy. Complete Book of Etiquette, A Guide to Gracious Living. Garden City, N. Y.: Doubleday and Co., 1952.

Books about home, family, and community life

Bell, Margaret E. Watch for a Tall White Sail. New York: William Morrow and Co., 1948.

Daly, Maureen. Seventeenth Summer. New York: Dodd, Mead and Co., 1942.

Davies, Valentine. Miracle on 34th Street. New York: Harcourt, Brace and Co., 1947.

Emery, Anne. Going Steady. Philadelphia: Westminster Press, 1950.

Gilbreth, Frank B. and Carey, Ernestine M. G. Cheaper by the Dozen. New York: Thomas Y. Crowell Co., 1948.

Gunther, John. Death Be Not Proud. New York: Harper and Bros., 1949.

Kimbrough, Emily. The Innocents from Indiana. New York: Harper and Bros., 1950.

Lewis, Sinclair. Main Street. New York: Grosset and Dunlap, Inc., 1922.

174

McDonald, Betty. The Egg and I. Philadelphia: J. B. Lippincott Co., 1945.

McKenney, Ruth. Love Story. New York: Harcourt, Brace and Co., 1950.

McKenney, Ruth. My Sister Eileen. New York: Harcourt, Brace and Co., 1938.

McLean, Kathryn. Mama's Bank Account. New York: Harcourt, Brace and Co., 1943.

Moody, Ralph. Little Britches; Father and I Were Ranchers. New York: W. W. Norton and Co., Inc., 1950.

Neagöe, Peter. A Time to Keep. New York: Coward-McCann, Inc., 1949.

Rawlings, Marjorie K. Cross Creek. New York: Charles Scribner's Sons, 1942.

Rose, Anna P. Room for One More. Boston: Houghton Mifflin Co., 1950.

Ross, Nancy Wilson. The Left Hand Is the Dreamer. New York: William Sloane Associates, Inc., 1947.

Streeter, Edward. Father of the Bride. New York: Simon and Schuster, Inc., 1949.

Taber, Gladys. Especially Father. Philadelphia: Macrae Smith Co., 1949.

Tarkington, Booth. Seventeen. New York: Grosset and Dunlap, Inc., 1946.

Toombs, Alfred. Raising a Riot. New York: Thomas Y. Crowell Co., 1949.

Walker, Mildred. Winter Wheat. New York: Harcourt, Brace and Co., 1944.

Yates, Elizabeth. Nearby. New York: Coward-McCann, Inc., 1947.

Books about animals

Anderson, Clarence W. Horses Are Folks. New York: Harper and Bros., 1950.

Anderson, Clarence W. Tomorrow's Champion. New York: Macmillan Co., 1946.

Benchley, Belle (Jennings). My Animal Babies. Boston: Little, Brown and Co., 1945.

Brentano, Francis (ed.). Big Cats, Kings of the Jungle in Fact and Fiction. Chicago: Ziff-Davis Pub. Co., 1949.

Clarke, Frances E. (comp.). Cats—and Cats; Great Cat Stories of Our Day. New York: Macmillan Co., 1937.

Clemens, Samuel L. (Mark Twain, pseud.). A Dog's Tale. New York: Harper and Bros., 1904.

Crawford, Nelson. Cats in Prose and Verse. Drawings by Diane Thorne. New York: Coward-McCann, Inc., 1947.

Ditmars, Raymond L. Strange Animals I Have Known. New York: Harcourt, Brace and Co., 1931.

Dobre, James F. The Mustangs. Boston: Little, Brown and Co., 1952.

Ehrlich, Bettina. A Horse for the Island. New York: Harper and Bros., 1952.

Favorite Stories About Horses and Dogs by Famous Authors. New York: Dial Press, 1935.

Ford, Corey and MacBain, Alastair. A Man of his Own and Other Dog Stories. New York: McGraw-Hill Book Co., Inc., 1949.

Henderson, J. Y. and Taplinger, Richard. Circus Doctor. Boston: Little, Brown and Co., 1951.

James, Will. Smoky, the Cow Horse. New York: Charles Scribner's Sons, 1926.

Joseph, Michael. Charles, the Story of a Friendship. New York: Prentice-Hall, Inc., 1952.

Kellino, Pamela and Mason, James. The Cats in Our Lives. New York: A. A. Wyn, 1949.

Kipling, Rudyard. Collected Dog Stories. Garden City, N. Y.: Doubleday and Co., 1934.

Lintz, Gertrude D. Animals Are My Hobby. New York: R. M. McBride and Co., 1942.

London, Jack. Call of the Wild. New York: Grosset and Dunlap, Inc., 1950.

Mally, Emma L. A Treasury of Animal Stories. New York: Citadel Press, 1946.

Mann, Thomas. A Man and His Dog. New York: Alfred A. Knopf, Inc., 1930.

O'Hara, Mary. My Friend Flicka. Philadelphia: J. B. Lippincott Co., 1941.

Rawlings, Marjorie K. The Yearling. New York: Charles Scribner's Sons, 1940.

Rosman, A. G. Nine Lives; A Cat of London in Peace and War. New York: G. P. Putnam's Sons, 1941.

Self, Margaret C. A Treasury of Horse Stories. New York: A. S. Barnes and Co., 1945.

Van de Water, Frederic F. Members of the Family. New York: John Day Co., Inc., 1946.

Van Vechten, Carl. Lords of the Housetops: Thirteen Cat Tales. New York: Alfred A. Knopf, Inc., 1921.

Van Vechten, Carl. The Tiger in the House. New York: Alfred A. Knopf, Inc., 1936.

Books about careers

Eberle, Irmengarde. Nurse! The Story of a Great Profession. New York: Thomas Y. Crowell Co., 1944.

Hamrin, Shirley A. 4-Square Planning for Your Career. Chicago: Science Research Assoc., Inc., 1948.

Harrington, Ruth L. Your Opportunities in Television. New York: Medill McBride Co., 1949.

Heiser, Victor. An American Doctor's Odyssey. New York: W. W. Norton and Co., Inc., 1936.

Heywood, Anne. There Is a Right Job for Every Woman. Garden City, N. Y.: Doubleday and Co., 1951.

Kamen, Ira and *Dorf, Richard.* TV and Electronics as a Career. New York: John F. Rider, Publisher, Inc., 1951.

Lariar, Lawrence. Careers in Cartooning. New York: Dodd, Mead and Co., 1949.

McGuire, John G. and *Barlow, Howard M.* An Introduction to the Engineering Profession. Cambridge, Mass.: Addison-Wesley Press, 1950.

Moon, George Robert. How to Become a Doctor. Philadelphia: Blakiston Co., 1949.

Murray, Mary. Sky Girl. New York: Duell, Sloan and Pearce, Inc., 1951.

Russell, Sheila M. A Lamp Is Heavy. Philadelphia: J. B. Lippincott Co., 1950.

Sharpe, William. Brain Surgeon. New York: Viking Press, Inc., 1952.

Thruelsen, Richard. Men at Work. New York: Harper and Bros., 1950.

Books about history, government, and current affairs

Allen, Frederick Lewis. The Big Change: America Transforms Itself 1900-1950. New York: Harper and Bros., 1952.

Beard, Charles A. and *Beard, Mary R.* A Basic History of the United States. New York: New Home Library, 1944.

Brown, Ina C. Race Relations in a Democracy. New York: Harper and Bros., 1949.

Chase, Eugene P. The United Nations in Action. New York: McGraw-Hill Book Co., Inc., 1950.

Eisenhower, Dwight D. Crusade in Europe. Garden City, N. Y.: Doubleday and Co., 1948.

Ellis, William D. The Bounty Lands. Cleveland, Ohio: World Pub. Co., 1952.

Fenichell, Stephens. The United Nations: Blueprint for Peace. Philadelphia: John C. Winston Co., 1951.

Findlay, Bruce Allyn and *Findlay, Esther Blair.* Your Rugged Constitution (Textbook Edition). Chicago: Science Research Assoc., Inc., 1952.

Floherty, John J. Our F.B.I.; An Inside Story. Philadelphia: J. B. Lippincott Co., 1951.

Gunther, John. Inside U.S.A. (Rev. ed.) New York: Harper and Bros., 1951.

Mauldin, William H. Bill Mauldin in Korea. New York: W. W. Norton and Co., Inc., 1952.

Roosevelt, Eleanor and *Ferris, Helen.* Partners: The United Nations and Youth. Garden City, N. Y.: Doubleday and Co., 1950.

Settel, Arthur. This Is Germany. New York: William Sloane Assoc., Inc., 1950.

Stebbins, Richard P. and the *Research Staff of the Council on Foreign Relations.* United States in World Affairs, 1949. New York: Harper and Bros., 1950.

Stensland, Per and *Dennis, Larry.* Keeping Up with the News. Chicago: Science Research Assoc., Inc., 1951.

Wilson, Donald P. My Six Convicts. New York: Rinehart and Co., 1951.

Books about science and mathematics

Bendick, Jeanne. Electronics for Young People. New York: McGraw-Hill Book Co., Inc., 1947.

Berkeley, Edmund C. Giant Brains or Machines That Think. New York: John Wiley and Sons, Inc., 1949.

Carson, Rachel L. The Sea Around Us. New York: Oxford University Press, 1951.

Clarke, Arthur C. The Exploration of Space. New York: Harper and Bros., 1951.

Cooke, David C. Young America's Aviation Manual. New York: Medill McBride Co., 1951.

Curie, Eve. Madame Curie. Garden City, N. Y.: Doubleday and Co., 1949.

Dunlap, Orrin E. Radar: What Radar Is and How It Works. (Rev. ed.) New York: Harper and Bros., 1948.

Everson, George. The Story of Television. New York: W. W. Norton and Co., Inc., 1949.

Glasstone, Samuel. Sourcebook on Atomic Energy. New York: D. Van Nostrand Co., Inc., 1950.

Hogben, Lancelot T. Mathematics for the Millions. New York: W. W. Norton and Co., Inc., 1940.

Jaffe, Bernard. Men of Science in America. New York: Simon and Schuster, Inc., 1944.

Jordan, E. L. Nature Atlas of America. Maplewood, N. J.: C. S. Hammond and Co., 1952.

Lewellen, John. Primer of Atomic Energy. Chicago: Science Research Assoc., Inc., 1952.

Ley, Willy. Conquest of Space. New York: Viking Press, Inc., 1949.

Leyson, B. W. Modern Wonders and How They Work. New York: E. P. Dutton and Co., 1949.

Osborn, Fairfield. Our Plundered Planet. Boston: Little, Brown and Co., 1948.

Books of and about drama, poetry, art, music, and religion

Cerf, Bennett and *Cartmell, Van H.* (comps.). S.R.O.; the Most Successful Plays in the History of the American Stage. Garden City, N. Y.: Doubleday and Co., 1944.

Costain, Thomas B. The Silver Chalice. Garden City, N. Y.: Doubleday and Co., 1952.

Dike, Helen. Stories from the Great Metropolitan Operas. New York: Random House, Inc., 1943.

Downer, Marion. Discovering Design. New York: Lothrop, Lee and Shepard Co., 1947.

Frost, Robert. The Road Not Taken; An Introduction to Robert Frost. New York: Henry Holt and Co., Inc., 1951.

Gassner, John. Best Plays of the Modern American Theater. New York: Crown Publishers, 1947.

Goldstein, Harriet I. Art in Everyday Life. New York: Macmillan Co., 1941.

Gombrich, E. H. The Story of Art. New York: Oxford University Press, 1950.

Graham, Alberta P. Strike Up the Band. New York: Thomas Nelson and Sons, 1949.

Haskell, Arnold L. How to Enjoy the Ballet. New York: William Morrow and Co., 1951.

Johnstone, Margaret Blair. Create Your Own Tomorrow. Garden City, N. Y.: Doubleday and Co., 1950.

Lloyd, Margaret. The Borzoi Book of Modern Dance. New York: Alfred A. Knopf, Inc., 1949.

Millay, Edna St. Vincent. Renascence and Other Poems. New York: Harper and Bros., 1941.

Morley, Christopher. Mince Pie. Philadelphia: J. B. Lippincott Co., 1947.

Oursler, Fulton. The Greatest Story Ever Told. Garden City, N. Y.: Doubleday and Co., 1949.

Sandburg, Carl. Complete Poems. New York: Harcourt, Brace and Co., 1950.

Shakespeare, William. **Four Great Comedies.**
New York: Pocket Books, Inc., 1952.

Simpson, Martha. **Art Is for Everyone.**
New York: McGraw-Hill Book Co., Inc.,
1951.

Books about entertainment, sports, and fun

Allen, Lee. **100 Years of Baseball.** New
York: Bartholomew House, Inc., 1950.

Aller, Doris. **Sunset Wood Carving Book.**
Menlo Park, Calif.: Lane Pub. Co., 1951.

Anderson, Clarence W. **Heads Up—Heels
Down: A Handbook of Horsemanship
and Riding.** New York: Macmillan Co.,
1944.

Andrews, Roy C. **My Favorite Stories of
the Great Outdoors.** New York: Grey-
stone Press, 1950.

Benchley, Robert. **Inside Benchley.** New
York: Harper and Bros., 1942.

Benchley, Robert. **Pluck and Luck.** New
York: Blue Ribbon Books, 1925.

Carhart, Arthur H. **Fishing Is Fun.** New
York: Macmillan Co., 1950.

Cerf, Bennett A. **Good for a Laugh.** Garden City, N.Y.: Hanover House, 1952.

Cerf, Bennett. **Laughing Stock.** New York:
Grosset and Dunlap, Inc., 1945.

Cerf, Bennett. **Try and Stop Me.** New York:
Simon and Schuster, Inc., 1945.

Daley, Arthur. **Times at Bat: A Half Century of Baseball.** New York: Random
House, Inc., 1950.

Daly, Sheila J. **Party Fun.** New York: Dodd,
Mead and Co., 1948.

Duncan, Julia Hamlin and *D'Amico, Victor.*
**How to Make Pottery and Ceramic
Sculpture.** New York: Museum of
Modern Art, 1947.

Dunlop, Ronald O. **How to Paint for
Pleasure.** New York: Pellegrini and
Cudahy, Inc., 1952.

Farrell, Johnny. **If I Were in Your Golf
Shoes.** New York: Henry Holt and Co.,
Inc., 1951.

Feller, Robert W. **How to Pitch.** New York:
A. S. Barnes and Co., 1948.

Hartley, Paul. **How to Paint.** New York:
Harper and Bros., 1951.

Hobson, Howard A. **Basketball Illustrated.**
New York: A. S. Barnes and Co., 1948.

Holman, Nathan. **Holman on Basketball.**
New York: Crown Publishers, 1950.

MacGillicuddy, Cornelius. **Connie Mack's
Baseball Book.** New York: Alfred A.
Knopf, Inc., 1950.

Rice, William S. **Block Prints, How to
Make Them.** Milwaukee, Wis.: Bruce
Pub. Co., 1941.

Snead, Sam. **How to Play Golf.** Garden City,
N. Y.: Garden City Books, 1946.

Tilden, William. **How to Play Better Ten-
nis.** New York: Simon and Schuster, Inc.,
1950.

Turoff, Muriel P. **How to Make Pottery
and Other Ceramic Ware.** New York:
Crown Publishers, 1949.

Weiss, Mike. **100 Handy Hints on How to
Break 100.** New York: Prentice-Hall,
Inc., 1951.

Books about interesting people

Baker, Rachel. **The First Woman Doctor.**
New York: Julian Messner, Inc., 1944.

Eaton, Jeanette. **David Livingstone, Foe of
Darkness.** New York: William Morrow
and Co., 1947.

Edward VIII, King of Great Britain (ab-
dicated 1936). **A King's Story; the
Memoirs of the Duke of Windsor.** New
York: G. P. Putnam's Sons, 1951.

Floherty, John J. **The Courage and the
Glory.** Philadelphia: J. B. Lippincott Co.,
1942.

Freidel, Frank. **Franklin D. Roosevelt, the
Apprenticeship.** Boston: Little, Brown
and Co., 1952.

Gollomb, Joseph. **Albert Schweitzer.** New
York: Vanguard Press, Inc., 1949.

Grace, Dick. **Visibility Unlimited.** New
York: Longmans, Green and Co., 1950.

Graham, Shirley and *Lipscomb, G. D.* **Dr.
George Washington Carver.** New York:
Julian Messner, Inc., 1944.

Hall, Anna G. Nansen. New York: Viking Press, Inc., 1940.

Hemingway, Ernest. The Old Man and the Sea. New York: Charles Scribner's Sons, 1952.

Lawrence, Marjorie. Interrupted Melody. New York: D. Appleton-Century-Crofts Co., Inc., 1949.

Nuttall, Madeleine. The Gift. New York: A. A. Wyn, 1951.

Porter, William Sidney (O. Henry, pseud.). The Best Stories of O. Henry. New York: The Modern Library, 1945.

Roosevelt, Eleanor. This I Remember. New York: Harper and Bros., 1949.

Smith, Hannah. For Heaven's Sake. Boston: Little, Brown and Co., 1949.

Spaeth, Sigmund G. Dedication: The Love Story of Clara and Robert Schumann. New York: Henry Holt and Co., Inc., 1950.

Stewart, Anna. Young Miss Burney. Philadelphia: J. B. Lippincott Co., 1947.

Stuart, Jessie. The Thread That Runs So True. New York: Charles Scribner's Sons, 1949.

Taubman, Hyman H. The Maestro; the Life of Arturo Toscanini. New York: Simon and Schuster, Inc., 1951.

Thorp, Louise H. The Peabody Sisters of Salem. Boston: Little, Brown and Co., 1950.

Thorpe, Niels. Peter Nielsen's Story. Minneapolis: Univ. of Minnesota Press, 1949.

Vandercook, John W. Great Sailor: A Life of the Discoverer, Captain James Cook. New York: Dial Press, 1951.

Wong, Su-ling and *Cressy, Earl Herbert.* Daughter of Confucius, A Personal History. New York: Farrar, Straus, and Young, Inc., 1952.

Books about adventure and travel

Bell, W. D. M. Karamojo Safari. New York: Harcourt, Brace and Co., 1949.

Bronte, Emily. Wuthering Heights. New York: Random House, Inc., 1943.

Clemens, Samuel L. (Mark Twain, pseud.). The Adventures of Huckleberry Finn. New York: Chanticleer Press, Inc., 1950.

Cooke, David C. (ed.). Best Detective Stories of the Year 1952. New York: E. P. Dutton and Co., 1952.

Dewey, Thomas E. Journey to the Far Pacific. Garden City, N. Y.: Doubleday and Co., 1952.

Doyle, Sir Arthur Conan. The Case Book of Sherlock Holmes. New York: Pocket Books, Inc., 1950.

Floherty, John J. Five Alarm. Philadelphia: J. B. Lippincott Co., 1949.

Fuller, Iola. The Loon Feather. New York: Harcourt, Brace and Co., 1940.

Guthrie, Alfred B. The Way West. New York: William Sloane Assoc., 1949.

Hammond-Innes, Ralph. Campbell's Kingdom. New York: Alfred A. Knopf, Inc., 1952.

Hersey, John. The Wall. New York: Alfred A. Knopf, Inc., 1950.

Heyerdahl, Thor. Kon-Tiki. Chicago: Rand McNally Co., 1950.

Hilliard, Jan. The Salt-Box. New York: W. W. Norton and Co., Inc., 1951.

Kipling, Rudyard. Captains Courageous. Garden City, N. Y.: Doubleday and Co., 1949.

Koestler, Arthur. Darkness at Noon. New York: Macmillan Co., 1941.

Lane, Rose. Let the Hurricane Roar. New York: Longmans, Green and Co., 1933.

Lothrop, Eleanor B. Throw Me a Bone: What Happens When You Marry an Archaeologist. New York: McGraw-Hill Book Co., Inc., 1948.

Mackintosh, Elizabeth (Josephine Tey, pseud.). Brat Farrar. New York: Macmillan Co., 1950.

Mauldin, William H. Back Home. New York: William Sloane Assoc., 1947.

Maule, Harry E. (ed.). The Pocket Book of Western Stories. New York: Pocket Books, Inc., 1945.

Michener, James A. Return to Paradise. New York: Random House, Inc., 1951.

Michener, James A. **Tales of the South Pacific.** New York: Pocket Books, Inc., 1946.

Mowat, Farley. **People of the Deer.** Boston: Little, Brown and Co., 1952.

Murphy, Grace E. **There's Always Adventure.** New York: Harper and Bros., 1951.

Norway, Nevel S. **The Legacy.** New York: William Morrow and Co., 1950.

Roberts, Kenneth. **Northwest Passage.** Garden City, N. Y.: Doubleday and Co., 1937.

Scott, Sir Walter. **Ivanhoe.** (Riverside Book Shelf). Boston: Houghton Mifflin Co., 1913.

Seton, Ernest Thompson. **Lives of the Hunted.** New York: Charles Scribner's Sons, 1915.

Sperry, Armstrong. **Danger to the Windward.** Philadelphia: John C. Winston Co., 1944.

Sperry, Armstrong. **Storm Canvas.** Philadelphia: John C. Winston Co., 1944.

Stefansson, Vilhjalmur (ed.). **Great Adventures and Explorations.** New York: Dial Press, 1947.

Stern, Philip Van Doren (ed.). **The Pocket Book of Adventure Stories.** New York: Pocket Books, Inc., 1945.

Stevenson, Robert L. **The Black Arrow.** New York: Grosset and Dunlap, Inc., 1947.

Verne, Jules. **Twenty Thousand Leagues under the Sea.** New York: Charles Scribner's Sons, 1925.

Williams, Eric. **The Wooden Horse.** New York: Harper and Bros., 1950.

Wouk, Herman. **The Caine Mutiny.** Garden City, N. Y.: Doubleday and Co., 1951.

How-to-do-it books

Better Homes and Gardens Handyman's **Book.** Des Moines, Ia.: Meredith Publishing Co., 1950.

Betty Crocker Picture Cook Book. Minneapolis, Minn.: General Mills Co., 1950.

Flynn, Jack and others. **Develop, Print, and Enlarge Your Own Pictures.** New York: McGraw-Hill Book Co., Inc., 1952.

Hauser, Bengamin Gayelord. **Look Younger, Live Longer.** New York: Farrar, Straus, and Young, Inc., 1950.

McCoy, Robert A. **Practical Photography.** Bloomington, Ill.: McKnight and McKnight, 1950.

Bibliographies of good books

The Booklist. (Monthly periodical). Chicago: American Library Association.

Book Review Digest. (Monthly periodical). New York: H. W. Wilson Co.

Grim, Frances M. (ed.). (Rev. ed.) **By Way of Introduction.** Chicago: American Library Association, 1947.

Herzberg, Max J. and Center, Stella. **Books for Home Reading for High School.** Chicago: National Council of Teachers of English, 1937.

Kuder, G. Frederick and Crawford, Lura. **Kuder Book List.** Chicago: Science Research Assoc., Inc., 1951.

Lenrow, Elbert. **Reader's Guide to Prose Fiction.** New York: D. Appleton-Century-Crofts Co., Inc., 1940.

Neville, Mark (chairman). **Books for You.** Chicago: National Council of Teachers of English, 1945. (Supplement, 1948).

Steffurud, Alfred (ed.). **The Wonderful World of Books.** (A Mentor Book.) New York: The New American Library of World Literature, Inc., 1953.

Strang, Ruth M. and others. **Gateways to Readable Books.** New York: H. W. Wilson Co., 1944.

Taba, Hilda and others. **Reading Ladders for Human Relations.** Washington, D. C.: The American Council on Education, 1947.

Townsend, Atwood H. (ed.). **Good Reading: A Guide to the World's Best Books.** (A Mentor Book.) New York: The New American Library of World Literature, Inc., 1948.

Books on reading improvement

Barnes, Duane C. **Wordlore.** New York: E. P. Dutton and Co., 1948.

Brown, James I. Efficient Reading. Boston: D. C. Heath and Co., 1952.

Cage, Mabel. Reading in High Gear. New York: Harper and Bros., 1938.

Center, Stella S. The Art of Book Reading. New York: Charles Scribner's Sons, 1952.

Dale, Edgar. How to Read a Newspaper. Chicago: Scott, Foresman and Co., 1941.

Funk, Wilfred and *Lewis, Norman.* 30 Days to a More Powerful Vocabulary. New York: Wilfred Funk, Inc., 1942.

Kelley, Victor H. and *Greene, Harry A.* Better Reading and Study Habits. Yonkers, N. Y.: World Book Co., 1947.

Knight, Pearle and *Traxler, Arthur.* Read and Comprehend. (Rev. ed.) Boston: D. C. Heath and Co., 1949.

Lewis, Norman. How to Read Better and Faster. (Rev. ed.) New York: Thomas Y. Crowell Co., 1951.

Numberg, Maxwell W. and *Rhodes, W. T.* How to Build a Better Vocabulary. New York: Prentice-Hall, Inc., 1949.

Picturesque Word Origins. Springfield, Mass.: G. and C. Merriam Co., 1933.

Roos, Jean C. What Shall We Read Next? New York: H. W. Wilson Co., 1935.

Simpson, Elizabeth. SRA Better Reading Books. Chicago: Science Research Assoc., Inc., 1950-51.

Smith, Samuel S. How to Double Your Vocabulary. New York: Thomas Y. Crowell Co., 1947.

Wayne, E. How to Use a Book. New Brunswick, N. J.: Rutgers Univ. Press, 1947.

Witty, Paul. Streamline Your Reading. Chicago: Science Research Assoc., Inc., 1949.

General reading exercises

1 through 20

Here are the directions

for doing a general reading exercise

AT THE END OF each lesson in this book, you will do a general reading exercise. Through this exercise, you will check upon your reading rate, comprehension, and vocabulary.

Your reading rate is measured by the number of words you read per minute. Your reading comprehension is measured by the number of items that you mark correctly in a 20-item comprehension test. And your reading vocabulary is measured by the number of words that you mark correctly in a 10-item vocabulary test.

You will keep a record of your reading rates and scores in the *Reading Progress Folder* that appears near the end of this book.[1] You will write your answers to the tests in this *Progress Folder*.

How do you do a general reading exercise?

This book has 20 general reading exercises that appear on pages 186-304. How you are to do each of these exercises is described next.

Each general reading exercise is made up of four parts: (1) a suggested reading practice; (2) an article to read; (3) a reading test; and (4) a vocabulary test. In doing each exercise, as said before, you use the *Progress Folder*. It helps you to keep track of your reading improvement.

Here is how you do a reading practice

To do a reading practice,[2] read in any book, magazine, or newspaper that you like very much. You will find a list of interesting books to read on pages 174-181. In reading one of these, see how many pages you can read in 10 minutes. Have someone ask you questions about what you have just read. Record this reading practice on page 8 of the *Progress Folder*.

Here is how you test your reading rate

Before you begin reading an article, record your starting time in the *Progress Folder*. Then read the article as fast as

---

[1]If you should not write in this book, you can keep your record in a separate copy of the *SRA Reading Progress Folder*. You can get this copy from your reading instructor.

[2]You may do your reading practice on a reading device such as the *SRA Reading Accelerator*. If your school, college, or library has one of these devices, you may use it to increase your reading rate and comprehension.

you can, but make sure you understand what you are reading. As soon as you finish reading the article, record your finishing time in the *Progress Folder*. Later, you will figure out your reading time and your reading rate. Then you will enter your rate in the Reading Rate Graph of the *Progress Folder*.

Here is how you take a reading comprehension test

Immediately after you read an article, take the reading comprehension test that covers this article. The test is made up of 20 items.

After reading Article 1, "Last Warning," you may recall something from the first paragraph, which was:

"All day John Muir had been stringing wire for the south pasture. He was hot and tired and dirty. Yet he sat lightly in the saddle, a figure to draw the eyes of men as well as women."

The first item in Comprehension Test 1 reads as follows:

> John Muir was a (A) well-built man
> (B) clumsy man
> (C) strong man
> (D) happy man
> (E) wealthy man

1. Read the first part of the item. In the example, the first part is, "John Muir was a".

2. Read the second part of the item. In the example, the second part gives five answers—one correct answer and four incorrect answers.

3. Select the answer that you believe is correct. In the example, suppose that you select the answer "well-built man." Thus, you believe that the test item correctly reads: "John Muir was a well-built man."

4. Mark a check (✔) at the left of the correct answer.[3] After you answer all 20 items in the test, copy the letters of your selected answers in the *Progress Folder*. In the example, your selected answer is "a well-built man"; its letter is A. Print this letter under Test 1 and at the right of item number 1 on the Answer Record on page 4 of the *Progress Folder*.

After you copy your answers to all 20 items of Test 1 in the *Progress Folder*, correct your answers. You will find the correct answers in the Answer Key on page 6 of the folder. Count the number of answers that you had correct. This number is your reading comprehension score. Write this score at the bottom of the Answer Record in the *Progress Folder*. Also enter this score in the Reading Comprehension Graph on page 3 of this folder.

> To learn exactly what steps you take in doing a general reading exercise, read carefully pages 1 and 10 of the *Progress Folder;* also study each of the other pages in the folder. Then read the last page in this book; it gives the time-to-rate table for changing your reading time into your reading rate.

Here is how you take a vocabulary test

After you record your reading rate and your reading comprehension score in the *Progress Folder*, take the vocabulary test on the article you have just read. This test presents ten of the harder words that appear in the article. Here is an example of one of these words from Article 1, "Last Warning."

1. foe: (A) fear (B) fight (C) enemy

[3]If you should not mark in this book, you will enter the letter of the correct choice in your separate copy of the *SRA Reading Progress Folder*.

Read the word at the left. In the example, the word at the left is "foe." Then find the word at the right that has the same meaning. In the example, that word is "(C) enemy." Draw a heavy line under this word.[4] After you mark all the items in the test, copy the letters of your answers on page 9 of the *Progress Folder* in this book. For the example, your answer would look like this:

I	C

After you answer all 10 items in the vocabulary test, correct your answers. The correct answers appear on page 11 of the *Progress Folder*. Next, count the number of answers that you had correct. This number is your vocabulary score. Enter that score on page 9 of the *Progress Folder*.

---

[4]If you should not mark in this book, write your answers to the vocabulary test on a separate sheet of paper. Then enter your vocabulary score at the bottom of page 4 or 7 in your separate copy of the *SRA Reading Progress Folder*, just below your score on the comprehension test.

Because you want to improve your vocabulary, you should follow up each word that you marked incorrectly. Suppose that, in the example, you wrote the answer "A"; you thought that the word "foe" meant "fear." If so, you should skim the article, "Last Warning," and find the sentence in which the word "foe" appears. Here is the sentence:

"She was of the house of the foe, but between them was a tie on his side at least closer than friendship."

By studying this sentence, you probably learn that "foe" and "friend" have opposite meanings. Another word meaning the opposite of "friend" is "enemy." Therefore, you rightly conclude that "foe" and "enemy" have the same or about the same meaning.

If you still are not sure about the meaning of the word "foe," look it up in a dictionary. Read all the meanings given there until you find the meaning that best fits the sense in which the word is used in the sentence.

Follow-up each test item that you answered wrongly. After you complete a reading comprehension test or a vocabulary test, take these steps:

1. Read again each test item that you answered incorrectly.

2. In the article, find quickly and read carefully the sentence or paragraph that gives the correct answer.

3. Try to determine why you selected the wrong choice for the test item, and why the choice given in the Answer Key is the only right answer.

Through these follow-up steps, you will definitely help to improve your comprehension and your vocabulary.

ARTICLE 1

*Last warning**

by William MacLeod Raine

READING PRACTICE 1 In a book, magazine, or newspaper that you like, practice reading for speed and comprehension. Make a record of each such practice in Chart 3 on page 8 of the PROGRESS FOLDER. Then do Reading Article 1.

READING ARTICLE 1 Before you begin reading Article 1, record your starting time in the Time Record on page 4 of the PROGRESS FOLDER. Then read Article 1. Read it as fast as you can, but make sure you understand what you are reading.

ALL DAY John Muir had been stringing wire for the south pasture. He was hot and tired and dirty. Yet he sat lightly in the saddle, a figure to draw the eyes of men as well as women.

Riding across the floor of Sweet Springs park toward his cabin in the pines was one who made him forget his fears and his weariness. She was of the house of the foe, but between them was a tie on his side at least closer than friendship.

"I came," she said when near him, "because I overheard two of our men talking and what they said worried me. I caught your name and listened. One of them said it would be with you the way it was with Barry and the other added, 'Unless he lights out sudden.' What did they mean about Barry? I know he left suddenly."

The homesteader's smile was thin and grim. "Nobody knows for sure what happened to Barry. He had been warned to get out or take the consequences." As the two rode up to the cabin, they saw a yellow paper tacked to the closed door.

*Condensed and adapted from Short Stories Magazine, January 10, 1943. Copyright, 1942, by Short Stories, Inc. Reprinted with permission of the publisher and the author.

Rose Durbin read it aloud: "Get out, you damned rustler, before 24 hours. This is your last warning."

There was no signature. Muir did not need one to know who was responsible for the notice. It came from Hank Durbin of the Bar Double S, though he had not nailed it there himself.

"Are you going to leave?" She asked.

"No."

"Then what are you going to do?"

"I don't know."

"You're not just going to stay and let them—kill you?"

"Not if I can help it."

"Come to the Bar Double S and stay with us until the danger is over. Father will give you a job if you want to work."

"No," Muir told her harshly. "I have to play my own hand."

After she had gone, Muir lit a fire, washed himself, and prepared supper. He did not want food, but he had to carry on the routine of life. Frenault would shoot him from ambush, though the gunfighter could meet him in the open with small risk. Muir had never fired a gun at a man. Even if he were given a chance he might be weak and unnerved at the critical moment.

Before daylight Muir rose, saddled a horse, and started for River Fork. There were a few loose ends of business he wanted to clear up while he could. After a restless night at home, Rose too was up early, in time to see her father and Frenault riding down the road that led to town. After a hurried breakfast she had a horse saddled and set out to have another talk with John Muir. If she could persuade him to marry her at once, her father might spare her lover.

John Muir knew that he was safer in River Fork than on his own land. He called at the office of Jim Baylor, lawyer, and made his will. While he was at the general store settling a bill, he heard that Durbin and Frenault were at the Cowman's Rest.

For a full minute Muir hesitated, then walked down the street to Cowman's Rest. Durbin and Frenault were at the bar drinking. Hank caught sight of Muir in the doorway and called to the nester. "I hear you're leaving. Come in and have a drink with us before you go."

Muir could not draw back now. "I'm not leaving," he answered quietly.

"My mistake." Durbin's great midriff shook like a jelly. "I heard the climate didn't agree with you."

"I'd like to talk with you, Mr. Durbin," the homesteader went on, his voice low and pleading. "I'm running only a two-by-four spread and I've fenced just one water hole. That won't interfere with your stock. There's feed and water enough for both of us."

"I don't give a tinker's damn whether it's one or twenty," Durbin replied. "I'll fight for my rights. If I let you get away with this some other guy will try it."

"I'm not looking for trouble," Muir said. "You know that, Mr. Durbin. But I have rights too. The law says . . ."

"Who cares about law?" The cattleman brushed it aside with a sweep of his plump hand. "This is cow territory—no good for anything else. It belongs to the man who uses it first. The Sweet Springs water and grass are mine. Get that in your thick skull while there is time."

A man who had come in and ordered a bottle of beer became aware of the tensity. Hurriedly he drank his beer and departed without paying for it. Mike, the bartender, did not remind him of the obligation.

"Don't go crazy with the heat, you lunkhead," Durbin warned. "I've offered to buy. Last chance, Muir."

"You didn't offer me one-fourth of what my spread is worth."

"I offered you all it's worth to me. I don't give a cuss whether you accept or don't. I'll get it anyhow."

"I'm not going to let anybody rob me," Muir said thickly.

The eyes of the cattleman and his killer met. A message passed from one to the other. Without another word Durbin turned and clumped out of the building. Muir knew the showdown had come.

Before the swing doors had settled to rest, somebody from outside pushed through them. " 'Lo, Frenault," he said. "Heard you were in town and brought the twenty bucks I owe you."

The gunfighter turned his head to the newcomer. "Hand it to Mike," he said. "I'm busy right now."

Muir picked up the empty beer bottle and pressed the rim of the narrow end against the back of the desperado's neck. "Don't move," he warned.

Frenault stood rigid. He did not move while Muir slipped the .45 from the scabbard at the man's side.

"Keep your hands at your sides, Frenault," Muir warned. "You may turn now." As Frenault turned, his right arm moved upward swiftly. It brushed under his coat and continued to lift without stopping.

With his left hand Muir slapped down the barrel of the revolver and at the same time fired. The bullet from Frenault's second gun crashed through the floor.

The hired killer caught at his heart. From his slack fingers the .45 clattered to the ground. He swayed, took a step forward, and plunged down beside his gun. The body twitched and lay motionless.

Muir fought down the sickness that ran through him and said in a low voice, "I wasn't armed."

"Not armed?" Mike looked at him in wonder. "And with a beer bottle you rubbed out the worst killer ever in this part of the country."

Muir pushed through the swing doors and stood outside. A big man with a lumbering body was clumping up the street toward the Cowman's Rest. He pulled up abruptly. The man at the entrance to the saloon with the gun in his hand was not the one he had expected to see there.

At sight of Durbin all of Muir's agitation was sloughed away. He said quietly, "We'll settle this business now."

Already a crowd was beginning to gather. From stores and offices, men came running.

The cattleman lifted a fat hand in frightened protest. "Lemme explain, Muir. Don't rush this. We can fix it up all right. Whatever you say."

"You're through running this country," Muir told him. "You'll never interfere again with any homesteader who wants to take up government land. Better start at once. Fork your horse and get out of town."

Plodding across the street to the hitch rack where his horse was tied, Durbin swung heavily to the saddle and rode away.

Through the crowd a girl pushed her way to Muir.

"You here?" he cried.

"I was afraid I would be too late." Rose was trembling from the reaction to the fear that had driven her all through her long ride.

He took both her hands in his and looked down into her eyes. "You're just in time," he told her.

As soon as you finish reading Article 1, record your finishing time in the Time Record on page 4 of the PROGRESS FOLDER. *Then read Test 1 that appears next in this book.*

READING TEST 1   LAST WARNING

Read each test item and select the answer you believe is correct. Print the letter of your answer in the Answer Record on page 4 of the PROGRESS FOLDER.

---

1. John Muir was a   (A) well-built man
                        (B) clumsy man
                        (C) strong man
                        (D) happy man
                        (E) wealthy man

2. When Muir saw the young woman riding toward him, he forgot his fears and his weariness because he
   - (A) liked her
   - (B) loved her
   - (C) knew her
   - (D) admired her
   - (E) trusted her

3. According to the woman's story, the two men said that what happened to Barry would also happen to Muir unless he
   - (A) paid what he owed them
   - (B) left the country suddenly
   - (C) stayed on his own land
   - (D) let their cattle drink at his spring
   - (E) kept his fence in good repair

4. In the message tacked to the cabin door, the writer told Muir
   - (A) to leave before sunset
   - (B) to go to the nearest town
   - (C) to leave his gun at home
   - (D) to keep his pasture gates open
   - (E) to get out within 24 hours

5. Muir knew that if he did not do what the message said, he would probably be
   - (A) shot to death
   - (B) tarred and feathered
   - (C) horse-whipped
   - (D) put in jail
   - (E) stabbed to death

6. Rose Durbin wanted Muir
   - (A) to fence in his land
   - (B) to fight for his property
   - (C) to play his own hand
   - (D) to work for her father
   - (E) to move into town

7. While in his cabin that evening, Muir feared that, if he had to shoot to save his own life, he would
   - (A) be killed or wounded by Durbin
   - (B) be arrested for shooting another man
   - (C) have to leave his farm and livestock forever
   - (D) lose the nerve needed to aim his gun and fire it
   - (E) never be able to marry the one he loved

8. The next morning, while Muir was riding to town, Rose was riding toward Muir's cabin in order to ask him
   - (A) to give up his farm
   - (B) to look for Barry
   - (C) to marry her
   - (D) to have dinner at her home
   - (E) to protect her from Frenault

9. John Muir did not expect to live very long because soon after he arrived in River Fork, he
   - (A) saw Durbin and Frenault together
   - (B) called on his doctor and an undertaker
   - (C) made his will and paid his bills
   - (D) gave both his guns to a close friend
   - (E) decided to kill both his enemies

10. In the Cowman's Rest, Durbin told Muir that he had heard the homesteader was leaving because Muir
    - (A) had found that the climate did not agree with him
    - (B) was afraid that Frenault would kill him
    - (C) had been warned to get out of the country right away
    - (D) planned to elope with Durbin's daughter
    - (E) did not really own the land that he was farming

11. Muir tried to persuade Durbin to let him alone by talking about the
    - (A) selfishness and cruelty of the Bar Double S owner
    - (B) need to work together instead of against each other
    - (C) townspeople who liked farmers better than ranchers
    - (D) poor grass and spring at Sweet Springs park
    - (E) small size of his farm and its one water hole

12. Durbin said that the territory belonged to the man who
    - (A) had a lawful title to it
    - (B) took it with his gun
    - (C) fenced it in
    - (D) grazed his cattle on it
    - (E) used it first

13. As things turned out later, Muir had good luck because a man
    - (A) did not pay the bartender for his beer
    - (B) left an empty beer bottle on the bar
    - (C) bought Frenault a large number of drinks
    - (D) let him borrow a revolver
    - (E) said Frenault was a killer

14. When Muir told Durbin he had offered only one-fourth of what Muir's farm was worth, Durbin said that he would
    - (A) pay more for the farm
    - (B) tear the farm's fences down
    - (C) kill Muir instead of paying more for the farm
    - (D) get the farm anyhow
    - (E) put the heat on Muir to accept the offer

15. After Durbin left the saloon, Muir was able to push the bottle against Frenault's neck because Frenault
    - (A) was paying the bartender for another man's beer
    - (B) raised his hands to scratch his head
    - (C) was handling the money a newcomer gave him
    - (D) put his head down to fix his boots
    - (E) turned his head toward a newcomer

16. When Frenault moved his right arm upward swiftly, he was
    - (A) putting his first gun back in its holster
    - (B) drawing his second gun from its holster
    - (C) trying to take the beer bottle away from Muir
    - (D) getting ready to push Muir's gun aside
    - (E) starting to shake hands with Muir

17. If Muir had not shot Frenault when he did, Frenault would certainly have
    - (A) killed Muir
    - (B) laughed at Muir
    - (C) forced Muir to leave his farm
    - (D) challenged Muir to a duel
    - (E) arrested Muir

18. Muir ordered Durbin to leave town because he wanted to make sure that Durbin never again interfered with

   (A) Rose and Muir who planned to marry and settle down
   (B) Muir who wished to keep his Sweet Springs farm
   (C) everyone who wanted to live peacefully in River Fork
   (D) any homesteader who wanted government land
   (E) any rustler who was trying to sell cattle

19. Rose said: "I was afraid I would be too late." By this, she probably meant she feared that Muir had

   (A) killed her father
   (B) left the country very suddenly
   (C) been killed by Frenault
   (D) decided to marry another girl
   (E) sold his farm to her father

20. The best headline for this Western story is:

   (A) Rancher loses homesteader's land
   (B) Poor homesteader woos cattleman's daughter
   (C) Last warning boomerangs
   (D) Beer bottle saves homesteader's life
   (E) Cattleman gives last warning

NEXT — *Follow the directions (Steps 8-17) on page 1 of the* PROGRESS FOLDER.

ARTICLE 2

*They ask to be killed**

by David G. Wittels

READING PRACTICE 2 *In a book, magazine, or newspaper that you like, practice reading for speed and comprehension. Make a record of each such practice in Chart 3 on page 8 of the* PROGRESS FOLDER. *Then do Reading Article 2.*

READING ARTICLE 2 *Before you begin reading Article 2, record your starting time in the Time Record on page 4 of the* PROGRESS FOLDER. *Then read Article 2. Read it as fast as you can, but make sure you understand what you are reading.*

IF A BULLET missed us by a few inches or feet, or even if a gun went off by accident anywhere near us, we understandably would have the jitters for at least hours and probably would tell and retell

for days the graphic tale of how we were "nearly killed." There would be the same reaction if we scrambled over a fence just ahead of a charging bull. But a 3000-pound automobile or a 20,000-pound truck is more dangerous than a charging bull and far more deadly than a bullet. We have become so conditioned to re-

*Condensed and adapted from *The Saturday Evening Post*, January 1, 1949. Copyright 1949, by the Curtis Publishing Company, Philadelphia. Reprinted with permission of the publisher and the author.

peated brushes with sudden death in traffic that we hardly notice the incidents and do not think of them as truly narrow escapes from being killed.

Yet in 1950 more than 8,700 pedestrians, mostly children less than 15 years old and people past middle age, were killed by motor vehicles and 180,000 were injured. When bicyclists, who in a sense also are pedestrians, are added, the score rises to more than 9,000. That's more people than live in any one of the vast majority of American towns. And that was in a so-called "good" year.

Impressive statistics are cited to buttress the claim that it's mostly the poor pedestrian's own fault. A survey by the National Safety Council indicates that "more than half of the pedestrians killed by motor vehicles were either violating a traffic law or acting in an obviously unsafe manner." In New Jersey, the State Motor Vehicle Department reports that 75 percent of the pedestrians killed there last year were victims of their own carelessness, such as stepping from behind parked cars, strolling in the roadway, and jaywalking.

These figures sounded so unbelievable and so unfair to the pedestrian, that I became suspicious. I voiced these suspicions to William S. Canning, engineering director of the Keystone Automobile Club.

He talked me into a ride from Philadelphia to Baltimore, where we cruised the business section and some residential streets. We rode some 125 miles with our eyes really open, actively looking for and registering traffic incidents. It was a shocking experience. The wonder is not that so many pedestrians are killed or mangled, but why only so few.

Canning is not only a noted safety expert but an extraordinarily skilled driver

who did not once break or even slightly bend a traffic rule. Yet on that trip, we nearly killed 27 pedestrians and saw 79 more nearly killed by other cars.

We hardly got started from downtown Philadelphia when we saw an almost perfect example of how otherwise intelligent pedestrians invite sudden death in the streets. A very well-dressed man of about forty, carrying a brief case, stepped off the curb almost directly in front of us. He started diagonally across a heavily trafficked street in the middle of the block, against the lights, and without even glancing to see what was coming. Only Canning's alertness saved that man from immediately becoming an item in the pedestrian-toll statistics.

Outside the city limits, the first thing worthy of note was a man getting out of a parked car. That act changed him from motorist to pedestrian. His first step in the latter role almost cost him his life. To save himself the trouble of sliding across the seat to the curb side of the car, he got out on the traffic side. A light delivery truck whizzed so close to him that the slip stream billowed his shirt.

Outside Chester, Pennsylvania, we neared two men plodding along the highway. They had their backs to us. They were so engrossed in conversation that they didn't even glance at us as we passed. I watched them in the rearvision mirror as long as I could. They never once looked back to see what was coming. I didn't list these two men as "nearly killed," but perhaps I should have. Most of the 1,000 persons killed while walking in roadways were walking with their backs to traffic instead of facing it.

On 3rd Street in Chester, we saw an attractive young woman step into traffic from behind a parked truck. A boy on a bicycle had to brake so hard to avoid her that he fell off. If it had been an automobile, she wouldn't have had a chance. An automobile swerved just in time to miss the fallen boy. In so doing, it nearly hit another car.

One obvious way to get killed by an automobile is to walk into traffic without looking.

In Baltimore we saw a man step off the pavement, take two paces into the path of traffic, then stand there with his back to the on-rushing cars. We missed him, and so did about a dozen other cars, but if any of the drivers had been forced to swerve or had looked away at the wrong moment, that man would have been a hospital or morgue case.

At Light Street and East Camden, into which we turned, a whole bevy of chattering girls stepped off the curb directly into our path, without a look in our direction . . . or any direction. Their pretty legs and figures remained unbroken and unscarred only because Canning stepped on the brake fast and hard.

A very good way to get killed by an automobile is to cross an intersection against the lights or to cut diagonally across it in order to save a few steps.

But the surest way to get killed by an automobile is to try to cross the street in the middle of a block or anywhere away from an intersection. This practice, the most popular form of jaywalking, cost approximately 600 pedestrians their lives in 1950, and caused about 20,000 others to be injured in varying degrees.

On Orleans Street above Kenwood we saw three nearly grown boys and a smaller one dart through traffic halfway across the street, then get stuck in the center. They stood there trapped, looking for an opening, while cars zipped by, only inches away on either side of them. We saw the same thing happen to a girl who tried to cross North Howard Street below Saratoga, and to two workmen crossing Liberty Street near Fayette.

One survey indicates that you are 51 times more likely to be killed trying to cross in the middle of the block than at an intersection. Even excellent drivers relax somewhat between intersections, not expecting pedestrians to pop up elsewhere.

What is to be done with pedestrians such as these, to save them from themselves? Most experts are agreed that they should be treated like reckless drivers —that is, arrested or at least handed summonses and forced to pay fines.

Washington began emphasizing pedestrian control in 1939, and still does it. If a pedestrian starts to cross against a light in central Washington, a policeman whistles or waves him back. If the pedestrian persists, the policeman takes his name and address and hands him a traffic ticket, unless the pedestrian can prove he is a stranger, in which case he is let off with a warning.

In the first five months of that method, pedestrian accidents in central Washington dropped nearly 17 percent. In the first full year of getting tough with pedestrians, Washington jumped into first place in the national ratings. It has remained near the top ever since.

Arrests and summonses cannot, however, be applied to the child-pedestrian problem. Though safety teaching in the schools, safety patrols and the posting of policemen at school intersections have steadily cut the toll of children, that still remains a serious problem. In 1950, about 850 children under five were killed by automobiles while walking or playing on the streets, and 1050 others under fifteen. Another 370 were run down and killed while riding bicycles. In the majority of the cases the children were doing something wrong.

In the final analysis, it is up to pedestrians to save their own lives, not only by being more careful but by demanding that officials give them at least an even break in the battle of motorist vs. pedestrian.

As soon as you finish reading Article 2, record your finishing time in the Time Record on page 4 of the PROGRESS FOLDER. Then read Test 2 that appears next in this book.

READING TEST 2   THEY ASK TO BE KILLED

Read each test item and select the answer you believe is correct. Print the letter of your answer in the Answer Record on page 4 of the PROGRESS FOLDER.

1. If we were nearly killed in a gun accident, we would probably
   - (A) forget about it fairly soon
   - (B) learn to handle a gun more safely
   - (C) think and talk a lot about it
   - (D) stay away from guns all the time
   - (E) keep the muzzles of our guns in the air

2. We hardly notice it when we are nearly killed in traffic because we have
   - (A) had so many close brushes with death in the streets
   - (B) read so many news stories about pedestrian deaths
   - (C) obeyed the laws and rules for safe walking
   - (D) seen so many people jaywalk without being injured
   - (E) ridden in cars which barely missed hitting pedestrians

3. Most of the pedestrians who are killed by motor vehicles are
   - (A) small children and teen-agers
   - (B) small children and older adults
   - (C) teen-agers and young adults
   - (D) young and middle-aged adults
   - (E) babies and older adults

4. In 1950, a so-called good year, automobiles killed about this number of pedestrians:
   - (A) 1,400
   - (B) 8,700
   - (C) 5,700
   - (D) 700
   - (E) 50,300

5. More than half of the pedestrians who are killed lose their lives because they are
   - (A) hit by law-breaking motorists
   - (B) ignorant about the rules for safe walking
   - (C) breaking traffic laws and safety rules
   - (D) blind or deaf, or in need of glasses or hearing aids
   - (E) injured too far from a doctor or a hospital

6. When the author rode through the cities looking for law-breaking pedestrians, he was surprised to see that
   - (A) so few pedestrians were hurt or killed
   - (B) so many pedestrians were hurt or killed
   - (C) so many motorists were such careless drivers
   - (D) so many pedestrians obeyed traffic laws
   - (E) so few good motorists were also careful pedestrians

7. In crossing the street, which thing did the middle-aged pedestrian *not* do?

(A) He crossed the street in the middle of the block.
(B) He stepped off the curb in front of a car.
(C) He crossed the street at an intersection.
(D) He walked against a red traffic light.
(E) He did not look to see what was coming.

8. One motorist who had parked his car was nearly hit by a delivery truck because he

(A) walked from in front of his car into traffic
(B) stood behind a car which was backing up
(C) had put his car on the left side of the street
(D) did not signal the truck to be careful
(E) got out of his car on the traffic side

9. On the highway the author saw two men who were taking a dangerous chance with their lives. They were

(A) walking in the center of the road
(B) walking on the left side of the road
(C) running across the road without looking
(D) walking on the right side of the road
(E) hitch-hiking to the next town

10. The chain of near-accidents that could have involved two cars, a woman, and a boy on a bicycle was started by

(A) the woman stepping from behind a parked truck
(B) one car trying to overtake and pass the other car
(C) the bicyclist riding on the wrong side of the street
(D) the motorist swerving to miss the bicyclist
(E) the driver parking his truck too far from the curb

11. A good way to get killed is to walk into a street

(A) with your face toward onrushing cars
(B) with a heavy package in your hand
(C) with a friend who never talks
(D) with your eyes looking first to the left
(E) with your eyes looking only straight ahead

12. At a street corner in Baltimore, the author's car almost hit a group of girls because they were

(A) stopping and looking
(B) talking to each other
(C) racing across the street
(D) playing a game
(E) pushing each other around

13. Most pedestrians lose their lives because they

(A) cross an intersection against the lights
(B) cut diagonally across an intersection
(C) walk on the right side of a street
(D) cross the street in the middle of a block
(E) look to the left before crossing a street

14. If you dodge cars and get trapped in the center of the street you are very

(A) brave
(B) wise
(C) skillful
(D) timid
(E) foolish

15. When crossing a street, your chances of being killed in the middle of a block are about

    (A) 50 times greater than at an intersection
    (B) 100 times greater than at an intersection
    (C) 10 times greater than at an intersection
    (D) the same as at an intersection
    (E) 25 times less than at an intersection

16. Traffic experts believe that one of the best ways to save pedestrians from themselves is

    (A) to lecture the jaywalker
    (B) to educate the jaywalker
    (C) to fine the jaywalker
    (D) to make fun of the jaywalker
    (E) to warn the jaywalker

17. In Washington, D.C., a pedestrian who is crossing the street against a traffic light is warned and then is

    (A) taken to court by a policeman
    (B) made fun of by a policeman
    (C) asked to show his walker's license by a policeman
    (D) given a ticket by a policeman
    (E) told to stay out of town by a policeman

18. Among all large cities, Washington, D.C., has a high rating in pedestrian safety because its police are

    (A) kind to ignorant jaywalkers
    (B) brutal to habitual jaywalkers
    (C) courteous to out-of-town jaywalkers
    (D) helpful to crippled jaywalkers
    (E) tough on local jaywalkers

19. Schools have reduced the number of traffic accidents to children mainly through

    (A) building underpasses on school streets
    (B) safety teaching and safety patrols
    (C) keeping automobiles off of school streets
    (D) giving young pedestrians the right of way
    (E) putting up buildings on quiet side streets

20. Most of the 2,200 children killed while walking or playing on the streets in 1950 were

    (A) disobeying their parents
    (B) observing traffic rules
    (C) going to school or home
    (D) doing something wrong
    (E) enjoying their summer vacation

NEXT — *Follow the directions (Steps 8-17) on page 1 of the* Progress Folder.

ARTICLE 3

*How to handle an outdoor cook fire**

by James E. West and William Hillcourt

READING PRACTICE 3 *In a book, magazine, or newspaper that you like, practice reading for speed and comprehension. Make a record of each such practice in Chart 3 on page 8 of the* PROGRESS FOLDER. *Then do Reading Article 3.*

READING ARTICLE 3 *Before you begin reading Article 3, record your starting time in the Time Record on page 4 of the* PROGRESS FOLDER. *Then read Article 3. Read it as fast as you can, but make sure you understand what you are reading.*

WHAT ABOUT IT? Getting hungry? Time for a snack?

OK! Get out the grub. Then start your fire.

Yeah—grub first, fire next!

That's where a tenderfoot often gets off the track. He starts a fire first, then unpacks. And what's the result? He wastes a lot of heat and fuel. He winds up with a blaze before he's ready to cook over it.

You may have heard the story of the old Indian who visited some white men's camp. He stalked up to their camp fire, looked at it, and grunted: "White man, him heap fool. Him make big fire—can't git near. Indian, him make small fire—git close. Good!"

The fire you want is the Indian fire. It is a small fire. It is smokeless. It can be regulated easily, and it is suitable for the kind of cooking you want to do, with "flames for boiling—coals for broiling."

*Adapted from *Scout Field Book*, Boy Scouts of America. Copyright 1948, by Boy Scouts of America, 2 Park Ave., New York. Reprinted with permission of the publisher.

Gathering wood

Right off the bat: What'll you use for *kindling?*

Well, look around.

Any evergreens? On the trunks are tiny dead twigs that seem to sprout right from the bark. Take in a supply and put them where they will keep dry. And while you are at it, there should be some cones around. They make good kindling. So does pitch wood chipped off an old pine stump.

In birch country, you have the ideal kindling. Peel a piece of bark off a *dead* tree. Put a match to it. It burns furiously, wet or dry. Many old-time campers carry a tiny roll of birch bark in their packs all the time for quick fire-making on a rainy day. Why not you? Cedar bark from a *dead* tree isn't too bad either.

If everything else is wet, split open a fairly thick, dead log. You are pretty certain to find it dry in the center. Quarter the log and cut the center part into kindling sticks. "Fuzz" up some of the sticks with a knife, leaving long shavings attached to them, Christmas-tree-like.

For *firewood* you need some pencil-thick branches, others as thick as a thumb, others still thicker.

In dry weather, there are plenty of dry sticks on the ground.

Better are dead branches still on trees—the so-called "squaw wood." It is named for the Indian women who used it for their cooking. Break off the dead branches within reach. Throw a rope over the branches up high and pull them down.

Use wood that snaps easily. Branches that just bend are too green for a fire. "If you can't snap it, SCRAP IT!"

A standing, dead tree will provide fire wood aplenty. Drop it and log it into suitable pieces, then split the pieces. Split wood burns much easier than whole logs.

And, by all means, gather and prepare enough wood for your whole meal *before* you strike your match.

Clearing the spot

Pick a spot in an open space more than *ten feet away* from brush and the nearest tree. Be sure there are no overhanging branches that will be damaged by the heat. Then *clear a circle*, at least ten feet in diameter. Scrape away dry leaves, dry grass, twigs, pine needles, until you get right down to mineral earth. On grassy soil, it pays to dig up the turf with a trench shovel. Store the turf on a moist, shady spot, so that you can replace it later without a trace.

If the ground is wet, lay a "floor" of sticks or bark of dead trees to build your fire on. In winter weather, scrape the snow away before laying the "floor."

Making your fire

The pyramid fire is the most commonly used fire. To start it, place the kindling in the center of the cleared spot, in the shape of a small pyramid. Lean some of the thin pieces of firewood against the pyramid, on the side away from the wind.

Now you can really get down to business:

Crouch in front of the wood with your back to the wind. Strike a match. Turn it in such a way that the tiny flame licks up along the matchstick. Let it burn into a real flame while you cup your hands around it for protection. Apply it to the kindling close to the ground. Whoopee! It caught!

Let the kindling burn a moment. Then feed the fire, first with small, then with gradually larger sticks. Continue feeding it slowly until it has reached the size you want. Keep in mind that a flame burns upward and away from the wind and needs lots of air.

After you have started your fire, stay close by it! IT IS CRIMINAL TO LEAVE A FIRE UNATTENDED.

Hanging your pots

The moment the fire is going, you are ready for most primitive cookery. But for cooking with pots or pans you need a way of placing them over the fire.

A single pot may be suspended from a *dingle stick*. That's just a straight stick put up in a slanting position over the fire. The stick is held in place by a couple of rocks or forked sticks. Cut a notch in the upper side of the dingle stick to hold the pot handle.

For several pots erect a *crane* of two forked sticks and a cross bar—the "lug pole." The best fork for this purpose is a straight stick with a side branch, rather than a true fork. At opposite sides of your fire, hammer the two forked sticks into the ground with the fork up. Then lay the lug pole so that it rests in the forks of the two uprights and extends above your fire.

If you are the kind of camper who is prepared for all emergencies, you'll have a couple of pieces of thin wire or twine in your knapsack. Then for your uprights you can use straight sticks which do not have forks. All you need to do is to lash the lug pole with wire or twine to the tops of the two upright sticks.

Hang your pots from the lug pole on *pot hooks*. Sometimes these are called "hakes," "gallow crooks," "pot claws," or "gibs." Make your pot hooks by cutting down a sapling—a small tree. Before you start chopping, make sure that you have permission from the landowner to chop down this tree.

For each pot hook, cut the trunk in two about four inches below a crotch—that is, below where a branch is growing. Then cut the trunk again about two feet above the crotch. Next cut off the branch about six inches from the crotch.

To finish the pot hook, chop notches in the long end of this stick. Now hang your stick upside down on the lug pole. The crotch of the stick will hook over the pole. In one of the notches in the long end, you can hang your pot. By shifting the pot from one notch to another, you can regulate the height of the pot over the fire. You can lower the pot for fast boiling; you can raise it for simmering.

Putting out the fire

Golly! What a meal that was! Now you burn all your trash. You were smart enough *not* to burn scrap paper while you were cooking. You didn't want paper ashes to get into your food pots. Pretty smart of you, too, to put a pot of water on for dishwashing when you had finished cooking!

Now that you have no further use for the fire, put it out. Or rather, not just "out," but "OUT!!!"

A fire is not OUT until you are SURE that the last spark has been DROWNED!

Sprinkle (do not pour) water on the embers. Stir with a stick until only soaking wet ashes remain. Turn logs and sticks and drench both sides. Wet the ground around the fire. Finally cover the place with dirt. Bury all garbage, tin cans, and bottles. *Make the spot so clean that no one will ever see that you have been there.*

As soon as you finish reading Article 3, record your finishing time in the Time Record on page 4 of the PROGRESS FOLDER. *Then read Test 3 that appears next in this book.*

READING TEST 3   **HOW TO HANDLE AN OUTDOOR COOK FIRE**

Read each test item and select the answer you believe is correct. Print the letter of your answer in the Answer Record on page 4 of the PROGRESS FOLDER.

1. In starting to cook out-doors, you should always
(A) start your fire, then unpack your food
(B) unpack your food, then start your fire
(C) start your fire, then get your water
(D) start your fire, then look for more firewood
(E) take care of your fire and food at the same time

2. According to the story, the old Indian said that he made a small fire mainly so that he could
   - (A) keep it from spreading
   - (B) put it out easily
   - (C) keep it going with little firewood
   - (D) get close to it
   - (E) hide from his enemies

3. To get the best natural kindling to start your cook fire, you should look for and use
   - (A) dead twigs and cones from evergreens
   - (B) bark strips from a live birch tree
   - (C) branches and cones from live evergreens
   - (D) leaves and branches from dead oak trees
   - (E) old newspapers and magazines

4. In order to make a fire quickly on a rainy day, old-time campers carry this type of natural kindling:
   - (A) A small package of pine needles
   - (B) A small flint-and-steel set
   - (C) A small bottle of kerosene
   - (D) A small bag of pine chips
   - (E) A small roll of birch bark

5. If everything else is wet, you can usually get dry wood to make a "fuzz" stick from this part of a log:
   - (A) The twigs
   - (B) The leaves
   - (C) The center
   - (D) The branches
   - (E) The bark

6. For starting and building up your cook fire, the best sticks to use are dead branches which are
   - (A) lying on the ground
   - (B) still on trees
   - (C) nearest to your fire
   - (D) covered with twigs
   - (E) buried under leaves

7. If you bend a branch and it snaps, the branch is likely to be
   - (A) rotten
   - (B) green
   - (C) wet
   - (D) strong
   - (E) dry

8. After you chop down a dead tree and saw it into logs for firewood, you should do this:
   - (A) Peel the logs with a knife.
   - (B) Saw the logs into small pieces.
   - (C) Split the logs with an ax.
   - (D) Let the logs dry out thoroughly.
   - (E) Push the logs gradually into the fire.

9. Before building a cook fire, you should clear a circle ten feet across mainly because it helps
   - (A) to obtain dirt for putting out your fire
   - (B) to keep your food clean
   - (C) to get the kindling you need
   - (D) to prevent your fire from spreading
   - (E) to protect nearby-by trees from your fire

10. If you dig up grassy turf   (A) sprinkle that turf with water
    to make your cook fire,   (B) put that turf back in place
    later you should always   (C) turn that turf upside down
                                 (D) get new turf to replace the old turf
                                 (E) plant grass seed on the bare spot

11. If the ground under your   (A) lay a floor of dead sticks
    fire place is wet, you   (B) build a roof of live branches
    should first   (C) wait for the ground to dry out
                                 (D) dig a deep hole with a shovel
                                 (E) put in a layer of dry sand

12. After you light a pyra-   (A) just below the wind
    mid fire, you should place   (B) toward the wind
    thin pieces of wood on   (C) parallel with the wind
    the side that is   (D) just above the wind
                                 (E) away from the wind

13. When you are lighting   (A) face the wind and light the kindling very quickly
    the kindling of your   (B) strike your match and let it burn for a while
    pyramid fire, you should   (C) cup your hands around the flaming match
    not   (D) crouch near-by with your back to the wind
                                 (E) light the kindling very close to the ground

14. After the kindling has   (A) rapidly with small, then larger, sticks
    burned for a moment,   (B) slowly with large, then smaller, sticks
    you should feed your fire   (C) evenly with both small and large sticks
                                 (D) rapidly with large, then smaller, sticks
                                 (E) slowly with small, then larger, sticks

15. In cooking, you may   (A) your hands
    hang your pot on a dingle   (B) two crossbars
    stick which is held in   (C) grassy turf
    position by   (D) some rocks
                                 (E) firewood

16. To hang pots over your   (A) dingle stick
    cook fire, you can put up   (B) lug pole
    a crane that is made of   (C) pot hook
    two forked sticks and a   (D) fuzz stick
                                 (E) pyramid

17. You can make a pot hook   (A) piece which has a notch in it
    from a sapling by cut-   (B) branch which has a twig on it
    ting a   (C) stick which has a crotch in it
                                 (D) section which has a knot in it
                                 (E) part which has a crook in it

18. You cut several notches
in each pot hook so that
you can

    (A) fasten the pot hook to the crossbar
    (B) keep the pot hook from catching fire
    (C) hold each forked stick very steadily
    (D) change the height of your pot above the fire
    (E) remove the pot from the cook fire

19. In order to keep paper
ashes out of your food,
you always

    (A) burn your trash after cooking
    (B) bury your trash before cooking
    (C) cover your pots with tight lids
    (D) eat your meal away from the fire
    (E) place your trash at the side of the fire

20. After you use your cook
fire, always do each of
these things except one.
Which should you *not*
do?

    (A) Sprinkle water on the embers.
    (B) Drench both sides of each stick and log.
    (C) Leave after all the wood has become ashes.
    (D) Wet the ground around the fire.
    (E) Cover the place with dirt.

NEXT — *Follow the directions (Steps 8-17) on page 1 of the* PROGRESS FOLDER.

ARTICLE 4

*The romance of a busy broker**

by O. Henry

READING PRACTICE 4 *In a book, magazine, or newspaper that you like, practice reading for speed and comprehension. Make a record of each such practice in Chart 3 on page 8 of the* PROGRESS FOLDER. *Then do Reading Article 4.*

READING ARTICLE 4 *Before you begin reading Article 4, record your starting time in the Time Record on page 4 of the* PROGRESS FOLDER. *Then read Article 4. Read it as fast as you can, but make sure you understand what you are reading.*

PITCHER, confidential clerk in the office of Harvey Maxwell, broker, allowed a look of mild interest and surprise to visit his usually expressionless countenance when his employer briskly entered at half-past nine in company with his young lady stenographer. With a snappy "Good-morning, Pitcher," Maxwell dashed at his desk as though he were intending to leap over it, and then plunged into the great heap of letters and telegrams waiting there for him.

The young lady had been Maxwell's

stenographer for a year. She was beautiful in a way that was decidedly unstenographic. She forewent the pomp of the alluring pompadour. She wore no chains, bracelets, or lockets. She had not the air of being about to accept an invitation to luncheon. Her dress was gray and plain, but it fitted her figure with fidelity and discretion. In her neat black turban hat was the gold-green wing of a macaw. On this morning she was softly and shyly radiant. Her eyes were dreamily bright, her cheeks genuine peach-blow, her expression a happy one, tinged with reminiscence.

Pitcher, still mildly curious, noticed a difference in her ways this morning. Instead of going straight into the adjoining room, where her desk was, she lingered, slightly irresolute, in the outer office. Once she moved over by Maxwell's desk, near enough for him to be aware of her presence.

The machine sitting at that desk was no longer a man; it was a busy New York broker, moved by buzzing wheels and uncoiling springs.

"Well—what is it? Anything?" asked Maxwell, sharply. His opened mail lay like a bank of stage snow on his crowded desk. His keen gray eye, impersonal and brusque, flashed upon her half impatiently.

"Nothing," answered the stenographer, moving away with a little smile.

"Mr. Pitcher," she said to the confidential clerk, "did Mr. Maxwell say anything yesterday about engaging another stenographer?"

"He did," answered Pitcher. "He told me to get another one. I notified the agency yesterday afternoon to send over a few samples this morning. It's 9.45 o'-clock, and not a single picture hat or piece of pineapple chewing gum has showed up yet."

"I will do the work as usual, then," said the young lady, "until some one comes to fill the place." And she went to her desk at once and hung the black turban hat with the gold-green macaw wing in its accustomed place.

He who has been denied the spectacle of a busy Manhattan broker during a rush of business does not know how really busy that business is.

And this day was Harvey Maxwell's busy day. The ticker began to reel out jerkily its fitful coils of tape, the desk telephone had a chronic attack of buzzing. Men began to throng into the office and call at him over the railing, jovially, sharply, viciously, excitedly. Messenger boys ran in and out with messages and telegrams. The clerks in the office jumped about like sailors during a storm. Even Pitcher's face relaxed into something resembling animation.

On the Exchange there were hurricanes and landslides and snowstorms and glaciers and volcanoes, and those elemental disturbances were reproduced in miniature in the broker's offices. Maxwell shoved his chair against the wall and transacted business after the manner of a toe dancer. He jumped from ticker to 'phone, from desk to door with the trained agility of a harlequin.

In the midst of this growing and important stress the broker became suddenly aware of a high-rolled fringe of golden hair under a nodding canopy of velvet and ostrich tips, and imitation sealskin sacque and a string of beads as large as hickory nuts, ending near the floor with a silver heart. There was a self-possessed young lady connected with these accessories; and Pitcher was there to construe her.

"Lady from the Stenographer's Agency to see about the position," said Pitcher.

Maxwell turned half around, with his hands full of papers and ticker tape.

"What position?" he asked, with a frown.

"Position of stenographer," said Pitcher. "You told me yesterday to call them up and have one sent over this morning."

"You are losing your mind, Pitcher," said Maxwell. "Why should I have given you any such instructions? Miss Leslie has given perfect satisfaction during the year she has been here. The place is hers as long as she chooses to retain it. There's no place open here, madam. Countermand that order with the agency, Pitcher, and don't bring any more of 'em in here."

The silver heart left the office, swinging and banging itself independently against the office furniture as it indignantly departed. Pitcher seized a moment to remark to the bookkeeper that the "old man" seemed to get more absent-minded and forgetful every day of the world.

The rush and pace of business grew fiercer and faster. On the floor they were pounding half a dozen stocks in which Maxwell's customers were heavy investors. Orders to buy and sell were coming and going as swift as the flight of swallows. Some of his own holdings were imperilled, and the man was working like some high-geared, delicate, strong machine—strung to full tension, going at full speed, accurate, never hesitating, with the proper word and decision and act ready and prompt as clockwork. Stocks and bonds, loans and mortgages, margins and securities—here was a world of finance, and there was no room in it for the human world or the world of nature.

When the luncheon hour drew near there came a slight lull in the uproar.

Maxwell stood by his desk with his hands full of telegrams and memoranda, with a fountain pen over his right ear

and his hair hanging in disorderly strings over his forehead. His window was open, for the beloved janitress, Spring, had turned on a little warmth through the waking registers of the earth.

And through the window came a wandering—perhaps a lost—odor—a delicate, sweet odor of lilac that fixed the broker for a moment immovable. For this odor belonged to Miss Leslie; it was her own, and hers only.

The odor brought her vividly, almost tangibly before him. The world of finance dwindled suddenly to a speck. And she was in the next room—twenty steps away.

"By George, I'll do it now," said Maxwell, half aloud. "I'll ask her now. I wonder I didn't do it long ago."

He dashed into the inner office with the haste of a short trying to cover. He charged upon the desk of the stenographer.

She looked up at him with a smile. A soft pink crept over her cheek, and her eyes were kind and frank. Maxwell leaned one elbow on her desk. He still clutched fluttering papers with both hands and the pen was above his ear.

"Miss Leslie," he began, hurriedly, "I have but a moment to spare. I want to say something in that moment. Will you be my wife? I haven't had time to make love to you in the ordinary way, but I really do love you. Talk quick, please—those fellows are clubbing the stuffing out of Union Pacific."

"Oh, what are you talking about?" exclaimed the young lady. She rose to her feet and gazed upon him, round-eyed.

"Don't you understand?" said Maxwell, restively. "I want you to marry me. I love you, Miss Leslie. I wanted to tell you, and I snatched a minute when things had slackened up a bit. They're calling me for the 'phone now. Tell 'em to wait a minute, Pitcher. Won't you, Miss Leslie?"

The stenographer acted very queerly. At first she seemed overcome with amazement; then tears flowed from her wondering eyes; and then she smiled sunnily through them, and one of her arms slid tenderly about the broker's neck.

"I know now," she said, softly. "It's this old business that has driven everything else out of your head for the time. I was frightened at first. Don't you remember, Harvey? We were married last evening at 8 o'clock in the Little Church around the Corner."

As soon as you finish reading Article 4, record your finishing time in the Time Record on page 4 of the PROGRESS FOLDER. *Then read Test 4 that appears next in this book.*

READING TEST 4   THE ROMANCE OF A BUSY BROKER

Read each test item and select the answer you believe is correct. Print the letter of your answer in the Answer Record on page 4 of the PROGRESS FOLDER.

1. When Harvey Maxwell entered his office with his young lady stenographer, Pitcher, the clerk, was mildly
   - (A) angry
   - (B) afraid
   - (C) jealous
   - (D) surprised
   - (E) pleased

2. The young lady had been Maxwell's stenographer for this period of time:
   - (A) One week
   - (B) One month
   - (C) Six months
   - (D) One year
   - (E) Two years

3. The young lady stenographer
   - (A) was flashily dressed and looked anxious
   - (B) was poorly dressed and looked sad
   - (C) was becomingly dressed and looked happy
   - (D) was well dressed and looked surprised
   - (E) was stylishly dressed and looked proud

4. Pitcher noticed a difference in the stenographer's behavior this morning because she
   - (A) went immediately to her desk in the inner office
   - (B) stopped to talk to Maxwell's other stenographers
   - (C) went out with Maxwell for a cup of coffee
   - (D) smiled and winked at Maxwell
   - (E) lingered in the outer office near Maxwell's desk

5. The young lady went over to Maxwell's desk probably because she wanted to ask him whether
   - (A) he had hired another stenographer
   - (B) he had rush work for her to do
   - (C) she might have the afternoon off
   - (D) she could answer letters for him
   - (E) she might resign from her position

6. When Pitcher told the young lady that "not a picture hat had shown up yet," he indicated that he
   - (A) liked a stenographer's dress more than her ability
   - (B) liked picture hats better than he liked turbans
   - (C) wanted a law passed against wearing picture hats
   - (D) had little respect for the typical stenographer
   - (E) wished more stenographers would wear picture hats

7. This was Harvey Maxwell's busy day. Each of these things except one happened. Which one did *not* happen?
   - (A) The ticker reeled out tape and the phone kept ringing.
   - (B) Many men came into the office and called at Maxwell.
   - (C) Maxwell went into his office and locked the door.
   - (D) Boys ran in and out of the office with messages.
   - (E) Office clerks ran around like sailors in a storm.

8. The broker's office reproduced in miniature the hurricanes and other disturbances that were occurring
   - (A) in Harvey Maxwell's life
   - (B) in many New York department stores
   - (C) in the heart of the young lady stenographer
   - (D) on the New York Stock Exchange
   - (E) all over the world

9. After Maxwell shoved his chair against the wall, he carried on his business much like a
   - (A) jack-in-the-box
   - (B) toe dancer
   - (C) chameleon
   - (D) marionette
   - (E) jack rabbit

10. In the midst of his rush of business, Maxwell became suddenly aware of the presence of a
    - (A) flashily dressed young lady
    - (B) well-dressed young man
    - (C) tastefully dressed young woman
    - (D) hurrying messenger boy
    - (E) prosperous looking customer

11. When Pitcher announced that the lady from the agency was here to see about the position, Maxwell said:
    - (A) "Send her in."
    - (B) "Put her to work."
    - (C) "What agency?"
    - (D) "Where is she?"
    - (E) "What position?"

12. When Pitcher said Maxwell had told him to call the agency, which one of these things did Maxwell *not* say?
    - (A) "I want a lady, not a clothes horse, for a stenographer."
    - (B) "You are losing your mind."
    - (C) "Miss Leslie's work has been perfectly satisfactory."
    - (D) "Miss Leslie can keep the position."
    - (E) "Tell the agency not to send any more stenographers."

13. Pitcher remarked to the bookkeeper that every day "the old man" appeared to get more
    - (A) thoughtful and courteous
    - (B) efficient and businesslike
    - (C) gentle and understanding
    - (D) angry and sharp-tongued
    - (E) absent-minded and forgetful

14. While Harvey Maxwell was buying and selling stocks, he acted most like
 - (A) a careful, methodical, and stout workhorse
 - (B) a quick, nervous, and intelligent ape
 - (C) a rapid, accurate, and strong machine
 - (D) a wild, angry, and stubborn bull
 - (E) a bright, scholarly, and friendly professor

15. The uproar of the office quieted down for the first time just before
 - (A) closing time
 - (B) lunch time
 - (C) the middle of the morning
 - (D) the middle of the afternoon
 - (E) dinner time

16. During the business lull, Maxwell felt that Miss Leslie was near him when he
 - (A) smelled the odor of lilacs
 - (B) saw roses in bloom
 - (C) felt a warm breeze
 - (D) heard a robin sing
 - (E) listened to Miss Leslie's voice

17. Just as soon as Maxwell thought of Miss Leslie, he
 - (A) called her on the telephone
 - (B) asked Pitcher to tell her to come in
 - (C) daydreamed about her for an hour
 - (D) remembered he had a date with her
 - (E) rushed into the inner office to see her

18. While Maxwell was telling Miss Leslie that he loved her, he again and again seemed to want
 - (A) to take a long honeymoon trip with her
 - (B) to get back to his business
 - (C) to be alone in the office with her
 - (D) to go into a quieter kind of work
 - (E) to let Pitcher manage the office that day

19. When Maxwell again asked Miss Leslie to marry him, she acted as if she were overcome with
 - (A) love
 - (B) annoyance
 - (C) amazement
 - (D) hope
 - (E) amusement

20. Miss Leslie tenderly slid her arm around Maxwell's neck and told him that
 - (A) Pitcher was holding the phone for him
 - (B) they had been married the evening before
 - (C) his new stenographer was in the other office
 - (D) they had a dinner engagement that evening
 - (E) he should not work so hard

NEXT — *Follow the directions (Steps 8-17) on page 1 of the* PROGRESS FOLDER.

ARTICLE 5

Give the heart[*]

by Sylvie Schuman

READING PRACTICE 5 In a book, magazine, or newspaper that you like, practice reading for speed and comprehension. Make a record of each such practice in Chart 3 on page 8 of the PROGRESS FOLDER. *Then do Reading Article 5.*

READING ARTICLE 5 Before you begin reading Article 5, record your starting time in the Time Record on page 4 of the PROGRESS FOLDER. *Then read Article 5. Read it as fast as you can, but make sure you understand what you are reading.*

IT WAS STILL snowing as Abby rode to work. A feathery dancing snow that laid a soft down on roofs and lawns and started a tingling anticipation in her. It would be a white Christmas.

This year Christmas held triple promise. She was earning her own money at a part-time job she'd obtained through her high school. And this year there was Dan, too.

A confusion of pain and tenderness welled in her at the thought of him. She had really taken the job at Kane's Department Store to be near Danny. To cement some definite bond between them. Now she had him, now she didn't. It had been fun the past summer. But fall had somehow sobered and deepened her, starting new demands. She wanted assurance from him, some little word or gesture. But Danny remained as light and elusive as those snowflakes tumbling past the bus window.

The question kept circling in her head. With such a touch-and-go relationship between them, should she—could

she—buy Danny a Christmas present without making a fool of herself?

She walked into the store and made her way to her counter. Suddenly she caught sight of Danny's red hair. As he brought his truck to a perilously sudden halt before the hobby counter, she darted forward, calling his name.

"Hi, Abigail!" he said.

He nodded toward the glass counter. "Nice set of X-acto knives, those. You could really operate on balsa with them."

She had learned finally that balsa wood was used for building model airplanes; that dope was lacquer, not an insult; what the difference was between free-flight and control-line.

"Long time no see, Danny," she said before she could stop herself.

"I'm building a control-line job for the national contest. Been tied up. There's an M.I.T.[*] scholarship for the winner."

Lamely she said, "Oh—I hope you win it."

He didn't pick up her cue. He didn't even try to be tactful.

That evening Abby went to see her

---

[*]Massachusetts Institute of Technology.

best friend, Meg Dearing. She tried to explain about Danny, but it came out garbled. "I'm botching it," she said. "It's hard to put into words. The point is if I buy Dan a present and he doesn't buy me one, I'll feel like a dope. Also I'll embarrass him. Also I might chase him away. He might think I'm pursuing him. On the other hand, if I don't buy him a present, and he does buy me one, I'll be sorry. Because—well, because—." She fumbled for words to hide the intensity of her feeling. "Because he's a nice guy."

The doorbell rang downstairs, and Abby jumped. It was George, Meg's boy friend, no doubt. Meg paid no heed.

"My grandma taught us a rhyme when we were kids," she said. Her voice chanted reminiscently:

> Some give rings,
> Some give strings.
> For my part,
> I give the heart.

The words struck at Abby oddly, reaching and yet not reaching her, like a cryptogram of which she knew only half the letters. She wanted to ask what she meant, but Meg was saying, "I've got to go. I'll phone you Monday."

She chewed over the verse. Somewhere hidden in it was the meaning which eluded her.

Looking back on her last date with Danny, Abby could find no new signpost to his feeling for her. If anything, he had been more flip. Anger stabbed at her, recalling his offhand "Be seein' you!" That did it. She made up her mind in that moment and she was sticking to it. She was not buying Daniel Keel a present.

The decision should have made her feel better. Somehow it left her as fidgety as before.

"I've definitely decided," she told Meg on the phone that night. "It's all too 'iffy.' I'm not getting him anything."

Meg said, "Oh—." And silence buzzed in the phone.

Abby didn't want to talk about it anymore. "How was your evening with George? Super as usual?"

Meg said in a distant, tired voice, "We had a quarrel. A bad one."

"Oh, Meg. I'm sorry. Is there anything I can do to help?"

"No. Look, Abby, I don't feel much like yaketing. Just wanted to know how you made out. I'll ring off now, mind?"

"Of course not, Meg—and take it easy." As she replaced the receiver, Abby sighed. She had never heard such a listless note in Meg's voice before. Men could be so confusing. . . .

The five days left till Christmas dwindled to four, then three. The weather was cold and grey, matching Abby's mood.

On Saturday, Meg came into the store. "Couldn't wait to show you." Her face beamed as she pointed to a long, clumsily wrapped package. "Got 'em upstairs."

"Skis!" Abby said. Confusion creased her brow. "But. . . ." She studied Meg's dancing eyes. "Did you make up with George?"

Meg nodded. "I had to swallow some pride. But it just wouldn't be a Christmas without him. It's all quite simple. I happen to like the guy."

The sincerity in her voice caught at Abby and illumined something in her. And suddenly she knew what Meg's rhyme meant.

Abby couldn't wait for the evening shift to take over. She handed her salary check to the cashier. "Could you cash this for me? Christmas shopping, you know."

The toy department was raucous. She approached the hobby counter, excitement quickening her pulses. "I want that set of X-acto knives," she said.

In her room later she placed it on her desk under the student lamp. Contentment flowed through her—such as she had not felt in weeks.

She had been acting out of petty pride, not out of her real feelings for Danny. That's what Meg had been trying to tell her. That's what Meg's gesture had shown her.

"Ab. .by. . ." her mother's voice caroled up the stairs. "Phone for you." That was probably Meg. But when she picked up the receiver, it was a masculine voice— Danny's voice—and her hand trembled.

"I looked for you at work today. And say . . ." he paused, as though embarrassed, "there's a good holiday show downtown tomorrow. I was wondering if we might go—or is it too short notice?"

"No," she said, "not at all. Only couldn't we stay home instead? I'd like that for a change."

"Sure," he said. "Fine." There was a silence again. "See you tomorrow then, Abby."

Now she could give him the gift instead of mailing it.

It snowed, Christmas, as though to order. When Danny arrived he was wearing a tweed suit instead of his regulation sweater and flannels. His hair was subjugated by tonic. They said "Merry Christmas" together and laughed. When the family had drifted out, discreetly, Abby picked up a package from beneath the tree.

"For you, Danny," she said softly.

His eyes were circles. "For me?" Quickly he untied the ribbon.

"Abby! You're a doll. You're an angel. Why, I had my eye on these! If you knew how I wanted them!"

He plunged his hand into his pocket. Awkwardly he pushed a small package at her.

For a moment Abby just stood there with the package in her hands. Then her fingers fumbled with the string, and finally she had it open. She gasped. Perfume— in the most beautiful little bottle.

"It's perfect, Danny," she said.

He took her hand and pulled her down on the sofa. Danny's voice was different than she'd ever heard it. "There are Christmas presents and Christmas presents. I want this one to mean something."

Then Danny said, "Maybe I've given you the wrong impression. Just because I spend a lot of time building planes. . . . You know, I'm an ambitious guy. You've got to understand that about me." He paused for words. "There are a lot of things to do before a fellow can get serious."

She understood. A new warmth glowed in Abby. It didn't come from the firelight, or even from Danny's hand comfortingly around hers. It came from a new, rich feeling about Christmas—from the knowledge that to give from the heart was its own reward.

As soon as you finish reading Article 5, record your finishing time in the Time Record on page 4 of the PROGRESS FOLDER. *Then read Test 5 that appears next in this book.*

READING TEST 5   GIVE THE HEART

Read each test item and select the answer you believe is correct. Print the letter of your answer in the Answer Record on page 4 of the PROGRESS FOLDER.

1. Christmas held promise for Abby because, in addition to the usual celebration, she
   - (A) had a part-time job and a boy friend
   - (B) received plenty of Christmas money from her father
   - (C) was having holiday guests and a party for them
   - (D) planned to exchange gifts with Danny
   - (E) had new ice skates and skating clothes

2. When thinking of Danny, Abby had a feeling of
   - (A) pain and tenderness
   - (B) warmth and assurance
   - (C) indifference and disgust
   - (D) anger and dislike
   - (E) pleasure and certainty

3. Abby took the job at Kane's Department Store mainly because she wanted
   - (A) to earn money for Christmas shopping
   - (B) to be near Danny
   - (C) to be with her girl friends
   - (D) to get sales experience
   - (E) to have something to do during Christmas vacation

4. Abby worried about buying Danny a Christmas gift because she did *not*
   - (A) have enough spending money
   - (B) like him as well as he liked her
   - (C) want him to buy her a present
   - (D) want to make a fool of herself
   - (E) know where to buy a present for him

5. As Abby made her way to her counter, she saw Danny come to a sudden halt before the hobby counter and look at a
   - (A) stamp collector's album
   - (B) model airplane motor
   - (C) model airplane box
   - (D) book on airplane design
   - (E) set of wood-carving knives

6. Abby tried to get Danny to show some interest in her by saying:
   - (A) "How's tricks?"
   - (B) "Hope you win that scholarship."
   - (C) "Long time no see."
   - (D) "Hail! Hail! The gang's all here."
   - (E) "I like airplanes, but . . ."

7. In talking with Meg, Abby said that if Danny bought her a present and she did not buy him one, she would
   - (A) feel like a fool
   - (B) embarrass him
   - (C) chase him away
   - (D) be sorry
   - (E) return his present

8. Meg tried to help Abby solve her problem by
   - (A) talking to Danny
   - (B) reading a story
   - (C) asking her grandmother
   - (D) giving her advice
   - (E) reciting a rhyme

9. At first Abby felt that Danny's remark, "Be seein' you," was very
   - (A) serious
   - (B) casual
   - (C) hopeful
   - (D) friendly
   - (E) courteous

10. After Abby finally decided not to buy Danny a gift, she felt
   - (A) ashamed
   - (B) pleased
   - (C) restless
   - (D) relieved
   - (E) angry

11. When Abby telephoned Meg to tell of her decision, Meg was *not* enthusiastic because she
   - (A) had quarreled with George
   - (B) felt sorry for Abby
   - (C) liked Danny better than George
   - (D) had bought a gift for George
   - (E) wanted Abby to forget about Danny

12. On the fifth and fourth days before Christmas, Abby's mood matched the weather, which was
   - (A) windy and snowy
   - (B) cold and grey
   - (C) warm and sunny
   - (D) chilly and clear
   - (E) moderate and calm

13. On Saturday when Meg came into the store with a long package, Abby was
   - (A) excited
   - (B) happy
   - (C) sad
   - (D) disappointed
   - (E) confused

14. The meaning of the statement, "I give the heart," became perfectly clear to Abby when Meg said:
   - (A) "It's all quite simple."
   - (B) "I happen to like the guy."
   - (C) "I got these skis upstairs."
   - (D) "I made up with George."
   - (E) "I couldn't wait to show you."

15. Abby bought a nice present for Danny immediately after
   - (A) the store closed for the day
   - (B) she saw Danny near the hobby counter
   - (C) she finished her workday
   - (D) she spent a sleepless night
   - (E) her mother told her to go ahead

16. Abby had been acting not
out of her real feeling
for Danny but from
- (A) anger
- (B) fear
- (C) pride
- (D) love
- (E) unhappiness

17. When her mother called
Abby to the phone, Abby
was sure the person on
the other end of the line
was
- (A) Abby's boss
- (B) Meg's grandmother
- (C) George
- (D) Meg
- (E) Danny

18. Abby was pleased that
they were going to stay
at home instead of going
to a show because then
she could
- (A) hand her gift to Danny
- (B) open Danny's gift to her
- (C) play some of her new dance records
- (D) help Danny save money for college
- (E) have Danny to herself

19. Abby knew that Danny
really cared for her when
he said that he wanted
- (A) her present to him to mean everything
- (B) her always to be his doll and his angel
- (C) her to understand that he was an ambitious guy
- (D) to be as serious about her as he was about airplanes
- (E) his present to her to mean something

20. A new warmth glowed in
Abby because she now
knew that
- (A) Danny was in love with her
- (B) the surest way to a man's heart is through a gift
- (C) the greatest gift in life is friendship
- (D) a gift from the heart is its own reward
- (E) she would "never look a gift horse in the mouth"

NEXT — *Follow the directions (Steps 8-17) on page 1 of the* PROGRESS FOLDER.

ARTICLE 6

Buying dynamite*

by Raymond L. Ditmars

READING PRACTICE 6 *In a book, magazine, or newspaper that you like, practice reading for speed and comprehension. Make a record of each such practice in Chart 3 on page 8 of the* PROGRESS FOLDER. *Then do Reading Article 6.*

READING ARTICLE 6 *Before you begin reading Article 6, record your starting time in the Time Record on page 4 of the* PROGRESS FOLDER. *Then read Article 6. Read it as fast as you can, but make sure you understand what you are reading.*

OBTAINING NEW specimens is one of the most fruitful sources of adventure in my position as curator of the Bronx Zoo in New York City. One morning I received a telephone call from one of the older animal dealers whose disordered gloomy places are fast disappearing. The man was excited and urged me to hurry down, that he had two big king cobras loose. We wanted to buy a pair of these creatures, but I didn't relish the job of capturing them. Nevertheless, the head keeper and I started downtown. We carried a large fiber satchel in which were two deep, burlap bags, and a staff with a noose at the end.

The king cobra holds the palm as the largest and most active of all poisonous serpents. It grows to be fifteen feet long and is built like a great whip. From its size and extremely deadly venom it is by far the most formidable of all snakes. But added to all this is the cobra's alert mentality or intelligence, and its common

*Condensed and adapted from *Strange Animals I Have Known*. Copyright 1931, by Raymond L. Ditmars. Reprinted by permission of Harcourt, Brace and Company, Inc.

habit of deliberately pursuing and attacking humans.

We found the dealer in a bad state of excitement. He had knocked off part of the cover of a case expecting to find the highly piled coils of the Indian python. Instead, he saw many loops of pale olive, no thicker than a man's wrist. At once, an orange-colored head with glowing eyes rose straight up. As he backed for the door, the cobra continued to rise directly upward until it had reared to the level of the man's chest. Just as he closed the door, he caught the flash of a second cobra rearing beside the first, the two like great candlesticks.

When we arrived, the first thing the dealer did was to unlock the door. Then he backed off while we peeked in. The room was about eighteen feet square. It was filled with trash, broken boxes, and their covers, which were piled waist and shoulder high.

There was nothing in sight. Fortunately, there was some cleared space on our side. We stepped inside and I momentarily closed the door to make more room. The head keeper picked up a stout piece of wooden strip which was loose on the floor. We also had the two burlap bags and the stick with the noose.

Next we cautiously peered around, gently shoving a broken box here and there before we saw the first snake. A greenish fold stuck out from beneath a case. The cobra was asleep.

"Go around behind me and open the door so we have a getaway; I'm going to stir him up!" I cautioned the head keeper. He quietly moved behind me and grasped the handle. *The door was locked!*

We were in a fine mess! The door was too strong to be kicked through and the windows were covered with heavy wire mesh. So I told my companion not to hesitate, but to swing hard and disable the cobra if he came at us. As there was nothing to do but start, I poked the greenish coil.

Instantly there was a hiss like a muffled sneeze—and out and up the serpent came, turning to us with his intent stare. His neck slowly expanded into the long narrow hood of his species, showing black and white spots between the scales.

That slow expanding of the hood was a favorable sign. The snake was hesitating between anger and surprise. I knew that here was the critical moment to get him. If the noose didn't work, he would get one of us—or there would be a dead cobra.

My assistant slowly waggled his stick as I reached forward and upward with the noose. I saw the cobra's intent eyes giving a flicking glance at the noose. There was also a slight movement of his head. But instantly the eyes gathered intensity in their gaze at me. Quickly the thin noose slipped over his head. But still he didn't move. A side swing of the pole tightened the noose and we pulled him down. The tightening cord narrowed

his hood about three inches from the head.

The way that long body poured out from under the boxes was terrifying. There were fully twelve feet of him. He furiously chewed the stick, embedding his fangs again and again in it. When my assistant got his stick across the snake's head, I grasped the brute by the neck. This is not as dangerous as it sounds if one knows how to do it. The idea was to back him into our bag. Meanwhile he was throwing his body around and crashing over boxes right and left. I yanked my end toward a corner. The other man pulled the serpent hand over hand toward the bag and then started to shove the tail part in.

We were successfully backing our first cobra in when we saw the other one. She gave us more of a shock than the first, being high on the boxes and rearing fully four feet besides. She looked over the scene like an avenger about to descend.

"Swing for that one!" I shouted, gathering the bag around the first snake. This snake was helping, if anything, in backing into the bag in his effort to pull his head away. As he yanked back, I let go of his head quickly with one hand and spun the bag with the other. In this way I sealed the serpent inside.

Then there was an awful clatter beside me. It was my assistant trying to hold down the head and neck of the second snake. Now it was my turn to waggle the noose staff and stand ready. The lady pulled loose once and made a magnificent sweep at us, but missed by a couple of feet. We nearly climbed the wall in our scrambling jumps to duck that strike.

It was the cobra or ourselves. I was prepared to end it with a kill when the head keeper made a swing between a blow and a push. He pinned the creature's neck against the top of a tilting case. The case lay fairly firm. I followed this by jamming the noosing staff nearer the head. I held it with all my strength as she lashed and whipped her body all around the room.

"I have a good grip—pin the head!" I yelled. My man's stick advanced over the head. All at once we had her, grasped firmly by the neck like the first. Here was victory! We backed number two into a bag. This was a lively but not difficult act as there was nothing else to bother us.

The next thing for us to do was to get the heaviest piece of wood in the room and batter down that door. The racket we made in the job was satisfying to both of us. We split one panel in several places. A moment later we would have had splinters flying into the hall. Then the door opened and the owner peeked in. The dealer, who was an oldish man, was as pale as clay, perspiring and shaking. He

gasped for a statement of results and I told him we had both cobras.

I have never seen a man recover his poise so quickly. He was keen for a dicker. Within five minutes he was rubbing his hands and telling us what a fine pair of cobras we had. The head keeper gave me a slow wink. We were also recovering our own poise and breath.

King cobras were sold for about $100 apiece in those days before the war, a price that meant a good profit for the dealer.

"I'll give you $100 for the *two* snakes," I told the dealer.

He wouldn't listen to such a price, but he was crafty enough to ask a bit less than $100 for each snake. I turned to the head keeper:

"Take them both upstairs and turn them loose where we found them."

That was enough. It closed the deal. It was our revenge for the locked door.

As soon as you finish reading Article 6, record your finishing time in the Time Record on page 4 of the Progress Folder. *Then read Test 6 that appears next in this book.*

READING TEST 6   BUYING DYNAMITE

Read each test item and select the answer you believe is correct. Print the letter of your answer in the Answer Record on page 4 of the Progress Folder.

---

1. Ditmars decided to go to the animal dealer's place because he wanted
   - (A) to keep the cobras from killing the dealer
   - (B) to buy a pair of cobras for the zoo
   - (C) to get more experience in handling cobras
   - (D) to secure these cobras without paying for them
   - (E) to write another cobra adventure story for his book

---

2. To capture the cobras, Ditmars and the head snake keeper took this thing with them:
   - (A) A strong net with a long handle
   - (B) A large flour sack with a cord at the top
   - (C) A big leather suitcase with a strong lock
   - (D) A large fiber basket with a heavy lid
   - (E) A long stick with a loop at the end

3. The king cobra is the most dangerous poisonous snake because of each of these things except one. Which is *not* true?
   - (A) It is the largest.
   - (B) It is the most active.
   - (C) It is the most intelligent.
   - (D) It most often attacks people.
   - (E) It frequently hypnotizes its prey.

4. When the dealer had knocked off part of the cover of the snake box, he had expected to find
   - (A) an anaconda
   - (B) a rattlesnake
   - (C) a python
   - (D) a cobra
   - (E) a gila monster

5. As the dealer backed toward the door, the first cobra
   - (A) rose until its head was chest-high
   - (B) crawled until half its body was out of the box
   - (C) struck again and again until it was tired out
   - (D) hissed until the man left the room
   - (E) lifted its head until it was near the ceiling

6. When Ditmars and the head keeper peeked into the room, they saw that it was
   - (A) fairly large and well-lighted
   - (B) guarded by two angry cobras
   - (C) filled with trash and broken boxes
   - (D) lined with neatly-arranged animal cases
   - (E) nearly empty

7. At first Ditmars and the head keeper
   - (A) climbed on top of a very tall box
   - (B) asked the dealer to close the door behind them
   - (C) stepped into a cleared space in the room
   - (D) opened up both of the heavy burlap bags
   - (E) put the cover back on the snake case

8. When the two men saw the first cobra, it was
   - (A) asleep beneath a case
   - (B) crawling toward a window
   - (C) raised up ready to strike
   - (D) heading for the doorway
   - (E) looking for its mate

9. In order to make a getaway if the cobras attacked, Ditmars told the head keeper
   - (A) to break the door down with a big stick
   - (B) to take the heavy screens off the windows
   - (C) to move all the boxes away from the door
   - (D) to build a small fire in front of the door
   - (E) to open the door

10. When Ditmars found the door locked, he told his companion to do this if a cobra came near:
   - (A) Grab the cobra just behind the head.
   - (B) Shout to the dealer to bring a shotgun.
   - (C) Hit the cobra with his stick.
   - (D) Throw an empty box over the cobra.
   - (E) Trap the cobra in a burlap bag.

11. Ditmars was pleased when the cobra crawled out, rose, and expanded its hood, because this meant the snake was
    - (A) hesitating between anger and surprise
    - (B) looking around for the other snake
    - (C) getting ready to retreat to its own box
    - (D) watching the head keeper instead of him
    - (E) undecided between fear and bravery

12. As the cobra stared intently at Ditmars, he skillfully used his pole
    - (A) to pin its head against the floor
    - (B) to take its attention away from the keeper
    - (C) to lift its body into the air
    - (D) to slip a noose over its head
    - (E) to push its head into a burlap bag

13. While Ditmars held the cobra firmly just behind its head, his companion
    - (A) kept his stick firmly on its body
    - (B) looked around for the other cobra
    - (C) scratched the back of its head to quiet it
    - (D) tried to throw the bag over its head
    - (E) worked to put it tail-first into the bag

14. The second cobra frightened the men more than the first cobra did because she
    - (A) crawled toward them behind their backs
    - (B) reared up near them while she was high on the boxes
    - (C) struck at them before the first snake was bagged
    - (D) fastened her fangs in their noose stick
    - (E) tried to rescue her mate from them

15. As Ditmars let go of the head of the first cobra with one hand, he used his other hand to close the bag by
    - (A) pulling its draw string
    - (B) pinning it
    - (C) folding it
    - (D) twirling it
    - (E) holding it

16. When the second cobra slipped out of the noose and struck at the two men, they nearly
    - (A) trapped the snake in a burlap bag
    - (B) let the first cobra out of the bag
    - (C) broke down the door of the room
    - (D) climbed the wall of the room
    - (E) knocked over all the boxes

17. To save their lives, Ditmars was ready to kill the second cobra when the keeper used his stick
    - (A) to fasten a loop around the snake's neck
    - (B) to pin the snake's head against a case
    - (C) to knock the snake unconscious for a moment
    - (D) to hold the snake's jaws wide open
    - (E) to get the snake to look somewhere else

18. Just after the men had both cobras in the bags, they
    - (A) shouted to the dealer to unlock the door
    - (B) sat down to rest and talk
    - (C) put the snake bags into the fiber valise
    - (D) used a heavy stick to batter down the door
    - (E) tried to get out through a window

19. Immediately after the dealer learned that the men from the zoo had both cobras in the bag, he
    - (A) quieted down and talked business
    - (B) became pale, perspiring, and shaky
    - (C) thanked and paid them for their work
    - (D) told them to take the snakes away
    - (E) asked for more money than the snakes were worth

20. Ditmars told the head keeper to turn the cobras loose upstairs, probably because he wanted
    - (A) to make the dealer clean up his animal room
    - (B) to get even with the dealer for locking the door
    - (C) to show the dealer how to catch cobras
    - (D) to secure the snakes as cheaply as possible for the zoo
    - (E) to get something for the dangerous work he had done

NEXT — *Follow the directions (Steps 8-17) on page 1 of the* PROGRESS FOLDER.

ARTICLE 7

*The gladsome washing machine season**

by Ruth McKenney

READING PRACTICE 7 *In a book, magazine, or newspaper that you like, practice reading for speed and comprehension. Make a record of each such practice in Chart 3 on page 8 of the* PROGRESS FOLDER. *Then do Reading Article 7.*

READING ARTICLE 7 *Before you begin reading Article 7, record your starting time in the Time Record on page 4 of the* PROGRESS FOLDER. *Then read Article 7. Read it as fast as you can, but make sure you understand what you are reading.*

OTHER PEOPLE may go around caroling about spring and violets and things, but I regard the gladsome May season with considerable sourness. It makes me think of washing machines.

For my father used to hold himself in all during the blustery winter months, a little restless, but still fairly content with his *Saturday Evening Post* and a few rounds of bridge on Saturday nights. But come the first warm day, and Father was

off on his quest of the perfect washing machine.

Father was a man of regular habits, and year after year, the storm always broke in exactly the same fashion. Father would come whistling down to breakfast, always a sign of trouble on the wing, and start off merrily with, "Well, well, well, I guess today's washing day, isn't it?"

He knew perfectly well it was, of course. The breakfast room was just over the section of the basement where Belle, the laundress, was hard at work at the family washing machine. You could hear the

---

*Condensed and adapted from *My Sister Eileen.* Copyright 1938, by Ruth McKenney. Reprinted by permission of Harcourt, Brace & Company.

groan and whine and swoosh of the machine with perfect distinctness as you gulped your morning shredded wheat.

"Uhmmmmmm," the whole family would murmur warily, in reply.

"Well, I guess today's just as good as any day to give a try to the new model."

When the argument finally broke out, Father was always very much grieved that none of his own kith and kin took the slightest interest in his career. Here he was, the manager of a home electric appliance factory ("Mother's Best Helper") and did his family care whether his new fall model washing machine was going to be a success or not? No. He worked himself to the bone, day and night, to provide food, and yes, luxuries for his little brood and look what he got in return! A lot of carping talk about whether Belle would quit or not if he brought the experimental model home. A man's own basement was no longer, he supposed, his castle. He liked Belle, but was Belle going to ruin his business career? He would be mighty sorry when we had Belle and no money to pay her with. You can't pay Belle on what you get from selling pencils on street corners.

Besides, he absolutely guaranteed that this new model was past the experimental stage and it really would not squirt oil all over the best tablecloth like the spring before.

And for the last time, a laboratory was no place to give a final test to a washing machine. You needed practical home conditions to see if it would really stand up under the wear and tear housewives would give it next fall. Housewives are all dumb and continually pull the wrong lever and jam up the works and you need to see if a washing machine that works fine in a laboratory will stand the strain of a lot

of feeble-minded women running it backwards all the time.

So about nine-fifteen that morning a large truck would draw up in our driveway and a crew of four or five husky men in oil-stained overalls would jump out and start to yell, "Easy, easy there, boys, they ain't got this thing screwed together very tight."

Belle, who was suspicious of machinery at its best, regarded Father's spring washing machine models as creatures of the devil. They were infernal contraptions invented by Satan himself to plague her poor old soul and body.

Some years the new model blew up the moment Belle touched the motor button. There would be a five-minute silence after the truck and the delivery crew left, while Belle put a batch of clothes and the appropriate amounts of soap chips and hot water in the new machine. Then suddenly, as she turned the switch, a low roar, a grinding noise, and then a loud plop, plop, plop, followed by a hysterical shriek of bolts, gears, and motor, rising finally to a mighty climax with an explosion that rocked the neighborhood or anyhow the house next door. As quiet slowly settled down again, we could hear Belle saying her prayers in the coal bin, whither she had fled for refuge.

The disintegration of the new model was usually not quite so rapid, however, although nearly always as spectacular. Sometimes Belle would get half the family washing done before a low peculiar whine caught her alert ear. She would leap to turn off the motor, not always before the whine blossomed into the mighty roar of the whole machine shaking apart before her very eyes. Other years, Belle would learn that something had gone a little wrong when she took the cover off the tub to remove the freshly washed clothes, only to find them floating in a sea of black oil.

But in the whole era of new spring experimental models, the wash day never passed without Father being summoned home from his factory by his hysterical family. He would arrive on these occasions riding on the repair truck. With him he brought the entire experimental department, including seven bright young men only recently graduated from Massachusetts Institute of Technology and four hard-bitten practical mechanics who had no use for the college geniuses.

The truck would pull up briskly beside the basement door and the enthralled neighbor ladies would watch twelve strong men and true march into the McKenney house, presumably to fix up one little old washing machine. Presently, by keeping a sharp ear cocked, they would hear the sound of bitter controversy leaking out from the basement windows. Men raised their voices in bold denial of bolder accusations.

After an hour's loud argument, one of the inventors would come brusquely up the stairs, stamp to the telephone without so much as a kind word for the assembled and anxious womenfolk. He spread a film of oil and grease over the living-room carpet and leaned against the wallpaper as he juggled the receiver professionally against a dirty ear. The wallpaper always had to be cleaned after the washing machine season.

"Hello," the young man would growl, "listen, that bunch of saps in my department thinks we got a little differential trouble in the new model. So send us over some parts, will yuh?"

Then he would name off various high-sounding contraptions while Belle would be at his elbow, demanding, "How soon are they going to get it fixed? I got to get my washing done."

Getting the washing done was always the least of Father's troubles. After several hours' work, Father would bawl up the basement stairs, ordering sandwiches and beer and other nutritious items for himself and his crew which had now expanded considerably. For the man who brought the parts also arrived in a truck with two other gentlemen from some obscure department in the factory, who stayed around to see what was up. Then one of the executives of the company, getting word of the trouble, would arrive in a big Packard. By late afternoon the McKenney driveway would be crowded with trucks, Packards, and other vehicles, while the basement would be swarming with inventors, toolmakers, mechanics, worried general managers, excited sales managers, and Father.

At last, as dusk fell, all hands would admit temporary defeat and the trucking crew would reappear to haul the poor new model, now considerably denuded, back to the factory. With a roar of motors and the grinding of many sets of gears, the little band of inventors, company executives, and mechanics would depart, leaving Belle mourning over a pile of dirty clothes in the basement.

Some years it took five different tries to get the experimental model to run through a day's washing. Before Father's inventors finally solved their differential trouble, Belle would be driven to the verge of giving notice, and the Cleveland Heights Flat and Fancy Laundry Company, Inc., would get plenty of rush trade from the McKenney family. But eventually peace and calm would settle down over the basement regions of the household and Belle would resign herself to doing the washing all year on the now renovated experimental model.

As soon as you finish reading Article 7, record your finishing time in the Time Record on page 4 of the PROGRESS FOLDER. *Then read Test 7 that appears next in this book.*

READING TEST 7   THE GLADSOME WASHING MACHINE SEASON

Read each test item and select the answer you believe is correct. Print the letter of your answer in the Answer Record on page 4 of the PROGRESS FOLDER.

---

1. According to the author (Ruth), she and her sister Eileen thought of May as a season of
   - (A) gladness and electric washers
   - (B) sourness and washing machines
   - (C) spring and violets
   - (D) fatigue and housecleaning
   - (E) work and many visitors

---

2. During the winter months, Father was fairly content with
   - (A) trying out a new washing machine
   - (B) taking care of the furnace
   - (C) reading and card-playing
   - (D) fixing things inside the house
   - (E) building a new washer in the basement

---

3. One spring day every year the family knew that Father was ready to try out a new washing machine, when this happened: Father
   - (A) stayed late at the office
   - (B) came whistling down to breakfast
   - (C) said he wished every day was washing day
   - (D) asked the family to go to the factory
   - (E) wanted to sell the old washer

---

4. While Ruth was having breakfast on wash day, she could hear
   - (A) Belle swearing at the old washing machine
   - (B) the old washing machine breaking down
   - (C) the noise of the old washing machine
   - (D) her father working on the old washing machine
   - (E) a repairman fixing the old washing machine

---

5. When Father said that he guessed today was washing day, the whole family said carefully:
   - (A) "Please"
   - (B) "Ohhhhhh"
   - (C) "Wrong"
   - (D) "Right"
   - (E) "Uhmmmmm"

---

6. Father was unhappy because his own family did not seem interested in his factory. There he was the
   - (A) superintendent
   - (B) owner
   - (C) head mechanic
   - (D) manager
   - (E) chief technician

---

7. Father always mentioned that he worked very hard
- (A) to develop a new and better model machine
- (B) to keep all his men on the job the year around
- (C) to provide necessities and luxuries for the family
- (D) to make washing easier for many housewives
- (E) to keep Belle from quitting as the family laundress

8. Father said that he had to be successful in business so that he could
- (A) pay money to Belle
- (B) get rid of Belle
- (C) buy a better washing machine for Belle
- (D) hire an assistant for Belle
- (E) let Belle have a vacation

9. Father guaranteed that the new model machine would *not*
- (A) squirt oil over the family's best tablecloth
- (B) break down after a few minutes
- (C) tear the family's nicest curtains
- (D) bring his men tramping through the house
- (E) make Belle angry or drive her crazy

10. Father said that he wanted to see whether the new model would stand the strain of being run by
- (A) experienced laundresses
- (B) bright older girls
- (C) hen-pecked husbands
- (D) dumb housewives
- (E) alert homemakers

11. The truck crew yelled "Easy, easy" in handling the machine because they believed it might
- (A) crash to the pavement
- (B) be hard to install
- (C) fall apart
- (D) be too heavy for them
- (E) start running too soon

12. Belle regarded Father's new washing machine as a
- (A) welcome addition to the home
- (B) modern wonder to aid her
- (C) good fairy to help her
- (D) sign of spring to awaken her
- (E) creature of the devil to bother her

13. Just after the new washing machine broke down and exploded, Belle usually
- (A) fled to the coal bin and said her prayers
- (B) called to Father to take the machine away
- (C) closed her eyes and put her fingers in her ears
- (D) soaked and scrubbed the washing by hand
- (E) telephoned the laundry to come and get the clothes

14. While using the new model, Belle would sometimes find that the machine had
- (A) torn many of the articles of clothing in it
- (B) broken much of the cement of the basement floor
- (C) crashed in a big heap on the floor
- (D) leaked out all of the soapy water
- (E) covered all the clothing inside with black oil

15. Soon after the new model had broken down, Father would arrive on the repair truck with a crew of
    - (A) practical housewives and college home economists
    - (B) practical businessmen and college heads
    - (C) practical salesmen and college teachers
    - (D) practical mechanics and college geniuses
    - (E) practical clean-up men and college handymen

16. The neighbor ladies who gathered around the basement door soon heard
    - (A) Belle telling the men to get out
    - (B) the men inside arguing
    - (C) the washing machine running nicely again
    - (D) Ruth's mother asking the men to clean up
    - (E) one of the mechanics telephoning the factory

17. When one of the inventors came upstairs to telephone the factory, the family found that he always
    - (A) spent too much time on the telephone
    - (B) spread oil and grease on the carpet and wallpaper
    - (C) told the women why the machine did not work
    - (D) told Belle she would soon finish the washing
    - (E) showed Ruth's mother how to operate the machine

18. Father seemed to be least interested in
    - (A) seeing the excited sales managers
    - (B) talking with a worried company executive
    - (C) obtaining the needed parts from the factory
    - (D) supplying the working crew with free food and beer
    - (E) getting the family washing done

19. After one crew of men worked all day on the washing machine, another crew
    - (A) hauled the machine back to the factory
    - (B) continued working until late at night
    - (C) brought another machine of the same model
    - (D) took the machine to a junk yard
    - (E) showed up the next day to work on the machine

20. While the men were trying to get the experimental model so that it worked properly,
    - (A) Father was "Mother's Best Helper"
    - (B) Belle quit working for the family
    - (C) all the women helped with the laundry
    - (D) Belle did the family washing by hand
    - (E) the family sent its laundry out

NEXT — *Follow the directions (Steps 8-17) on page 1 of the* PROGRESS FOLDER.

ARTICLE 8

The man who rode a shark*

by Wilmon Menard

READING PRACTICE 8 *In a book, magazine, or newspaper that you like, practice reading for speed and comprehension. Make a record of each such practice in Chart 3 on page 8 of the* PROGRESS FOLDER. *Then do Reading Article 8.*

READING ARTICLE 8 *Before you begin reading Article 8, record your starting time in the Time Record on page 4 of the* PROGRESS FOLDER. *Then read Article 8. Read it as fast as you can, but make sure you understand what you are reading.*

A FEW MONTHS before I came to the South Pacific coral atoll of Nukurua (Amanu), I witnessed a sight at the island of Rapa, to the south of Tahiti, that has made me a shark's enemy for life.

Native divers, working pearl shell beds under water, have been seized by sharks. Sometimes the monsters, with a mad wrench, strip off the skin and flesh, leaving lengths of white bone exposed. Several divers in the Dangerous Isles (the Tuamotus) with whom I have talked have been attacked by sharks while descending, and the brutes have sheared off parts of their jaws and cheeks, leaving their gleaming teeth visible forever after.

But the most wonderful story in the Dangerous Isles is the tale of how a giant Tuamotuan, Mopi by name, rode on the back of a huge shark. French traders, schooner captains, and colonial officials verified the account, as follows. While gathering pearl shells under water at the pearl-diving atoll of Hikueru, Mopi bumped heads with a shark. The creature,

fully twelve feet long, circled swiftly and attacked him. Mopi, caught off guard, was forced to seek refuge in a coral cavern. But the shark lunged in after him, and Mopi, seeing no escape, struggled desperately onto its back and buried his strong fingers in the wide, deep gills.

The shark, enraged and startled, headed with great speed for the surface. There the brute barrel-rolled and leaped clear out of the water with terrifying impact, trying to free itself of its rider. It suddenly shot to the bottom again, crashing wildly through brittle coral trees and slashing Mopi cruelly. Again it zoomed to the surface, blood gushing from its torn gills. This time it headed toward a submerged reef near the native village, and there it accidentally beached itself.

The villagers, who had lined the coral strand to watch Mopi's amazing ride, attacked the shark with spears and clubs. Mopi walked unaided to the beach, his entire body torn and bleeding from the shark's rough skin and from collisions with coral. Then, seized with blind rage, he whirled around suddenly, ran back to the shark, and gave it a smashing blow on the snout above the jaws with his fist.

But at that moment, the shark's jaws flashed wide—and Mopi's hand was gone!

I had always hoped to meet this extraordinary Tuamotuan, and one morning on Amanu my wish was fulfilled. A loud, yodeling call aroused me just after dawn, and when I stuck my head out of my palm-leaf hut, I saw a Polynesian giant standing beside a beached sailing canoe. He wore only a blue-and-white *pareu* tied around his strong, bulging loins. His muscular body was marked by long, serrated, livid scars, the telltale decorations of a veteran shark-killer. His head was massive, with tight, crisp ringlets of hair hanging low over his wide forehead. His eyes were large and liquid, tender though giving the impression of absolute fearlessness.

When he saw me, he grinned and waved gaily. His right hand was severed at the wrist.

" 'Ullo, big boy!" he cried in a deep, booming voice. "My name Mopi! I been Frisco! I walk down Market Street! *Yah! Vera ka hau!* Hot stuff!"

(Mopi had once voyaged to San Francisco on a copra schooner, and he had picked up an amazing vocabulary of English words.)

He rushed up to me and threw his injured arm around my shoulders in a rough hug.

"I come Amanu. I hear you no like sharks!" he shouted.

Mopi shared my simple breakfast with me, and not long afterward I had an opportunity to see him under water with sharks. We hurriedly launched the canoe across the lagoon and paddled to the foraging ground of the sea gangsters. The surface of the lagoon was unruffled, and the marine garden that spread out below us could be seen as clearly as if viewed under an immense magnifying glass. The sunlight was reflected from the coarse, sandy bottom and cast shadows in coral caverns where the monsters of the lagoon were possibly ensconced. Now and again a shaft of light would transfix the sliding body of a barracuda or a small lagoon shark or the green, slimy sheen of a twisting moray. It was like an amazing kaleidoscope.

When I turned around to speak to Mopi, who was in the stern paddling, I saw that he was affixing to his injured wrist a leather stirrup ending in a brass cap. In the center of the brass end was a threaded hole. He reached down, grinning, and lifted up an object wrapped in an oily cloth. When he unrolled it, I saw that it was a long three-edged knife. This he screwed securely into the threaded hole of the guard.

He shouted truculently and waved it in the air. The canoe rocked suddenly and Mopi was over the side, with hardly a ripple to mark his descent. Through the water, I watched him go down feet first, the knife flashing brightly in the clear water. Then, at a depth of about ten feet, he turned and shot like a torpedo, head first, for the bottom. A huge shark was cruising slowly among smaller ones. The smaller sharks took instant flight, but the monster he had singled out circled him warily at a distance. Mopi swam toward the shark boldly, the knife-arm extended. The killer swam deeper, and Mopi followed him, until I could see only a shadowy outline of shark and man. A few seconds later, they rose higher, and I suddenly saw Mopi make a quick lunge at the shark.

Mopi's face was upturned now, and I could see that he was "making faces" at the shark. Then his fixed sword flashed out, and a small jet of gray smoke was ejected from the belly of the monster. (Blood in sea water at this distance appears gray in color.) The shark was furious. It circled quickly and charged Mopi, who nimbly somersaulted, swam deeper, and then came up under the brute for another hard knife thrust. Again the native swam nimbly around a coral fan and pricked the thrashing, enraged shark. Then—danger!

A small though dangerous-sized shark came into the scene, attracted by the blood of the large one. It first saw Mopi and headed toward him; but the Tuamotuan was not to be caught napping, and when the small shark swam past, flashing its jaws for a bite, Mopi sank the knife deeply into its neck just back of the gills. The shark was moving away from him at the time, and, by its own momentum, drew the knife out clean, without jerking Mopi around.

But the large shark was still to be reckoned with. It rushed in for a swift attack on Mopi, and the native jerked his body aside just in time to save his limbs from a cruel bite. Mopi apparently realized that with so much blood in the water he was exposing himself need-

lessly to danger, so he quickly reached out and grabbed a fluke of the big shark. He twisted his body under its stomach and, at the same time, sank his knife deeply into its belly. Then he released his hold on its fluke and allowed the force of the shark's motion to rip open its stomach.

The battle over, Mopi came to the surface, blowing his nose lustily. He was breathing in whistling gasps through his clenched teeth in the peculiar way of Tuamotuan divers, to relieve his strained lungs and accustom his lung muscles to normal action. Then he climbed unaided into the canoe, unscrewed his bayonet, wrapped it in the fish-oil rag.

He gestured down into the depths of the lagoon. "Now you do go down and give it to them."

I gave Mopi a long, dubious stare. "My good friend," I said grinning, "when I want to cut short my life, I'll find pleasanter ways of doing it than rubbing noses with sharks!"

Mopi gave me a broad, understanding smile. "Maybe you right."

As soon as you finish reading Article 8, record your finishing time in the Time Record on page 4 of the PROGRESS FOLDER. *Then read Test 8 that appears next in this book.*

READING TEST 8   THE MAN WHO RODE A SHARK

Read each test item and select the answer you believe is correct. Print the letter of your answer in the Answer Record on page 4 of the PROGRESS FOLDER.

1. The natives of Amanu in the South Pacific are most often attacked by sharks while they are diving for
   - (A) coral
   - (B) coins
   - (C) pearls
   - (D) fun
   - (E) seafood

2. While Mopi was under water, he was attacked by a large shark just after
   - (A) he cut the shark with his knife
   - (B) he and the shark bumped heads
   - (C) the shark slashed his leg
   - (D) he hit the shark with his fists
   - (E) he and the shark were scratched by a coral reef

3. To save himself, Mopi struggled onto the shark's back and used his fingers to hold onto the shark's
    - (A) gills
    - (B) fins
    - (C) jaws
    - (D) tail
    - (E) skin

4. As the shark tried to free itself of its rider, it did each of these things except one. Which did it *not* do?
    - (A) It crashed through coral trees.
    - (B) It sped to the surface and leaped out.
    - (C) It suddenly shot to the bottom.
    - (D) It snapped at Mopi's legs.
    - (E) It rolled over and over like a barrel.

5. The shark was captured because it
    - (A) was tired out by Mopi
    - (B) swam into a strong fish net
    - (C) was harpooned by Mopi's friends
    - (D) caught itself on a fish hook
    - (E) beached itself on a coral reef

6. When Mopi walked onto the beach, his whole body was torn and bleeding from cuts made by
    - (A) the sharp coral
    - (B) the shark's fins
    - (C) the shark's teeth
    - (D) his own knife
    - (E) the underwater shells

7. The villagers attacked the shark with
    - (A) knives and swords
    - (B) pistols and guns
    - (C) spears and clubs
    - (D) ropes and nets
    - (E) hands and feet

8. Mopi lost his right hand when he
    - (A) hit the shark just above the mouth
    - (B) rode the shark through sharp coral beds
    - (C) rubbed the shark's rough skin
    - (D) grabbed the shark's strong jaws
    - (E) scraped the shark's top fin

9. When the author first met Mopi, he noticed each of these things except one. Which did he *not* notice?
    - (A) Mopi's body and head were large.
    - (B) Mopi's voice was high and soft.
    - (C) Mopi's body had many long scars.
    - (D) Mopi's eyes appeared kind but fearless.
    - (E) Mopi's hair was long and curly.

10. Mopi had learned many English words when he
    - (A) worked on a sailboat to Australia
    - (B) went to a missionary school near his home
    - (C) talked with American soldiers and sailors
    - (D) sailed on a schooner to San Francisco
    - (E) traded goods with tourists to his island

11. When Mopi met the author, he was very
 - (A) timid
 - (B) rude
 - (C) friendly
 - (D) quiet
 - (E) suspicious

12. When Mopi took the author in a canoe across the lagoon, the
 - (A) sea was rough and muddy
 - (B) tide was going out fast
 - (C) sky was cloudy and dark
 - (D) water was calm and clear
 - (E) sharks had frightened all smaller fish away

13. Into the metal cap that was strapped to his right wrist, Mopi screwed a
 - (A) double fishhook
 - (B) long knife
 - (C) short harpoon
 - (D) short dagger
 - (E) long spear

14. When Mopi left the canoe to go into the water, he
 - (A) dived head first and swam to the bottom
 - (B) slid feet first and then shot to the bottom
 - (C) swam slowly for a while and then did a surface dive
 - (D) swam rapidly under water just below the surface
 - (E) slid feet first from the surface to the bottom

15. Mopi first thrust at the shark while the shark was
 - (A) circling around him
 - (B) swimming toward the bottom
 - (C) turning a somersault
 - (D) heading toward him
 - (E) swimming toward the surface

16. When Mopi withdrew his weapon, there came from the shark's belly what looked like a stream of
 - (A) red blood
 - (B) black ink
 - (C) green water
 - (D) white milk
 - (E) gray smoke

17. The small but dangerous shark that tried to bite Mopi had come because it was attracted by
 - (A) the rich marine garden
 - (B) the sight of a man in the water
 - (C) Mopi's canoe
 - (D) a school of smaller fish
 - (E) the blood of the large shark

18. After Mopi had thrust his weapon into the underside of the large shark, he
 - (A) stabbed the shark just behind a gill
 - (B) cut off one of the shark's great jaws
 - (C) forced his weapon down the shark's throat
 - (D) allowed the shark's motion to rip open its belly
 - (E) held onto the shark's fluke until the fish died

19. When Mopi first came to the surface, he
   (A) coughed up the water in his throat
   (B) filled his lungs and held his breath for a while
   (C) gasped air through his closed teeth
   (D) gulped air through his open mouth
   (E) breathed deeply and rapidly through his nose

20. When invited to kill a shark, the author said that when he wanted to shorten his life, he would find
   (A) pleasanter ways of doing it
   (B) easier ways of doing it
   (C) more interesting ways of doing it
   (D) safer ways of doing it
   (E) quicker ways of doing it

NEXT — *Follow the directions (Steps 8-17) on page 1 of the* PROGRESS FOLDER.

ARTICLE 9

My convict*

by Charles Dickens

READING PRACTICE 9 *In a book, magazine, or newspaper that you like, practice reading for speed and comprehension. Make a record of each such practice in Chart 3 on page 8 of the* PROGRESS FOLDER. *Then do Reading Article 9.*

READING ARTICLE 9 *Before you begin reading Article 9, record your starting time in the Time Record on page 4 of the* PROGRESS FOLDER. *Then read Article 9. Read it as fast as you can, but make sure you understand what you are reading.*

MY FIRST MOST vivid and broad impression of the identity of things, seems to me to have been gained on a memorable raw afternoon towards evening. At such a time I found out for certain, that this bleak place overgrown with nettles was the churchyard; and that my father, Philip Pirrip, late of this parish, and also Georgiana wife of the above, were dead and buried; and that the dark flat wilderness beyond the churchyard was the marshes; and that the distant savage lair from which the wind was rushing, was the sea; and that the small bundle of shivers growing afraid of it all and beginning to cry, was myself, Pip.

"Hold your noise!" cried a terrible voice, as a man started up from among the graves at the side of the church porch.

A fearful man, all in coarse grey, with a great iron on his leg. A man with no hat, and with broken shoes, and with an old rag tied around his head.

The man, after looking at me for a moment, turned me upside down, and emptied my pockets. There was nothing in

---

*Condensed and adapted from *Great Expectations*, by Charles Dickens. First published 1860-61.

them but a piece of bread which he ate ravenously.

"Ha!" he muttered then, considering. "Where d'ye live—supposin' you're kindly let to live which I han't made up my mind about?"

"With my sister, sir—Mrs. Joe Gargery —wife of Joe Gargery, the blacksmith, sir."

"Blacksmith, eh?" said he. And he looked down at his leg.

"Now, lookee here," he said. "You bring me, tomorrow morning early, a file and some wittles and you never dare to say a word concerning your having seen such a person as me, and you shall be let to live. You fail, and your heart and your liver shall be tore out, roasted and ate. There's a young man hid with me, in comparison with which young man I am a angel. That young man has a secret way pecooliar to himself, of getting at a boy, and at his heart, and at his liver. Now, what do you say?"

I said that I would get him the file, and I would get him what broken bits of food I could, and I would come to him at the old Battery, early in the morning. Then I ran home without stopping.

I was afraid to sleep that night. I was in mortal terror of the young man who wanted my heart and liver; I was in mortal terror of myself, who had promised to rob Mrs. Joe's pantry; and I was in mortal terror of Mrs. Joe, who had a hard and heavy hand. As soon as darkness began to lift, I got up and went downstairs. I stole some bread, some rind of cheese, about half a jar of mincemeat, some brandy from a stone bottle, and a beautiful round compact pork pie. Then I got a file from among Joe's tools and ran for the misty marshes.

I had just crossed a ditch which I knew to be very near the Battery, when I saw the man sitting before me. His back was towards me, and he had his arms folded, and was nodding forward, heavy with sleep. I went forward softly and touched him on the shoulder. He instantly jumped up, and it was not the same man, but another man!

And yet this man was dressed in coarse grey, too, and had a great iron on his leg, and was lame, and hoarse, and cold, and was everything that the other man was; except that he had not the same face, and had a flat-broad-brimmed, low-crowned felt hat on. He swore an oath at me, made a hit at me, and then he ran into the mist, stumbling twice as he went, and I lost him.

"It's the young man!" I thought, feeling my heart shoot as I identified him. I dare say I should have felt a pain in my liver, too, if I had known where it was.

I soon found the right man, hugging himself and limping to and fro, waiting for me. He did not turn me upside down, this time, but left me right side upwards while I opened the bundle and emptied my pockets.

The man took strong sharp sudden bites of the food, just like a dog. He swallowed, or rather snapped up every mouthful, too soon and too fast; and he looked sideways here and there while he ate, as if he thought there was danger of somebody's coming to take the pie away.

"I am afraid you won't leave any of it for the young man. That you spoke of. That was hid with you," said I timidly.

"Oh, ah!" he returned, with something like a gruff laugh. "Him? Yes, yes! *He* don't want no wittles."

"I thought he looked as if he did," said I.

The man stopped eating, and regarded

me with the keenest scrutiny and the greatest surprise.

"Looked? When?"

"Just now."

"Where?"

"Yonder," said I pointing; "over there, where I found him nodding asleep, and thought it was you."

He looked in the direction indicated for an instant. Then he was down on the rank wet grass, filing at his iron like a madman, and not minding me at all.

I told him I must go, but he took no notice, so I thought the best thing I could do was to slip off. The last I heard of him, I stopped in the mist to listen, and the file was still going.

When we had finished dinner that day, my sister went out to get the pork pie to lay atop it. She returned empty-handed, to stop short and stare, in her wondering lament of "Gracious goodness, gracious me, what's gone—with the—pie!" I was sure she would accuse me.

But just then a party of soldiers arrived at the door. They were on a chase of two convicts who had escaped from a prison-ship. Joe proposed that we should go down with the soldiers and see what came of the hunt, so we did.

The soldiers were moving on in the direction of the old Battery, and we were moving on a little way behind them, when, all of a sudden, we heard a long shout. The sergeant ordered that his men should make towards it "at the double." As we came nearer to the shouting, it became more and more apparent that it was made by more than one voice. We could hear one voice calling, "Murder!" and another voice, "Convicts! Runaways! Guard! This way for the runaway convicts!"

Water was splashing, and mud was flying, and oaths were being sworn, and blows were being struck. Some of the men went down and dragged out, separately, my convict and the other one.

As we prepared to march back to the prison ship, my convict looked round him for the first time, and saw me. I looked at him eagerly, and slightly moved my hands and shook my head. I had been waiting for him to see me, that I might try to assure him of my innocence. It was not at all expressed to me that he even comprehended my intention, for he gave me a look that I did not understand, and it all passed in a moment.

It had grown dark and the soldiers lit torches to guide us back. After we reached the wharf, my convict turned to the sergeant and remarked:

"I wish to say something respecting this escape. It may prevent some persons laying under suspicion alonger me.

"A man can't starve; at least I can't. I took some wittles, up at the willage over yonder—where the church stands a'most out of the marshes.

"And I'll tell you where from. From the blacksmith's. It was some broken wittles —that's what it was—and a dram of liquor, and a pie."

The boat had returned, and his guard was ready, and we saw him taken up the side of the prison ship and disappear.

As soon as you finish reading Article 9, record your finishing time in the Time Record on page 4 of the PROGRESS FOLDER. *Then read Test 9 that appears next in this book.*

READING TEST 9   MY CONVICT

Read each test item and select the answer you believe is correct. Print the letter of your answer in the Answer Record on page 4 of the PROGRESS FOLDER.

---

1. Pip found out for sure each of these things except one. Which did he *not* find out for sure?
   - (A) The place overgrown with nettles was the churchyard.
   - (B) His father and his mother were dead and buried.
   - (C) Beyond the churchyard was the wild marshland.
   - (D) The convict who shouted at him was an innocent man.
   - (E) The small, shivering, fearful, crying bundle was Pip.

---

2. The man who suddenly stood up among the graves first told Pip
   - (A) to look at him
   - (B) to give him some money
   - (C) to stay there
   - (D) to trust him
   - (E) to hold his noise

---

3. Pip noticed that the fearful man wore
   - (A) a battered old hat
   - (B) fairly good shoes
   - (C) rough grey clothes
   - (D) a handcuff on his wrist
   - (E) a coarse neckerchief

---

4. When the man emptied Pip's pockets, he found a
   - (A) piece of bread
   - (B) few copper coins
   - (C) rusty knife
   - (D) broken comb
   - (E) fishline

---

5. The man was very interested when he learned that Pip lived with his sister, the wife of Joe Gargery who was a
   - (A) shoemaker
   - (B) tailor
   - (C) minister
   - (D) blacksmith
   - (E) soldier

---

6. The man ordered Pip to bring him the next morning something to eat and a
   - (A) saw
   - (B) chisel
   - (C) file
   - (D) bottle of ale
   - (E) suit of clothes

---

7. If Pip told on him, the man said, someone would tear out, roast, and eat the boy's
   - (A) tongue and brains
   - (B) heart and liver
   - (C) arms and legs
   - (D) eyes and ears
   - (E) lungs and kidneys

8. When the man said that he was "a Angel" compared to the young man, he meant that the young man was even more
   (A) daring
   (B) hungry
   (C) fatigued
   (D) terrible
   (E) human

9. Just after Pip promised to do what the man said, the boy
   (A) hid in the churchyard
   (B) ran home without stopping
   (C) walked rapidly toward town
   (D) prayed near his parents' graves
   (E) shouted loudly for help

10. That night Pip was afraid to sleep. He feared not only the young man but also his own sister who would
    (A) put him to bed for sneaking away
    (B) scold him sharply for going to the churchyard
    (C) whip him badly for taking the file
    (D) paddle him severely for helping the two men
    (E) spank him hard for stealing food

11. When Pip left home at dawn, he took each of these things except one. Which did he *not* take?
    (A) Plum pudding
    (B) Bread and cheese
    (C) Mincemeat and pork pie
    (D) Some brandy
    (E) A file

12. When Pip arrived near the battery, he saw the back of a man who was
    (A) sitting down and nodding sleepily
    (B) standing up and tottering drunkenly
    (C) kneeling and weaving from side to side
    (D) lying down and fast asleep
    (E) running into the mist-covered marsh

13. As soon as Pip found the right man, he
    (A) asked why the young man had run away
    (B) invited the man to go home with him
    (C) asked the man to take him along
    (D) opened his bundle and emptied his pockets
    (E) told the man to give himself up

14. The man ate the food like a dog mainly because he was very
    (A) afraid
    (B) hungry
    (C) greedy
    (D) rushed
    (E) happy

15. The man stopped eating and seemed surprised when Pip said that he thought the young man
    (A) seemed very worried
    (B) did not want any food
    (C) had gone to sleep
    (D) looked very angry
    (E) looked hungry

16. Just after Pip left the
man, he heard the sound
of the

    (A) two men fighting over the brandy
    (B) bloodhounds hunting the two men
    (C) file scraping a leg iron
    (D) alarm guns of the prison ship
    (E) voices of the approaching soldiers

17. When Pip's sister found
the pork pie gone, she
would have accused him
if this had not happened
soon:

    (A) Joe and Pip went on a hunt for the convicts.
    (B) His sister and her husband started drinking brandy.
    (C) His sister's husband asked where the file was.
    (D) Pip said that he had given the pie to two men.
    (E) A party of soldiers looking for the convicts arrived.

18. The party of soldiers
finally captured the two
escaped convicts imme-
diately after the soldiers

    (A) sent Pip ahead to deliver food to the convicts
    (B) heard some men shouting and saw them fighting
    (C) saw the convicts wading through the marsh
    (D) noticed the small fire which the convicts had started
    (E) followed the convicts' footprints in the mud

19. When the first convict
looked at Pip, Pip moved
his hands and head to
try to show that he (Pip)

    (A) had not betrayed the convicts to the soldiers
    (B) hoped the soldiers would not hurt the convict
    (C) believed the convict was a friendly man
    (D) was sorry the convict was so miserable
    (E) wanted to go wherever the convict went

20. Just before Pip's convict
was taken back to the
prison ship, he said that
he had

    (A) taken some food and drink from the blacksmith
    (B) stolen the blacksmith's file to remove the leg iron
    (C) gotten some wittles, liquor, and a pie from Pip
    (D) plotted his escape with the younger convict
    (E) wanted to die before being returned to prison

NEXT — *Follow the directions (Steps 8-17) on page 1 of the* PROGRESS FOLDER.

ARTICLE 10

What makes a hero?*

by Henry Lee

READING PRACTICE 10 *In a book, magazine, or newspaper that you like, practice reading for speed and comprehension. Make a record of each such practice in Chart 3 on page 8 of the* PROGRESS FOLDER. *Then do Reading Article 10.*

READING ARTICLE 10 *Before you begin reading Article 10, record your starting time in the Time Record on page 4 of the* PROGRESS FOLDER. *Then read Article 10. Read it as fast as you can, but make sure you understand what you are reading.*

A SURVEYOR for a Southern railroad was riding his handcar up a mountain track one pleasant day. Suddenly he saw the afternoon express train, ahead of schedule. It was speeding around a long curve toward him.

As he stopped his handcar, wild ideas flashed through his head. He first thought of jumping to save himself. But he knew that the half-ton handcar would throw the train off the track. He next thought of riding his handcar downhill, trying to beat the express to the nearest side track. Then he realized he never could make it.

Finally he did the impossible. He *lifted* the handcar off the track and the express roared safely past.

Later, railroad engineers studied carefully what had occurred. They knew the speed of the handcar and of the train. From these facts they figured out that the surveyor had moved the handcar off the track in only about 30 seconds. Where the accident had nearly happened, he tried to do the same thing again. "No

matter how hard I tried," he said, "I could never do it again."

Young and old, many of us have much more strength and coolness than we realize. Our whole being, mind and body, fuses burningly on the immediate emergency so that we rise above fear or pain. We might call this the "X" stuff of courage, the stuff of which heroes are made.

Among the bravest spontaneous heroes are children. In a small Southern town, a 14-year-old boy found that his best friend was lying unconscious on a damp patch of ground. His friend's hand was locked to a steel rod which crackled with 2,300 volts of electricity.

The boy tried to break his friend's grip with a blow of his fist, but the electricity hurled him flat. He got up and kicked the wire, and again was thrown down. Still game, he hunted around until he found a tree branch with a Y-shaped twig. As he hooked the twig onto the rod, voltage flowed through the branch to him, shaking his arm, but the current was endurable now. He pressed the end of the twig against the branch, making a tight loop. Then he jerked the rod from the hand of his unconscious friend. Thanks to this

---

*Condensed and adapted from *Coronet*, August, 1948. Copyright 1948, by Esquire, Inc., Chicago, 1948. Reprinted with permission of the publisher and the author.

young hero's bravery, the other boy lived.

In Fort Lauderdale, Florida, Joseph R. Arcaris is an animal trainer. One day he heard an awful sound coming from a cage which housed five untrained lions. A person was screaming and the animals were roaring. He ran to the cage and found that the lions had cornered and knocked down a young caretaker. Now they were closing in for the kill.

Arcaris did not have time to go back for a gun or even a chair, which trainers often use. He knew, too, that his usual tricks would not work. But, because he had the X-stuff of courage, he picked up a stick and walked in.

The beasts snarled and tried to circle behind him. He waved the stick as though it were a snapping whip. And he faced down the angry lions.

While he held the animals at a safe distance, the caretaker crawled to safety. Then, as the lions crawled nearer, Arcaris backed to the door and made his own escape. For this, he won a Carnegie hero medal.

Policemen, firemen, and others who are trained and disciplined can usually face emergencies bravely. Yet curiously, just ordinary people often show surprising courage. In Illinois, a small and timid farm wife saw a bull butting the hired man against the earth. She ran from the house, picked up an ax, and with one blow stunned the bull. Then she half-carried the injured man to safety.

You wonder what makes people carry on when common sense must tell them to hold back and call for help. It is difficult to find out because these are mostly shy heroes, fast of action but slow of tongue. They know only that they have to aid a fellow who is in distress—that they can't stand idly by.

At least part of the mystery, science tells us, can be explained in terms of glands. When a person gets excited, his glands, particularly the adrenal and the thyroid glands, pour extra fluids into his bloodstream. These help to make his body stronger and more ready for action.

If a person is less anxious, psychologists say, he is freer to fasten all his energies on the one, immediate goal. He does not hold back because of fear or worry. But there is another explanation, perhaps a better one. That is that a person is moved to action by love and faith.

In Poughkeepsie, New York, James Hines, a 36-year-old Negro was spending a pleasant July afternoon with his four small children. They were ten months to four years old. With him were his wife, another mother with her five-year-old daughter, and a third woman. Without warning, fire swept the house. Hines was trapped on the third floor with the three women and five children. Their escape seemed cut off.

The only possible route to safety was a window that overlooked a small garage. It was a straight drop of two stories, but Hines decided to take the chance.

The jump smashed his left leg badly. Every movement sent hot agony through his body, and nausea and faintness swept him in waves. Then the X-stuff of courage began to work.

Standing on his good leg, bracing himself as best he could, Hines called to his wife to drop the children to him. One after another, he caught them, staggering back each time in pain, but not dropping one. He caught his ten-month-old daughter and each of his three young sons. When the fifth child, a girl, twisted in the air, he had to reach forward to catch her, wrenching his broken leg. But he caught and held her.

Fire bells now were clanging in the

distance, but Hines' job wasn't done. A ladder was standing near-by. Crawling along the garage roof, he reached it and, with almost his last strength, swung it against the burning building. Then, before he collapsed, he helped the three trapped women to safety.

Theodore Bonawitz, a truck driver, was passing through the outskirts of a small Eastern town when a workman called weakly to him. Pointing to an entrance, he told Bonawitz that 140 feet down the steep-sloping tunnel, a 17-year-old laborer was lying unconscious. The youth, Harold Nelson, had been knocked out by carbon monoxide from a gasoline-driven pump.

Bonawitz had never been in the place before. He had never known Nelson. But he was a simple man who lived by the Golden Rule. That is why Bonawitz went down.

As Bonawitz felt his way toward Nelson, he stumbled into foot-deep holes between the ties of the tunnel's track. It was so dark that he couldn't find the youth until he stepped on his body. Almost at once the carbon monoxide began to make him sleepy.

Bonawitz carried Nelson a few feet and then tripped, burning his hand against the exhaust pipe of the pump. He got up and alternately dragged and carried Nelson toward daylight. Twenty-five feet from the tunnel's mouth, he collapsed.

Two men came down, in answer to Bonawitz's cries. Between the three of them, they carried Nelson another five feet. Bonawitz's legs then became numb and he had to crawl ahead to the open air. He collapsed again. He begged bystanders to go in for Nelson, but they refused.

After a moment's rest, Bonawitz staggered back. Two men, feeling ashamed, followed him. At last they carried Nelson to safety. Then for the first time, Bonawitz saw the face of the stranger for whose life he had almost sacrificed his own.

Although Bonawitz himself did not know it, his brave deed was another inspiring example of the "X" stuff of courage—the mysterious but powerful thing that turns ordinary, everyday people into heroes when the need for heroism arises.

As soon as you finish reading Article 10, record your finishing time in the Time Record on page 4 of the PROGRESS FOLDER. *Then read Test 10 that appears next in this book.*

READING TEST 10   WHAT MAKES A HERO?

Read each test item and select the answer you believe is correct. Print the letter of your answer in the Answer Record on page 4 of the PROGRESS FOLDER.

---

1. The surveyor who was riding his handcar up a mountain track was in danger because the express train was
   (A) on the wrong track
   (B) behind schedule
   (C) ahead of schedule
   (D) on time
   (E) out of sight

---

2. As the express train came nearer, the surveyor first thought that he would

   (A) ride the handcar downhill to a side track
   (B) jump off the handcar leaving it on the track
   (C) run up the track and flag the train to stop
   (D) set off a torpedo to warn the train of danger
   (E) lift the handcar off the track

3. Experts figured out that the surveyor had moved the handcar off the track in 30 seconds after determining

   (A) the strength of the surveyor
   (B) the train's regular schedule
   (C) the bravery of the surveyor
   (D) the speeds of the handcar and the train
   (E) the weights of the handcar and the train

4. In an emergency, we who become heroes have or do each of these things except one. Which do we *not* have or do?

   (A) We have more strength and coolness than we realize.
   (B) We give all of our mind and body to the danger.
   (C) We have the "X" stuff of courage.
   (D) We are able to rise above fear or pain.
   (E) We practice safety first for ourselves and for others.

5. When the 14-year-old boy found his friend lying unconscious on damp ground, the friend had a steel rod

   (A) over his leg
   (B) under his arm
   (C) in his hand
   (D) over his body
   (E) under his foot

6. The teen-age boy finally rescued his friend from the high-voltage rod in this way:

   (A) He knocked the rod away with his foot.
   (B) He hit the rod with his fist.
   (C) He pulled the rod away with a branch.
   (D) He removed the rod with his hands.
   (E) He pushed the rod away with a board.

7. When the animal trainer heard a man scream and ran to the cage, he found that the five untrained lions had

   (A) smashed the caretaker's chair
   (B) injured the caretaker
   (C) seized the caretaker's whip
   (D) knocked down the caretaker
   (E) disobeyed the caretaker

8. When the animal trainer entered the lion cage, he carried a

   (A) gun
   (B) stick
   (C) chair
   (D) whip
   (E) rope

9. In saving the caretaker and himself, the animal trainer

   (A) fed the lions and patted them gently
   (B) stood up before the lions and faced them down
   (C) forced the lions to go into another cage
   (D) let the lions move around anywhere in the cage
   (E) walked up to the lions and whipped them

10. During emergencies, surprising courage is often shown by everyday
    - (A) lifeguards
    - (B) policemen
    - (C) soldiers
    - (D) firemen
    - (E) people

11. In Illinois, a small and timid housewife rescued the hired man from an angry bull in this way:
    - (A) She waved her apron in front of the bull.
    - (B) She struck the bull with her fists.
    - (C) She twisted the bull's tail.
    - (D) She grabbed the bull's horns.
    - (E) She hit the bull with an ax.

12. During an emergency, the person who becomes a hero usually knows only that he has
    - (A) to go to the aid of a fellow in danger
    - (B) to think twice before risking his life
    - (C) to use common sense in saving a fellow
    - (D) to stay alive to rescue a fellow in distress
    - (E) to remember exactly why he saved a fellow

13. A person's body is made ready for action by the extra fluids that are being poured into his bloodstream by the
    - (A) pineal and thymus glands
    - (B) liver and kidney glands
    - (C) sweat and olfactory glands
    - (D) salivary and digestive glands
    - (E) adrenal and thyroid glands

14. When James Hines saved eight persons from his burning house, he was most probably moved to action by
    - (A) fear
    - (B) pain
    - (C) love
    - (D) worry
    - (E) strength

15. When Hines jumped from the third story of his burning house, he
    - (A) wrenched his back
    - (B) smashed one of his legs
    - (C) burned his face and hands
    - (D) broke one of his arms
    - (E) called loudly for help

16. As Hines stood below, he called to his wife
    - (A) to stay there until the firemen came
    - (B) to jump with two children in her arms
    - (C) to cover each child with a wet blanket
    - (D) to drop each child into his arms
    - (E) to lower each child with a rope made of sheets

17. Before Hines collapsed from his injury and pain, he rescued the women by
    - (A) swinging a ladder against the building up to them
    - (B) catching each of them in his arms after she jumped
    - (C) going up the blazing stairway of the house for them
    - (D) making them wait for the safety net to arrive
    - (E) throwing one end of a long strong rope to them

18. Harold Nelson, who was lying unconscious 140 feet down a sloping tunnel, had been knocked out by

    (A) electric shock from a high-voltage power line
    (B) a fallen timber from the roof of the tunnel
    (C) natural gas from a vein of soft coal
    (D) carbon monoxide from a gasoline-driven pump
    (E) several cars breaking loose from their engine

19. Bonawitz started down the tunnel after Nelson because Bonawitz lived by this rule:

    (A) A friend in need is a friend indeed.
    (B) Everybody's business is nobody's business.
    (C) Do unto others as you would have others do unto you.
    (D) The Lord helps those who help themselves.
    (E) Always look before you leap.

20. While Bonawitz was dragging and carrying Nelson up toward the mouth of the tunnel, Bonawitz

    (A) nearly lost his own life
    (B) was saving his best friend
    (C) believed others would soon come to the rescue
    (D) hoped to become a hero
    (E) felt his body was getting stronger

NEXT — *Follow the directions (Steps 8-17) on page 1 of the* PROGRESS FOLDER.

ARTICLE 11

Not with beat of drum*

by Victor G. Heiser

READING PRACTICE 11 *In a book, magazine, or newspaper that you like, practice reading for speed and comprehension. Make a record of each such practice in Chart 3 on page 8 of the* PROGRESS FOLDER. *Then do Reading Article 11.*

READING ARTICLE 11 *Before you begin reading Article 11, record your starting time in the Time Record on page 7 of the* PROGRESS FOLDER. *Then read Article 11. Read it as fast as you can, but make sure you understand what you are reading.*

IN THE MOUNTAINOUS interior of Northern Luzon, in the Philippine Islands, lived three hundred thousand wild tribesmen. They were untamed wards of the government who, for lack of a better name, were commonly called non-Christians. But they were not savages. Because they had so recently abandoned the practice, they were sensitive to the disgrace conveyed by the term head-hunter.

The principal reason for their long isolation was geographical. The narrow passes which led into the mountains could

*Condensed from *An American Doctor's Odyssey*, by Victor G. Heiser. Copyright 1936, by the author. Reprinted with permission of W. W. Norton & Company, New York.

be easily defended against a considerable military force. Furthermore, the land was poor and the people fierce and warlike. It had never been worth the Spaniards' time or money to conquer them. For centuries also a feud had smoldered between Christian lowlander and animistic mountain dweller. For a long time it was questionable whether friendly relations between the two could be established.

In general, the mountain people were exceptionally healthy and sturdy. The normal death rate from disease was not so high as in the lowlands, although many children died of malnutrition or improper feeding. The mothers used to chew up rice, camotes, and meat, and feed infants of a few days directly from their own mouths, as a squab is fed.

Our first step in peaceful penetration was to provide medical service for these mountain dwellers whom civilization had overlooked. In the Igorot country which lay just beyond our doors, we began the attempt to relieve some of the suffering caused by yaws—a so-called "skin disease" similar to syphilis. We were making slow progress with the potassium iodide treatment, when luck unexpectedly came our way. Dr. Paul Ehrlich sent some of his newly developed salvarsan (606) to Dr. Richard P. Strong, who experimented with it, and found it marvelously effective in yaws, working miraculous cures. Armed anew with this discovery, we opened a small dispensary on the edge of the Igorot territory.

The healthy Igorot wore nothing but a breech clout, but when he fell ill he immediately took his blanket and wrapped himself into his misery. There was no clock, no sun-dial, no hourglass in the Mountain Province, but the sun rose every day. Every medicine man, brown, black, yellow, or white, often practices hocus-

pocus. To an Igorot whose sufferings had overcome his suspicions, we handed a stick with fifteen loops of string tied around it.

"Be up at dawn each morning," he was admonished solemnly. "Have your bolo ready. Watch carefully. Just as you see the first yellow tip of the sun, cut off one loop. Do not take off your blanket. Do not look at your skin. At every sunrise cut one more loop. When the last one is gone, throw aside your blanket. You will be well."

Having pronounced these words, we injected the 606, and sent the Igorot on his way.

One of our doctors was most anxious to describe the magic treatment for a medical journal. He had selected six particularly interesting cases, and sent for a photographer from the Bureau of Science, asking the six Igorots to be present on a certain morning. The morning came, and so did the photographer, but no Igorots.

"That's just the way with these ungrateful people," the doctor irritably exclaimed. "You cure them with great trouble and cost, but when you ask some little favor, that's the last you see of them."

Two weeks later the doctor heard a great hullabaloo. He went to the door of the dispensary, and there were his six "ungrateful" patients, triumphantly leading several hundred of their afflicted brethren, all coming for their sticks with the fifteen loops.

By healing the people we gradually extended our dispensaries, until we had penetrated into the heart of the non-Christian country. The tribesmen began flocking to them, carrying their sick in litters and welcoming physicians and nurses into their homes.

When we first went into the mountain country, tribe warred against tribe, all hunting each others' heads. The mutual ferocity and hatred was unbelievable. The people were compelled to huddle into villages for protection from their head-hunting neighbors, and spent hours traveling from their distant fields to their homes. Men from Village A would not even carry our baggage as far as Village B. They would go half way, lay down their loads and retire, whereupon those from Village B would come forward and pick them up.

Almost every house had its head rack, and the number of skulls, which ranged from two to several dozen, indicated the social standing and prestige of the owner. Head-hunting was a sort of game; if one village took three heads, the enemy village had to prove its manhood by securing four in return. There were great ceremonies, with speeches and songs, when the heads were carried home in triumph. Any warrior decapitated in one of these encounters was considered to have cast such discredit on his community that he was buried under a trail where his resting place would be trampled upon. The Igorots had a fundamental sporting instinct; they would send timely warning to the village to be attacked, and sometimes met by mutual appointment.

In later years the warriors would stage sham head-hunting battles for us with spear, head axe, and shield of stout wood lashed with rattan. It was a beautiful sight to see with what accuracy they could hurl the wickedly barbed, long steel-tipped spear, but gruesome to watch them manipulate, even in play acting, the terrible head axe, pointed at one end to puncture the enemy's skull, and fashioned and sharpened at the other to cut off his head.

Head-hunting was forbidden by law, but the enforcement of such laws is not easy. In most backward countries, the white man's usual method is to shoot the offenders; we did it chiefly by changing the nature of the rivalry. We substituted athletics, reduced to their simplest terms. Instead of allowing the villagers to cut each other's heads off, we would say to those of Village A, "Choose eight of your strongest men. Village B is going to do the same. Then you will meet in a tug of war and whichever team can pull the other over the line has proved that he belongs to the better village." These contests became life-and-death matters; in this way the tribesmen sublimated the violent emotions which formerly had found outlet in bloodshed.

I made many solitary trips into the Igorot country, usually forewarned by anxious friends that I would certainly be killed, because I could not tell when the savages would turn upon me. I was going along one day in a remote part of the country when my ears were startled by the most stupendous uproar of yelling and shouting. It sounded ominous, but there was no help for it. I had to go on. These agile runners could have outdistanced me and cut off any possible escape had they been so minded. The only thing to do was to keep quietly on as unconcernedly as possible.

The din increased as I proceeded. Suddenly I emerged into a clearing. Instead of spears and bolos, my eyes were startled with the sight of bats and balls, and the fantastic picture of a savage, naked save for a string around his middle and a great wire catcher's mask before his face. An inter-village baseball game was in progress. Nobody paid any attention to me; nobody knew or cared whether I had arrived. The teams were fairly matched, and I was soon raised to almost the same pitch of excitement. With one man on first base, a young Igorot came to bat and, with a resounding crack, hit the ball into left field. The man on first started for second, but it seemed almost certain he would be put out. With one accord the cry arose from the throats of the wild men, "Slide, you devil, slide!"

The Igorots had watched the games of the American soldiers at the hill station, and were letter-perfect in their lines. So civilization gradually took root in the wilds of the Philippines.

As soon as you finish reading Article 11, record your finishing time in the Time Record on page 7 of the PROGRESS FOLDER. *Then read Test 11 that appears next in this book.*

READING TEST 11   NOT WITH BEAT OF DRUM

Read each test item and select the answer you believe is correct. Print the letter of your answer in the Answer Record on page 7 of the PROGRESS FOLDER.

1. The story is about Igorot tribesmen who lived on one of the
   - (A) Hawaiian Islands
   - (B) Marianas Islands
   - (C) Philippine Islands
   - (D) Japanese Islands
   - (E) Fiji Islands

2. The tribesmen did not like to be called head-hunters because they had recently
   - (A) become Christians
   - (B) heard about white men's wars
   - (C) taken up this practice again
   - (D) given up this practice
   - (E) taught other tribes this practice

3. The tribes had been isolated for a long time mainly because they
   - (A) were very fierce and well-armed
   - (B) lived on such poor land
   - (C) worshiped animals instead of gods
   - (D) lived in the mountains
   - (E) hated the Spanish invaders

4. In general, the adults among these mountain people were very
   - (A) healthy and strong
   - (B) tall and heavy
   - (C) hungry and starved
   - (D) ill and weak
   - (E) fearful and worried

5. The author's first step in making friends with the mountain people was
   - (A) to take photographs of them
   - (B) to provide medical service
   - (C) to teach reading, writing, and arithmetic
   - (D) to supply baseballs, bats, and gloves
   - (E) to give away large knives

6. In treating the mountain people for yaws, the doctor gave the patients
   (A) penicillin
   (B) doses of quinine
   (C) thermometers
   (D) warm blankets
   (E) salvarsan

7. When an Igorot became very ill, he usually
   (A) put on his breech clout
   (B) wrapped himself in his blanket
   (C) went off into the woods
   (D) stayed away from his family
   (E) wanted to go to the hospital

8. The doctor handed each sick Igorot a stick with loops of string, mainly because he knew that the patient
   (A) believed in hocus-pocus
   (B) kept his bolo near him
   (C) liked something to handle
   (D) could hit at the evil spirit
   (E) could whittle the stick with his knife

9. By having the Igorot cut the string loops on his stick, the doctor helped make sure that his patient
   (A) stayed quietly wrapped in his blanket for 15 days
   (B) came back to the doctor 15 days later
   (C) was safe from a head-hunter for 15 days
   (D) kept the medicine man away for 15 days
   (E) was cared for by his family for 15 days

10. On the day scheduled for photographs, the doctor was angry mainly because the six Igorots
    (A) brought in hundreds of their fellow tribesmen
    (B) wanted more of the string-covered sticks to use
    (C) failed to show up as they had promised to do
    (D) carried their bolos and blankets with them
    (E) had cost so much of the doctors' time and medicines

11. To protect themselves against their head-hunting neighbors, the members of an Igorot tribe usually
    (A) stayed close together in their own village
    (B) moved to a place far from their enemies
    (C) took the shortest route from their farms to their homes
    (D) tried to make a treaty of peace with their enemies
    (E) asked the white men to give them guns

12. The men of Village A would carry the author's baggage only half way to Village B because they were
    (A) uncertain whether the author would pay them enough
    (B) all tired out after carrying the heavy load
    (C) not sure of the right trail to follow
    (D) afraid of being killed by the men of Village B
    (E) sure the men of Village B would pick up the load

13. The number of skulls which a tribesman had on the head rack of his house indicated his
    (A) wish to frighten as many of his enemies as possible
    (B) desire to guard all families in his tribe
    (C) ability to keep his bolo razor-sharp
    (D) fierceness in the eyes of the white doctors
    (E) standing among the men in his own tribe

14. If a warrior actually lost his head, his fellow tribesmen
   - (A) had an impressive funeral with speeches and songs
   - (B) buried his body and trampled on the grave
   - (C) honored and cared for the warrior's family
   - (D) asked the enemy tribe to return the warrior's head
   - (E) stopped fighting the enemy tribe for a while

15. The Igorots showed their sporting instinct in this way:
   - (A) They tried to take more heads than the enemy took.
   - (B) They asked the white doctors to referee the battle.
   - (C) They shook hands after every fight was over.
   - (D) They warned the enemy's village of a coming attack.
   - (E) They quit the fight after one man was killed.

16. When the tribesmen staged sham battles, the author found that the sight of a warrior using a head axe was
   - (A) beautiful
   - (B) skillful
   - (C) gruesome
   - (D) unusual
   - (E) pleasant

17. Where the white man has a law forbidding the practice of head-hunting, his government usually
   - (A) imprisons the offender
   - (B) educates the offender
   - (C) shoots the offender
   - (D) disarms the offender
   - (E) exiles the offender

18. The author found that a good substitute for head-hunting between two villages was to arrange for a
   - (A) sham battle
   - (B) man of war
   - (C) treaty of peace
   - (D) family picnic
   - (E) tug of war

19. When the author heard a group of tribesmen yelling and shouting, he decided
   - (A) to use his gun if necessary to save his life
   - (B) to teach the tribesmen how to play baseball
   - (C) to give the tribesmen the medical care they wanted
   - (D) to run back to his camp as fast as possible
   - (E) to walk ahead as though nothing were wrong

20. The two tribes whom the author watched playing baseball had learned this game from
   - (A) Spanish missionaries at the town church
   - (B) American soldiers at the hill station
   - (C) American doctors at the nearest dispensary
   - (D) their sons who were attending an American school
   - (E) radio programs of the American World Series

NEXT — *Follow the directions (Steps 8-17) on page 1 of the* PROGRESS FOLDER.

ARTICLE 12

The divine story of Handel's Messiah*

by Stefan Zweig

READING PRACTICE 12 *In a book, magazine, or newspaper that you like, practice reading for speed and comprehension. Make a record of each such practice in Chart 3 on page 8 of the* PROGRESS FOLDER. *Then do Reading Article 12.*

READING ARTICLE 12 *Before you begin reading Article 12, record your starting time in the Time Record on page 7 of the* PROGRESS FOLDER. *Then read Article 12. Read it as fast as you can, but make sure you understand what you are reading.*

ON THE AFTERNOON of April 13, 1737, George Frederick Handel returned to his London home in a terrible fury from an orchestra rehearsal. The great German composer angrily banged the front door. He now was pacing the floor of his room so that the ceiling below trembled.

Suddenly a heavy thud, followed by the sound of breaking glass, came from upstairs. Handel's manservant raced to the master's study. There he saw Handel's great body lying on the floor. As the servant stared in frozen horror, Christopher Smith, the composer's assistant, rushed into the room. Together the two men raised the heavy body.

Smith cried: "Sprinkle his face with water while I go for a doctor!" Hastening to Fleet Street, he found Dr. Jenkins and dragged him to a carriage.

Jenkins entered the maestro's study and used his knife to make a cut for bloodletting. As he did so, a deep sigh came from Handel's mouth. Then his lips

moved. "I'm finished—no strength—don't want—live—"

The doctor noticed that one of Handel's eyes stared without seeing. Then he raised the sick man's arm. It dropped, lifeless.

"Apoplexy," said Dr. Jenkins. "Right side paralyzed. We may save the man—but the musician is lost forever. His brain has been permanently injured."

For four long months Handel could neither walk nor write nor play even a key of his harpsichord. When friends made music for him, his eyes would light up and his body would try to move with the rhythm. But the arm and leg on one side could not move, and horror was in his eyes.

After trying out everything he knew, Jenkins ordered that Handel take the hot baths at Aix-la-Chapelle. And just as under the earth's surface there boiled the strange springs, so within the unmoving body of the great musician there stirred a mysterious force. His will had not been touched by the stroke; the undying fire refused to be quenched.

A week after arriving at Aix-la-Chapelle, Handel was able to walk; another week, and he could raise his arm. On the day of leaving Aix, he entered the cathedral. There stood the huge organ. He touched the keys with his stricken right hand. Soon, glorious chords rose and fell, filling the vaulted shrine with echoing sound.

Handel, his head bowed in humility, played and played. Again he had found the language in which he talked with God, with his fellow men, and with eternity. Once again he would compose music.

Back in London, Handel hurled himself into composition. He wrote an opera, then a second, a third, a fourth. It was as if a spring, long pent up, had been loosed.

Even so, fate soon turned against him. Queen Caroline, his patron, died and his pension was stopped. The Spanish wars came, and houses of entertainment were closed. His creditors pressed him, and the public remained indifferent.

Handel began to roam the streets of London. People just looked at him and walked on. He became so lonely he could hardly stand it. Then, on August 21, 1741, he came home with a single thought in his mind: Rest, sleep, oblivion. Slowly he climbed to his study. Like a machine, he lighted the candles of his work table. Then suddenly he frowned.

What was that large package on the table? A letter from Charles Jennens, poet who had written the librettos of *Saul* and *Israel*. He was sending Handel a copy of his new poem. He hoped that the greatest genius in music would speed forth the lumbering words on the wings of undying melody.

Handel dropped the letter. Was Jennens laughing at him? That was a mean thing to do to a dying man, stricken as he was! The maestro tore the letter to shreds and stamped upon them. Then, feeling dead and lost, he threw himself upon the bed.

But he could not sleep, for a storm was raging within him. Finally he got up and relit the candles. He then pushed the copy of the poem nearer the light. On the first page he read the word "Messiah." Another oratorio! All his latest efforts to compose such music had been failures. Yet he turned the title page and began to read.

The first words caught his attention. "Comfort ye!" A marvelous beginning, a call of angels to his weary heart. Hardly had he read them when they began to take form as music, swelling, calling, singing forth into the sky. Once more, Handel heard musical tones after the long drought of inspiration. His weariness disappeared.

With trembling fingers Handel turned the pages. Then suddenly he read the sentence, "The Lord gave the Word." Handel held his breath in wonder. Surely the Lord Himself had inspired this poet! "The Lord gave the Word" . . . divine mercy had rained down from on high.

Again and again must the words be repeated: "Hallelujah! Hallelujah! Hallelujah!" The voices of mankind must be joined in a mighty chorus—high voices and low, sweet notes from the fiddles merging with the rougher notes from the brass, the whole sustained by the organ's powerful undertones.

Tears flooded Handel's eyes as the fires of inspiration swept through him. He took up his pen and jotted notes; faster and faster the queer little signs began to cover paper. Darkness lay over the huge city, but light flooded his own soul, and the study was alive with music.

Day and night, he kept at his task, living wholly in the realm of rhythm and tone. He strummed on the harpsichord, he sang, he worked with his fingers until they gave out. Never before had he so lived and fought with music.

At last, in three weeks—a miracle in music—the great work was finished. Soon after, when Dr. Jenkins heard the composer sing and play the "Amen" chorus, he muttered: "Never have I heard the like of this. You must be possessed of the Devil." And, with hanging head, Handel whispered: "I think, rather, that God has visited me . . . ."

It was Handel's wish that the first performance of *The Messiah* take place in Dublin, where receipts were sure to be large. But he did not want to profit from his work. Instead, he directed that the money be devoted to the care of prisoners, orphans and the sick.

On the evening of April 13, 1742, crowds were waiting in Fishamble Street for the doors to open. Ladies had come in narrow skirts. Gentlemen had left their swords at home so that there might be room for a great audience. First, breathless silence. Then the oratorio opened. There came a tremor as the massed chorus of singers from two cathedrals began with a hurricane of energy.

Handel stood close by the organ in a dream. When the final Amen resounded he joined in the chorus, singing as he had never sung before. Then when the storms of applause began, he slipped away. From this night onward, the stream of public acclaim for Handel flowed on, year after year.

On April 6, 1759, a broken man of 74, he drove to the concert hall. He stood among the musicians and singers whom he could no longer see. But as the waves of sound came to his ears, his tired face lighted up one last time. Then he staggered and nearly fell.

When friends got him to bed, he murmured: "I should like to die on Good Friday." Good Friday would be April 13— the day on which, years before, fate had struck him down—the day on which, with *The Messiah*, his temporal resurrection had been accomplished in Dublin.

The man's strong will had power over death as well as life. By April 13 he was very weak. Handel could not see or hear or feel. Yet to his inner senses came the sound of faraway music by others—music stranger and more splendid than any he had ever wrought in imagination.

And the next day, before the Easter bells began to ring, there perished all that was mortal of George Frederick Handel.

As soon as you finish reading Article 12, record your finishing time in the Time Record on page 7 of the PROGRESS FOLDER. *Then read Test 12 that appears next in this book.*

READING TEST 12   THE DIVINE STORY OF HANDEL'S MESSIAH

Read each test item and select the answer you believe is correct. Print the letter of your answer in the Answer Record on page 7 of the PROGRESS FOLDER.

1. When Handel, the German composer, returned to his London home on April 13, 1737, he was very
   (A) fearful
   (B) happy
   (C) afraid
   (D) angry
   (E) tired

2. After Handel's servant and assistant heard a crash, they rushed into his room. There they found that Handel had

(A) fallen to the floor
(B) thrown a chair
(C) slammed the door
(D) broken a mirror
(E) smashed the harpsichord

3. While Dr. Jenkins was examining Handel, the composer sighed and said that he wanted

(A) to write music
(B) to take a vacation
(C) to get well
(D) to go to sleep
(E) to die

4. The physician believed that Handel would never again be able to write music because the composer's

(A) brain was injured
(B) right arm was paralyzed
(C) eyesight was gone
(D) attitude was hopeless
(E) hearing was lost

5. For four months after Handel was first paralyzed, he was able only to do this:

(A) He took short walks with the help of his friends.
(B) He wrote some music using his good left hand.
(C) He played his harpsichord for a few minutes daily.
(D) He listened to music played by his friends.
(E) He took easy exercises to strengthen his body.

6. Handel's will to write music was like the

(A) hot baths provided at Aix-la-Chapelle
(B) caves formed by rushing water
(C) springs boiling under the earth's surface
(D) rocks standing along sea coasts
(E) rivers flowing into the oceans

7. On the day Handel left Aix, he used his stricken right hand

(A) to play the piano in his bedroom
(B) to play the organ in the cathedral
(C) to play the harpsichord in a small church
(D) to compose the first part of an oratorio
(E) to write a letter of thanks to Dr. Jenkins

8. When Handel first found that he could compose music again, he felt very

(A) strong
(B) humble
(C) kind
(D) afraid
(E) proud

9. In London, Handel faced each of these difficulties except one. Which difficulty did Handel *not* face?

(A) Handel was able to write only a few compositions.
(B) When the Queen died, Handel's pension stopped.
(C) Because of the wars, concert houses were closed.
(D) Handel's creditors pressed him to pay his debts.
(E) The public paid little attention to Handel's music.

10. When Handel returned home on August 21, 1741, he wanted most
- (A) to tell people to let him alone
- (B) to eat, drink, and be merry
- (C) to write the greatest composition ever
- (D) to sleep for ever and ever
- (E) to play great music for his friends

11. As Handel read Jennen's letter, he thought that the poet was
- (A) encouraging him
- (B) fooling him
- (C) feeling sorry for him
- (D) laughing at him
- (E) cheating him

12. When Handel read the sentence, "The Lord gave the word," he felt that the poet had been inspired by
- (A) Handel's music
- (B) God Himself
- (C) the Bible
- (D) great hymns
- (E) Heaven itself

13. Handel felt that mankind should join in a mighty chorus when in the poem he read this word again and again:
- (A) Hail the Messiah (Welcome the Savior)
- (B) Amen (So be it)
- (C) Hallelujah (Praise the Lord)
- (D) Joy to the world
- (E) Comfort ye (Peace to you)

14. Handel labored day and night composing the music for *The Messiah* mainly because he was so
- (A) anxious to get out of debt
- (B) eager to please Jennens
- (C) afraid his death was near
- (D) glad to have something to do
- (E) inspired by the work itself

15. After hearing the "Amen" chorus, Dr. Jenkins said: "You must be possessed of the Devil." Handel replied:
- (A) "I think, rather, that Christ has been with me."
- (B) "I think, rather, that the angels have lifted me."
- (C) "I think, rather, that God has visited me."
- (D) "I think, rather, that you have strengthened me."
- (E) "I think, rather, that a great poet has inspired me."

16. Handel directed that the profits from the first performance of *The Messiah* be given to helping
- (A) paralyzed persons
- (B) needy people
- (C) young poets
- (D) the church
- (E) aged composers

17. After *The Messiah* was first performed, Handel's compositions were
- (A) acclaimed by the public for many years
- (B) criticized by the public for many years
- (C) liked by the public for a few years
- (D) ignored by the public for many months
- (E) misunderstood by the public for a few years

18. When Handel for the last time attended a performance of *The Messiah*, he
    - (A) watched the performers closely
    - (B) sang loudly with the chorus
    - (C) listened happily to the music
    - (D) felt like a young man again
    - (E) conducted the orchestra and chorus

19. At the age of 74, Handel died on
    - (A) the day just before Good Friday
    - (B) the date of his first heart attack
    - (C) the night before Christmas
    - (D) New Year's Day
    - (E) the day just before Easter

20. While Handel was on his deathbed, the great composer may have heard splendid music coming from
    - (A) a harpsichord
    - (B) a near-by concert hall
    - (C) a cathedral choir
    - (D) a radio station
    - (E) a heavenly chorus

NEXT — *Follow the directions (Steps 8-17) on page 1 of the* PROGRESS FOLDER.

ARTICLE 13

*Our plundered planet**

by Fairfield Osborn

READING PRACTICE 13 *In a book, magazine, or newspaper that you like, practice reading for speed and comprehension. Make a record of each such practice in Chart 3 on page 8 of the* PROGRESS FOLDER. *Then do Reading Article 13.*

READING ARTICLE 13 *Before you begin reading Article 13, record your starting time in the Time Record on page 7 of the* PROGRESS FOLDER. *Then read Article 13. Read it as fast as you can, but make sure you understand what you are reading.*

YESTERDAY MORNING more than 175,000 mothers looked down upon the vague uncomprehending eyes of their newborn babes. Today a similar number are doing likewise, and tomorrow and the next day.

*Condensed and adapted from *Our Plundered Planet*, by Fairfield Osborn. Copyright 1948 by the author. Reprinted with permission of Little, Brown & Company, Boston.

These are the children of the earth, the daily host reproducing the human species the world over. Each day, on the average, there are a few more than the day before. So it is known to have been for the last three centuries.

Throughout most of recorded history, there are no reliable data as to the total world population. In the early part of the seventeenth century, however, enough figures were gathered together from every continent and every country to indicate that the total number somewhat exceeded 400,000,000. In the year 1630, then, one could, for the first time, have some idea as to how many "neighbors" there were on the planet.

For another two centuries there was a steady increase so that by the year 1830 the total world population had doubled. Then came the violent explosive upsurge in human numbers. By the year 1900, or within three generations, the world population doubled again, touching the figure of 1,600,000,000 persons. By 1940 the figure rose well over the 2,000,000,000-mark and is still steadily increasing. The rate of increase is now approximately one percent per year. If this rate were to be continued, it would mean a doubling of the present world population in about 70 years.

No matter what their total number in the next century may be, the peoples of the earth today, whether they will it so or not, are bound together by common interests and needs. The most basic are, of course, food supply and other primary living requirements. These come, all of them, from nature and from nature alone —from the forests, the soils, and the waterways.

Although this has always been true, man has injured vast fertile areas in various parts of the earth, many of them so ruined that they have become deserts and uninhabitable. In such places, flourishing civilizations have disappeared, their cities buried under wastes of sand, their inhabitants scattered to new lands. But *now*, with isolated and inconsequential exceptions, there are no fresh lands, anywhere. Human civilization has permeated virtually every living area of the earth's surface.

We are apt to forget that almost three-quarters of the earth is covered by water and that at least one-half of all the land is uninhabitable because it lies in the polar regions or is extremely mountainous or is desert land. In the world's habitable areas, the productive soil is now so limited that there are probably not more than 4,000,000,000 acres of arable land left to fill the needs of more than 2,000,-000,000 people. This means that there are less than two acres per capita.

Contrasted with this it is a generally accepted computation that two and one-half acres of land of *average productivity* are required to provide even a minimum adequate diet for each person. Many countries have less than an acre of productive land per capita. No wonder there are world-wide shortages, and that the people of a number of nations are facing starvation.

As far as the habitable and cultivable portions of the earth's surface are concerned, there are four major elements that make possible not only our life, but to a large degree, the industrial economy upon which civilization rests. These elements are: water; soil; plant life, from bacteria to forests; and animal life, from protozoa to mammals. The last two of these elements, being alive and capable of reproduction, are referred to by conservationists as "renewable resources."

Water is, of course, the element that makes life possible to all the others. The function of water in the life scheme is obvious. Vegetation is composed mostly of water; more than 70 percent of our human body weight is water. Consequently, water must be generally available, and at all seasons, in habitable areas.

A regular and adequate water supply

is dependent upon the preservation of extensive forests, especially in the watershed areas where streams and rivers have their sources. Water supply is also dependent upon vegetation cover in open country. When these natural conditions are too greatly disturbed, water supply diminishes or disappears. The water is not held on the surface long enough to percolate slowly into the ground. Springs dry up owing to the lowering of the underground water table. Further, rains falling upon exposed lands, which have been improperly stripped of forest or other vegetation cover, are not held in the soils and consequently rush to stream or river beds. Violent fluctuations of drought and flood conditions are started, becoming cumulatively more severe.

Another element, perhaps the most vital of all, is productive soil—that is, topsoil. *When that goes we go with it.* In the United States, topsoil is estimated to lie originally at an average depth of about seven or eight inches over the face of the land. As nearly as can be ascertained, it takes nature, under the most favorable conditions, including a good cover of trees, grass, or other protective vegetation, anywhere from 300 to 1000 years or more to build a single inch of topsoil. Yet what may have taken a thousand years to build can be, and in places has been, removed by erosion in a year or even in a single day.

On sloping lands, comprising the great majority of the earth's cultivable areas, erosion is active and eventually fatal unless man controls it, which he too rarely does. In flat country the processes of erosion are less apparent though still present.

It would be hard to enumerate all the many causes of man-made erosion throughout the world, though the sequence of events has much the same aspect wherever it may be found. To produce food,

man makes clearings in forests or, in areas of natural grasslands, turns the protective sod for planting. He plants his grain or other crops one year, and then the next year, and then the next. Too often he leaves his fields bare and unprotected from the elements in the stormy seasons between harvests. And, as man's yield of food from a field dwindles with each harvest, he looks about for a new place to plant, leaving the old one to the fate that erosion will complete.

Another cause of erosion is overgrazing of grasslands, where herdsmen try to maintain the largest possible number of animals on a limited range. These graze at all times, seasonable and unseasonable, and so destroy the grass and bushes to such an extent that nothing is left but nearly barren ground. Such abused land soon becomes gullied by the rains, or suffers sheet erosion, or is subject to the more dramatic and terrible wasting by violent winds and torrential rains.

The indiscriminate cutting down or burning of forests is one of the most widespread causes of erosion. Too close lumbering, especially on sloping lands, is nearly as damaging as the forest fires which we all have come to dread. When the forest is down, the land that was once protected by it suffers from flash runoffs of the water whenever there is a heavy rainfall.

Proper agricultural methods, now well understood, are capable of preventing this destructive cycle of events. Yet over great areas of the earth until recently, man still moved from place to place, wearing out the land without a thought save for his immediate physical needs.

The day when new fresh lands can be found is now almost over. Man's inheritance of the earth is now in truth a completed fact. But as an heir he has already destroyed a large part of his inheritance. He has failed so far to recognize that he is a child of the earth and that, this being so, he must for his own survival work with nature in understanding rather than in conflict. While in some countries corrective steps are being taken, the fact remains that the turning point of land recovery and reclamation has not yet been reached in this country or elsewhere.

As soon as you finish reading Article 13, record your finishing time in the Time Record on page 7 of the PROGRESS FOLDER. *Then read Test 13 that appears next in this book.*

READING TEST 13   OUR PLUNDERED PLANET

Read each test item and select the answer you believe is correct. Print the letter of your answer in the Answer Record on page 7 of the PROGRESS FOLDER.

1. Every day throughout the world the total number of babies born is about

   (A)   1,750
   (B)   17,500
   (C)   175,000
   (D)   1,750,000
   (E)   17,500,000

2. During the past 300 years, the total number of births each day has been

   (A) falling greatly
   (B) falling slightly
   (C) staying about the same
   (D) rising greatly
   (E) rising slightly

3. At the present time, the world's population is estimated to be about

   (A)   400,000,000
   (B)   800,000,000
   (C)   1,600,000,000
   (D)   2,000,000,000
   (E)   4,000,000,000

4. If the world's population increases as it has since 1830, the present population will double in about

   (A) 70 years
   (B) 10 years
   (C) 40 years
   (D) 20 years
   (E) 100 years

5. All of the peoples of the world are bound together mainly by the common and basic need for

   (A) recreation
   (B) religion
   (C) government
   (D) food
   (E) family life

6. Flourishing civilizations have disappeared and their sites have become deserts mainly because man has
   - (A) fought bloody wars
   - (B) wasted the land
   - (C) killed all the wildlife
   - (D) moved to more fertile areas
   - (E) suffered from natural floods

7. Large numbers of people cannot move from poor to better lands because all of the world's habitable lands are
   - (A) empty
   - (B) eroded
   - (C) too cold
   - (D) too hot
   - (E) occupied

8. Of the world's total land area, the proportion which is habitable is about
   - (A) 10 percent
   - (B) 50 percent
   - (C) 90 percent
   - (D) 25 percent
   - (E) 75 per cent

9. Of the world's cultivable land, there is on the average this area per person:
   - (A) 100 acres
   - (B) 25 acres
   - (C) Five acres
   - (D) Two acres
   - (E) One-half acre

10. In many countries, the peoples are hungry year after year mainly because there is not enough
    - (A) grazing land per person
    - (B) farm machinery per person
    - (C) imported food per person
    - (D) cultivable land per person
    - (E) food preservation per person

11. The life of our people depends upon four basic natural elements. Which of these is *not* such an element?
    - (A) Manpower
    - (B) Animal life
    - (C) Plant life
    - (D) Soil
    - (E) Water

12. The importance of water to life is shown by the fact that water makes up this part of the weight of the human body:
    - (A) 90 percent
    - (B) 50 percent
    - (C) 70 percent
    - (D) 10 percent
    - (E) 30 percent

13. A regular and adequate water supply during all seasons of the year depends mainly upon a good
    - (A) system of dams, lakes, and irrigation canals
    - (B) supply of rain every month of the year
    - (C) cover of wheat, corn, cotton, and other crops
    - (D) system of deep wells and storage tanks
    - (E) cover of forests and grasses

14. When men destroy the natural vegetation, the water from rainfall

    (A) seeps too deeply into the ground
    (B) raises the water table too high
    (C) runs off the land too fast
    (D) evaporates too quickly from the soil
    (E) stays in one place too long

15. Within a single day, water can wash away an inch of topsoil which nature took this many years to build:

    (A) 3,000 to 10,000 years
    (B) 300 to 1,000 years
    (C) 100 to 200 years
    (D) 25 to 75 years
    (E) Five to 10 years

16. Erosion causes the most damage when the land is

    (A) bare and sloping
    (B) covered with grass or forests
    (C) used to graze livestock
    (D) planted in corn or cotton
    (E) flat or slightly rolling

17. Because man often leaves his fields bare during the stormy seasons between harvests, the

    (A) value of his fields stays about the same
    (B) number of weeds in his fields increases rapidly
    (C) plowing of his fields is more and more difficult
    (D) discovery of new fields is harder and harder
    (E) yield of his fields goes down and down

18. The main cause of the widespread erosion of grasslands is this:

    (A) The winds blowing across the range are too strong.
    (B) Man plants too little grass on barren areas.
    (C) Man puts too many animals on a limited range.
    (D) Rainfall is too light in grassland areas.
    (E) Man kills off too many wolves and other predators.

19. Heavy rainfall always cuts deep gullies in the sides of hills and mountains when man

    (A) cuts down all the trees
    (B) allows too much underbrush to grow
    (C) starts to plant new trees
    (D) builds a highway along a slope
    (E) allows a few cattle to graze there

20. According to the author, in handling the farm lands of the earth man has

    (A) understood the importance of working with nature
    (B) destroyed a large part of his inheritance
    (C) saved most of his inheritance for future generations
    (D) added more to his inheritance than he has wasted
    (E) hoarded his inheritance instead of using it

NEXT — *Follow the directions (Steps 8-17) on page 1 of the* PROGRESS FOLDER.

ARTICLE 14

*We flew eight miles up**

by Wesley Price

READING PRACTICE 14 *In a book, magazine, or newspaper that you like, practice reading for speed and comprehension. Make a record of each such practice in Chart 3 on page 8 of the* PROGRESS FOLDER. *Then do Reading Article 14.*

READING ARTICLE 14 *Before you begin reading Article 14, record your starting time in the Time Record on page 7 of the* PROGRESS FOLDER. *Then read Article 14. Read it as fast as you can, but make sure you understand what you are reading.*

THE LIEUTENANT handed me a printed form with blank spaces to fill in—whom to notify in case of accident, and you promise not to sue the Navy.

"Just a formality," he said. "You won't have to bail out or anything like that."

I hoped he was right, I sincerely hoped so. Within the hour I would be strapped into the radarman's seat of a jet night fighter, the X-F3D Skyknight. (The X meant she was experimental.) The pilot, lanky Lieutenant Charles B. Smith, would climb steeply from the Naval Air Test Center at Patuxent River, Maryland. Soon we would be eight blue miles straight up, leveling off for stability tests over Washington, D.C.

I was thinking that the bailing out isn't so good above 40,000 feet. In air that thin, a plunging man accelerates to 220 miles an hour. If he opens a conventional parachute at this speed, the shock of deceleration can break his neck. Anyway, there is no future for him, dangling up there without oxygen at sixty-seven degrees below

*Condensed from *The Saturday Evening Post*, May 6, 1950. Copyright 1950, by The Curtis Publishing Company. Reprinted with permission of the publisher and the author.

zero. So the instructions go: Fall free, keep on falling, until the air gets thick enough to slow you down, thick enough to breathe; now pull the rip cord. But how could I tell how low was low enough?

"Don't worry," said Lieutenant Smith. He produced a smile. "We won't be making any parachute jumps."

I wasn't worried, I didn't give it another thought, hardly. When we drove to the hangar I was telling jokes, that's how relaxed I was.

The gear an airman wears is enough to suggest that he may soon be replaced by robot missiles. He carries bottled oxygen for high-altitude bailouts, and breathes through a new kind of mask that is fully automatic. The one lent me at the Naval Air Test Center delivers plain air at sea level, mixing in richer and richer doses of oxygen as you climb. At 29,000 feet, cabin altitude, the gas comes undiluted. At 35,-000 feet the pressure kicks on. The pressure pushes your tongue back, so you talk through clenched teeth. It pops the mask away from your face. Jets of oxygen spray your eyes, bringing tears, and the edges of the mask thrum on your cheeks.

It's like being slapped by a rubber-bladed electric fan.

Crash helmets fit closely. I tried on four. One felt as if my head was jammed in a plumber's vise; just right, said Gus Widhelm, the director of Tactical Test. The Mae West life jacket, for a sea landing, came with attached flashlight, packets of sea stain, cartridges for making signal smoke or flares.

We found the X-F3D Skyknight outside the hangar. The Navy had asked for the utmost in a night fighter, but a thoroughly practical and usable one; something that could whip up to the sub-stratosphere, cruise there for hours and knock down the bombers blind, with radar-sighted cannon. To meet the order, Douglas Aircraft crammed gear and fuel tanks into an expansive fuselage, doubled up on the engines and spread the wings to take hold of rarefied air.

We climbed into the plane and the roof hatch thudded shut. We buttoned oxygen masks to our helmets. Lieutenant Smith told the tower that Four-Five-Eight was ready to taxi, and the jets urged us down the runway, slowly at first, gently. We weighed eleven tons. Then we were being booted along, faster, faster, the speed read 90, lots of runway left, 100 . . . 110—we were off. The large hand on the altimeter scurried round and round to keep pace with the climb. Our speed left the roaring of jet exhausts miles behind.

Altitude, 30,000 feet. The horizon, a rim that always seems at eye level, was no longer rising with us. It sank a trifle, rounding off. We were beginning to get out of this world.

Altitude, 35,000 feet. Frost speckled the windscreen. Lieutenant Smith turned on more heat. The frost melted, and so did I. Oxyen blinker okay.

Altitude, 40,000 feet. Everything below had shrunk to neat, maplike dimensions. At a glance I took in the entire length of Chesapeake Bay. Both the Appalachian Mountains and the Atlantic Ocean were in view, and I could identify Baltimore to the north, Norfolk down south. Washington, D.C.? A brown spot below, the size of a cooky; those glinting, sugary bits are public buildings.

The stupendous view was dimmed for me by vague discomforts. I was sweating, I imagined myself short of breath, and I felt trapped. The straps pinning me to the seat, the helmet jammed on my head, the mask clutching my nose and mouth, hinting at suffocation—all implied that I'd got myself stuck in a drain pipe. Yet all space was before me, and the altimeter was still registering climb.

Navy jetmen will tell you that high flying isn't spectacularly different from low flying. In the next breath, they mention a "hot flash," one of the milder symptoms of aeroembolism, otherwise known as the bends, the chokes or the staggers. Aeroembolism is caused by tiny gas bubbles expanding in the body during an abrupt climb past the six-mile level. A severe case can double up a man with pain. Yet aeroembolism is less feared than oxygen deficiency, which has alcoholic effect on one's judgment and senses. It is suspected that oxygen-starved pilots have held ships in fatal dives, laughing like crazy.

But give the pilot pressurized oxygen and he can soar to the eight-mile level. Add pressure to his cabin, and he can ascend further.

When we lost our aileron boost over Washington, Smith thoughtfully neglected to discuss it. We had been making vertical turns. The Skyknight was standing on a wing tip when something failed in the mechanism which helps the pilot move the stick. Lieutenant Smith had to put his shoulder into it to bring the wing up. That was the end of capering. The Skyknight went stiffly to 42,500 feet and leveled off. The interphone delivered his voice fogged by altitude.

"Too bad," he said. "I was going to make you a member of the There-I-Was-Upside-Down-at-Forty-Thousand-Feet-Over-Washington Club. It's very exclusive." A moment later: "Turn on your radio."

"Four-Five-Eight, this is Five-Four-One. I say again, coming up on your starboard side."

Visitors in the substratosphere. I looked over my right shoulder. A Banshee materialized, flying formation on us. White contrails—condensed moisture—streamed from her tail pipes. Five-Four-One was only ten feet away: I could see her pilot's eyelashes. Or was she fifty feet off our wing; or a hundred? Eight miles above the dusty earth, the air was so clean, the sunshine so brilliant, that everything seemed close by.

"Anything else you'd like to see?" asked Lieutenant Smith.

"Lunch on the table," I said.

The lieutenant popped the dive brakes and nudged the stick forward. The al-timeter spun backward, reeling toward Maryland at 6000 feet a minute. Norfolk gently subsided, Baltimore sidled away, and an old-fashioned horizon rose to meet the eye. It seemed that I had been gone a long time.

On the downwind leg I ripped off my oxygen mask and inhaled deeply. Plain air, how good it is! Pressurized exactly right, oxygen content a perfect 20.96 per cent, no rubber tubes needed to get it up your nose, and the supply inexhaustible.

When we reached Gus Widhelm's office, he said accusingly, "You didn't get to fifty thousand; you didn't even join the club."

"Come back when we have the production model," Lieutenant Smith suggested.

The F3D Skyknight with the X knocked off will have more potent engines. In the Navy's book she will be the best night and bad-weather interceptor in the country. She carries tail-warning radar, intercept radar, and gun-laying radar. Tactical Test still isn't satisfied. They're going to get an electronic computer that will fly the airplane, find the target, calculate deflection, take aim and automatically fire the guns.

"All this," commented Gus, "is so we can grow old with our children."

As soon as you finish reading Article 14, record your finishing time in the Time Record on page 7 of the PROGRESS FOLDER. *Then read Test 14 that appears next in this book.*

READING TEST 14   WE FLEW EIGHT MILES UP

Read each test item and select the answer you believe is correct. Print the letter of your answer in the Answer Record on page 7 of the PROGRESS FOLDER.

---

1. Before entering the airplane, the author filled out a printed form. On it he promised he would *not*
   - (A) bail out of the plane unless told to do so
   - (B) sue the Navy in case of an accident
   - (C) give away any military secrets
   - (D) talk to the pilot while in the air
   - (E) become airsick during the flight

---

2. The Skyknight, in which the author flew, was one of the Navy's experimental jet
   - (A) day bombers
   - (B) night bombers
   - (C) day fighters
   - (D) observation planes
   - (E) night fighters

---

3. At 40,000 feet above sea level, the air is always very
   - (A) thick and cold
   - (B) thin and cold
   - (C) thick and warm
   - (D) thin and warm
   - (E) cloudy and windy

---

4. A man who bails out of an airplane at 40,000 feet should pull the rip cord of his parachute when
   - (A) the airplane is about a mile away
   - (B) he is falling at a speed of 220 miles per hour
   - (C) the air gets thick enough to slow his fall
   - (D) the temperature is just above freezing
   - (E) the atmosphere is fairly easy to breathe

---

5. After the pilot said not to worry about having to make any parachute jumps, the author was
   - (A) somewhat relaxed
   - (B) very happy
   - (C) quite upset
   - (D) still worried
   - (E) still hopeful

---

6. The author wore a special kind of mask which, as the plane climbed, automatically
   - (A) kept him in touch by phone with the pilot
   - (B) supplied him with more and more oxygen
   - (C) shut out more and more noise and chill
   - (D) kept his goggles clear of moisture and ice
   - (E) provided him with increasing amounts of air

---

7. At 35,000 feet and above, the author found that he had difficulty in talking because the
   - (A) pressure outside his mask was so light
   - (B) thin air made him very faint
   - (C) pressure inside his mask was so great
   - (D) high altitude made him very dizzy
   - (E) front of his mask pressed hard against his mouth

---

8. The author put on a Mae West which was designed to help save his life if
(A) he landed on his back instead of his feet
(B) his parachute caught in the top of a tree
(C) he had to bail out at a high altitude
(D) his plane crash-landed in mountainous country
(E) he parachuted into the sea

9. The Skyknight has each of these features except one. Which feature does this plane *not* have?
(A) It can fly rapidly upward to the sub-stratosphere.
(B) It can cruise for hours at high altitudes.
(C) It can drop bombs on enemy airplanes.
(D) It can knock down enemy bombers.
(E) It can fire "blind" with its radar-sighted guns.

10. The Skyknight left the runway at a speed of about
(A) 110 miles per hour
(B) 180 miles per hour
(C) 140 miles per hour
(D) 90 miles per hour
(E) 80 miles per hour

11. While the Skyknight was climbing rapidly, the horizon at first seemed
(A) to sink lower than the plane
(B) to stay at the same eye-level
(C) to disappear from view
(D) to rise with the plane
(E) to come closer to the plane

12. When the Skyknight was 40,000 feet above Washington, D.C., the author looked north and was able to identify
(A) the Atlantic Ocean
(B) Baltimore
(C) Norfolk
(D) the Appalachian Mountains
(E) Philadelphia

13. As the airplane climbed, the author more and more noticed the safety straps, helmet, and mask. He felt that he had
(A) protected himself against all possible dangers
(B) flown higher than any other man
(C) made himself as comfortable as possible
(D) gotten himself stuck in a drain pipe
(E) put on too much flying gear for parachuting

14. If a pilot has a severe case of aeroembolism,
(A) he feels like he had drunk a lot of whisky
(B) his hands and feet swell greatly
(C) his body is doubled up with pain
(D) he puts more oxygen in his air supply
(E) his whole body relaxes and rests

15. The pilot of a climbing airplane who has an oxygen mask is most afraid of
(A) aeroembolism—expanding air bubbles in his body
(B) oxygen deficiency—too little oxygen for his lungs
(C) air sickness due to many large air pockets
(D) parachute paralysis—fear of bailing out
(E) fuel shortage due to a leak in the gas tanks

16. The Skyknight's pilot found it hard to move his steering stick just after the

  (A) fuel tank became nearly empty
  (B) oxygen-boosting pump went dead
  (C) altimeter needle would no longer move
  (D) aileron-boosting device stopped working
  (E) grease lubricating the stick almost froze

17. As the Banshee flew near, the author had difficulty in judging its distance from the Skyknight because the

  (A) air was so clear and sunshiny
  (B) clouds were so white and thick
  (C) planes were moving so smoothly and fast
  (D) windshield was covered by so much mist and frost
  (E) exhaust was so filled with condensed moisture

18. The author told the pilot he would like "to see lunch on the table." By this the author meant that he

  (A) was getting very hungry for a good meal
  (B) would be very happy when the plane landed safely
  (C) wished to take off his hood and breathe plain air
  (D) would be very glad to fly again after lunch
  (E) liked to eat at a table instead of at a lunch counter

19. The Naval Test Center was trying to develop an airplane that flies, finds the target, and fires its guns

  (A) accurately
  (B) automatically
  (C) atomically
  (D) systematically
  (E) rapidly

20. Gus Wilhelm said: "All this is so we can grow old with our children." He hoped to develop planes that give us

  (A) the best chance to develop aviation
  (B) the most time to be with our children
  (C) the best protection against enemy bombers
  (D) the greatest chance to take off from our airfields
  (E) the best weapon for conquering the world

NEXT — *Follow the directions (Steps 8-17) on page 1 of the* PROGRESS FOLDER.

ARTICLE 15

Ring out, wild bells*

by Wolcott Gibbs

READING PRACTICE 15 *In a book, magazine, or newspaper that you like, practice reading for speed and comprehension. Make a record of each such practice in Chart 3 on page 8 of the* PROGRESS FOLDER. *Then do Reading Article 15.*

READING ARTICLE 15 *Before you begin reading Article 15, record your starting time in the Time Record on page 7 of the* PROGRESS FOLDER. *Then read Article 15. Read it as fast as you can, but make sure you understand what you are reading.*

WHEN I FINALLY got around to seeing Max Reinhardt's cinema version of "A Mid-summer-Night's Dream," and saw a child called Mickey Rooney playing Puck, I remembered suddenly that long ago I had taken the same part.

Our production was given on the open-air stage at the Riverdale Country School. The scenery was only the natural scenery of that suburban dell, and the cast was exclusively male, ranging in age from eleven to perhaps seventeen. While we had thus preserved the pure Elizabethan note of the original, it must be admitted that our version had its drawbacks. The costumes were probably the worst things we had to bear, and even Penrod, tragically arrayed as Launcelot in his sister's stockings and his father's drawers, might have been embarrassed for us. Like Penrod, we were costumed by our parents, and like the Schofields, they seemed on the whole a little weak historically. Half of the ladies were inclined to favor the Elizabethan, and they had constructed rather bunchy ruffs and farthingales for their offspring; others, who had read as far as the stage directions and learned that the action took place in an Athenian wood, had produced something vaguely Athenian, usually beginning with a sheet. Only the fairies had a certain uniformity. For some reason their parents had all decided on cheesecloth, with here and there a little ill-advised trimming with tinsel.

My own costume was mysterious, but spectacular. As nearly as I have ever been able to figure things out, my mother found her inspiration for it in a Maxfield Parrish picture of a court jester. Beginning at the top, there was a cap with three stuffed horns; then, for the main part, a pair of tights that covered me to my wrists and ankles; and finally slippers with stuffed toes that curled up at the ends. The whole thing was made out of silk in alternate green and red stripes, and (unquestionably my poor mother's most demented stroke) it was covered from head to foot with a thousand tiny bells. Because all our costumes were obviously perishable, we never wore them in rehearsal, and naturally nobody knew that I was invested with these peculiar sound effects until I made my entrance at the beginning of the second act.

*Reprinted by permission, Copyright 1936, The New Yorker Magazine, Inc.

Our director was a man who had strong opinions about how Shakespeare should be played, and Puck was one of his favorite characters. It was his theory that Puck, being "the incarnation of mischief," never ought to be still a minute, so I had been coached to bound onto the stage, and once there to dance up and down, cocking my head and waving my arms.

"I want you to be a little whirlwind," this man said.

Even as I prepared to bound onto the stage, I had my own misgivings about those dangerously abundant gestures, and their probable effect on my bells. It was too late, however, to invent another technique for playing Puck, even if there had been room for anything but horror in my mind. I bounded onto the stage.

The effect, in its way, must have been superb. With every leap I rang like a thousand children's sleighs, my melodies foretelling God knows what worlds of merriment to the enchanted spectators. It was even worse when I came to the middle of the stage and went into my gestures. The other ringing had been loud but sporadic. This was persistent, varying only slightly in volume and pitch with the vehemence of my gestures. To a blind man, it must have sounded as though I had recklessly decided to accompany myself on a xylophone. A maturer actor would probably have made up his mind that an emergency existed, and abandoned his gestures as impractical under the circumstances. I was thirteen, and incapable of innovations. I had been told by responsible authorities that gestures went with this part, and I continued to make them. I also continued to ring—a silvery music, festive and horrible.

If the bells were hard on my nerves, they were even worse for the rest of the cast, who were totally unprepared for my new interpretation. Puck's first remark is addressed to one of the fairies, and it is mercifully brief.

I said, "How now, spirit! Whither wander you?"

This unhappy child, already embarrassed by a public appearance in cheese-cloth and tinsel, was also burdened with an opening speech of sixteen lines in verse. He began bravely:

"Over hill, over dale,
    Through brush, through brier,
    Over park, over pale,
    Through flood, through fire. . ."

At the word "fire," my instructions were to bring my hands up from the ground in a long, wavery sweep, intended to represent fire. The bells pealed. To my startled ears, it sounded more as if they exploded. The fairy stopped in his lines and looked at me sharply. The jingling, however, had diminished; it was no more than as if a faint wind stirred my bells, and he went on:

"I do wander everywhere,
    Swifter than the moone's sphere . . ."

Here again I had another cue, for a sort of swoop and dip indicating the swiftness of the moone's sphere. Again the bells rang out, and again the performance stopped in its tracks. The fairy was clearly troubled by those interruptions. He had, however, a child's strange acceptance of the inscrutable, and was even able to regard my bells as a last-minute adult addition to the program, nerve-racking but not to be questioned. I'm sure it was only this that got him through that first speech.

My turn, when it came, was even worse. By this time the audience had succumbed to a helpless gaiety. Every time my bells rang, laughter swept the spectators, and this mounted and mingled with the bells until everything else was practically inaudible. I began my speech, another long one, and full of incomprehensible references to Titania's changeling.

"Louder!" said somebody in the wings. "You'll have to talk louder."

It was the director, and he seemed to be in a dangerous state.

"And for heaven's sake, stop that jingling!" he said.

I talked louder, and I tried to stop the jingling, but it was no use. By the time I got to the end of my speech, I was shouting and so was the audience.

All this had a very bad effect on the fairy, who by this time had many symptoms of a complete nervous collapse. However, he began his next speech:

"Either I mistake your shape and
    making quite,
Or else you are that shrewd and knav-
    ish sprite
Called Robin Goodfellow: are you
    not he
That . . ."

At this point I forgot that the rules had been changed and I was supposed to leave out the gestures. There was a furious jingling, and the fairy gulped.

"Are you not he that, that. . ."

He looked miserably at the wings, and the director supplied the next line, but the tumult was too much for him. The unhappy child simply shook his head.

"Say anything!" shouted the director desperately. "Anything at all!"

The fairy only shut his eyes and shuddered.

"All right!" shouted the director. "All right, Puck. You begin your next speech."

By some miracle, I actually did remember my next lines, and had opened my mouth to begin on them when suddenly the fairy spoke. His voice was a high, thin monotone, and there seemed to be madness in it, but it was perfectly clear.

"Four score and seven years ago," he began, "our fathers brought forth on this continent a new nation, conceived . . ."

He said it right through to the end, and it was certainly the most successful speech ever made on that stage. I don't remember, if I ever knew, how the rest of us ever picked up the dull, normal thread of the play after that extraordinary performance, but we must have, because I know it went on. I only remember that in the next intermission the director cut off my bells with his penknife, and after that things quieted down and got dull.

As soon as you finish reading Article 15, record your finishing time in the Time Record on page 7 of the PROGRESS FOLDER. *Then read Test 15 that appears next in this book.*

READING TEST 15   RING OUT, WILD BELLS

Read each test item and select the answer you believe is correct. Print the letter of your answer in the Answer Record on page 7 of the PROGRESS FOLDER.

---

1. The author suddenly remembered that he had once had a part in "A Midsummer Night's Dream" when he
    - (A) heard this play on a radio program
    - (B) saw this play in a motion picture
    - (C) saw this play on a television show
    - (D) saw this play on the stage
    - (E) reread this play in a book

---

2. According to Shake-
   speare, the author of the
   play, the action took
   place in a forest near

   (A) Riverdale
   (B) Rome
   (C) Stratford
   (D) Athens
   (E) London

3. In getting ready for and
   in giving the play, the
   boys found that the worst
   things they had to bear
   were the

   (A) many lines to be memorized
   (B) different stage sets to be constructed
   (C) sales of tickets to friends
   (D) costumes made by parents
   (E) jokes made by brothers and sisters

4. All the costumes of the
   fairies were made of

   (A) mosquito netting and bells
   (B) cheesecloth and tinsel
   (C) muslin and ribbon
   (D) ruffs and farthingales
   (E) sheets and pillowcases

5. The author wrote that
   his costume was most like
   a Maxfield Parrish picture of a

   (A) king
   (B) fairy
   (C) prince
   (D) troubadour
   (E) jester

6. The costume worn by
   the author as a boy had
   each of these parts except one. Which did his
   costume *not* have?

   (A) A cap with three stuffed horns
   (B) Tights made of green and red silk stripes
   (C) Tinsel trimming on both cap and suit
   (D) Shoes with stuffed and curled-up toes
   (E) Tiny bells sewed everywhere on the clothing

7. Before Puck went on
   stage, no one knew he
   would make peculiar
   sounds because the boys
   were not allowed

   (A) to wear their perishable costumes at rehearsals
   (B) to try on their perishable costumes before the play
   (C) to show each other their perishable costumes
   (D) to make any changes in their perishable costumes
   (E) to fool around at all during the dress rehearsal

8. The director told Puck
   to keep moving about the
   stage because Puck was
   the spirit of

   (A) restlessness
   (B) happiness
   (C) laughter
   (D) evil
   (E) mischief

9. Just before Puck went
   onto the stage, he was
   most worried that his
   movements would cause

   (A) the bells to sound too noisily
   (B) everybody to laugh out loud
   (C) him to get tired too soon
   (D) the director to take him out of the play
   (E) his perishable costume to rip

10. To a blind man, Puck must have sounded as though he were accompanying himself on a
    - (A) tenor drum
    - (B) xylophone
    - (C) violin
    - (D) piano
    - (E) mouth harp

11. Puck continued to ring his bells mainly because he was
    - (A) helping fill in when another boy forgot his part
    - (B) trying to wait until he could recall his lines
    - (C) having so much fun making the audience laugh
    - (D) making the gestures he had been told to make
    - (E) enjoying the sound of the many tinkling bells

12. The bells were very hard on the nerves of the other boys mainly because their sound was so
    - (A) pleasant
    - (B) musical
    - (C) surprising
    - (D) sad
    - (E) expected

13. When a boy spoke just after Puck's first remark, that boy was already embarrassed by the
    - (A) hard words in his speech
    - (B) difficulty of making himself heard
    - (C) fairy costume he wore
    - (D) noise of Puck's many bells
    - (E) laughter of the audience

14. When Puck swept his arms upward as the boy said, "Through fire," the boy stopped in his lines and
    - (A) looked sharply at Puck
    - (B) told Puck to quit moving
    - (C) asked Puck to leave the stage
    - (D) stared sadly at the audience
    - (E) whispered softly to the director

15. The fairy was able to finish his lines probably because he felt the bells had been added by
    - (A) boys
    - (B) mistake
    - (C) the director
    - (D) Puck
    - (E) adults

16. When Puck began his speech, no one could hear what he was saying because every time his bells rang
    - (A) the director shouted
    - (B) the other boys giggled
    - (C) he forgot his lines
    - (D) the audience laughed
    - (E) babies in the audience cried

17. The director told Puck to talk louder and to stop his
    - (A) coughing
    - (B) fooling
    - (C) jingling
    - (D) stuttering
    - (E) bounding

18. The fairy forgot his lines completely and stood silently when
 (A) Puck's bells started ringing again
 (B) the audience kept on shouting
 (C) the director told him to leave the stage
 (D) his costume ripped down the back
 (E) Puck's funny cap fell off

19. Just as Puck was about to begin his next lines, the fairy recited all of
 (A) Washington's Farewell Address
 (B) the Declaration of Independence
 (C) Burke's essay on liberty
 (D) Puck's longest speech
 (E) Lincoln's Gettysburg Address

20. The author remembers that after the director cut off all of Puck's bells, this happened:
 (A) Puck refused to go back onto the stage again.
 (B) Things quieted down and got dull.
 (C) The fairy apologized for making the wrong speech.
 (D) The director bawled out all the boys in the cast.
 (E) Everyone got more excited and amused.

NEXT — *Follow the directions (Steps 8-17) on page 1 of the* PROGRESS FOLDER.

ARTICLE 16

Chink: the development of a pup*

by Ernest Thompson Seton

READING PRACTICE 16 *In a book, magazine, or newspaper that you like, practice reading for speed and comprehension. Make a record of each such practice in Chart 3 on page 8 of the* PROGRESS FOLDER. *Then do Reading Article 16.*

READING ARTICLE 16 *Before you begin reading Article 16, record your starting time in the Time Record on page 7 of the* PROGRESS FOLDER. *Then read Article 16. Read it as fast as you can, but make sure you understand what you are reading.*

CHINK WAS JUST old enough to think himself a very remarkable little dog; and so he was, but not in the way he fondly imagined. He was neither fierce nor dreadful, strong nor swift, but he was one of

*Reprinted from *Lives of the Hunted* by Ernest Thompson Seton; copyright 1901, 1929, by Ernest Thompson Seton; used by permission of the publishers, Charles Scribner's Sons.

the noisiest, best-natured, silliest pups that ever chewed his master's boots to bits. His master, Bill Aubrey, was an old mountaineer who was camped below Garnet Peak in Yellowstone Park.

The little dog was always trying to do some absurd or impossible thing. He slowly realized that there were long whips and big, fierce dogs with wagons; that horses have teeth in their heels; that calves have relatives with clubs on their heads; that a slow cat may turn out a skunk; and that wasps are not butterflies.

Chink's crowning blunder was a large coyote who lived not far from our camp. He evidently realized, as all the animals there do, that no man is allowed to shoot, trap, hunt, or in any way molest the wild creatures in the Park—above all, in this part, close to the military patrol, with soldiers always on watch. Secure in the knowledge of this, the coyote used to come about the camp each night for scraps. Then growing bolder, he came occasionally in the daytime.

One morning, as he sat on a bank some fifty yards away, one of us, in a spirit of mischief, said to Chink: "Chink, do you see that coyote over there grinning at you? Go and chase him out of that."

Chink always did as he was told. He dashed after the coyote, who loped lightly away, and there was a pretty good race for a quarter of a mile. But it was nothing to the race which began when the coyote turned on his pursuer.

Chink realized all at once that he had been lured into the power of a Tartar, and strained every muscle to get back to camp. The coyote was swifter, and soon overtook the dog, nipping him first on one side, then on the other. Chink yelped and howled and ran his hardest; and we, I am afraid, laughed with the coyote. The puppy did not get the sympathy he deserved for his trouble in doing as he was told.

One more experience like this was enough to dampen even Chink's enthusiasm. He decided to let that coyote very much alone in the future. Not so the coyote, however. He had discovered a new and delightful amusement. He came daily now and hung about the camp and sought every opportunity to tease the dog.

One day Aubrey moved his camp a mile up-stream, and we saw less of the coyote, for the reason that he moved a mile up-stream too.

Aubrey gave it out that he had moved camp to get better horse-feed. It soon turned out, however, that he wanted to be alone while he enjoyed the contents of a whiskey-flask that he had obtained somewhere. But one flask was a mere starter for him. The second day he mounted his horse, said, "Chink, you watch the tent," and rode away over the mountains to the nearest saloon. He left Chink obediently curled up on some sacking.

There was some bacon in the tent wrapped in a bag, but that was sacred. His master had told him to "watch it," and Chink would have starved rather than touch it.

He ventured out on the flat in hope of finding a mouse or something to stay the pangs of hunger, when suddenly he was pounced on by that brute of a coyote, and the old chase was repeated as Chink dashed back to the tent.

Chink was a mere puppy yet, and a little fool in many ways, but away back of all was a fibre of strength that would grow with his years. The moment that coyote tried to follow into the tent—his master's tent—Chink forgot all his own fears, and turned on the enemy like a little demon.

The coyote backed off, growling savagely, and vowing, in coyote fashion, to tear that dog to ribbons very soon. All the same, he did not venture to enter the tent, as he clearly had intended doing.

Then began a literal siege; for the coyote came back every little while, and walked round the tent. He scratched contemptuously with his hind feet, or marched up to the open door, to be met at once, face to face, by poor little Chink. The dog, really half dead with fear, was brave again as soon as he saw any attempt to injure the things in his charge.

All this time Chink had nothing to eat. He could slip out and get a drink at the near-by stream once or twice a day, but he could not get a meal in that way. He could have torn a hole in the sack and eaten some bacon, but he would not, for that was in trust. Or, he could have watched his chance to desert his post and sneak off to our camp, where he would have been sure of a good meal. But no; he would not betray his master's trust in any way.

For four days and four nights of misery did this heroic little dog keep his place, and keep tent and stuff from the coyote that he held in mortal terror.

On the fifth morning old Aubrey had awakened to the fact that he was not at home, and that his camp in the mountains was guarded only by a small dog. He was tired of his spree now, and he got on his horse and set out over the hills, sober but very shaky. When he was about half-way on the trail, it suddenly dawned on his clouded brain that he had left Chink without any food.

"Hope the little beast hain't spoiled all my bacon," he thought, and he pressed on more briskly till he came to the ridge commanding a view of his tent. There it was, and there at the door, exchanging growls and snapping at each other, were the big, fierce coyote and poor little Chink.

"Wal, I be darned!" exclaimed Aubrey. "I forgot all about that blasted coyote. Poor Chink! he must 'a' had a mighty tough time. Wonder he ain't all chawed up an' the camp in tatters."

There Chink was, bravely making his last stand. When Aubrey galloped up and saw the untouched bacon, he realized that Chink had eaten nothing since he left. When the puppy, trembling with fear and weakness, crawled up and looked in his face and licked his hand as much as to say, "I've done what you told me," it was too much for old Aubrey. The tears stood in his eyes as he hastened to get food for the little hero.

Then he turned to him and said: "Chink, old pard, I've treated you dirty, an' you always treated me white. I'll never go on another spree without takin' you along, Chink, an' I'll treat you as white as you treated me. 'Tain't much more I kin do for you, pard, but I reckon I kin lift the biggest worry out o' yer life, an' I'll do it, too."

Then from the ridge-pole he took down the pride of his heart, his treasured repeating rifle. Regardless of consequences, he broke the government seals, and went to the door.

The coyote was sitting off a little way with a Mephistophelian grin on his face, as usual; but the rifle rang, and Chink's reign of terror was at an end.

What matter if the soldiers did come out and find that the laws of the Park had been violated? What matter to Aubrey if his gun was taken from him and destroyed, and he and his outfit expelled from the Park, with a promise of being jailed if ever he returned?

"It's all right," said old Aubrey. "I done the squar' thing by my pard—my pard, that always treated me white."

As soon as you finish reading Article 16, record your finishing time in the Time Record on page 7 of the PROGRESS FOLDER. Then read Test 16 that appears next in this book.

READING TEST 16   CHINK: THE DEVELOPMENT OF A PUP

Read each test item and select the answer you believe is correct. Print the letter of your answer in the Answer Record on page 7 of the PROGRESS FOLDER.

1. Chink was a remarkable pup because he was really so very
   - (A) fierce, dreadful, and bad-tempered
   - (B) quiet, smart, and tricky
   - (C) strong, swift, and sure of himself
   - (D) large, heavy, and awkward
   - (E) noisy, good-natured, and silly

2. Chink's master, Bill Aubrey, was an old
   - (A) soldier
   - (B) mountaineer
   - (C) miner
   - (D) ranger
   - (E) rancher

3. While Chink was always trying to do something crazy or impossible, he slowly learned
   - (A) what animals could hurt him
   - (B) why animals could frighten him
   - (C) when animals could play with him
   - (D) how animals could outrun him
   - (E) where animals could hide from him

4. In Yellowstone Park the law provided that a man was allowed to shoot a wild animal
   - (A) during a short open season
   - (B) only when he was starving
   - (C) at no time of the year
   - (D) if that animal was very old or sick
   - (E) to save his own life

5. At first the large coyote came to Aubrey's camp each night and then in the daytime mainly in order to
   - (A) frighten Chink
   - (B) watch Aubrey
   - (C) steal food scraps
   - (D) have fun with the pup
   - (E) get warm inside the tent

6. Chink started for the coyote because he
   - (A) was an obedient dog
   - (B) hated the coyote's grin
   - (C) wished to get away from camp
   - (D) saw the coyote sitting near
   - (E) wanted the coyote's bone

7. As Chink dashed back toward camp, the coyote
   - (A) bit him on one side and then the other
   - (B) yelped and howled as loudly as possible
   - (C) seemed to laugh at the little dog
   - (D) shook him from side to side
   - (E) knocked him to the ground several times

8. The coyote came again and again to Aubrey's camp because he seemed to enjoy

(A) racing Chink
(B) stealing Chink's food
(C) teasing Chink
(D) grinning at Aubrey
(E) bringing home the bacon

9. Aubrey moved his camp a mile upstream because he wanted

(A) to find better grass for his horse
(B) to get Chink away from the coyote
(C) to pan for gold in a new place
(D) to put up his tent on a drier spot
(E) to drink a bottle of whiskey

10. Just before Aubrey mounted his horse and rode away, he told Chink

(A) to chase the coyote away
(B) to stay home
(C) to guard the bacon
(D) to watch the tent
(E) to curl up on some sacking

11. Chink tried to get something to eat by

(A) searching outside for some meat scraps
(B) looking outside for a mouse
(C) tearing the rinds off the bacon in the bag
(D) seizing a bone dropped by the coyote
(E) opening a box of dog biscuits

12. When the coyote started to enter the tent, Chink

(A) fought him off like a demon
(B) stood guard like a fool over the bag of bacon
(C) whined and cried for his master
(D) hid for a while under a blanket
(E) attacked him from behind

13. The coyote acted as if he were just about

(A) to get Chink to chase him
(B) to make a fool of Chink
(C) to pull the tent down around Chink
(D) to tear Chink into ribbons
(E) to force Chink to give up the bacon

14. Every time the coyote marched up to the door of the tent, Chink

(A) scratched his hind feet furiously
(B) sat down firmly on the bag of bacon
(C) barked for his master
(D) chased his enemy far away
(E) stood bravely facing his enemy

15. While Chink was guarding the tent, he

(A) caught some field mice in the tent
(B) went to the camp down-stream for food
(C) spent nearly all his time resting and sleeping
(D) sneaked out to a near-by stream for water
(E) chewed grass and roots to keep alive

16. On the fifth morning, while Aubrey was on the way back to his camp, he was most afraid that
    - (A) Chink was very, very hungry
    - (B) he was too drunk to take care of Chink
    - (C) the coyote had hurt or killed Chink
    - (D) the stream had washed away his tent
    - (E) Chink had spoiled all his bacon

17. When Aubrey first saw Chink and the coyote, he was most surprised that the coyote had *not*
    - (A) been wounded by his dog
    - (B) left the camp for good
    - (C) torn up his dog and tent
    - (D) dug up the garbage pit
    - (E) brought in other coyotes to fight

18. When Chink crawled up to Aubrey and looked into his master's eyes, the little dog seemed to say,
    - (A) "May I have something to eat?"
    - (B) "I've done what you told me."
    - (C) "I hope you shoot that coyote."
    - (D) "Stop crying. Everything's all right."
    - (E) "Take me with you next time."

19. Aubrey decided to shoot the coyote mainly because he wanted
    - (A) to leave the Park with his little dog
    - (B) to lift the biggest worry from Chink's life
    - (C) to provide some fresh meat for Chink
    - (D) to protect his small supply of bacon
    - (E) to frighten the coyote away from his camp

20. Aubrey knew that, for killing the coyote, each of these things except one would probably happen. Which would *not?*
    - (A) Soldiers would find he had broken the Park's laws.
    - (B) Soldiers would take his precious gun and destroy it.
    - (C) Soldiers would force him to leave the Park.
    - (D) Soldiers would take Chink away from him.
    - (E) Soldiers would put him in jail if he returned.

NEXT — *Follow the directions (Steps 8-17) on page 1 of the* PROGRESS FOLDER.

ARTICLE 17

*The story-teller**

by Saki (H. H. Munro)

READING PRACTICE 17 *In a book, magazine, or newspaper that you like, practice reading for speed and comprehension. Make a record of each such practice in Chart 3 on page 8 of the* PROGRESS FOLDER. *Then do Reading Article 17.*

READING ARTICLE 17 *Before you begin reading Article 17, record your starting time in the Time Record on page 7 of the* PROGRESS FOLDER. *Then read Article 17. Read it as fast as you can, but make sure you understand what you are reading.*

IT WAS A HOT afternoon, and the railway carriage was correspondingly sultry, and the next stop was at Templecombe, nearly an hour ahead. The occupants of the carriage were a small girl, and a smaller girl, and a small boy. An aunt belonging to the children occupied one corner seat, and the further corner seat on the opposite side was occupied by a bachelor who was a stranger to their party. Both the aunt and the children were conversational in a limited, persistent way, reminding one of the attentions of a housefly that refused to be discouraged. Most of the aunt's remarks seemed to begin with "Don't," and nearly all of the children's remarks began with "Why?" The bachelor said nothing out loud.

"Come over here and listen to a story," said the aunt, when the bachelor had looked twice at her and once at the communication cord.

The children moved listlessly towards the aunt's end of the carriage. Evidently her reputation as a story-teller did not rank high in their estimation.

In a low, confidential voice, interrupted at frequent intervals by loud, petulant questions from her listeners, she began an unenterprising and deplorably uninteresting story about a little girl who was good, and made friends with every one on account of her goodness, and was finally saved from a mad bull by a number of rescuers who admired her moral character.

"Wouldn't they have saved her if she hadn't been good?" demanded the bigger of the small girls. It was exactly the question that the bachelor had wanted to ask.

"Well, yes," admitted the aunt lamely, "but I don't think they would have run quite so fast to her help if they had not liked her so much."

"It's the stupidest story I've ever heard," said the bigger of the small girls, with immense conviction.

"I didn't listen after the first bit, it was so stupid," said Cyril, the small boy.

"You don't seem to be a success as a story-teller," said the bachelor suddenly from his corner.

*Slightly condensed from "The Story-Teller" from *The Short Stories of Saki* by H. H. Munro. Copyright 1930, by The Viking Press, Inc. Reprinted by permission of The Viking Press, Inc., New York. Also by permission of John Lane, The Bodley Head Limited, London.

The aunt bristled in instant defense at this unexpected attack.

"It's a very difficult thing to tell stories that children can both understand and appreciate," she said stiffly.

"I don't agree with you," said the bachelor.

"Perhaps you would like to tell them a story," was the aunt's retort.

"Tell us a story," demanded the bigger of the small girls.

"Once upon a time," began the bachelor, "there was a little girl called Bertha, who was extraordinarily good."

The children's momentarily-aroused interest began at once to flicker; all stories seemed dreadfully alike, no matter who told them.

"She did all that she was told, she was always truthful, she kept her clothes clean, ate milk puddings as though they were jam tarts, learned her lessons perfectly, and was polite in her manners."

"Was she pretty?" asked the bigger of the small girls.

"Not as pretty as any of you," said the bachelor, "but she was horribly good."

There was a wave of reaction in favour of the story; the word horrible in connection with goodness was a novelty that commended itself. It seemed to introduce a ring of truth that was absent from the aunt's tales of infant life.

"She was so good," continued the bachelor, "that she won several medals for goodness, which she always wore, pinned on to her dress. There was a medal for obedience, another for punctuality, and a third for good behaviour. They were metal medals and they clicked against one another as she walked.

"Everybody talked about her goodness, and the Prince of the country got to hear about it, and he said that as she was so very good she might be allowed once a week to walk in his park, which was just outside the town. It was a beautiful park, and no children were ever allowed in it, so it was a great honour for Bertha to be allowed to go there."

"Were there any sheep in the park?" demanded Cyril.

"No," said the bachelor, "there were no sheep."

"Why weren't there any sheep?" came the inevitable question arising out of that answer.

The aunt permitted herself a smile, which might almost have been described as a grin.

"There were no sheep in the park," said the bachelor, "because the Prince's mother had once had a dream that her son would either be killed by a sheep or else by a clock falling on him. For that reason the Prince never kept a sheep in his park or a clock in his palace."

The aunt suppressed a gasp of admiration.

"Was the Prince killed by a sheep or by a clock?" asked Cyril.

"He is still alive, so we can't tell whether the dream will come true," said the bachelor unconcernedly; "anyway, there were no sheep in the park, but there were lots of little pigs running all over the place."

"What colour were they?"

"Black with white faces, white with black spots, black all over, grey with white patches, and some were white all over."

The story-teller paused to let a full idea of the park's treasures sink into the children's imaginations; then he resumed:

"There were lots of other delightful things in the park. There were ponds with gold and blue and green fish in them, and trees with beautiful parrots that said clever things at a moment's notice, and humming birds that hummed all the popular tunes of the day. Bertha walked up and down and enjoyed herself immensely, and thought to herself: 'If I were not so extraordinarily good I should not have been allowed to come into this beautiful park and enjoy all that there is to be seen in it.' Just then an enormous wolf came prowling into the park to see if it could catch a fat little pig for its supper.

"The first thing that it saw in the park was Bertha; her pinafore was so spotlessly white and clean that it could be seen from a great distance. Bertha saw the wolf and saw that it was stealing towards her, and she began to wish that she had never been allowed to come into the park. She ran as hard as she could, and the wolf came after her with huge leaps and bounds. She managed to reach a shrubbery of myrtle bushes and she hid herself in one of the thickest of the bushes. The scent of the myrtle was so strong that the wolf could not sniff out where Bertha was hiding, and the bushes were so thick that he might have hunted about in them for a long time without catching sight of her, so he thought he might as well go off and catch a little pig instead.

"Bertha was trembling very much at having the wolf prowling and sniffing so near her, and as she trembled the medal for obedience clinked against the medals for good conduct and punctuality. The wolf was just moving away when he heard the sound of the medals clinking and stopped to listen; they clinked again in a bush quite near him. He dashed into the bush, and dragged Bertha out and devoured her to the last morsel. All that was left of her were her shoes, bits of clothing, and the three medals for goodness."

"It is the most beautiful story that I ever heard," said the bigger of the small girls, with immense decision.

"It is the only beautiful story I have ever heard," said Cyril.

A dissentient opinion came from the aunt.

"A most improper story to tell to young children! You have undermined the effect of years of careful teaching."

"At any rate," said the bachelor, collecting his belongings preparatory to leaving the carriage, "I kept them quiet for ten minutes, which was more than you were able to do."

"Unhappy woman!" he observed to himself as he walked down the platform of Templecombe station. "For the next six months or so those children will assail her in public with demands for an improper story!"

As soon as you finish reading Article 17, record your finishing time in the Time Record on page 7 of the PROGRESS FOLDER. *Then read Test 17 that appears next in this book.*

READING TEST 17   THE STORY-TELLER

*Read each test item and select the answer you believe is correct. Print the
letter of your answer in the Answer Record on page 7 of the* PROGRESS FOLDER.

1. On the hot afternoon of
the story, the railway
carriage was occupied by

   (A) five persons
   (B) three persons
   (C) six persons
   (D) four persons
   (E) seven persons

2. Most of the conversation
between the aunt and the
small children was made
up of these two words:

   (A) "Please!" and "What?"
   (B) "Stop!" and "When?"
   (C) "Do!" and "How?"
   (D) "Don't!" and "Why?"
   (E) "You!" and "Who?"

3. The children moved
slowly toward the aunt
to hear her story prob-
ably because they

   (A) were tired out from the long train ride
   (B) wanted to talk with the bachelor
   (C) preferred to look out the car window
   (D) wished to act like pesky houseflies
   (E) disliked her stories

4. The aunt told the children a story about a good
little girl who was res-
cued by her admirers
from a mad

   (A) dog
   (B) bull
   (C) pig
   (D) wolf
   (E) man

5. When the girl asked if
the story girl's friends
wouldn't have saved her
if she hadn't been good,
the aunt said: "I don't

   (A) think they were near enough to help her."
   (B) think they really wanted to help her."
   (C) think they would have run so fast to help her."
   (D) think they would have tried to help her."
   (E) think they were brave enough to help her."

6. The bigger girl and the
small boy both said that
their aunt's story was

   (A) funny
   (B) exciting
   (C) stupid
   (D) good
   (E) sad

7. When the bachelor criticized her story, the aunt
said that it was very difficult to tell stories that

   (A) children can both remember and repeat
   (B) children can learn from and apply
   (C) children can enjoy and recall
   (D) children can read and write down
   (E) children can understand and appreciate

8. When the bachelor began his story about Bertha, the children lost interest immediately because such stories seemed
   - (A) terribly different
   - (B) awfully frightening
   - (C) dreadfully alike
   - (D) much too long
   - (E) about little girls

9. The bachelor told the children that Bertha did each of these things except one. Which did she *not* do?
   - (A) She told the truth.
   - (B) She tried to be very pretty.
   - (C) She learned her lessons perfectly.
   - (D) She kept her clothes clean.
   - (E) She was polite in her manners.

10. When the bachelor said Bertha was "horribly good," the children wanted to hear more because these words
    - (A) made the story seem false and imaginary
    - (B) made the story seem fresh and truthful
    - (C) made the story seem helpful and useful
    - (D) made the story seem happy and ordinary
    - (E) made the story seem good and cheerful

11. According to the bachelor's story, which of these things was *not* true about Bertha's medals?
    - (A) They were for obedience, punctuality, and goodness.
    - (B) The children's aunt gave Bertha the medals.
    - (C) She always wore the medals pinned onto her dress.
    - (D) When Bertha walked, the medals clicked together.
    - (E) The medals were large and were made of metal.

12. The Prince allowed Bertha to walk in his park. This was a great honor because he
    - (A) had made the park such a beautiful place
    - (B) allowed only his own family in the park
    - (C) did not allow children in the park
    - (D) allowed wolves to run wild in the park
    - (E) often walked with Bertha in the park

13. When the boy asked the bachelor why the park had no sheep, the aunt thought the bachelor would
    - (A) have trouble answering the boy's question
    - (B) have to say that wolves had killed all the sheep
    - (C) tell the boy to stop asking so many questions
    - (D) pay little or no attention to the boy's question
    - (E) have to ask her for the answer

14. The Prince had never kept a clock in the palace because his mother had dreamed that he would
    - (A) be kept awake at night by the clock
    - (B) never learn to tell the time
    - (C) take the clock apart
    - (D) be killed by a falling clock
    - (E) throw a clock at the sheep

15. The bachelor said the park had each of these things except one. Which thing did the park *not* have?
    - (A) Little pigs colored with black, white, and gray
    - (B) Ponds with gold, blue, and green fish
    - (C) Wolves that were dressed in sheep's clothing
    - (D) Trees with beautiful and clever-talking parrots
    - (E) Hummingbirds that hummed all the popular tunes

16. The wolf first noticed Bertha because from a long distance he
    (A) saw her large shining medals
    (B) heard her laughing
    (C) smelled her body
    (D) tracked her footprints
    (E) saw her white dress

17. For a while the wolf could not find Bertha who was hiding in the thick myrtle bushes because
    (A) the scent of the bushes was so strong
    (B) there were so many little pigs in the bushes
    (C) the wind was blowing so strongly
    (D) Bertha moved so quietly from place to place
    (E) the bushes had so many sharp thorns

18. The wolf finally found Bertha because he
    (A) could not find a fat little lamb
    (B) was so hungry for a good little girl
    (C) waited for her to tremble with fear
    (D) heard her medals clinking together
    (E) listened to her cry for help

19. After the bachelor finished the story about Bertha, the aunt said that it was
    (A) the best story to tell young children again and again
    (B) the most beautiful story her children had ever heard
    (C) the first story to keep the children quiet for a while
    (D) the silliest story anyone could tell to young children
    (E) a most improper story to tell young children

20. In this story, the author makes fun of persons who are
    (A) namby-pamby
    (B) willy-nilly
    (C) wishy-washy
    (D) goody-goody
    (E) hoity-toity

NEXT — *Follow the directions (Steps 8-17) on page 1 of the* PROGRESS FOLDER.

ARTICLE 18

*To walk alone**

by Virginia Conroy

READING PRACTICE 18 *In a book, magazine, or newspaper that you like, practice reading for speed and comprehension. Make a record of each such practice in Chart 3 on page 8 of the* PROGRESS FOLDER. *Then do Reading Article 18.*

READING ARTICLE 18 *Before you begin reading Article 18, record your starting time in the Time Record on page 7 of the* PROGRESS FOLDER. *Then read Article 18. Read it as fast as you can, but make sure you understand what you are reading.*

SOMETHING IS happening to the world, I thought. It's going too fast. So, faster and faster I ran until my breath came short and my heart pounded, but I could not catch up with it.

And then one day it fell to pieces. I was on Forty-Second Street in New York City when it happened. Suddenly the buildings were mountains of stone that would crumble and crush me; the pavement opened and the subway was a black, roaring pit of hell yawning below. People were enemies, attacking me, trampling me down. My clothes dropped from me, charred rags at my feet.

I fled in panic from the scene, seeking the security of my home. But destruction had reached it before me. The beautiful facade had cracked. The blinds hung crazily. I could hardly recognize it—the place I had lived in for years. In my bed I lay for days, weeping, covering my head with a blanket to shut out this terrible thing that had happened to the world. Then they brought My Friend to see

me. He took the blanket away. "Come," he said, "this won't do, you know. You can't stay here."

"I dare not move," I sobbed. "I dare not even tread upon the floor. It will collapse under me. There was an earthquake. My own home is no longer safe."

"Then we will strengthen it," he replied. "We will go to the cellar and inspect the foundations."

A year passed before we came out of the cellar—a year in which he drove me relentlessly, tearing down and rebuilding, strengthening the foundations of my house which had always been weak beneath its facade of assurance. When I cried for mercy he said, "I cannot do it alone. We must work together." But when we left it at last, the foundations were strong, the floor was clean, the rubble of a lifetime had been cleared away and not a single cobweb was left in the rafters.

When we came back upstairs he asked: "Where do you spend your time in your home?"

Gaining courage, I went ahead of him and opened a door.

"But this is the nursery," he said, "and you have grown up these many years."

*Condensed from *Today's Health*, January, 1951. Copyright 1951, by the American Medical Association. Reprinted with permission of the publisher and the author.

"I play with my toys," I protested, "and I love them, and I won't give them up."

There they were in the corner, scarred of paint, leaking sawdust on the floor, those playthings that should have been discarded years ago. And my defiance turned to shame. "Burn them!" I cried. "Burn them all in the fireplace." And I watched, triumphant, while he did it.

Then he turned to my fairy tale books. "And these, too, of course. These must go."

Unrelentingly he pulled them from the shelf and gave them to the flame.

"I hate you!" I cried. "I hate you. Because of you I am only ashes in the fireplace. I am nothing. This is what you have done to me."

But after a time we were friends again. For years, he explained, I had lived within the pastel protection of nursery walls, spooning cereal from a plastic bowl, while my place was set in the adult banquet hall, with china and crystal and silver and fine linen. I must hurry, I thought, hurry to make up for all the spilt time and the tears that had flowed under the bridge. I must get to the banquet hall before they took my place away.

And so for three months we talked about these things and then he said, "It is almost time for you to dress and go out into the world again."

I went to the closet and looked at my clothes and they were a bedraggled lot indeed. Most of them had been given to me. They had been imposed upon me by other people—cut to their patterns. They had never fitted.

Angrily I asked, "Why did they do this to me? Why did they make me wear their clothes?"

"Why did you accept them?" he challenged. "Why did you not reject them and make your own?"

I hung my head, chagrined, and then

I looked up at him hopefully. "But there is an old trunk in the attic. I can find material there. Is it too late for me to make my own?"

His eyes twinkled. "I was waiting for you to say that."

And so we went to the attic and delved deep into the overflowing trunk.

"Here is a generous length of religious faith," he said, "faded a little. But the material is strong and if you like it, we can dye it to its original richness. It will be as good as new, a warm cloak against the wind."

"And here is a good relationship," I caroled. "I might just turn it and it will make a lovely dress."

He nodded and we went on assembling the clothing. Garments to be cut after my own pattern in colors that pleased me. Mine.

At the bottom of the trunk I found something that sparkled.

"What is this?" I asked puzzled, and then I recalled it. "Oh, I remember, it is a little talent I had once. I packed it away years ago and forgot it."

"Let me see it," he commanded.

"Oh," I laughed, "it is nothing valuable, really. Just costume jewelry."

"You are wrong," he said. "It is a real gem. See how it sparkles in the light. Polish it, have it reset and you will wear it with pride all your life."

And so the days passed, happily now, fruitfully, and soon I was dressed.

"Tomorrow you will go out into the world," he said, "but before you go I shall give you my parting gift. This little red feather to stick in your hat."

"What is it really?" I asked delightedly.

"Men call it many things, but perhaps it will be simplest to say that it is a sense of proportion. As long as you wear it you will be protected. It is a magic talisman. This thing that happened to you can never happen again."

We went through the hallway onto the porch.

"Couldn't we sit on the porch a bit first, before I go out on the sidewalk—just to watch?"

"If you like," he said, "but only for a short time. Then we must be on our way."

At last he pulled me gently down the steps and I walked with people again, holding tightly to his hand.

"Where are you taking me?"

"To Forty-Second Street."

"I stopped in my tracks. "But you don't understand. That was where it happened. Forty-Second Street fell apart."

"No," he said kindly. "Forty-Second Street is still there. Nothing happened to it. It didn't fall apart. You did."

Because I knew by then that he was My Friend, because I knew he was wise and kind and good, I let him lead me there, but it was not easy.

"Now," he said, stopping on the very spot from which I had run in terror. "What do you see?"

"Just buildings, and pavements and people."

"All intact?"

"All intact."

"Now you know."

"Yes," I smiled.

"Good," he replied. "Then I will leave you here."

"Oh—no!" I wailed. "Not here. Not now."

"It must be here and now."

"But I thought we would be together always. You are everything to me. I love you. I admire you. I want to tell you so over and over."

"To forget me is the greatest compliment you can give me," he smiled, "and that is all I ask."

Still I clung. "I can't bear to see you disappear in the crowd. Don't desert me. Don't walk away from me."

"Then you must walk away from me."

I drew a deep breath. "I'll try, but I'm not sure that I can."

"You can walk alone through the crowd. You can walk without me—without anybody else in the world."

I met his eyes and I knew that it was true.

"Goodbye, Doctor," I said, and I dropped his hand and walked down Forty-Second Street—alone.

As soon as you finish reading Article 18, record your finishing time in the Time Record on page 7 of the PROGRESS FOLDER. *Then read Test 18 that appears next in this book.*

READING TEST 18   TO WALK ALONE

Read each test item and select the answer you believe is correct. Print the letter of your answer in the Answer Record on page 7 of the PROGRESS FOLDER.

1. At the beginning of the story, the author (Virginia Conroy) felt that the world was

   (A) falling so quickly she could not escape it
   (B) moving so slowly she could not wait for it
   (C) turning so noisily she could not hear herself think
   (D) becoming so quiet she could not stay awake
   (E) going so fast she could not catch up with it

2. One day while on 42nd Street in New York, Virginia suddenly felt that the buildings and people were about

(A) to hide her
(B) to confuse her
(C) to uplift her
(D) to crush her
(E) to capture her

3. After Virginia arrived home, she stayed in bed for days, weeping, because she believed that

(A) the best doctor had refused to come to see her
(B) all her friends had left her alone in the world
(C) a terrible thing had happened to the world
(D) crying was the best way to relieve her tensions
(E) everything would be all right after a while

4. Virginia and her friend worked a whole year in the cellar of her house. During that time she was *really*

(A) trying to improve her appearance
(B) cleaning up the house's basement
(C) letting her friend do most of the work
(D) getting ready to move to another home
(E) strengthening the base of her life

5. When Virginia told her friend to burn all the toys, she really meant that she wanted

(A) to rid herself of childish thoughts and habits
(B) to buy new and better toys for her friend
(C) to destroy all memories of her childhood
(D) to make the room as clean and neat as possible
(E) to show her friend she did not care what happened

6. After Virginia's fairy tale books had been burned, she told her friend that because of him she was only

(A) child-like
(B) ashes
(C) human
(D) smoke
(E) flames

7. Virginia's friend said that, for years, she had lived as a child while a beautiful place waited for her as

(A) an adult
(B) a teen-ager
(C) a healthy person
(D) a homemaker
(E) an intelligent woman

8. Virginia felt that she had to hurry because she had to

(A) finish her dinner
(B) get back to Forty-Second Street
(C) gain the respect of her friend
(D) build up her own library
(E) make up for lost time

9. When Virginia looked in her closet, which of these things did she *not* think or say?

(A) The clothes when new looked fairly good on her.
(B) The clothes appeared soiled and unpressed.
(C) Other people had given her the clothes.
(D) The clothes had never fitted her.
(E) Other people had made her wear their clothes.

10. In telling the story about the clothes in her closet, Virginia really meant this: I should
   - (A) see myself as others see me
   - (B) be myself, not what others want me to be
   - (C) do unto others as I would have them do unto me
   - (D) realize that fine feathers do not make fine birds
   - (E) remember that everybody should be well-dressed

11. When Virginia's friend suggested that she make her own clothes, Virginia recalled that she had some material
   - (A) stored in an old box in the cellar
   - (B) stored in an old suitcase in the closet
   - (C) stored in an old trunk in the attic
   - (D) stored in an old wardrobe in the sewing room
   - (E) stored in an old dresser in the guest room

12. Virginia's friend discovered that she had something strong, warm, and enriching. It was a
   - (A) religious faith
   - (B) pot of gold
   - (C) happy childhood
   - (D) special talent
   - (E) good friend

13. When Virginia found a little talent that she had forgotten, her friend suggested that she should
   - (A) try to build all of her different talents
   - (B) practice this talent after she was well
   - (C) remember this talent and the happiness it brought
   - (D) use this talent and be proud of it
   - (E) find her strongest talent and develop it

14. Virginia's friend pointed out that the red feather for her hat stood for a sense of
   - (A) humor
   - (B) decency
   - (C) disaster
   - (D) proportion
   - (E) optimism

15. Just after Virginia and her friend went out the front door, she wanted
   - (A) to walk with other people along the street
   - (B) to go back inside the house right away
   - (C) to tell her friend everything was all right
   - (D) to take a taxicab ride through the park
   - (E) to sit on the porch for a while

16. Virginia let her friend lead her back to Forty-Second Street mainly because she
   - (A) believed in him
   - (B) wanted to see what had happened
   - (C) was no longer afraid
   - (D) liked to hold his hand
   - (E) was tired of staying home

17. Virginia told her friend that she did not want him to leave her then and there because she
   - (A) wanted him to meet her family
   - (B) loved him
   - (C) needed a doctor's care
   - (D) was so unhappy
   - (E) knew he was kind and good

18. Virginia's friend told her that she could pay him the greatest compliment if she

    (A) worked with him
    (B) forgot him
    (C) remembered him
    (D) thanked him
    (E) paid him

19. When Virginia told about leaving her friend and walking alone through the crowd, she meant this:

    (A) She felt more lonely than ever before.
    (B) She knew she could always go back to the doctor.
    (C) She was well enough to face the world by herself.
    (D) She no longer believed strangers would help her.
    (E) She liked being with many other people again.

20. In treating Virginia, which thing did her doctor *not* do? He helped her

    (A) to rebuild the foundation of her life
    (B) to be herself instead of what others wanted her to be
    (C) to replace childish attitudes with adult attitudes
    (D) to realize her illness was only imaginary
    (E) to gain confidence in herself and her abilities

NEXT — *Follow the directions (Steps 8-17) on page 1 of the* PROGRESS FOLDER.

ARTICLE 19

*A wild ride in the Waverly**

by Emily Kimbrough

READING PRACTICE 19 *In a book, magazine, or newspaper that you like, practice reading for speed and comprehension. Make a record of each such practice in Chart 3 on page 8 of the* PROGRESS FOLDER. *Then do Reading Article 19.*

READING ARTICLE 19 *Before you begin reading Article 19, record your starting time in the Time Record on page 7 of the* PROGRESS FOLDER. *Then read Article 19. Read it as fast as you can, but make sure you understand what you are reading.*

A YEAR AFTER we had moved to Blackstone Avenue in Chicago, my father bought a Waverly electric for Mother. I was thirteen years old.

*Condensed and adapted from *The Innocents from Indiana*, by Emily Kimbrough. Copyright 1950, by the author. Published by Harper & Brothers, New York. Reprinted with permission of the author and publisher.

An electric was a small car, powered by a motor that drew electricity from a storage battery. In an electric the driver's place was on the left side of the back seat. Two parallel metal bars stood upright at the left of the driver. The longer one was for steering, the shorter for speed control. If you wished to turn left, you pushed the long bar away, or pulled it toward you to turn right. Pushing the shorter bar away would send the machine from first, through the notches of higher speeds, to fifth. Before it would start, however, you had to insert a thick, flat key in a slot. This would turn on the current.

Mother liked the Waverly the minute she saw it. All that month we went for a ride every pleasant evening.

In April that year I went to spend my spring vacation with my grandparents. While I was there, Grandfather taught me to drive Grandmother's Waverly.

When I returned to Chicago at the end of vacation, I was lofty about my driving, and Mother worked out a plan for me. I was to drive myself to and from school on the two days when we had afternoon sessions. Walking home alone in the late afternoon was dangerous, she thought. It was, however, on the three-block trip in the Waverly, that I came to grief.

I was driving home from class when the speed lever stuck between third and fourth speeds. I couldn't budge it. It was frozen, and I was rounding the corner at a clip of about twenty miles an hour, or better. I couldn't stop because I had been severely warned that in an electric, if you put on the brake while the current was on, you burned out the motor after first setting it on fire. And the motor was immediately under the driver's seat. You could tap the brake lightly for a very slight pause, but for a genuine slowing down, you had to pull the speed lever back to neutral, and then apply the brake.

I tapped my way around the corner at Fiftieth and Blackstone. Simultaneously, I began to ring the bell, which was a button at the end of the steering rod. I had only half a block to go before reaching

our apartment. I knew I couldn't stop there, but I thought I might attract someone's attention.

The first time past brought no results, so I went on around the block, brake-tapping at the corners, though the seat beneath me was beginning to feel hot. As I approached the apartment on the second try, I stopped ringing the bell, braced my knee against the steering rod to hold a steady course, leaned out the window, my hands cupped around my mouth, and roared over and over, "Mother, come help! Mother, help! *Mother!*"

Miraculously Hilda, our maid, heard and recognized my voice and the bell of our electric. I saw her out on the porch my next time around the block. But she shook her finger crossly as I flashed by and yelled after me, "Shame on you."

Part way around the block I was confused by this; then I guess she had thought I was showing off how I could drive no-handed, and wouldn't on any account let Mother see. But the next time past, I saw Mother beside Hilda on the porch. "Come in this minute," she called down very loud and she repeated it. This prevented her from hearing what I was saying. Going around the corner, I burst into tears. I had been sure that once I got Mother's attention, she would know what was wrong and what to do.

When I rounded on to Blackstone Avenue again, Mother had guessed that I couldn't stop. She was standing in the middle of the street. As I reached her, I tapped the brake so hard that the motor sizzled under me. She swung on to the running board on the side opposite me. "You're doing nicely," she said. "What's the matter? Stop crying."

"The speed lever's stuck." I jiggled it to show her, and I stopped crying. When she had satisfied herself that the lever *was* stuck, she straightened up, looked over the top, and shouted, first to people in our way, then equally loud but sticking her face suddenly through the window, to me.

"Out of our way, little boy . . . We could keep on driving 'til the power dies . . . Look out, *please*, we're out of control. . . Not around and around like this, Emily, we'll be dizzy . . . Keep *back*, please . . ."

"Where do you want me to go?" I asked her. She had an inspiration. "Go across Fifty-first Street," she directed, "and up Lake Park. There's a nice garage somewhere along that block. Mrs. Dyer told me. Very courteous, she said. We can ask which it is."

We crossed Fifty-first Street, turned left, and right on Lake Park Avenue. There seemed to be several garages on each side of the street.

Mother changed the plan of approach. "Don't ring," she ordered, "shout 'ahoy' with me. That's more unusual. It may bring someone."

It did. It brought two or three men out of almost every garage on the run.

Mother said, "Quiet, Emily," and straightened to her full height. "Are you Mrs. Dyer's garage?" she called as we whirled by. No one answered.

"I surprised them, I think," Mother said as we went around the block again. "You have to present ideas slowly to people like that. They work with their hands. It makes them deliberate. And yet surgeons, they tell me, respond quickly to a crisis. Broader preliminary education probably."

We turned into Lake Park again. Some of the men who had come out at our shouts were still in front of the garages. Mother addressed them, leaning out from the running board, her arm upraised.

"My daughter," she said rapidly but clear and loud, "my daughter has had an accident. Not really an accident. She only drives three blocks. To Miss Faulkner's School . . . for basketball. I am Mrs. H. C. Kimbrough, 5019 Blackstone avenue." We passed the last garage . . . "and dancing, on Wednesdays," she called back.

We had reached the corner. Mother didn't talk as we made the next circuit, but at Fifty-first and Lake Park she got ready again. This time I saw only one man in the whole block. He was young and thin and dirty. He slouched over to the curb as we rushed toward him and dropped into the gutter a cigarette he'd been smoking. He was on my side of the machine. I don't think Mother even saw him. She called down to me, "Ring again, Emily, and shout. We'll have to start all over again."

I was watching the young man. He stepped into the street and put up his hand, palm toward me, like a traffic policeman. I tapped the brake as hard as I dared. He stepped with no particular effort on the running board next me. I stopped tapping and the Waverly shot forward again. He held the sill of my window in one hand, leaned inside, reached down beside me and pulled out the key that connected the current. The machine slowed down. I put on the brake hard and we stopped.

Mother apparently didn't realize at once that we had stopped. Her face appeared in the window, and she seemed about to speak to me when she saw the face of the man in the opposite window. She spoke to him instead.

"Oh," she said, "I'm glad to see you. Are you Mrs. Dyer's garage?"

"No, ma'am," he said finally, "I don't think so." He looked at me, and pointed to the speed lever. "That happens every once in a while," he said. "All you got to do is disconnect the current. People never seem to think of it. They don't think quick, I guess."

As soon as you finish reading Article 19, record your finishing time in the Time Record on page 7 of the PROGRESS FOLDER. *Then read Test 19 that appears next in this book.*

READING TEST 19   A WILD RIDE IN THE WAVERLY

Read each test item and select the answer you believe is correct. Print the letter of your answer in the Answer Record on page 7 of the PROGRESS FOLDER.

1. In the Waverly which Emily's father bought for her mother, the driver sat
   - (A) on the left side of the back seat
   - (B) on the left side of the front seat
   - (C) on the right side of the front seat
   - (D) on the right side of the back seat
   - (E) in the middle of the front seat

2. If you wanted to turn the Waverly to the left, you did this with the steering bar:
   - (A) You pulled it toward you.
   - (B) You pushed it toward the roof.
   - (C) You pushed it away from you.
   - (D) You pulled it toward the floor.
   - (E) You twisted it in your hands.

3. Emily learned to drive a Waverly with the help of
   - (A) her mother
   - (B) her grandfather
   - (C) a young man
   - (D) her father
   - (E) a car salesman

4. Emily drove the car from school because her mother thought that walking home was
   - (A) tiring
   - (B) harmful
   - (C) unpleasant
   - (D) dangerous
   - (E) slow

5. While Emily was driving home one day, she could not stop the Waverly because the
   - (A) brake stuck
   - (B) steering bar stuck
   - (C) speed bar stuck
   - (D) starting key stuck
   - (E) front door stuck

6. Emily did not press the brake down hard and hold it there to stop the car because this would have
   - (A) caused the car to skid
   - (B) burned out the motor
   - (C) set the battery on fire
   - (D) worn out the tires
   - (E) broken the speed bar

7. When Emily was about half a block from home, she started ringing the Waverly's bell because she hoped that

    (A) all the other automobiles would get out of the way
    (B) the storage battery would run down
    (C) her father would come to the rescue
    (D) the car would stop in front of her house
    (E) she would attract someone's attention

8. On the second time around the block, Emily did this while near her home:

    (A) She rang the car's bell again and again.
    (B) She leaned out the window and shouted, "Mother!"
    (C) She let the car steer itself down the street.
    (D) She stood up to get off the car's hot seat.
    (E) She put on the brake and held it firmly.

9. When Hilda, the maid, first saw Emily driving by, she thought that Emily was trying

    (A) to stop the car
    (B) to talk to her mother
    (C) to keep the car under control
    (D) to show off
    (E) to make the car go faster

10. When Emily drove past her home the third time, her mother could not hear what her daughter was saying because

    (A) her mother kept shouting, "Come in this minute!"
    (B) Emily kept crying, "Mother! I can't stop the car!"
    (C) the maid yelled again and again, "Shame on you!"
    (D) other cars blew their horns so loudly
    (E) the Waverly was making so much noise

11. When Emily's mother guessed what the trouble was and jumped on the running board, she tried

    (A) to help Emily steer the car
    (B) to make Emily get out of the car
    (C) to calm Emily down
    (D) to turn the car into the driveway
    (E) to scold Emily severely

12. As soon as Emily's mother found out that the car could not be stopped, she

    (A) jumped off and ran ahead of the car
    (B) reached over and steered the car herself
    (C) decided never to let Emily drive the car again
    (D) tried to turn off the electric current
    (E) shouted to people to get out of the way

13. Emily's mother told her not to drive the car around and around the block because this might make both of them

    (A) dizzy
    (B) weak
    (C) sick
    (D) tired
    (E) sleepy

14. Emily's mother told her to drive up Lake Park Avenue because this street had a nice

    (A) pavement
    (B) curb
    (C) garage
    (D) park
    (E) filling station

15. In order to get assistance, Emily's mother had them both shout:

    (A) "Out of our way!"
    (B) "Danger!"
    (C) "Tally-ho!"
    (D) "Help!"
    (E) "Ahoy!"

---

16. When the garage men did not answer or do anything, Emily's mother told her that people like that were

    (A) fast-acting
    (B) easily confused
    (C) not helpful
    (D) slow-thinking
    (E) very awkward

---

17. While Emily's mother was explaining to the men why Emily was driving the car, they probably thought that she was

    (A) making fun of them
    (B) teaching Emily to drive
    (C) looking for Mrs. Dyer's garage
    (D) going to a basketball game
    (E) talking nonsense

---

18. As the Waverly rounded the corner the last time, Emily and her mother saw a young man

    (A) sitting in front of a garage
    (B) walking along a sidewalk
    (C) crossing the street
    (D) standing near the curb
    (E) driving in a near-by car

---

19. The young man who jumped on the Waverly's running board stopped the car in this way:

    (A) He pushed hard on the brake.
    (B) He pulled the key out of the slot.
    (C) He steered the car into a side street.
    (D) He dragged his left foot on the ground.
    (E) He let the battery run down.

---

20. The young man indicated that some people have trouble in stopping an electric car because they don't

    (A) think quickly
    (B) keep calm
    (C) steer correctly
    (D) shift properly
    (E) drive carefully

NEXT — *Follow the directions (Steps 8-17) on page 1 of the* PROGRESS FOLDER.

ARTICLE 20

The attack on Boonesborough*
by James Daugherty

READING PRACTICE 20 *In a book, magazine, or newspaper that you like, practice reading for speed and comprehension. Make a record of each such practice in Chart 3 on page 8 of the* PROGRESS FOLDER. *Then do Reading Article 20.*

READING ARTICLE 20 *Before you begin reading Article 20, record your starting time in the Time Record on page 7 of the* PROGRESS FOLDER. *Then read Article 20. Read it as fast as you can, but make sure you understand what you are reading.*

THERE WERE about fifty men and boys, besides the women and children, behind the log stockade when the Indians surrounded the clearing of Boonesborough. Instead of the usual sudden attack, an Indian came out of the woods with a white flag and by calling back and forth arranged for a parley. Every hour of delay meant a nearer hope of reinforcement coming in from Harrodsburg. Three of the defenders met Black Fish, Moluntha, and Catahecassa near the fort for a pow-wow. There was talk of friendship and peaceful surrender. The chief promised that the whites would be taken safely on horses to Detroit if they surrendered peaceably. There need be no bloodshed if the Americans would agree to abandon the fort.

Daniel Boone said he would explain to his people and in two days give an answer. He was glad to find that the Indians had heard from a white captive that there were several hundred defenders in the fort. The Indians believed their offer of safety was sure to be accepted.

*From *Daniel Boone*, by James Daugherty. Copyright 1939, by James Daugherty. Reprinted by permission of The Viking Press, Inc., New York.

Inside the fort the chances were talked over and argued and weighed after the democratic way of the backwoods. The odds were ten to one and worse against defense, and not a man, woman, or child would be spared if— But the tough cantankerous spirit of the frontier urged: "Go ahead or bust." They would not have been where they were if they had not been stubborn survivors of a rough, tough, restless race who lived and died in their own independent way by the rifle, the ax, the Bible, and the plow. So they sent back the eagle's answer: "No surrender," the answer of the sassy two-year-old baby democracy, the answer of Man the Unconquerable to the hosts of darkness—"No surrender."

The iron-faced chiefs and the ornery Frenchman DeQuindre took the answer grimly back to their council, while the settlers got in their cows, corn, and water from the spring without interference from the Indians. The next move was an Indian trick which was perfectly transparent to Boone, but he took the chances of playing it to win time.

The Indians proposed a grand council of nine on each side to sign a treaty of peace, after which they would depart, they said, like lambs. The council sat under the sycamore trees within rifle shot of the fort. At a wave of the hat from the delegates the riflemen in the fort were to open fire and cover the nine men's dash back when trouble started.

All day they sat in the shade and smoked, talked, and ate while a fancy treaty of peace, including a sworn allegiance to the British Crown, was agreed on, to be signed tomorrow at the same place. In the night an ambush of Indians was set around the treaty tree. The next day when the nine appeared from the fort, Black Fish met them with eighteen powerful young braves. After the signing came the two-to-one hand-shaking. Two Indians grabbed for each white man and a mob jumped from the laurel to finish the job. Then the nine Kentucky wildcats let loose with teeth and claws, and the fur flew. Shooting began and the nine raced for the fort. They had won the first round.

Next day there was great hubbub in the forest, bugles blowing and orders for retreat bawled out, and the pack horses were seen crossing the river at the ford. But the old border fox in the fort was not fooled. The gates of Boonesborough remained shut and the Indian trick failed. The real danger was an Indian rush on the gates under a heavy fire from all sides. This was what kept the riflemen waiting and watching at the portholes day and night.

But to charge across the clearing under the fire of Kentucky rifles was so contrary to the Indian way of fighting that all of DeQuindre's urging for a mass attack was useless. Instead, the savages remained under cover of the woods, firing continuously. Day and night under the heavy encircling fire of the enemy, the riflemen stuck to their posts, blazing away whenever an inch of Indian hide was exposed to view. The women passed out the scant rations and scarce water, loaded guns when the firing was fast, molded bullets, comforted the children, and prayed the prayers of the pioneer faith. Each slow day under the burning sun was an eternity; each night they thanked the God of their Fathers that some protecting angel had kept the gates.

Most serious was the tunnel which the enemy was driving toward the fort. It carried to the defenders the sinister fear of exploding mines that would breach the wooden walls. Day by day they could hear the digging coming nearer. It wore on their strained nerves like the gnawing of a rat in the night.

Hour by hour a week dragged on. In the inky blackness of the seventh night a bright flame suddenly shot across the clearing in a long arc and dropped on a cabin roof. It was the dreadful flaming arrow. Now they were dropping fast on the pine roofs of the cabins. Worse yet, the savages had crept across the clearing in the darkness and started fagot fires against the log palisade on all sides. The spreading glow lit up the clearing as the hungry little flames ran along the shingles. Against the glow the frantic silhouettes of the defenders trying to beat out the flames drew stinging gun fire from the enemy.

The fires along the stockade were taking hold and the last remaining buckets full of precious water would be of no avail. The riflemen were standing at their posts holding their fire, waiting for the final mass attack, and women stood clutching their children. To Boone it seemed the last card had been played and lost. As the red light flickered over his set face, suddenly he felt a drop of water strike the back of his hand, and as he looked up heavy drops struck his face. In a few minutes the God-sent rain streamed down in drenching sheets. The burning stockade hissed, steamed, glowed, and went out. Something beyond human power had saved Boonesborough by the skin of its teeth.

Still the firing from the forest kept up incessantly. No one knew how near the tunnel was, but it seemed almost under their feet. The September pouring rain had soaked everyone to the bone. They would soon be passing around the last ration of food. Hope held desperately to ever slimmer chances. No Indian attack on a fort had ever been known to keep up so long.

Utter darkness of a night of lashing rain set in on the ninth day of the siege. In the fierce movement of the storm it seemed as though the savage demons of all the wild valley had come down for vengeance. The riflemen stood grimly at their posts in the pouring rain and waited. In the darkness time stopped. They shifted and growled, trying to keep their powder dry, and muttered to each other.

At long last the night lifted. Out of the shapeless grayness the world was taking form. The morning came with no firing from the enemy, and the lookouts reported no signs of Indians in the forest. It looked like another false retreat. A scout or two came back with the news that the Indians were on the march this time for sure.

Then two white men crossed the clearing shouting and waving. One was Simon Kenton who had not been able to get through the lines. It was true that the Indians had gone. The white medicine was too strong. The spirits of the forest were beaten and the white gods prevailed. A surge of wild joy was in the hearts of Boonesborough when the log gates swung open and let out the starved cattle. There was whooping and firing to welcome eighty backwoodsmen from Harrodsburg, riding in too late for a rescue but in time for the celebration.

As soon as you finish reading Article 20, record your finishing time in the Time Record on page 7 of the PROGRESS FOLDER. *Then read Test 20 that appears next in this book.*

READING TEST 20   THE ATTACK ON BOONESBOROUGH

Read each test item and select the answer you believe is correct. Print the letter of your answer in the Answer Record on page 7 of the PROGRESS FOLDER.

1. The battle of Boonesborough described in the story occurred during
   - (A) the War of the American Revolution
   - (B) the French and Indian War
   - (C) the War of 1812
   - (D) King Phillip's War
   - (E) the War between the States

2. After the Indians surrounded the clearing at Boonesborough, they first
   - (A) asked for a parley with the fort's defenders
   - (B) attacked the fort suddenly
   - (C) did a war dance around the fort
   - (D) traded furs for cloth and beads
   - (E) pretended they were leaving the area

3. Daniel Boone did everything possible to delay
the Indians' attack be-
cause he hoped that

(A) a heavy rainstorm was on the way
(B) the Indians would get tired out waiting
(C) the defenders could sneak through the Indian lines
(D) the Indians would not kill the women and children
(E) help would come soon from the nearest town

4. The Indian chief prom-
ised that, if the whites
surrendered peacefully, he
would

(A) let the men join his war party
(B) allow the families to settle near the fort
(C) carry them safely in canoes to St. Louis
(D) take them safely on horses to Detroit
(E) hold the men only as prisoners

5. While the defenders inside the fort were talk-
ing over what to do, they
knew that the chances
were

(A) ten to one against the defenders
(B) ten to one against the attackers
(C) even for the defenders and the attackers
(D) two to one against the defenders
(E) two to one against the attackers

6. Pioneers like those inside
the fort depended mainly
on each of these things
except one. Which did
they *not* depend on?

(A) The rifle
(B) The Bible
(C) The ax
(D) The sword
(E) The plow

7. The defenders sent the
word, "No surrender," to
the Indian chief because
they

(A) feared the Indians would break their promise
(B) knew reinforcements were coming soon
(C) were a tough people fighting for independence
(D) thought the Indians could not take the fort
(E) had plenty of ammunition, food, and water

8. Just after the defenders
answered, "No surren-
der," the Indian chiefs
did this unusual thing:
The chiefs

(A) threatened to kill everyone inside the fort
(B) thought up ways to take the fort by trickery
(C) decided to attack the fort from all sides
(D) held a long council on what to do next
(E) let them bring cows, corn, and water into the fort

9. When the Indians pro-
posed a grand council to
sign a peace treaty,
Boone agreed to send
delegates because he

(A) thought the Indians wished to leave the area
(B) believed the Indians were trying to trick him
(C) felt the Indian chiefs really did not want bloodshed
(D) wanted to delay the Indian attack for a while
(E) was willing to lose a few men to save the others

10. When Black Fish and his
warriors started to seize
the white delegates, these
delegates

(A) attacked and chased the Indians away
(B) fought like wildcats and raced for the fort
(C) lay down while their comrades fired from the fort
(D) surrendered peacefully and were led away
(E) shook hands and made friends with the Indians

11. The Indians pretended that they were retreating in order to get the defenders
   - (A) to attack the enemy in the rear
   - (B) to obey the peace treaty
   - (C) to open the fort's gates
   - (D) to believe the Indians kept their promises
   - (E) to show how many men were in the fort

12. Large numbers of Indians did not charge across the clearing to attack the fort mainly because they were
   - (A) tired out from fighting the fort's delegates
   - (B) used to fighting under cover of the woods
   - (C) afraid of the guns of the fort's defenders
   - (D) running out of gunpowder and bullets
   - (E) fairly sure the fort would soon surrender

13. While the Indians fired at the stockade day and night, the riflemen
   - (A) sneaked out and captured small groups of Indians
   - (B) wounded or killed all the Indian chiefs
   - (C) stayed at their posts and fired back
   - (D) held their fire until the Indians came close
   - (E) molded bullets and loaded their guns

14. After a long hard day of fighting, the people inside the stockade offered thanks each night to
   - (A) the women for feeding and caring for them
   - (B) the men on the way to rescuing them
   - (C) Daniel Boone for leading them so wisely
   - (D) the Indians for not killing them
   - (E) the God of their Fathers for protecting them

15. The Indians first tried to get through one of the stockade's walls by
   - (A) chopping down and removing some of the logs
   - (B) digging a tunnel and exploding a mine in it
   - (C) creeping up and setting the wall afire
   - (D) hitting a weak spot with a battering ram
   - (E) digging a trench and causing the logs to fall

16. To the defenders the hours of the siege seemed to pass
   - (A) very quickly
   - (B) somewhat quickly
   - (C) somewhat slowly
   - (D) very slowly
   - (E) neither slowly nor quickly

17. On the seventh night the Indians started fires inside the fort by
   - (A) building stick fires
   - (B) exploding powder kegs
   - (C) shooting flaming arrows
   - (D) throwing buckets of flaming oil
   - (E) striking pieces of flint together

18. Boone believed that the Indians would soon take the blazing fort until he and the other defenders
   - (A) were soaked by a heavy rainstorm
   - (B) stamped out the fires on the cabins' roofs
   - (C) poured many buckets of water on the wall fires
   - (D) heard the shouts and shots of the rescue party
   - (E) killed or wounded many Indians in the clearing

19. When morning came, the fort's defenders were sure that the enemy had left the area when their

    (A) women heard the calls of returning birds
    (B) leaders saw no smoke from Indian campfires
    (C) riflemen heard no gunfire from the near-by woods
    (D) lookouts saw no Indians outside the clearing
    (E) scouts reported the Indians were on the march

20. The eighty men from Harrodsburg arrived just in time

    (A) to attack the retreating Indians
    (B) to rescue the defenders from the Indians
    (C) to celebrate the defenders' great victory
    (D) to help repair the fort's walls
    (E) to keep the defenders from starving to death

NEXT — *Follow the directions (Steps 8-17) on page 1 of the* PROGRESS FOLDER.

Vocabulary Tests 1 through 20

Read each test item and select the answer you believe is correct. Print the letter of your answer in the Answer Record on page 9 of the PROGRESS FOLDER.

VOCABULARY TEST 1   LAST WARNING

1. foe:	(A) fear	(B) fight	(C) enemy
2. rustler:	(A) dirt farmer	(B) trouble-maker	(C) cattle thief
3. ambush:	(A) shrubbery	(B) anger	(C) a trap
4. critical:	(A) most serious	(B) most exciting	(C) most unusual
5. nester:	(A) chicken-raiser	(B) homesteader	(C) rancher
6. tinker:	(A) thoughtful man	(B) repair man	(C) peddler
7. territory:	(A) large land area	(B) heaven	(C) great terror
8. showdown:	(A) undercover	(B) last warning	(C) final test
9. desperado:	(A) hero	(B) badman	(C) cowboy
10. agitation:	(A) mixture	(B) excitement	(C) concern

NEXT — *Follow the directions (Steps 15-17) on page 1 of the* PROGRESS FOLDER.

VOCABULARY TEST 2   THEY ASK TO BE KILLED

1. pedestrian:	(A) bicyclist	(B) driver	(C) walker
2. incident:	(A) happening	(B) accident	(C) carelessness
3. buttress:	(A) support	(B) argue	(C) overlook
4. registering:	(A) looking for	(B) arresting	(C) recording
5. mangled:	(A) mixed up	(B) lucky	(C) injured
6. alertness:	(A) watchfulness	(B) eyesight	(C) stupidity
7. billowed:	(A) cushioned	(B) blew out	(C) collapsed
8. swerved:	(A) switched	(B) turned aside	(C) upset
9. bevy:	(A) line	(B) group	(C) beautiful
10. intersection:	(A) middle of block	(B) corner	(C) diagonal

NEXT — *Follow the directions (Steps 15-17) on page 1 of the* PROGRESS FOLDER.

Please do not look back at the article while you are doing the vocabulary test. Please do not make any marks in this book unless the book is yours.

VOCABULARY TEST 3   HOW TO HANDLE AN OUTDOOR COOK FIRE

1. "grub": ....(A) dig ....(B) food ....(C) light
2. regulate: ....(A) control ....(B) command .....(C) put out
3. furiously: ....(A) queerly ....(B) quietly ....(C) fiercely
4. "squaw wood": ..(A) live branches ..(B) dead branches ..(C) low branches
5. turf: ....(A) carpet ....(B) diameter ....(C) sod
6. notch: ....(A) V-shaped cut ..(B) C-shaped cut ..(C) L-shaped cut
7. unattended: .....(A) not seen ......(B) not put out ....(C) not cared for
8. primitive: ....(A) civilized ......(B) modern ....(C) beginning
9. simmering: ......(A) broiling fast ..(B) boiling gently .(C) frying slowly
10. drench: ....(A) soak ....(B) stamp ....(C) sprinkle

NEXT — *Follow the directions (Steps 15-17) on page 1 of the* PROGRESS FOLDER.

VOCABULARY TEST 4   THE ROMANCE OF A BUSY BROKER

1. confidential: ....(A) deceitful ......(B) secret ....(C) fearful
2. countenance: ....(A) face ....(B) character .....(C) digestion
3. forewent: ....(A) went without ..(B) went with .....(C) went out
4. fidelity: ....(A) loyalty ....(B) strength ......(C) chagrin
5. reminiscence: ....(A) recollection ...(B) wandering ....(C) payment
6. irresolute: ....(A) determined ....(B) solving ....(C) changeable
7. macaw: ....(A) jacket ....(B) parrot ....(C) monkey
8. harlequin: ....(A) pendant ......(B) hairpin ....(C) buffoon
9. dwindled: ......(A) deceived ......(B) lessened ....(C) enlarged
10. restively: ....(A) uneasily ......(B) gracefully .....(C) leisurely

NEXT — *Follow the directions (Steps 15-17) on page 1 of the* PROGRESS FOLDER.

VOCABULARY TEST 5   GIVE THE HEART

1. anticipation: ....(A) reputation ....(B) formation .....(C) expectation
2. confusion: ......(A) destruction ....(B) disorder ......(C) discovery
3. elusive: ....(A) final ....(B) evasive ....(C) hopeless
4. perilously: ......(A) dangerously ...(B) carefully ......(C) angrily
5. airplane "dope": .(A) cryptogram ...(B) idiot ....(C) lacquer
6. decision: ....(A) idea ....(B) hope ....(C) conclusion
7. sincerity: ....(A) honesty ......(B) caution ....(C) silence
8. raucous: ....(A) painful ....(B) harsh ....(C) peaceful
9. discreetly: ......(A) loudly ....(B) regularly ......(C) thoughtfully
10. impression: ......(A) feeling ....(B) law ....(C) laundry

NEXT — *Follow the directions (Steps 15-17) on page 1 of the* PROGRESS FOLDER.

Read each test item and select the answer you believe is correct. Print the letter of your answer in the Answer Record on page 9 of the PROGRESS FOLDER.

VOCABULARY TEST 6   BUYING DYNAMITE

1. curator: ....(A) caretaker .....(B) doctor ....(C) visitor
2. satchel: ....(A) snake box .....(B) burlap sack ....(C) traveling bag
3. reared: ....(A) struck ....(B) backed ......(C) raised
4. stout: ....(A) slow ....(B) strong ....(C) stupid
5. waggle: ....(A) wag ....(B) push ....(C) lift
6. fangs: ....(A) rattles ....(B) hoods ....(C) teeth
7. avenge: ....(A) get even ......(B) anger ....(C) last
8. magnificent: .....(A) dangerous ....(B) grand ....(C) quick
9. poise: ....(A) breath ....(B) venom ....(C) balance
10. crafty: ....(A) high ....(B) sly ....(C) shy

NEXT — *Follow the directions (Steps 15-17) on page 1 of the* PROGRESS FOLDER.

VOCABULARY TEST 7   THE GLADSOME WASHING MACHINE SEASON

1. quest: ....(A) search ....(B) guess ....(C) answer
2. kin: ....(A) knowledge ....(B) relative ....(C) can
3. husky: ....(A) hairy ....(B) strong ....(C) tired
4. infernal: ....(A) devilish ....(B) inside ....(C) sick
5. disintegration: ...(A) falling to pieces(B) putting together (C) taking away
6. enthralled: ......(A) amused ....(B) gossiping ......(C) charmed
7. controversy: ....(A) discussion .....(B) argument .....(C) agreement
8. contraption: .....(A) wise device ...(B) usual device ...(C) crazy device
9. obscure: ....(A) dirty ....(B) small ....(C) unknown
10. verge: ....(A) thought ......(B) edge ....(C) push

NEXT — *Follow the directions (Steps 15-17) on page 1 of the* PROGRESS FOLDER.

VOCABULARY TEST 8   THE MAN WHO RODE A SHARK

1. witnessed: ......(A) heard about ...(B) saw ....(C) felt
2. refuge: ....(A) a strong place .(B) a happy place ..(C) a safe place
3. submerged: .....(A) above water ..(B) on the surface ..(C) underwater
4. collision: ....(A) crash ....(B) cut ....(C) escape
5. livid: ....(A) discolored ....(B) angry ....(C) alive
6. copra: ....(A) cocoa beans ...(B) coconut meat ..(C) poisonous snake
7. lagoon: ....(A) shallow pool ..(B) deep water ....(C) waterfall
8. kaleidoscope: ....(A) magnifying glass(B) telescope ......(C) changing scene
9. warily: ....(A) angrily ....(B) carefully ......(C) sharply
10. momentum: .....(A) movement ....(B) minute ....(C) important

NEXT — *Follow the directions (Steps 15-17) on page 1 of the* PROGRESS FOLDER.

Please do not look back at the article while you are doing the vocabulary test. Please do not make any marks in this book unless the book is yours.

VOCABULARY TEST 9   MY CONVICT

 1. vivid: ....(A) bloody ....(B) distinct ....(C) angry
 2. ravenously: .....(A) hungrily ......(B) bird-like ......(C) noisily
 3. "wittles": ....(A) wine ....(B) stomach ......(C) food
 4. rind: ....(A) outside layer ..(B) big piece .....(C) best part
 5. compact: ....(A) complete .....(B) tasty ....(C) compressed
 6. scrutiny: ....(A) close look .....(B) funny look ....(C) happy look
 7. lament: ....(A) surprise ....(B) sorrow ....(C) glee
 8. apparent: ....(A) confusing .....(B) relative ....(C) clear
 9. innocent: ....(A) not free ......(B) not false ......(C) not guilty
10. dram: ....(A) large drink ....(B) small drink ....(C) mean drink

NEXT — *Follow the directions (Steps 15-17) on page 1 of the* PROGRESS FOLDER.

VOCABULARY TEST 10   WHAT MAKES A HERO?

 1. surveyor: ....(A) train engineer .(B) safety expert ..(C) land measurer
 2. fuse: ....(A) melt together ..(B) separate ....(C) miss
 3. emergency: .....(A) foreseen event .(B) crisis ....(C) celebration
 4. spontaneous: ....(A) young ....(B) natural ....(C) trained
 5. conscious: ....(A) awake ....(B) asleep ....(C) afraid
 6. distress: ....(A) happiness .....(B) safety ....(C) danger
 7. nausea: ....(A) headache .....(B) stomach sickness (C) fatigue
 8. collapse: ....(A) break down ...(B) applaud ....(C) build up
 9. wrenching: ......(A) pulling ....(B) smashing ......(C) twisting
10. sacrifice: ....(A) give up ....(B) save ....(C) forget

NEXT — *Follow the directions (Steps 15-17) on page 1 of the* PROGRESS FOLDER.

VOCABULARY TEST 11   NOT WITH BEAT OF DRUM

 1. feud: ....(A) quarrel ....(B) fire ....(C) treaty
 2. penetration: .....(A) exit from .....(B) entrance into ..(C) by-pass
 3. hocus-pocus: ....(A) chanting ......(B) foolishness ....(C) trickery
 4. admonished: .....(A) punished ......(B) warned ....(C) reminded
 5. ferocity: ....(A) fierceness .....(B) friendliness ....(C) hatred
 6. prestige: ....(A) character .....(B) pressure ......(C) fame
 7. decapitated: .....(A) wounded .....(B) beheaded .....(C) defeated
 8. sham: ....(A) imitation ......(B) repeated ......(C) shameful
 9. sublimate: ....(A) elevate ....(B) undercut ......(C) burn out
10. fantastic: ....(A) noisy ....(B) unreal ....(C) clear

NEXT — *Follow the directions (Steps 15-17) on page 1 of the* PROGRESS FOLDER.

Read each test item and select the answer you believe is correct. Print the letter of your answer in the Answer Record on page 9 of the PROGRESS FOLDER.

VOCABULARY TEST 12   THE DIVINE STORY OF HANDEL'S MESSIAH

1. composer: ......(A) music writer ..(B) musician ......(C) libretto writer
2. harpsichord: .....(A) sour note .....(B) small organ ...(C) kind of harp
3. quench: ....(A) put out ....(B) twist ....(C) continue
4. shrine: ....(A) dark cave .....(B) sacred place ...(C) holy man
5. eternity: ....(A) ended past ...(B) endless time ...(C) certain time
6. oblivion: ....(A) learning nothing (B) recalling all ....(C) forgetting all
7. oratorio: ....(A) sacred music ..(B) serious talk ....(C) large chorus
8. realm: ....(A) music ....(B) kingdom ......(C) world
9. tremor: ....(A) fear ....(B) silence ....(C) quivering
10. resurrection: ....(A) salvation ......(B) rebirth ....(C) happiness

NEXT — *Follow the directions (Steps 15-17) on page 1 of the* PROGRESS FOLDER.

VOCABULARY TEST 13   OUR PLUNDERED PLANET

1. comprehending: .(A) understanding .(B) covering ......(C) confusing
2. surge: ....(A) rolling wave ..(B) dark blue .....(C) glancing blow
3. inconsequential: ..(A) unsure ....(B) unimproved ...(C) unimportant
4. permeate: ....(A) gather together (B) spread through .(C) fall below
5. element: ....(A) first part ......(B) basic part .....(C) light part
6. protozoa: ....(A) simple plants ..(B) rare minerals ...(C) tiny animals
7. adequate: ....(A) sufficient .....(B) water pipe ....(C) added to
8. comprising: .....(A) excluding .....(B) reclaiming ....(C) making up
9. indiscriminate: ...(A) unselective ....(B) unusual ......(C) criminal
10. cycle: ....(A) season ....(B) sickle ....(C) circle

NEXT — *Follow the directions (Steps 15-17) on page 1 of the* PROGRESS FOLDER.

VOCABULARY TEST 14   WE FLEW EIGHT MILES UP

1. stability: ....(A) moveability ...(B) standard ......(C) steadiness
2. accelerates: ......(A) slows down ...(B) stops ....(C) speeds up
3. undiluted: ......(A) pure ....(B) strengthened ...(C) deceived
4. vise: ....(A) great sin .....(B) holding device .(C) very intelligent
5. fuselage: ....(A) airplane body ..(B) oil tank ....(C) aileron
6. trifle: ....(A) little ....(B) accurate ......(C) playful
7. identify: ....(A) repay ....(B) recognize .....(C) forget
8. symptom: ....(A) seal ....(B) sign ....(C) cause
9. capering: ....(A) leaping ......(B) cutting ....(C) flying
10. intercept: ....(A) introduce .....(B) break ....(C) interrupt

NEXT — *Follow the directions (Steps 15-17) on page 1 of the* PROGRESS FOLDER.

Please do not look back at the article while you are doing the vocabulary test. Please do not make any marks in this book unless the book is yours.

VOCABULARY TEST 15 RING OUT, WILD BELLS

1. arrayed: ....(A) dressed ....(B) acted ....(C) played
2. farthingale: .....(A) hoop skirt ....(B) ruff collar .....(C) bird call
3. jester: ....(A) idiot ....(B) jumper ....(C) joker
4. misgiving: ......(A) wrong present . (B) loss of gift .....(C) some doubt
5. sporadic: ....(A) noisy ....(B) occasional .....(C) steady
6. innovation: ......(A) something old . (B) something new . (C) something bad
7. inscrutable: .....(A) mysterious ....(B) painful ....(C) childish
8. succumbed: .....(A) laughed at ....(B) gave way .....(C) took away
9. shrewd: ....(A) cunning ......(B) comic ....(C) dangerous
10. tumult: ....(A) costume ......(B) audience ......(C) uproar

NEXT — *Follow the directions (Steps 15-17) on page 1 of the* PROGRESS FOLDER.

VOCABULARY TEST 16 CHINK: THE DEVELOPMENT OF A PUP

1. remarkable: .....(A) ordinary ......(B) unusual ....(C) noisy
2. blunder: ....(A) coyote ....(B) mistake ....(C) enemy
3. lured: ....(A) chased ....(B) forced ....(C) attracted
4. pangs: ....(A) sharp pains ....(B) sharp teeth ....(C) sharp paws
5. demon: ....(A) fool ....(B) angel ....(C) devil
6. venture: ....(A) dare ....(B) betray ....(C) feel
7. mortal: ....(A) lively ....(B) deadly ....(C) constant
8. spree: ....(A) carouse ....(B) soberness ......(C) trip
9. regardless: ......(A) without regard (B) with less regard (C) with regard
10. expelled: ....(A) put in jail .....(B) asked to leave . (C) forced out

NEXT — *Follow the directions (Steps 15-17) on page 1 of the* PROGRESS FOLDER.

VOCABULARY TEST 17 THE STORY-TELLER

1. sultry: ....(A) very hot ......(B) very sunny ....(C) very small
2. listlessly: ....(A) persistently ...(B) silently ....(C) indifferently
3. conviction: .....(A) great crime ....(B) strong belief ...(C) happy thought
4. aroused: ....(A) angered ......(B) awakened ....(C) steadied
5. novel: ....(A) new ....(B) naughty ......(C) nice
6. inevitable: ......(A) uncertain .....(B) impolite ....(C) unavoidable
7. admiration: .....(A) gasp ....(B) appreciation ...(C) suppression
8. pinafore: ....(A) apron ....(B) dress ....(C) face
9. punctuality: .....(A) bad feeling ...(B) behavior ......(C) promptness
10. dissentient: ......(A) similar ....(B) indifferent ....(C) disagreeing

NEXT — *Follow the directions (Steps 15-17) on page 1 of the* PROGRESS FOLDER.

Read each test item and select the answer you believe is correct. Print the letter of your answer in the Answer Record on page 9 of the PROGRESS FOLDER.

VOCABULARY TEST 18 — TO WALK ALONE

		(A)		(B)		(C)	
1.	facade:	(A) foundation		(B) feeling		(C) front	
2.	collapse:	(A) applaud		(B) break down		(C) blow up	
3.	relentlessly:	(A) without letup		(B) without help		(C) without fear	
4.	defiance:	(A) attitude		(B) challenge		(C) pride	
5.	pastel:	(A) pasty shade		(B) soft tint		(C) childish	
6.	chagrined:	(A) frightened		(B) blushing		(C) humiliated	
7.	delved:	(A) dug		(B) looked		(C) fooled	
8.	talent:	(A) fastener		(B) jewel		(C) ability	
9.	talisman:	(A) charm		(B) storyteller		(C) feather	
10.	proportion:	(A) importance		(B) balance		(C) parts	

NEXT — *Follow the directions (Steps 15-17) on page 1 of the* PROGRESS FOLDER.

VOCABULARY TEST 19 — A WILD RIDE IN THE WAVERLY

1.	insert:	(A) take out	(B) turn over	(C) put in
2.	lofty:	(A) humble	(B) haughty	(C) certain
3.	pause:	(A) long time	(B) small place	(C) short stop
4.	simultaneous:	(A) at the same time	(B) soon afterward	(C) just before
5.	attract:	(A) draw to	(B) overlook	(C) push away
6.	miraculous:	(A) mirthful	(B) mirror-like	(C) marvelous
7.	jiggled:	(A) jerked	(B) jumped	(C) jammed
8.	Ahoy!:	(A) Hello there!	(B) Help us!	(C) Watch out!
9.	deliberate:	(A) hurried	(B) free	(C) leisurely
10.	circuit:	(A) shout	(B) round	(C) readiness

NEXT — *Follow the directions (Steps 15-17) on page 1 of the* PROGRESS FOLDER.

VOCABULARY TEST 20 — THE ATTACK ON BOONESBOROUGH

1.	parley:	(A) bet	(B) talk	(C) treaty
2.	cantankerous:	(A) seriously hurt	(B) very unsure	(C) bad tempered
3.	ornery:	(A) mean	(B) nice	(C) honorable
4.	allegiance:	(A) loyalty	(B) alliance	(C) statement
5.	siege:	(A) seizure	(B) lookout	(C) blockade
6.	sinister:	(A) strong	(B) evil	(C) savage
7.	scant:	(A) barely enough	(B) a big stick	(C) very tasty
8.	palisade:	(A) castle	(B) fagot	(C) fence
9.	silhouette:	(A) outlined object	(B) clear object	(C) silent object
10.	incessantly:	(A) continually	(B) stupidly	(C) unevenly

NEXT — *Follow the directions (Steps 15-17) on page 1 of the* PROGRESS FOLDER.

Reading Progress Folder

CONTENTS

NOTE: If you should not write in this book, use a separate copy of the *SRA Reading Progress Folder.* Get it from your instructor.

General directions for this folder

In using this *Progress Folder*, take these steps:

Step 1. Do a reading practice. Read in a book, magazine or newspaper that you like.

Step 2. Record your reading practice in Chart 3 on page 8 of this folder.

Step 3. Record your starting time. Before you begin reading an article, write down your starting time in the Time Record on page 4 or page 7 of this folder. (See Example 1 on page 10.)

Step 4. Read the article as fast as you can, but make sure you understand what you are reading.

Step 5. Record your finishing time. After you finish the article, write down your finishing time in the Time Record on page 4 or page 7 of this folder. (See Example 1 on page 10.)

Step 6. Take the comprehension test on the article. As you read each test item, select the correct answer for it.

Step 7. Record your answers to the comprehension test in the Answer Record on page 4 or page 7 of this folder. As you select your answer for each test item, mark the letter of this answer in the Answer Record. (See Example 2 on page 10.)

Step 8. Correct your answers to the comprehension test. Use the Answer Key on page 5 or page 6 of this folder.

Step 9. Score your answers to the comprehension test. Count the number of answers that you had correct. Write this score at the bottom of the Answer Record on page 4 or page 7 of this folder.

Step 10. Record your comprehension test score. Enter your score in Chart 2 on page 3 of this folder.

Step 11. Figure out your reading time for the article. Do this in the Time Record on page 4 or page 7 of this folder. (See Example 1 on page 10.)

Step 12. Change your reading time into your reading rate. Use the Time-To-Rate Table on the last page of this book.

Step 13. Record your reading rate. Enter your reading rate in the Time Record and in Chart 1 on page 2 of this folder. (See Example 3 on page 10.)

Step 14. Take the vocabulary test on the article. Mark your answers to the test in the Answer Record on page 9 of this folder.

Step 15. Correct your answers to the vocabulary test. Use the Answer Key on page 11 of this folder.

Step 16. Score your answers to the vocabulary test. Write this score at the bottom of the Answer Record on page 9 of this folder.

Step 17. Follow up each test item that you answered incorrectly. (See the suggestions on page 185 in this book.)

CHART 1. READING RATE RECORD FOR THE ARTICLES

Enter your reading rate for the article you have just read in the table and in the graph, below. For specific directions, see page 10 in this folder.

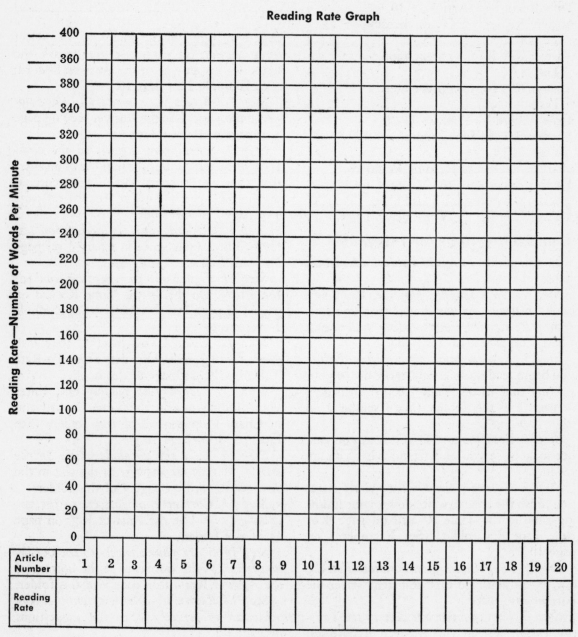

Reading Rate Graph

Reading Rate—Number of Words Per Minute

| 400 |
| 360 |
| 380 |
| 340 |
| 320 |
| 300 |
| 280 |
| 260 |
| 240 |
| 220 |
| 200 |
| 180 |
| 160 |
| 140 |
| 120 |
| 100 |
| 80 |
| 60 |
| 40 |
| 20 |
| 0 |

Article Number	1	2	3	4	5	6	7	8	9	10	11	12	13	14	15	16	17	18	19	20
Reading Rate																				

Reading Rate Table

CHART 2. READING COMPREHENSION RECORD FOR THE TESTS

Enter your reading comprehension score for the test you have just taken in the table and in the graph, below. For specific directions, see page 10 in this folder.

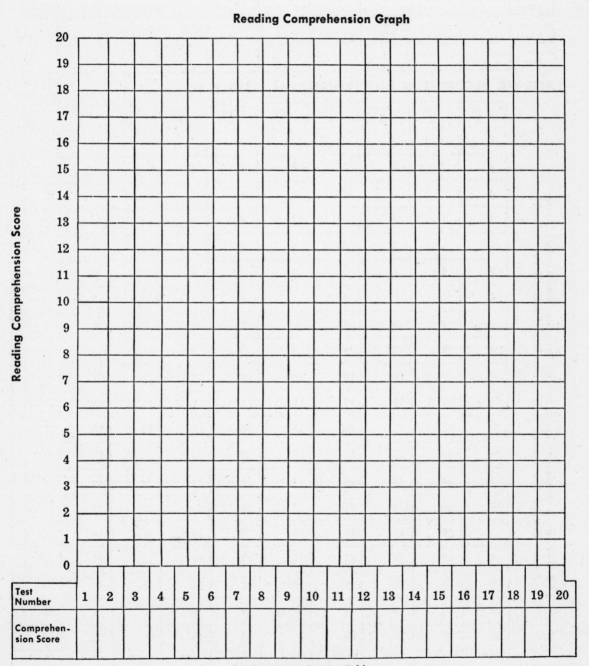

Reading Comprehension Graph

Test Number	1	2	3	4	5	6	7	8	9	10	11	12	13	14	15	16	17	18	19	20
Comprehension Score																				

Reading Comprehension Table

TIME RECORD FOR ARTICLES 1-10

	Article 1	Article 2	Article 3	Article 4	Article 5	Article 6	Article 7	Article 8	Article 9	Article 10
Finishing time										
Starting time										
Reading time										
Reading rate										

ANSWER RECORD FOR COMPREHENSION TESTS 1-10

Test 1	Test 2	Test 3	Test 4	Test 5	Test 6	Test 7	Test 8	Test 9	Test 10
1	1	1	1	1	1	1	1	1	1
2	2	2	2	2	2	2	2	2	2
3	3	3	3	3	3	3	3	3	3
4	4	4	4	4	4	4	4	4	4
5	5	5	5	5	5	5	5	5	5
6	6	6	6	6	6	6	6	6	6
7	7	7	7	7	7	7	7	7	7
8	8	8	8	8	8	8	8	8	8
9	9	9	9	9	9	9	9	9	9
10	10	10	10	10	10	10	10	10	10
11	11	11	11	11	11	11	11	11	11
12	12	12	12	12	12	12	12	12	12
13	13	13	13	13	13	13	13	13	13
14	14	14	14	14	14	14	14	14	14
15	15	15	15	15	15	15	15	15	15
16	16	16	16	16	16	16	16	16	16
17	17	17	17	17	17	17	17	17	17
18	18	18	18	18	18	18	18	18	18
19	19	19	19	19	19	19	19	19	19
20	20	20	20	20	20	20	20	20	20
SCORE	SCORE	SCORE	SCORE	SCORE	SCORE	SCORE	SCORE	SCORE	SCORE

NOTE: If you should not write in this book, keep your Time Record and your Answer Record in a separate copy of the *SRA Reading Progress Folder.*

ANSWER KEY FOR COMPREHENSION TESTS 11-20

Test 11	Test 12	Test 13	Test 14	Test 15	Test 16	Test 17	Test 18	Test 19	Test 20
1 C	1 D	1 C	1 B	1 B	1 E	1 A	1 E	1 A	1 A
2 D	2 A	2 E	2 E	2 D	2 B	2 D	2 D	2 C	2 A
3 D	3 E	3 D	3 B	3 D	3 A	3 E	3 C	3 B	3 E
4 A	4 A	4 A	4 C	4 B	4 C	4 B	4 E	4 D	4 D
5 B	5 D	5 D	5 D	5 E	5 C	5 C	5 A	5 C	5 A
6 E	6 C	6 B	6 B	6 C	6 A	6 C	6 B	6 B	6 D
7 B	7 B	7 E	7 C	7 A	7 A	7 E	7 A	7 E	7 C
8 A	8 B	8 B	8 E	8 E	8 C	8 C	8 E	8 B	8 E
9 A	9 A	9 D	9 C	9 A	9 E	9 B	9 A	9 D	9 D
10 C	10 D	10 D	10 A	10 B	10 D	10 B	10 B	10 A	10 B
11 A	11 D	11 A	11 D	11 D	11 B	11 B	11 C	11 C	11 C
12 D	12 B	12 C	12 B	12 C	12 A	12 C	12 A	12 E	12 B
13 E	13 C	13 E	13 D	13 C	13 D	13 A	13 D	13 A	13 C
14 B	14 E	14 C	14 C	14 A	14 E	14 D	14 D	14 C	14 E
15 D	15 C	15 B	15 A	15 E	15 D	15 C	15 E	15 E	15 B
16 C	16 B	16 A	16 D	16 D	16 E	16 E	16 A	16 D	16 D
17 C	17 A	17 E	17 A	17 C	17 C	17 A	17 B	17 E	17 C
18 E	18 C	18 C	18 B	18 A	18 B	18 D	18 B	18 D	18 A
19 E	19 E	19 A	19 B	19 E	19 B	19 E	19 C	19 B	19 E
20 B	20 E	20 B	20 C	20 B	20 D	20 D	20 D	20 A	20 C

ANSWER KEY FOR COMPREHENSION TESTS 1-10

Test 1	Test 2	Test 3	Test 4	Test 5	Test 6	Test 7	Test 8	Test 9	Test 10
1 A	1 C	1 B	1 D	1 A	1 B	1 B	1 C	1 D	1 C
2 B	2 A	2 D	2 D	2 A	2 E	2 C	2 B	2 E	2 B
3 B	3 B	3 A	3 C	3 B	3 E	3 B	3 A	3 C	3 D
4 E	4 B	4 E	4 E	4 D	4 C	4 C	4 D	4 A	4 E
5 A	5 C	5 C	5 A	5 E	5 A	5 E	5 E	5 D	5 C
6 D	6 A	6 B	6 D	6 C	6 C	6 D	6 A	6 C	6 C
7 D	7 C	7 E	7 C	7 D	7 C	7 C	7 C	7 B	7 D
8 C	8 E	8 C	8 D	8 E	8 A	8 A	8 A	8 D	8 B
9 C	9 D	9 D	9 B	9 B	9 E	9 A	9 B	9 B	9 B
10 A	10 A	10 B	10 A	10 C	10 C	10 D	10 D	10 E	10 E
11 E	11 E	11 A	11 E	11 A	11 A	11 C	11 C	11 A	11 E
12 E	12 B	12 E	12 A	12 B	12 D	12 E	12 D	12 A	12 A
13 B	13 D	13 A	13 E	13 E	13 E	13 A	13 B	13 D	13 E
14 D	14 E	14 E	14 C	14 B	14 B	14 E	14 B	14 B	14 C
15 E	15 A	15 D	15 B	15 C	15 D	15 D	15 E	15 E	15 B
16 B	16 C	16 B	16 A	16 C	16 D	16 B	16 E	16 C	16 D
17 A	17 D	17 C	17 E	17 D	17 B	17 B	17 E	17 E	17 A
18 D	18 E	18 D	18 B	18 A	18 D	18 E	18 D	18 B	18 D
19 C	19 B	19 A	19 C	19 E	19 A	19 A	19 C	19 A	19 C
20 C	20 D	20 C	20 B	20 D	20 B	20 E	20 A	20 A	20 A

TIME RECORD FOR ARTICLES 11-20

	Article 11	Article 12	Article 13	Article 14	Article 15	Article 16	Article 17	Article 18	Article 19	Article 20
Finishing time										
Starting time										
Reading time										
Reading rate										

ANSWER RECORD FOR COMPREHENSION TESTS 11-20

NOTE: If you should not write in this book, keep your Time Record and your Answer Record in a separate copy of the *SRA Reading Progress Folder.*

Test 11	Test 12	Test 13	Test 14	Test 15	Test 16	Test 17	Test 18	Test 19	Test 20
1	1	1	1	1	1	1	1	1	1
2	2	2	2	2	2	2	2	2	2
3	3	3	3	3	3	3	3	3	3
4	4	4	4	4	4	4	4	4	4
5	5	5	5	5	5	5	5	5	5
6	6	6	6	6	6	6	6	6	6
7	7	7	7	7	7	7	7	7	7
8	8	8	8	8	8	8	8	8	8
9	9	9	9	9	9	9	9	9	9
10	10	10	10	10	10	10	10	10	10
11	11	11	11	11	11	11	11	11	11
12	12	12	12	12	12	12	12	12	12
13	13	13	13	13	13	13	13	13	13
14	14	14	14	14	14	14	14	14	14
15	15	15	15	15	15	15	15	15	15
16	16	16	16	16	16	16	16	16	16
17	17	17	17	17	17	17	17	17	17
18	18	18	18	18	18	18	18	18	18
19	19	19	19	19	19	19	19	19	19
20	20	20	20	20	20	20	20	20	20
SCORE	SCORE	SCORE	SCORE	SCORE	SCORE	SCORE	SCORE	SCORE	SCORE

CHART 3. RECORD OF READING PRACTICES OUTSIDE THIS BOOK

DIRECTIONS: Select a book, magazine, or newspaper that you like. As you read it, keep trying to increase your reading rate and your reading comprehension.

Immediately after you do this reading practice, make a record of it in the blanks below. Fill in the right-hand column only if you use the *SRA Reading Accelerator*.

Date	I read this book, magazine, or newspaper:	I read these pages:	I believe that my reading rate was: (Check one)			I believe that my reading comprehension was: (Check one)			I read with the *Accelerator* set at this rate: (Words per min.)
			Fast	Ave.	Slow	Good	Ave.	Poor	
Example *Feb. 19*	*Streamline Your Reading*	25-39	✓				✓		*200*

ANSWER RECORD FOR THE VOCABULARY TESTS

NOTE: If you should not write in this book, write your answers to a vocabulary test on a separate sheet of paper.

Test 1	Test 2	Test 3	Test 4	Test 5	Test 6	Test 7	Test 8	Test 9	Test 10
1	1	1	1	1	1	1	1	1	1
2	2	2	2	2	2	2	2	2	2
3	3	3	3	3	3	3	3	3	3
4	4	4	4	4	4	4	4	4	4
5	5	5	5	5	5	5	5	5	5
6	6	6	6	6	6	6	6	6	6
7	7	7	7	7	7	7	7	7	7
8	8	8	8	8	8	8	8	8	8
9	9	9	9	9	9	9	9	9	9
10	10	10	10	10	10	10	10	10	10
SCORE	SCORE	SCORE	SCORE	SCORE	SCORE	SCORE	SCORE	SCORE	SCORE

Test 11	Test 12	Test 13	Test 14	Test 15	Test 16	Test 17	Test 18	Test 19	Test 20
1	1	1	1	1	1	1	1	1	1
2	2	2	2	2	2	2	2	2	2
3	3	3	3	3	3	3	3	3	3
4	4	4	4	4	4	4	4	4	4
5	5	5	5	5	5	5	5	5	5
6	6	6	6	6	6	6	6	6	6
7	7	7	7	7	7	7	7	7	7
8	8	8	8	8	8	8	8	8	8
9	9	9	9	9	9	9	9	9	9
10	10	10	10	10	10	10	10	10	10
SCORE	SCORE	SCORE	SCORE	SCORE	SCORE	SCORE	SCORE	SCORE	SCORE

Specific directions for this folder

Directions for the time record: Keep the Time Record as Example 1 shows.

1. If your starting time for Article 1 is exactly 12 minutes after the hour, write 12:00 to the right of "Starting time." (This is Step 3.)

2. If your finishing time is 19 minutes 18 seconds after the hour, write 19:18 to the right of "Finishing time." (This is Step 5.)

3. From your finishing time, 19:18, subtract your starting time, 12:00. The difference is 7:18—7 minutes 18 seconds. Write this difference to the right of "Reading time." (This is Step 11.)

4. Change your reading time into your reading rate, using the table on the last page of this book. Enter this rate as shown. (These are Steps 12 and 13.)

Example 1

TIME RECORD

	Article **1**
Finishing time	19:18
Starting time	12:00
Reading time	7:18
Reading rate	183

Directions for the answer record and the answer key:

1. Record your answers to the test in the Answer Record. In Example 2, the answers are recorded as follows: Item 1, C; Item 2, B; Item 3, B; and Item 4, D. (This is Step 7.)

2. Correct your answers to the test. Mark a check (√) at the right of each of your answers that is correct. (This is Step 8.)

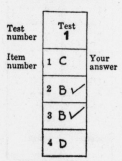

Example 2

ANSWER RECORD

Directions for Chart 1 (Reading Rate Record): On page 2 of this folder, record your reading rate for the article you have just read, as Example 3 shows.

1. Write your reading rate for the article in the reading rate table below the graph. In the example, the reading rate for Article 1 is 183 words per minute. For Article 2, it is 177 words. For Article 3, it is 197 words.

2. Enter your reading rate for the article in the reading rate graph, as shown in the example. Mark a heavy dot to show your reading rate for the article. Draw a circle around this dot to make it stand out. After you enter and encircle a dot for the next article, draw a heavy straight line connecting the two dots.

Directions for Chart 2 (Reading Comprehension Record): On page 3 of this folder, record your score for the comprehension test you have just taken. Write your score in the table below the graph. Then enter your score in the graph. Mark a dot; encircle it.

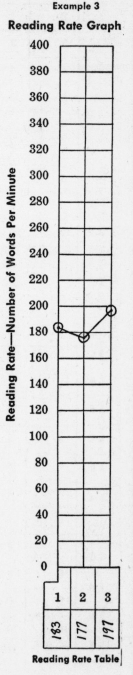

Example 3

Reading Rate Graph

Reading Rate—Number of Words Per Minute

Reading Rate Table

ANSWER KEY FOR THE VOCABULARY TESTS

Test 1	Test 2	Test 3	Test 4	Test 5	Test 6	Test 7	Test 8	Test 9	Test 10
1 C	1 C	1 B	1 B	1 C	1 A	1 A	1 B	1 B	1 C
2 C	2 A	2 A	2 A	2 B	2 C	2 B	2 C	2 A	2 A
3 C	3 A	3 C	3 A	3 B	3 C	3 B	3 C	3 C	3 B
4 A	4 C	4 B	4 A	4 A	4 B	4 A	4 A	4 A	4 B
5 B	5 C	5 C	5 A	5 C	5 A	5 A	5 A	5 C	5 A
6 B	6 A	6 A	6 C	6 C	6 C	6 C	6 B	6 A	6 C
7 A	7 B	7 C	7 B	7 A	7 A	7 B	7 A	7 B	7 B
8 C	8 B	8 C	8 C	8 B	8 B	8 C	8 C	8 C	8 A
9 B	9 B	9 B	9 B	9 C	9 C	9 C	9 B	9 C	9 C
10 B	10 B	10 A	10 A	10 A	10 B	10 B	10 A	10 B	10 A

Test 11	Test 12	Test 13	Test 14	Test 15	Test 16	Test 17	Test 18	Test 19	Test 20
1 A	1 A	1 A	1 C	1 A	1 B	1 A	1 C	1 C	1 B
2 B	2 C	2 A	2 C	2 A	2 B	2 C	2 B	2 B	2 C
3 C	3 A	3 C	3 A	3 C	3 C	3 B	3 A	3 C	3 A
4 B	4 B	4 B	4 B	4 C	4 A	4 B	4 B	4 A	4 A
5 A	5 B	5 B	5 A	5 B	5 C	5 A	5 B	5 A	5 C
6 C	6 C	6 C	6 A	6 B	6 A	6 C	6 C	6 C	6 B
7 B	7 A	7 A	7 B	7 A	7 A	7 B	7 A	7 A	7 A
8 A	8 B	8 C	8 B	8 B	8 A	8 A	8 C	8 A	8 C
9 A	9 C	9 A	9 A	9 A	9 A	9 C	9 A	9 C	9 A
10 B	10 B	10 C	10 C	10 C	10 C	10 C	10 B	10 B	10 A

Time-to-rate table for the general reading exercises

Use the Time-To-Rate Table on this page to change your reading time for an article into your reading rate for that article. This table shows reading time in minutes and seconds. It also shows reading rate in number of words per minute.

In the column headed, "Reading Time," find the time range which includes your reading time. At the right of this range, find the corresponding number in the column headed "Reading Rate." This number is your reading rate for the article.

Suppose that your reading time for Article 1 is 7:18 (7 minutes 18 seconds) as given on page 10 of the *Progress Folder*. This time, 7:18, is in the range, 7:15-7:29. For this time range, the reading rate is 183 words per minute. That is, if your reading time is 7:18, your reading rate is 183 words per minute. Write this rate in the *Progress Folder* (page 4 or 7).

TIME-TO-RATE TABLE FOR ARTICLES IN THE GENERAL READING EXERCISES

(each article contains about 1,350 words.)

Reading time	Reading rate	Reading time	Reading rate	Reading time	Reading rate
1:00-1:14	1209	7:00-7:14	190	13:00-13:14	103
1:15-1:29	988	7:15-7:29	183	13:15-13:29	101
1:30-1:44	835	7:30-7:44	177	13:30-13:44	99
1:45-1:59	723	7:45-7:59	172	13:45-13:59	97
2:00-2:14	638	8:00-8:14	166	14:00-14:14	96
2:15-2:29	570	8:15-8:29	161	14:15-14:29	94
2:30-2:44	516	8:30-8:44	157	14:30-14:44	92
2:45-2:59	471	8:45-8:59	152	14:45-14:59	91
3:00-3:14	433	9:00-9:14	148	15:00-15:14	89
3:15-3:29	401	9:15-9:29	144	15:15-15:29	88
3:30-3:44	373	9:30-9:44	140	15:30-15:44	86
3:45-3:59	349	9:45-9:59	137	15:45-15:59	85
4:00-4:14	328	10:00-10:14	133	16:00-16:14	84
4:15-4:29	309	10:15-10:29	130	16:15-16:29	82
4:30-4:44	292	10:30-10:44	127	16:30-16:44	81
4:45-4:59	277	10:45-10:59	124	16:45-16:59	80
5:00-5:14	264	11:00-11:14	121	17:00-17:14	79
5:15-5:29	252	11:15-11:29	119	17:15-17:29	78
5:30-5:44	240	11:30-11:44	116	17:30-17:44	77
5:45-5:59	230	11:45-11:59	114	17:45-17:59	76
6:00-6:14	221	12:00-12:14	111	18:00-18:14	75
6:15-6:29	212	12:15-12:29	109	18:15-18:29	74
6:30-6:44	204	12:30-12:44	107	18:30-18:44	73
6:45-6:59	197	12:45-12:59	105	18:45-18:59	72